Principles of Politica

Arthur Latham Perry

Alpha Editions

This edition published in 2024

ISBN 9789362513748

Design and Setting By
Alpha Editions
www.alphaedis.com
Email - info@alphaedis.com

Contents

PREFACE.

It is now exactly twenty-five years since was published my first book upon the large topics at present in hand. It was but as a bow drawn at a venture, and was very properly entitled "Elements of Political Economy." At that time I had been teaching for about a dozen years in this Institution the closely cognate subjects of History and Political Economy; cognate indeed, since Hermann Lotze, a distinguished German philosopher of our day, makes prominent among its only *five* most general phases, the "industrial" element in all human history; and since Goldwin Smith, an able English scholar, resolves the elements of human progress, and thus of universal history, into only *three*, namely, "the moral, the intellectual, and the productive."

During these studious and observant years of teaching, I had slowly come to a settled conviction that I could say something of my own and something of consequence about Political Economy, especially at two points; and these two proved in the sequel to be more radical and transforming points than was even thought of at the first. For one thing, I had satisfied myself, that the word "Wealth," as at once a strangely indefinite and grossly misleading term, was worse than useless in the nomenclature of the Science, and would have to be utterly dislodged from it, before a scientific content and defensible form could by any possibility be given to what had long been called in all the modern languages the "Science of Wealth." Accordingly, so far as has appeared in the long interval of time since 1865, these "Elements" were the very first attempt to undertake an orderly construction of Economics from beginning to end without once using or having occasion to use the obnoxious word. A scientific substitute for it was of course required, which, with the help of Bastiat, himself however still clinging to the technical term "Richesse," was discerned and appropriated in the word "Value"; a good word indeed, that can be simply and perfectly defined in a scientific sense of its own; and, what is more important still, that precisely covers in that sense all the three sorts of things which are ever bought and sold, the three only Valuables in short, namely, material Commodities, personal Services, commercial Credits. It is of course involved in this simple-looking but far-reaching change from "Wealth" to "Value," that Economics become at once and throughout a science of Persons buying and selling, and no longer as before a science of Things howsoever manipulated for and in their market.

For another thing, before beginning to write out the first word of that book, I believed myself to have made sure, by repeated and multiform inductions, of this deepest truth in the whole Science, which was a little after embodied (I hope I may even say *embalmed*) in a phrase taking its proper place in the book itself,—*A market for Products is products in Market*. The fundamental thus tersely expressed may be formulated more at length in this way: One cannot Sell without at the same instant and in the same act Buying, nor Buy anything without simultaneously Selling something else; because in Buying one pays for what he buys, which is Selling, and in Selling one must take pay for what is sold, which is Buying. As these universal actions among men are always voluntary, there must be also an universal motive leading up to them; this motive on the part of both parties to each and every Sale can be no other than the mutual satisfaction derivable to both; the inference, accordingly, is easy and invincible, that governmental restrictions on Sales, or prohibitions of them, must lessen the satisfactions and retard the progress of mankind.

Organizing strictly all the matter of my book along these two lines of Personality and Reciprocity, notwithstanding much in it that was crude and more that was redundant and something that was ill-reasoned and unsound, the book made on account of this original mode of treatment an immediate impression upon the public, particularly upon teachers and pupils; new streaks of light could not but be cast from these new points of view, upon such topics especially as Land and Money and Foreign Trade; and nothing is likely ever to rob the author of the satisfaction, which he is willing to share with the public, of having contributed something of importance both in substance and in feature to the permanent up-building of that Science, which comes closer, it may be, to the homes and happiness and progress of the People, than any other science. And let it be said in passing, that there is one consideration well-fitted to stimulate and to reward each patient and competent scientific inquirer, no matter what that science may be in which he labors, namely, this: Any just generalization, made and fortified inductively, is put thereby beyond hazard of essential change for all time; for this best of reasons, that God has constructed the World and Men on everlasting lines of Order.

As successive editions of this first book were called for, and as its many defects were brought out into the light through teaching my own classes from it year after year, occasion was taken to revise it and amend it and in large parts to rewrite it again and again; until, in 1883, and for the eighteenth edition, it was recast from bottom up for wholly new plates, and a riper title was ventured upon,—"Political Economy,"—instead of the original more tentative "Elements." Since then have been weeded out the slight typographical and other minute errors, and the book stands now in its ultimate shape.

My excellent publishers, who have always been keenly and wisely alive to my interests as an author, suggested several times after the success of the first book was reasonably assured, that a second and smaller one should be written out, with an especial eye to the needs of high schools and academies and colleges for a text-book within moderate limits, yet soundly based and covering in full outline the whole subject. This is the origin of the "Introduction to Political Economy," first published in 1877, twelve years after the other. Its success as a text-book and as a book of reading for young people has already justified, and will doubtless continue to justify in the future, the forethought of its promoters. It has found a place in many popular libraries, and in courses of prescribed reading. Twice it has been carefully corrected and somewhat enlarged, and is now in its final form. In the preface to the later editions of the "Introduction" may be found the following sentence, which expresses a feeling not likely to undergo any change in the time to come:—"I have long been, and am still, ambitious that these books of mine may become the horn-books of my countrymen in the study of this fascinating Science."

Why, then, should I have undertaken of my own motion a new and third book on Political Economy, and attempted to mark the completion of the third cycle of a dozen years each of teaching it, by offering to the public the present volume? One reason is implied in the title, "*Principles of Political Economy.*" There are three extended historical chapters in the earlier book, occupying more than one-quarter of its entire space, which were indeed novel, which cost me wide research and very great labor, and which have also proven useful and largely illustrative of almost every phase of Economics; but I wanted to leave behind me one book of about the same size as that, devoted exclusively to the Principles of the Science, and using History only incidentally to illustrate in passing each topic as it came under review. For a college text-book as this is designed to become, and for a book of reading and reference for technical purposes, it seems better that all the space should be taken up by purely scientific discussion and illustration. This does not mean, however, that great pains have not been taken in every part to make this book also easily intelligible, and as readable and interesting as such careful discussions can be made.

A second reason is, to provide for myself a fresh text-book to teach from. My mind has become quite too thoroughly familiarized with the other, even down to the very words, by so long a course of instructing from it, for the best results in the class-room. Accordingly, a new plan of construction has been adopted. Instead of the fourteen chapters there, there are but seven chapters here. Not a page nor a paragraph as such has been copied from either of the preceding books. Single sentences, and sometimes several of them together, when they exactly fitted the purposes of the new context, have been incorporated here and there, in what is throughout both in form and style a new book, neither an enlargement nor an abridgment nor a recasting of any other. I anticipate great pleasure in the years immediately to come from the handling with my classes, who have always been of much assistance to me from the first in studying Political Economy, a fresh book written expressly for them and for others like-circumstanced; in which every principle is drawn from the facts of every-day life by way of induction, and also stands in vital touch with such facts (past or present) by way of illustration.

The third and only other reason needful to be mentioned here is, that in recent years the legislation of my country in the matter of cheap Money and of artificial restrictions on Trade has run so directly counter to sound Economics in their very core, that I felt it a debt due to my countrymen to use once more the best and ripest results of my life-long studies, in the most cogent and persuasive way possible within strictly scientific limits, to help them see and act for themselves in the way of escape from false counsels and impoverishing statutes. Wantonly and enormously heavy lies the hand of the national Government upon the masses of the people at present. But the People are sovereign, and not their transient agents in the government; and the signs are now cheering indeed, that they have not forgotten their native word of command, nor that government is instituted for the sole benefit of the governed and governing people, nor that the greatest good of the greatest number is the true aim and guide of Legislation. I am grateful for the proofs that appear on every hand, that former labors in these directions and under these motives have proven themselves to have been both opportune and effective; and I am sanguine almost to certainty, that this reiterated effort undertaken for the sake of my fellow-citizens as a whole, will slowly bear abundant fruit also, as towards their liberty of action as individuals, and in their harmonious co-operation together as entire classes to the end of popular comforts and universal progress.

A. L. PERRY.

WILLIAMS COLLEGE,
    November 25, 1890.

CHAPTER I.
VALUE.

The first question that confronts the beginner in this science, and the one also that controls the whole scope of his inquiries to the very end, is: What is the precise subject of Political Economy? Within what exact field do its investigations lie? There is indeed a short and broad and full answer at hand to this fundamental and comprehensive question; and yet it is every way better for all concerned to reach this answer by a route somewhat delayed and circuitous, just as it is better in ascending a mountain summit for the sake of a strong and complete view to circle up leisurely on foot or on horseback, rather than to dash straight up to the top by a cog-wheel railway and take all of a sudden what might prove to be a less impressive or a more confusing view.

The preliminary questions are: What sort of facts has Political Economy to deal with, to inquire into, to classify, to make a science of? Are these facts easily separable in the mind and in reality from other kinds of facts perhaps liable to be confounded with them? Are they facts of vast importance to the welfare of mankind? And are the activities of men everywhere greatly and increasingly occupied with just those things, with which this science has exclusively to do? Let us see if we cannot come little by little by a route of our own to clear and true answers for all these questions.

If one should take his stand for an hour upon London Bridge, perhaps the busiest bit of street in the world, and cast his eyes around intelligently to see what he can see, and begin also to classify the things coming under his vision, what might he report to himself and to others? Below the bridge in what is called the "Pool," which was dredged out for that very purpose by the ancient Romans, there lie at anchor or move coming and going many merchant-ships of all nations, carrying out and bringing in to an immense amount in the whole aggregate tangible articles of all kinds to and from the remote as well as the near nations of the earth. All this movement of visible goods, home and foreign, is in the interest and under the impulse of Buying and Selling. The foreign goods come in simply to buy, that is, to pay for, the domestic goods taken away; and these latter go out in effect even if not in appearance to buy, that is, to pay for, the foreign goods coming in. At the same hour the bridge itself is covered with land-vehicles of every sort moving in both directions, loaded with salable articles of every description; artisans of every name are coming and going; merchants of many nationalities step within the field of view; and porters and servants and errand-boys are running to and fro, all in some direct relation to the sale or purchase of those visible and tangible things called in Political Economy *Commodities*. Moreover, vast warehouses built in the sole interest of trade on both sides the river above and below the bridge, built to receive and to store for a time till their ultimate consumers are found, some of these thousand things bought and sold among men, lift their roofs towards heaven in plain sight. Doubtless some few persons, like our observer himself, may be on the spot for pleasure or instruction, but for the most part, all that he can see, the persons, the things, the buildings, even the bridge itself, are where they are in the interest of *Sales* of some sort, mostly of Commodities. What is thus true of a single point in London is true in a degree of every other part of London, of every part of Paris and of Berlin, and in its measure of every other city and village and hamlet in the whole world. Wherever there is a street there is some exchange of commodities upon it, and wherever there is a market there are buyers and sellers of commodities.

If the curiosity of our supposed observer be whetted by what he saw on London Bridge, and if the natural impulse to generalize from particulars be deepened in his mind, he may perhaps on his return to America take an opportunity to see what he can see and learn what he can learn within and around one of the mammoth cotton mills in Lowell or Fall River or Cohoes. Should he take his stand for this purpose at one of these points, say Lowell, he will be struck at once by some of the differences between what he saw on the bridge and what he now sees in the mill. He will indeed see as before some commodities brought in and carried out, such as the raw cotton and new machinery and the finished product ready for sale, but in general no other commodities than the cotton in its various stages of manufacture, and those like the machinery and means of transportation directly connected with transforming the cotton into cloth and taking it to market.

But he sees a host of persons both within and without the mill, all busy here and there, and all evidently bound to the establishment by a strong unseen tie of some sort; he sees varying degrees of authority and subordination in these persons from the Treasurer, the apparent head of the manufactory, down to the teamsters in the yard and the common laborers within and without; he will not find the owners of the property present in any capacity, for they are scattered capitalists of Boston and elsewhere, who have combined through an act of incorporation their distinct capitals into a "Company" for manufacturing cotton; besides their Treasurer present, whose act is their act and whose contracts their contracts, he will see an Agent also who acts under the Treasurer and directly upon the Overseers and their assistants in the spinning and weaving and coloring and finishing rooms, and under these Operatives of every grade as skilled and unskilled; and lastly he will observe, that the direct representatives of the owners and all other persons present from highest to lowest are conspiring with a will towards the common end of getting the cotton cloth all made and marketed.

What is it that binds all these persons together? A little tarrying in the Treasurer's office will answer this question for our observer and for us. He will find it to be the second kind of Buying and Selling. At stated times the Treasurer pays the salary of the Agent, and his own. He pays the wages of the Overseers and the wages of all the Operatives and Laborers,—men and women and children. Here he finds a buying and selling on a great scale not of material commodities as before, but of personal services of all the various kinds. Every man and woman and child connected with the factory and doing its work sells an intangible personal service to the "Company" and takes his pay therefor, which last is a simple buying on the part of the unseen employers. Here, then, in this mill is a single specimen of this buying and selling of personal services, which is going on to an immense extent and in every possible direction in each civilized country of the world, and everywhere to an immensely increased volume year by year. Clergymen and lawyers and physicians and teachers and legislators and judges and musicians and actors and artisans of every name and laborers of every grade sell their intangible services to Society, and take their pay back at the market-rate. The aggregate value of all these services sold in every advanced country is probably greater than the aggregate value of the tangible commodities sold there. At any rate, both classes alike, commodities and services, are bought and sold under substantially the same economic principles.

The inductive appetite in intelligent persons, that is to say, their desire to classify facts and to generalize from particulars, almost always grows by what it feeds on; and our supposed observer will scarcely rest contented until he has taken up at least one more stand-point, from which to observe men's Buying and Selling. Suppose now he enter for this purpose on any business-day morning the New York Clearing-House. He will see about 125 persons present, nearly one half of these bank clerks sitting behind desks, and the other half standing before these desks or moving in cue from one to the next. The room is perfectly still. Not a word is spoken. The Manager of the Clearing with his assistant sits or stands on a raised platform at one end of the room, and gives the signal to begin the Exchange. No commodities of any name or nature are within the field of view. The manager indeed and his assistant and two clerks of the establishment who sit near him are in receipt of salaries for their personal services, and all the other clerks present receive wages for their services from their respective banks, but the exchange about to commence is no sale of personal services any more than it is a sale of tangible commodities. It is however a striking instance of the buying and selling of some valuables of the third and final class of valuable things.

At a given signal from the manager the (say) 60 bank messengers, each standing in front of the desk of his own bank and each having in hand before him 59 small parcels of papers, the parcels arranged in the same definite order as the desks around the room, step forward to the next desk and deliver each his parcel to the clerk sitting behind it, and so on till the circuit of the room is made. It takes but ten minutes. Each parcel is made up of cheques or credit-claims, the *property* of the bank that brings it and the *debts* of the bank to which it is delivered. Accordingly each bank of the circle receives through its sitting clerk its own *debits* to all the rest of the banks, and delivers to all through its standing messenger its own *credits* as off-set. In other words, each bank buys of the rest what it owes to each with what each owes to it. It is at bottom a mutual buying and selling of debts. There is of course a daily balance on one side or the other between every two of these banks, which must be settled in money, because it would never happen in practice that each should owe the other precisely the same sum on any one day; but substantially and almost exclusively the exchange at the Clearing-House is a simple trade in credit-claims. Each bank pays its debts by credits. A merchant is a dealer in commodities, a laborer is a dealer in services, and a banker is a dealer in credits. Each of the three is a buyer and seller alike, and the difference is only in the kind of valuables specially dealt in by each. In all cases alike, however, there is no buying without selling and no selling without buying; because, when one buys he must always pay for what he buys and that is selling, and when one sells he must always take his pay for what he sells and that is buying. This is just as true when one credit is bought or sold against a commodity or a service, and when two or more credits are bought and sold as against each other, as it is when two commodities or two services are exchanged one for the other.

But the Clearing-House is not by any means the only place where credits or debts (they are the same thing) are bought and sold. Every bank is such a place. Every broker's office is such a place. Every place is an establishment of the same kind where commercial rights, that is, claims to be realized in future time and for which a consideration is paid, are offered for sale and sold. The amount of transactions in Credits in every commercial country undoubtedly surpasses the amount in Commodities or that in Services.

Now our supposed observer and classifier, having noted on London Bridge the sale of material commodities, and in the Lowell Mill the sale of personal services, and within the New York Clearing-House the sale of credit-claims, has seen in substance everything that ever was or ever will be exhibited in the world of trade. He may rest. There is no other class of salable things than these three. Keen eyes and minds skilled in induction have been busy for two millenniums and a half more or less to find another class of things bought and sold among men, and have not yet found it or any trace of it. This work has been perfectly and scientifically done. The generalization is completed for all time.

The *genus*, then, with which Political Economy deals from beginning to end, has been discovered, can be described, and is easily and completely separable for its own purposes of science from all other kinds and classes and *genera* of things, namely, Salable things or (what means precisely the same) Valuable things or (what is exactly equivalent) Exchangeable things. In other words, the sole and single class of things, with which the Science of Political Economy has to do, is Valuables, whose origin and nature and extent and importance it is the purpose of the present chapter to unfold. We have fully seen already that this Genus, Valuables, is sub-divided into three *species*, and three only, namely, Commodities, Services, Credits. A little table here may help at once the eye and the mind:—

ECONOMICS.

The Genus   *Valuables*

The Species   { *Commodities*
                { *Services*
                { *Credits*

If only these three species of things are ever bought and sold, then it certainly follows that only six kinds of commercial exchanges are possible to be found in the world, namely these:—

- 1. *A commodity for a commodity.*

- 2. *A commodity for a personal service.*

- 3. *A commodity for a credit-claim.*

- 4. *A personal service for another service.*

- 5. *A personal service for a credit-claim.*

- 6. *One credit-claim for another.*

Though the kinds of possible exchanges are thus very few, the exchanges themselves in one or other of these six forms and in all of them are innumerable on every business day in every civilized country of the globe. And this point is to be particularly noted, that while buying and selling in these forms has been going on everywhere since the dawn of authentic History, it has gone on all the while in ever-increasing volume, it is increasing now more rapidly and variously than ever, and moreover all signs foretell that it will play a larger and still larger part in the affairs of men and nations as this old world gains in age and unity.

Damascus is one of the very oldest cities of the world, and its very name means a "*seat of trade.*" We are told in the Scriptures, that Abraham about 2000 years before Christ went up out of Egypt "very rich in cattle, in silver, and in gold," and the only possible way he could have acquired these possessions was by buying and selling. He afterwards purchased the cave and the field in Hebron for a family burial-place, and "weighed unto Ephron the silver which he had named in the audience of the sons of Heth, four hundred shekels of silver, current money with the merchant." We may notice here, that there were then "merchants" as a class, that silver by weight passed as "money" from hand to hand, and that in the lack of written deeds to land, as we have them, sales were "made sure" before the faces of living men, who would tell the truth and pass on the word. Abraham indeed seems to have given the pitch for the song of trade sung by his descendants, the Jews, from that day to this; for Jacob, his grandson, was a skilled trafficker, not to say a secret trickster, in his bargains; and wherever in the Old World or the New the Jews have been, *there* have been in fact and in fame busy buyers and sellers.

But the Jews have had no special privileges in the realm of trade; on the contrary, they have always been under special disabilities both legal and social. Even in England, the most liberal country in Europe, they were exiled for long periods, maltreated at all points of contact with other people, more or less put under the ban of the Common and the Statute law, often outrageously taxed on their goods and persons, and studiously kept out of the paths of highest public employment even down to a time within the memory of living men. Yet so natural is the impulse to trade, so universally diffused, so imperative also if progress is in any direction to be attained, that the English and all other peoples were as glad to borrow money, that is, buy the use of it, of the persecuted Jews, as the latter were to get money by buying and selling other things, and then to loan it, that is, sell the use of it, under the best securities (never very good) for its return with interest, that they could obtain. Happily, the mutual gains that always wait on the Exchanges even when their conditions are curtailed, of course attended the mutilated exchanges between Jews and Christians: otherwise, they would not continue to take place.

Christianity, however, as the perfected Judaism, gradually brought in the better conditions, the higher impulses, and the more certain rewards, of Trade, all which, we may be sure, were designed in the divine Plan of the world. What is called the Progress of Civilization has been marked and conditioned at every step by an extension of the opportunities, a greater facility in the use of the means, a more eager searching for proper expedients, and a higher certainty in the securing of the returns, of mutual exchanges among men. There have been indeed, and there still are, vast obstacles lying across the pathway of this Progress in the unawakened desires and reluctant industry and short-sighted selfishness of individuals, as well as in the ignorant prejudices and mistaken legislation of nations; but all the while Christianity has been indirectly tugging away at these obstacles, and Civilization has been able to rejoice over the partial or complete removal of some of them; while also Christianity directly works out in human character those chief qualities, on which the highest success of commercial intercourse among men will always depend, namely, Foresight, Diligence, Integrity, and mutual Trust; so that, what we call Civilization is to a large extent only the result of a better development of these human qualities in domestic and foreign commerce.

Contrary to a common conception in the premises, the sacred books of both Jews and Christians display no bias at all against buying and selling, but rather extol such action as praiseworthy, and also those qualities of mind and habits of life that lead up to it and tend too to increase its amount, and they constantly illustrate by means of language derived from traffic the higher truths and more spiritual life, which are the main object of these inspired writers. It is indeed true that the chosen people of God were forbidden to take Usury of each other, though they were permitted to take it freely of strangers, and that they were forbidden to buy horses and other products out of Egypt, for fear they would be religiously corrupted by such commercial intercourse with idolaters; but there is nothing of this sort in the law of Moses that cannot be easily explained from the grand purpose to found an agricultural commonwealth for religious ends, in which commonwealth no family could permanently alienate its land, and in which it was a great object to preserve the independence and equality of the tribes and families. Throughout the Old Testament there is no word or precept that implies that trade in itself is not helpful and wholesome; there were sharp and effective provisions for the recovery of debts; there were any number of exhortations to diligence in business, such as, "*In the morning sow thy seed, and at evening withhold not thy hand*"; King Solomon himself made a gigantic exchange in preparation for the temple with King Hiram of Tyre, by which the cedars of Lebanon were to be paid for by the grain and oil of the agricultural kingdom; chapter xxvii of the prophet Ezekiel is a graphic description of the commerce of the ancient world as it centered in the market of Tyre, a description carried out into detail both as to the nations that frequented that market and as to the products that were exchanged in it,—"*silver, iron, tin, lead, persons of men, vessels of brass, horses, horsemen, mules, horns of ivory, ebony-wood, carbuncles, purple work, fine linen, corals, rubies, wheat, pastry, syrup, oil, balm, wine of Helbon, white wool, thread, wrought iron, cassia, sweet* reed, cloth, lambs, rams, goats, precious spices, precious stones, splendid apparel, mantles of blue, embroidered work, chests of damask, and gold"; and chapter xxxi of Proverbs describes the model housewife in terms like these,—

"*The heart of her husband trusteth in her, And he is in no want of gain. She seeketh wool and flax, And worketh willingly with her hands. She is like the merchants' ships; She bringeth her food from afar. She riseth while it is yet night, And giveth food to her family, And a task to her maidens. She layeth a plan for a field and buyeth it; With the fruit of her hands she planteth a vineyard. She perceiveth how pleasant is her gain, And her lamp is not extinguished in the night. She putteth forth her hands to the distaff, And her hands take hold of the spindle. She maketh for herself coverlets; Her clothing is of fine linen and purple. She maketh linen garments and selleth them, And delivereth girdles to the merchants.*"

Still more explicit and instructive are the words and spirit of the New Testament. There cannot be the least doubt that the whole influence of Christianity is favorable to the freest commercial exchanges at home and abroad, because these depend largely on mutual confidence between man and man, of which confidence Christianity is the greatest promoter. It may be conceded at once that our Lord "*overthrew the tables of the money-changers and the seats of them that sold doves*" within the sacred precincts of the temple, but this, not because it is wrong to change money or sell doves, but because that was not the *place* for such merchandising; so He himself explained his own action in the sequel; provincial worshippers coming up to Jerusalem must needs have their coins changed into the money of the Capital, and must needs buy somewhere the animal victims for sacrifice; but the whip of small cords had significance only as to the *place*, and not at all as to the *propriety*, of such trading.

One of our Lord's parables, the parable of the Talents, sets forth in several striking lights the privilege and duty and reward of diligent trading. "*Then he that had received the five talents went and traded with the same, and made them other five talents.*" And when this servant came to the reckoning, and brought as the result of his free and busy traffic "*five talents more,*" the prompt and hearty approval of his lord—"well done, thou good and faithful servant"— becomes the testimony of the New Testament to the merit and the profit and the benefit of a vigorous buying and selling. For this servant could not have been authoritatively pronounced good and faithful if the results of his action commended had been in any way prejudicial to others. The truth is, as we shall abundantly see by and by with the reasons of it, that any man who buys and sells under the free and natural conditions of trade, benefits the man he trades with just as much as he benefits himself. But the parable has a still stronger word in favor of exchanges. There was another servant also entrusted with capital by his lord at the same time, when the latter was about to travel "*into a far country.*" We are expressly told that distribution was made "*to every man according to his several ability,*" and thus this servant was only entrusted with a single talent, the size of the capital given to him being in just proportion to the size of the man,—the smallest share falling of course to the smallest man. But he had the same opportunity as the two others. The world was open to him. Capital was in demand, if not in those parts then in some other, to which, like his lord, he might straightway take his journey. But when his time of reckoning came, and he had nothing to show for the use of his capital, he upbraided his lord as a hard man for expecting any increase, and brought out his bare talent wrapped in a napkin, saying, "*I was afraid, and I went and hid thy talent in the earth.*" His wise lord at once denounced this servant as "*wicked and slothful,*" insisted that his money ought to have been "*put to the exchangers,*" and said finally in a just anger "*cast ye the unprofitable servant into outer darkness.*"

It is moreover in incidental passages of the Scriptures, in which the methods of business are commended to the searchers after higher things, that we see their high estimate of those methods and gains. "*Buy the truth, and sell it not; buy wisdom and understanding*" (Prov. xxiii, 23). "*Buying up for yourselves opportunities*" (Col. iv, 5). "*I counsel thee to buy of me gold refined by fire, that thou mayest be rich; and white garments, that thou mayest be clothed; and eye-salve to anoint thine eyes, that thou mayest see*" (Rev. iii, 18). "*But rather let him labor, working with his hands at that which is good, that he may have to give to him that is in need*" (Eph. iv, 28). "*But if any one provideth not for his own, and especially for those of his own house, he hath denied the faith, and is worse than an unbeliever*" (1 Tim. v, 8).

Now, the universal test and proof of any truth is its harmony with some other truths. Does an alleged truth fall in with and fill out well some other demonstrated and accepted proposition, or a number of such other propositions? If so, then that truth is *proved.* Human reason can no further go. The mind rests with relish and content in a new acquisition. To apply this to the case in hand,—if men were designed of their Maker to buy and sell to their own mutual benefit and advancement, if mankind have always been buying and selling as towards that end and with that obvious result, and if the Future promises to increase and reduplicate the buying and selling of the Present in every direction without end, and all in the interest of a broad civilization and a true and lasting progress; and if, in harmony with these truths, the written revelation of God in every part of it assumes that buying and selling in its inmost substance and essential forms be good and righteous and progressive, and suitable in all its ends and methods to illustrate and enforce ends and methods in the higher kingdom of spiritual and eternal Life;—then these coördinate truths will logically and certainly follow, (1) that Trade is natural and essential and beneficial to mankind; (2)

that it constitutes in an important sense a realm of human thought and action by itself, separate from the neighboring realm of Giving, and equally from the hostile realm of Stealing; and (3) that a careful analysis of what buying and selling in its own peculiar nature is, a thorough ascertainment and a consequent clear statement of its fundamental laws, and a faithful exposure of what in individual selfishness and in subtle or open Legislation makes against these laws, *must be of large consequence to the welfare of mankind.*

Accordingly, let us now attempt such Analysis and Ascertainment and Exposure. This is precisely the task that lies before us in this book—just this, and nothing more. The term, "Political Economy," has long been and is still an elastic title over the zealous work of many men in many lands; but in the hands of the present writer during a life now no longer short, the term has always had a definite meaning, the work has covered an easily circumscribed field, and so the present undertaking concerns only Buying and Selling and what is essentially involved in that. This gives scope and verge enough for the studies of a life-time. This has the advantage of a complete sphere of its own. Terms may thus be made as definite as the nature of language will ever allow; definitions will thus cover things of one kind only; and generalizations, although they may be delicate and difficult, will deal with no incongruous and obstinate material.

1. The grandfather of the writer, an illiterate but long-headed farmer, was able to give good points to his three college-bred sons, by insisting that they look *"into the natur on't."* What, then, are the ultimate elements of Buying and Selling? What are the invariable conditions that precede, accompany, and follow, any and every act of Trade? Of course we are investigating now and throughout this treatise the deliberative acts of reasonably intelligent human beings, in one great department of their common foresight and rational action. We have consequently nothing to do here with Fraud or Theft or Mania or Gift. Acts put forth under the impulse of these are direct opposites of, or at best antagonistic to, acts of Trade. They tend to kill trade, and therefore they are no part of trade. These, then, and such as these, aside, we will now analyze a single Act of Exchange at one time and place,—which will serve in substance for all acts of exchange in all times and places, and just find out for ourselves what are the Fundamentals and Essentials of that matter, with which alone we have to do in this science of Political Economy.

Incidental reference was had a little way back to an Exchange once made between King Solomon of Jerusalem and King Hiram of Tyre. Let that be our typical instance. (a) *There were two persons*, Solomon and Hiram. Those two, and no more, stood face to face, as it were, to make a commercial bargain. They made it, and it was afterwards executed. The execution indeed concerned a great many persons on both sides, and occupied a long period of time; but the bargain itself, the trade, the exchange, the covenant, concerned only two persons, and occupied but a moment of time. It made no difference with the bargain as such, with the binding nature of it, with the terms of it, with the mutual gains of it, that each person represented a host of others, subordinates and subjects, who would have to coöperate in the carrying of it out, because each king had the right to speak for his subjects as well as for himself, for commercial purposes each was an agent as well as a monarch, the word of each concluded the consent and the action of others as well as his own. Nor did it make any, the least, difference with this exchange or the advantages of it, that each party to it belonged to, was even the head of, independent and sometimes hostile Peoples. Commerce is one thing, and nationality a totally different thing. The present point is, in the words of the old proverb,—"It takes two to make a bargain." And it takes *only* two to make a bargain. When corporations and even nations speak in trade, they speak, and speak finally, through one accredited agent. We reach, then, as the first bit of our analysis of Trade, the fact, that there are always two parties to it, "the party of the first part and the party of the second part."

(b) *There were two desires*, Solomon's desire for cedar-timbers to build the temple with, and Hiram's desire for wheat and oil with which to support the people of his sterile kingdom. "*So Hiram gave Solomon cedar-trees and fir-trees according to all his desire: and Solomon gave Hiram twenty thousand measures of wheat for food to his household, and twenty measures of pure oil.*" The desire of each party was personal and peculiar, known at first only to himself, but upon occasion became directed towards something in the possession of the other, and each at length became aware of the desire of the other, and also of his own ability to satisfy the want of the other. If Solomon could have satisfied his desire for timber by his own or his subjects' efforts directly, this trade would never have taken place; if Hiram or his subjects could have gotten the wheat and oil directly out of their narrow and sandy strips of sea-coast, this trade would not have taken place; and so there must be in every case of trade not only two desires each springing from a separate person, but also each person must have in his possession something fitted to gratify the desire of the other person, and each be willing to yield that something into the possession of the other for the sake of receiving from him that which will satisfy his own desire, and so both desires be satisfied indirectly.

Here is the deep and perennial source of exchanges. Men's desires are so many and various, and so constantly becoming more numerous and miscellaneous, and so extremely few of his own wants can ever be met by any one man directly, that the foundation of exchanges, and of a perpetually increasing volume of exchanges, is laid in the deep places of human hearts, namely, in Desires ever welling up to the surface and demanding their satisfaction through an easy and natural interaction with the ever swelling Desires of other men. Here too is a firm foundation (a chief foundation) of human Society. Reciprocal wants, which can only be met through exchanges, draw men together locally and bind them together socially, in hamlets and towns and cities and States and Nations, and also knit ties scarcely less strong and beneficent between the separate and remotest nationalities of the earth. It is certain that an inland commercial route connected the East of Asia with the West of Europe centuries before Christ, and that a traffic was maintained on the frontier of China between the Sina and the Scythians, in the manner still followed by the Chinese and the Russians at *Kiachta*. The Sina had an independent position in Western China as early as the eighth century before Christ, and five centuries later established their sway under the dynasty of Tsin (whence our word "China") over the whole of the empire. The prophet Isaiah exclaims (xlix, 12), "Behold! these shall come from far; and behold! these from the North and from the West; *and these from the land of Sinim.*" The second bit of our analysis leads to Desires as an essential and fundamental element in every commercial transaction.

(c) *There were two efforts*, those of the Tyrians as represented by King Hiram and those of the Israelites as represented by King Solomon. It was no holiday task that was implied in the proposition of Solomon to the party of the other part,—"*Send me now cedar-trees, fir-trees, and algum-trees out of Lebanon; for I know that thy servants are skilful to cut timber in Lebanon; even to prepare me timber in abundance, for the house which I am about to build shall be wonderfully great.*" On the other hand, the efforts insolved on the part of the people of Israel in paying for these timbers, and for their transportation by sea from Lebanon to Joppa, were equally gigantic. Solomon's offer in return for the proposed service of the Tyrian king was in these words,—"*And behold, I will give to thy servants, the hewers that cut timber, twenty thousand measures of beaten wheat, and twenty thousand measures of barley, and twenty thousand baths of wine, and twenty thousand baths of oil.*"

The reason why two efforts are always an element in every act of traffic, however small or however large the transaction may be, is the obvious reason, that the things rendered in exchange, whether they be Commodities, Services, or Credits, invariably cost efforts of some kind to get them ready to sell and to sell them, and no person can have a just claim to render them in exchange, who has not either put forth these efforts himself or become proprietor in some way of the result of such efforts. Efforts accordingly are central in all trade. Every trade in its inmost nature is and must be either an exchange of two Efforts directly, as when one of two farmers personally helps his neighbor in haying for the sake of securing that neighbor's personal help in his own harvesting, or an exchange of two things each of which is the result of previous Efforts of somebody, as when a man gives a silver dollar for a bushel of wheat. The third bit of the present analysis brings us to Efforts, perhaps the most important factor in the whole list.

(d) *There were also two reciprocal estimates*, the estimate of King Hiram of all the efforts requisite to cut and hew and float the timber, as compared with the aggregate of efforts needed to obtain the necessary wheat and barley and wine and oil in any other possible way; and the estimate of King Solomon of all the labors required to grow and market these agricultural products, as compared with what would otherwise be involved in getting the much-wished-for timbers. Such estimates invariably precede every rational exchange of products. It is not in human nature to render a greater effort or the result of it, when a lesser effort or the result of it will as well procure the satisfaction of a desire. Efforts are naturally irksome. No more of them will ever be put forth than is necessary to meet the want that calls them forth. No man in his senses will ever put more labor on anything, with which to buy something else, than is necessary to get that something else by direct effort or through some other exchange. Here we are on ground as solid as the very substance of truth can make it. The Jews of Solomon's time were too shrewd and sparing of irksome labor to devote themselves for years to the toils of the field and of the vat to get by traffic the materials for their temple, if they could have gotten those materials by a less expenditure of toil in any other way. Those Phœnicians of Tyre and Sidon, the born merchants of the East, the founders of commercial Carthage in the West, if they could have extorted from the reluctant sands of their coast the cereals and the vines and olives requisite for their own support with only so much of exertion as was needed to get that to market with which to buy them, would never have taken the indirect in preference to the direct method. They took the indirect, because it was the easier, and therefore the better.

It may, accordingly, be laid down as a maxim, that men never buy and sell to satisfy their wants but when that is the easiest and best way to satisfy them. It saves effort. It saves time. It saves trouble. It divides labor. It induces skill. It propels progress. But in order to determine which may be the easier way, requires constant *estimates* on the part of each party to a possible trade. Shall I shave myself or go to the barber? Before I decide, I estimate the direct effort in the light of the effort to get that with which to pay the barber for his service. If I trade with him, it is because I deem it easier, cheaper in effort, more convenient in time. Trade means comparisons in every case—comparisons by both parties—and in the more recondite and complicated cases, elaborate comparisons and often comprehensive calculations involving future time.

Now these estimates inseparable from exchanges, and these calculations which are a factor in all the far-reaching exchanges, are mental activities. They quicken and strengthen the *minds* of men. Trade is usually, if not always, the initial step in the mental development of individuals and nations. Desires stir early in the minds of all children; efforts more or less earnest are the speedy outcome of natural desires; direct efforts, however, to satisfy these soon reach their limits; it is now but a step over to simple exchanges, by which the desires are met indirectly; exchanges once commenced tend to multiply in all directions, and the estimates that must precede and accompany these are mental states,—the more of them, the greater the mental development, the higher the education; consequently, commerce domestic and foreign is a grand agency in civilization, a constant and broadening impulse towards progress in all its forms; and Christianity, as we have already seen, is friendly to commerce in its every breath. Those, therefore, who talk and preach about Trade as tending to *materialism*, do not know what they are talking about. Because Commodities are material things, and because a portion of the trade of the world concerns itself with commodities, these shallow thinkers jump to the conclusion that trade is materialistic. *It is just the reverse.* Let us hear no more from Professor Pulpit or Platform that buying and selling is antagonistic to men's higher intellectual and spiritual culture, because the present careful analysis has brought us indubitably to mental Estimates and prolonged comparisons, which are activities of Mind, as the fourth and a leading factor among the radical elements of Sale.

(e) *There were two renderings*, King Hiram's rendering at Joppa the desired cedars from the mountains of Lebanon, and King Solomon's rendering in return at Tyre the food products grown in his fertile country. These renderings were visible to all men. Unlike the desires and the estimates, which were subjective and invisible; the actual exchange of the products, the culmination of the previous efforts, the stipulated renderings by and to each party, were outward and objective—"known and read of all men." This is the reason why public attention is always strongly drawn to this particular link of the chain of events which we are now unlocking and taking apart, while other links of the series, that are just as essential, almost wholly escape observation. The ports and the markets are apt to be noisy and conspicuous, when the desires and the estimates and the satisfactions, without which in their place there would be no market-places, work in silence, and leave no records except the indirect one of the renderings themselves.

It is of great moment to note here, that each of the two parties to an exchange always has an advantage over the other, either absolute or relative, in the rendering his own product, whatever it may be, as compared with his present ability to get directly or through any other exchange the product he receives in return. Take the example in hand. Cedars and sandal-wood were natural to Mount Lebanon; there were no other workmen in those regions of country that could "*skill to hew timber like unto the Sidonians*"; the Mediterranean afforded a level and free and easy highway from its northern coast to the Judean seaport at Joppa; and all these natural and acquired facilities put King Hiram into a posture of advantage in the rendering of timber, not only over the Jews, but also over all the other peoples in the basin of the midland sea. Still this advantage, great as it was, could only be made a real and palpable gain to themselves, the proprietors of the timber, by means of some exchange with somebody else, by which some wants of their own greater than their present want of timber, could be supplied by means of the timber. They had more of that commodity, and more skill to fashion and transport it, than their present and immediately prospective needs could make use of; and the only way in which they could practically avail themselves of their advantages, was, to sell their surplus timber and buy with it something that they needed more. Otherwise their very advantage perished with them. God has scattered such a diversity of blessings and capacities and opportunities over the earth on purpose, that, through traffic, on which his special benediction rests, the good of each part and people may become the portion of other parts and peoples.

So, on the other hand, of the southern neighbors of the Tyrians. There the earth brought forth by handfuls. There was an abundance of corn in the land, even to the tops of the mountains. Its fruit did indeed shake like Lebanon. But there were no cedars there, no fir-trees, no sandal-woods. How short-sighted, then, and futile, would it have been for the Jews, to try to hang on in their own behoof to all the natural advantages that God had given to them, and to say, We will not part with the direct results of any of them, we will build treasure-cities as they did in Egypt, we will store up all the fruits of these fat years against the possible coming of some famine years in the time to come. That is anything in ordinary times but the divine plan. It is anything but the letter and spirit of the divine injunction: "*Him that keepeth back corn the people curse; but blessing shall be upon the head of him that selleth it*" (Prov. xii, 26). Had they talked and acted thus, no temple could then have been built in Jerusalem, and the people of that generation would have lost the moral and religious impulse and uplifting of their service and sacrifice. Their grain would have become worthless from its very abundance, and would have decayed on their hands. They would have missed a great gain for themselves, and would have snatched away from their neighbors to the northward a providential opportunity for an equal gain.

The general truth must not be lost sight of here, even in passing, that all trade whatsoever is based upon a Diversity of relative Advantage as between the parties exchanging products. If, for example, the Hills of Judah and the Mountains of Israel had been covered with timber suitable for building the temple, and the coasts of Tyre and Sidon and the foot-hills of Lebanon had been fertile stretches of arable land, this particular trade would never have been thought of and could never have been realized. There would have been no gain in it for either party, and unless there be a valid gain for both parties at least in prospect, no trade will ever spring into being, because there would be no motive, no impulse, no reason, in it. Unless the Jews could get the timber easier by raising grain to pay for it, and the Tyrians get the oil and wheat and barley easier by cutting and floating timber to pay for them,—no trade; but the greater easiness to each actually came about, because each had an Advantage both natural and acquired over the other in his own rendering, and the mutual gain of the trade was wholly owing to that circumstance. So far as that matter went, the Tyrians had no cause to envy their neighbors the superior soil of the south, for they reaped indirectly but effectively a part of those harvests for themselves; and the Jews had no reason to be jealous of their northern neighbors on account of the noble forests crowning their mountains, because through trade they secured easily to themselves a share of that vast natural advantage. Diversity of Advantage both natural and acquired is the sole ground of Trade both domestic and foreign; and consequently by means of trade the peculiar advantages of each are fully shared in by all.

It is perhaps less obvious but surely equally true, that the greater the relative diversity of advantage as between two exchangers, the more profitable does the exchange become to each. If the Vale of Sharon had been twice as fertile as it was, and the cedars of Lebanon twice as large and lofty as they were, the easier and better would Israel have gotten its timber, and the more secure and abundant would have become the food of Tyre and Sidon; and, therefore, the more unreasonable, or rather the more absurd and wicked, would have been any envy or jealousy of either of the superior advantages at any point or points of the other. So universally. By the divine Purpose as expressed in the constitution of Nature, in the structure of Man, and in the laws of Society, Trade in good measure and degree imparts to each the bounties of all, arms each with the power of all, and impels each by the progress of all.

One other important matter is closely connected with these two Renderings, which is the fifth bit in succession of our present analysis, namely this, that traffic renderings always make necessary new and better routes of travel and transportation. It is mainly for this reason, that persons and things have to be carried to distances less or greater in order to consummate these Renderings of home and foreign commerce, that roads by land and routes by sea have been sought for and found, made and made shorter, improved as to method and facilitated as to force, from the dawn of History until the present hour. It was to get the goods of India, and so find a market for the goods of Europe, that the earliest land routes between the two were tried and maintained. The ground-thought of Columbus, meditated on for years, was to discover a new commercial way to India; Magellan with the same intent sailed westward through the Straits that wear his name, and so circumnavigated the globe; repeated searches mainly with the mercantile view, never long intermitted, have attempted ever since the North-West or the North-East passage to India; Vasco da Gama in 1497 boldly accomplished the East passage, and thus changed for all the Continents the channels of trade; the West now trades with all the East through the Suez Canal, dug for that express purpose; and the words, "Panama" and "Nicaragua" are upon everybody's lips, simply because through Central America is the shortest and safest route for men and goods to and from all the Oceans.

Quite recently Dr. W. Heyd has announced through the Berlin Geographical Society the discovery of two commercial routes from India to the West not hitherto described. Trebizond (on the Black Sea) and Tana (at the mouth of the Don) were the chief distributing points. Through Tana passed westward the pepper and ginger and nutmeg and cloves; and the price of spices is said to have doubled in Italy, when the Italians were for a time shut out of Tana in 1343. The chief overland route from India to Tana ran through Cabul to Khiva by the Oxus, and then by land through Astrakhan. The other route to Trebizond passed through Persia, and came out by Tabriz to the Black Sea. It may perhaps be pardoned, if a far homelier, more modern, and even local, illustration be given of the present point, that trade makes roads. The western wall of Williamstown is the mountain range of the Taconics, whose general height is about 2000 feet above tide water at Albany. Within the limits of this town are four natural depressions or passes over this range, which is also the watershed between the Hoosac River on the east and the Little Hoosac on the west. About the beginning of this century, the population was quite sparse in both these valleys, while the impulse to travel and traffic over the barrier was sufficient to build (wholly at local expense) wagon roads over each of the four passes, one of which soon after became a turnpike between Northampton and Albany; and another was built mainly to accommodate the medical practice on the west side of the mountain of Dr. Samuel Porter—a Williamstown surgeon of local eminence. So soon as railroads were constructed to run down these parallel valleys (railroads themselves are perhaps the best illustration of the point in hand), the mountain roads were relatively deserted, and only two of them are now open to transient travel.

Lastly, (f) *There were two satisfactions*, the satisfaction of the southern king in actually obtaining the excellent timbers, without which the cherished national temple could not have gone up; and the satisfaction by the northern king in the easy receiving of the abundant food products for the daily maintenance of his court and kingdom. The simple story of these commercial transactions between Jew and Tyrian indicates clearly enough, what might have been anticipated and what always happens in such circumstances, not only a mutual satisfaction at the completion of each specific exchange, but also a general relation of contentment and peace in consequence of advantageous commercial intercourse. "*And Hiram, king of Tyre, sent his servants unto Solomon; for he had heard, that they had anointed him king in the room of his father; because Hiram was ever a lover of David. And it came to pass, when Hiram heard the words of Solomon, that he rejoiced greatly, and said, Blessed be the Lord this day, which hath given unto David a wise son over this great people; and there was peace between Hiram and Solomon; and they two made a league together.*"

It is plain to reason and to all experience, that mutual Satisfactions are the ultimate thing in exchanges. Our present analysis can go no further, for the reason, that we have now reached in Satisfactions the end, for the sake of which all the previous processes have been gone through with. Persons do not engage in buying and selling for the mere pleasure of it, but always for the sake of some satisfactions derivable to both parties from the issue of it. Ordinary self-inspection and foresight and industry being presupposed, the issue of exchanges is just what was expected by the two persons, the satisfaction of each follows as a matter of course, and stimulates to new exchanges in ever-widening circles.

Since the desires of all men, which the efforts of other men can satisfy through exchange, are indefinite in number and unlimited in degree, there is no end of human Satisfactions to be reached along this road of reciprocal trade; and since the very object of all trade and the actual result of all trade (the exceptions are infinitesimal) is to multiply and reduplicate continually mutual Satisfactions among men; we can see right here what a loss and wrong it is, what a wanton destruction of possible human happiness it is, what a bar to progress among men in comforts and powers it is, for nations to impede and to prohibit commerce by legislation! As we shall see more fully in a later chapter, Governments can have no moral or constitutional right to restrict the trade of their people, except in the sole interest of revenue or health or morals.

Such is the constitution of the universe, that a really good thing is usually cognate with and inseparable from a good many other good things. Buying and selling, as we have now clearly seen, springs right out of the nature of men in the circumstances in which they are providentially placed on the earth, and ends in the satisfaction of innumerable wants common to all men. This makes trade a thoroughly good thing in itself; and consequently it is intimately associated with many other good things. The scriptural instance, that we have been examining, gives a neat illustration of this: "*and there was peace between Hiram and Solomon; and they two made a league together.*" The mutually profitable exchange of commodities led to a feeling of amity between the two neighboring kings; the feeling of amity led to a treaty of Peace between the two adjacent nations; and the "*league*" so ratified not only kept out war from their borders, but also permitted the unhindered continuance of profitable exchanges between them.

So it is always. Peace waits on Commerce. Good-will among the nations is strengthened by the ties of interest and profit among their citizens. The mercantile classes as such are always averse to war, because war is the natural enemy of exchanges. Thus traffic leads to peace and tends to maintain it, and peace preludes increased prosperity, and commercial prosperity under freedom is wholly friendly to mental and moral progress, and Christianity walks before and all along this line of individual and national blessing. The commercial treaty of 1860 between France and England has tended powerfully, perhaps more powerfully than any other single cause, to keep those formerly inter-belligerent nationalities in peace and amity ever since.

We will now put into a little table the final results of the present analysis of Buying and Selling. The ultimate elements seem to be these:

1. *Two Persons.*   4. *Two Estimates.*

2. *Two Desires.*   5. *Two Renderings.*

3. *Two Efforts.*   6. *Two Satisfactions.*

The thoughtful reader will note in this table the fact, that three of these elements are objective, that is, outward and visible; and the other three are subjective, that is, inward and invisible. Persons, Efforts, Renderings, are seen and known of all men; Desires, Estimates, Satisfactions, can be directly known only to the persons who feel and make them. This is a peculiarity of Political Economy, that has been far too little observed even when it has been observed at all. Objective and subjective elements in it meet and mingle in each transaction. Indeed, they alternate, as is shown in the table above: first a Seen, and then an Unseen, Element throughout. It is this commingling of outward and inward, visible and invisible, that makes all the difficulty and gives all the fascination in Political Economy. Whatever carries us into the steady though billowy play of universal human nature is at once difficult and fascinating.

Quite contrary, however, to a common impression, the *certainty* both of action and prediction in all the other Sciences as well as in Economics lies rather in the unseen elements than in those that are seen. Take for an example the calculation of an eclipse: it is not so much from what is visible in the heavens and on the earth that the astronomer infers and predicts to the instant the shadow of one orb thrown upon another, as it is from the wholly hidden but ever-enduring forces of gravitation constantly relating these orbs one to the other. So it is of the Sciences generally; progress is made in them and certainties are reached in connection with them, "*while we look not at the things which are seen, but at the things which are not seen; for the things which are seen are but for a time; but the things which are not seen are everlasting.*" Invisible Desires and Satisfactions felt in connection with Exchanges are among the most constant elements of human nature; they, as it were, give birth to the relatively more transient (though visible) data of Efforts and Renderings; while inferences and conclusions and even predictions may be securely drawn from all of these, giving a solid ground for Political Economy to stand on,—almost as solid as the ground of the chief Physical Sciences.

2. We will next examine the inmost nature and the outward manifestations of *Value*. "Value" is by much the most important word in the Science of Economics; and we must, therefore, comprehend it thoroughly, root and branch. Nearly all the writers in English have used in place of this the word "Wealth" and those in other languages some equivalent and equally concrete word; but the present writer fully satisfied himself some twenty-five years ago, that it is impossible to use that word to any advantage in economical discussions, owing to its inherent ambiguities and concrete associations in the minds of men. He utterly discarded the word at that time, and has found not the least occasion to pick it up again since, and believes now that his substitution of the word "Value" in place of it will ultimately be seen to have been his greatest contribution to that Science, to which he devoted his life.

Even professed and excellent logicians, like John Stuart Mill, found the word "Wealth" an insoluble element in the science of Economics; he commenced his great work by writing, that it was not really needful to *define* the word which nevertheless he laid at the foundation of his discussions, that "every one has a notion sufficiently correct for common purposes of what is meant by Wealth"; he goes on, however, to give at least a half-dozen definitions of the word, no two of which are at all consistent with each other, only one of which embodies a clear and scientific conception, and even to this one he himself does by no means coherently adhere throughout his treatise. No wonder, that this great man died thoroughly dissatisfied with his own work in Economics, and wishing for longer life in which to recast and improve it! No wonder, too, that the crowd of writers both English and American, many of them able and thoughtful and otherwise logical, who have been content to continue to use this irreducible and utterly unscientific word at the bottom, have made a mess of it!

In dropping the word, "Wealth," accordingly, Political Economy has dropped a clog, and its movements are now relatively free and certain; and it is all the more incumbent on the Science for that very reason to define the good word that it substitutes for a bad one with absolute clearness, to explain it through and through until it become quite transparent, and then always to use it in its defined and economical sense, and none other, even though the same word be properly enough used in other senses in common speech and in other than scientific relations. Exactly that is what we are now going to attempt to do in a simple and consecutive order.

(a) Perhaps it will help us to find out precisely what Value *is* by seeing as clearly as possible at the outset what it is *not*. It is not *easy*, and never can be made so, to teach and to learn distinctly what Value is in its ultimate nature and constant changes. Here is the one unavoidable difficulty that lies at the very threshold of Political Economy; and this difficulty, which is not found as in the case of "Wealth" in the meaning of the word but in the complex character of that which the word describes, once overmastered, and one walks thereafter with ease and pleasure throughout the economic domain. It would be wrong and cruel to deny that just here is one hard place in the road for teacher and pupils to get over. It arises wholly from the nature of the subject, as we shall soon see, and not at all from the insufficiency of the word, Value. We have already seen fully, that Buying and Selling in each and every transaction is complex and relative, involving twelve elements every time; that Desires and Estimates and Renderings are especially relative,—each party to a trade desires something in possession of the other, estimates that something relatively to something in his own possession, and finally renders to the other his own something for the sake of receiving the other's something. Now everybody is used to all this and practically understands it perfectly, but it is complicated and reciprocal nevertheless, and Value, which is the single birth of the two Renderings, though perfectly intelligible to him that takes pains, is not a thing to be seized once for all at a passing trot.

Value, then, is *not* a quality of single things, belonging to them as if by nature, as hardness is a quality of a rock or gravity is an attribute of gold; because all physical qualities in physical things, all that which makes or helps to make anything such as it is, may be learned by a study of the things themselves by themselves; a careful examination and analysis of the mechanical and chemical properties of any physical thing will discover all its distinguishing characteristics, all that makes it that particular thing in distinction from all other things; but it is plain already, that the *Value* of anything (if it have value) cannot be found out by studying that particular thing by itself alone; the questioning of the senses however minute, the test of the laboratory however delicate, can never determine how much anything is *worth*, because that always implies a comparison between *two* things, or more strictly a comparison between two Renderings in exchange. Value is not an attribute of single things: not even if the things be physical and tangible.

Now two other kinds of things are bought and sold besides physical and tangible things, namely, personal services and commercial credits; and it is very plain, that Value cannot be a quality of any one personal service rendered, as looked at by itself, such as the service of a physician towards a fever patient, because the service in and of itself might be the same whether rendered to his own child or the child of one of his patrons, while in the former case there would be no value, and in the latter there would be; and so too the very name "commercial credit" implies an exchange of two Renderings, out of which Value always emerges, and not at all an attribute of one credit considered by itself. Value is no more a characteristic of single intangible services and claims than it is of single intangible commodities rendered.

And what makes all this still more certain is, that Value even in physical things, and perhaps still more in services and claims, is all the while changing under demand and supply, now rising and then falling, while the physical properties of things, that make them what they are, are fixed and unchangeable. A gold eagle, for example, has certain primary qualities as gold, without which it would not be gold; it is hard and heavy and colored: gold is gold the world over and in all ages: Value is not one of these primary qualities, nor even a secondary quality, nor any quality at all, of gold as such; because circumstances are readily conceived and have often occurred, in which gold has no Value even in exchange; for instance, among a crew abandoned at sea, a bag of gold belonging to one of the sailors might not buy even a biscuit belonging to another; all the natural qualities of the gold are present,—it is still yellow and weighty and solid,— but its Value has escaped altogether. Gold is always 19 times heavier than water: specific gravity is a *quality* and is constant in all physical things: Value is not a quality in this sense at all, inasmuch as it is something that is constantly changing, rising or falling, and not infrequently disappearing altogether, leaving no sign.

Ignorance of this vastly important truth has pecuniarily ruined thousands upon thousands of the people of this country during the last 20 years. They have gone into the mining of metals, gold and silver and copper, sometimes as individuals and more often as companies gathering in the driblets of investors, under the notion that if they could only get these metals out of the ground their Value would be just as secure and fixed as their physical qualities. They found out their mistake in bitterness of spirit. For example, the Value of an ounce of silver has gone down and down and down as the quantity of silver excavated has increased under zealous digging, in accordance with the universal and pitiless law of Supply and Demand. So of copper. And both these great monetary interests went to Congress and secured the passage of laws designed to lift artificially the Values that were sinking naturally under increased Supply, the silver men by a law requiring the United States to buy and mint at least $2,000,000 in silver each month whether the silver dollars were needed or not, and the copper men by a law imposing a tariff-tax on foreign copper that has actually lifted the price two cents a pound on the average of the whole 20 years above the average price of copper in the markets of the world.

Take another illustration of disappearing Values, this time in lands, long supposed to be the most stable in value of all human possessions. Whole tiers of farms in the writer's native town in New Hampshire, and for that matter all over New England as well, that in his boyhood supported large families, and when sold usually brought a fair price, are now abandoned of their owners as wholly or comparatively worthless, and are allowed to grow up into forest again, without a sign of present human habitation upon them. Value is something that needs to be studied carefully, if it is to be fully understood.

(b) Perhaps the origin of the word, "Value," will throw some light upon its nature and changes. Etymology can never be safely despised in scientific discussions, although words are perpetually changing their meaning in the mouths of men. No science can afford to build upon the transient meaning of a word; and yet it is clearly possible so to use words as to reach and describe ultimate and unchanging facts in science; and some knowledge of the original meaning of words is always a help in getting at those definitions and analyses of facts that are permanent in science. Let us hold fast to the cheering truth exemplified on all sides of every science, that a just analysis and exact description of ultimate facts in any department of knowledge are for all time, in spite of the transient meaning of current words.

The present word is derived from the Latin VALERE, *to pass for, to be worth*. There is a strong hint of a *comparison* in the original meaning of the word, and the current use of it both in Latin and English develops the hint into a certainty. In common language, when the Value of anything is asked for, the answer always comes in the terms of something else. If the question be, How much is it worth? the answer is, So many dollars or cents. Now the cents or dollars are very different things from those whose value is thus inquired after; and so we see again from another point of view that Value is a relative matter, since it clearly implies a comparison between two distinct things; and, if so, it is clearly enough not a quality of any one thing, and of course it would be useless to try to ascertain the Value of anything by a study of that thing alone. Etymology thus easily brings us up to our present vital question, and will assist us to solve it completely.

(c) *What is Value?* Plainly it is the result of a comparison instituted between two things, using the word, "things," here in its broadest sense. But who institutes the comparison? And who is competent to announce the result of it in Value? A comparison is required in order to ascertain the length of a stick of timber in feet and inches, and a carpenter's square is the instrument by which the comparison is made, and it makes no difference in the result whose the square is or whose the stick of timber is, since the square and the stick have in common the physical quality of length, and a simple comparison of square with stick determines the length of the latter, and one man in this case may determine the result by himself alone, and it is not needful that he be the *owner* of either of the things compared.

But it is a different kind of comparison from this that issues in Value. Let us suppose an exchange of a bushel of wheat for a mason's trowel: there is no common physical quality, as length, between the wheat and the trowel; and it is evident, that no *one* man can measure in any form one of these two commodities by means of the other. It is a peculiar kind of comparison that is involved in any and every trade; and the first peculiarity of it is, as we have already seen in another connection, that it always requires "two persons" to make it; and each of the two persons must always be the virtual *owner* of one of the two things exchanged. A thief may indeed go through the motions of selling a stolen horse, but as he is not the owner of the horse there can be no sale, and the actual owner may take his horse wherever he finds it even in the hands of an innocent third party. In other words, there must ever be "two efforts" also, two legitimate efforts giving a valid claim of ownership to each of the two parties in the exchange.

And there is a second distinctive peculiarity in that comparison that ends in Value, namely, the two things to be exchanged are not compared directly with each other at all, as square and stick are compared, but in the light of the "two desires" with which we are already familiar, and in that of the "two estimates" resulting therefrom. The owner of the wheat desires a trowel, and the owner of the trowel desires a bushel of wheat; the former estimates the effort it has already cost him to procure the wheat in a sort of comparison with the effort that it would otherwise cost him to procure the trowel, and he does not trade unless the trowel seem more and better to him than does the wheat; the latter estimates the effort it has cost him to procure the trowel in a sort of comparison with the effort it would cost him to procure otherwise the wheat that he wants, and he does not trade unless the wheat then and there seem more desirable than the trowel, which he already has; and these two relative estimates of the two owners must *coincide*, that is, the owner of the wheat must think more of the trowel than of the wheat, and the owner of the trowel must think more of the wheat than of the trowel, before these two parties can ever trade. So of all traffic whatsoever.

Now the third and last distinctive peculiarity of that kind of comparison out of which Value emerges is this,—an *action* is necessary in order to complete the comparison. Desires and estimates may have been never so busy, but no Value can ever be born until an outward action takes place in the "two renderings" of our former analysis. Then first we come out upon plain and solid ground. We leave the play of the subjective elements, which yet are essential in the premises, and touch firmly objective realities. *The trowel-maker passes over his tool in the sight of men to the wheat-grower in firm possession and ownership, and takes in return for it from him the grain, which the latter passes over to the former for the sake of receiving the trowel.* The two "satisfactions" follow as a matter of course, and that whole transaction as a commercial exchange and as the sole subject of Political Economy is ended.

But where is the "Value," of which we have been in search? The answer is easy and certain and unevadible. *The Value is in the Renderings, and nowhere else.* The value of the trowel is the wheat, that is actually given in exchange for it; and the value of the wheat is equally the trowel, for the sake of getting which the wheat was rendered. What was the Value of King Hiram's cedar-timbers? The oil and wheat actually returned in pay for them. What was the Value of the oil and wheat sent northward by King Solomon? The timbers rendered in direct exchange for the same. This is not merely the only possible answer to the question, *What is Value?* but it is also a perfectly complete and satisfactory answer. Common language here corresponds exactly with scientific language. "How much did the horse cost?" "One hundred dollars." The dollars have nothing whatever in common with the horse, except that they express his Value at the time; the horse has nothing in common with the dollars, except that it expresses the Value of the dollars at the time. It is just as exact to say, it means precisely the same thing to say, the dollars are worth the horse, as to say, the horse is worth the dollars.

In general terms, the Value of anything is something else received in return for it, when each owner renders the one *for the sake of* getting the other. This is the whole of it, so far as any specific valuable thing is concerned. We shall indeed need after a little, and shall have no trouble in finding, an abstract and universal definition of "*Value*," as an abstract and scientific term perfectly circumscribing the field of Economics. Here and now we are dealing with the simpler concrete question, What is the value of any specific valuable thing? The unvarying answer is, Some other specific valuable thing already exchanged for the first! There may be expected value, estimated value, but actual value there is none, until a real exchange has settled how much the value is. The value of anything is something else already exchanged for it. Value is not simply a relation subsisting between two things, the result of a careful comparison between them, but rather an actual fact established in connection with them. The universal formula of Value is *quid pro quo*, in which formula *quid* stands for one of the valuables and *quo* for the other, and *pro* unfolds the motive of each owner for the reciprocal receiving and rendering.

Here a caution is needful. Because nobody can tell what the value of anything is until something else has been put over against it in order to get it and actually received therefor, and because the only possible way to express the value of either is in the terms of the other,—the trowel is worth the wheat and the wheat is worth the trowel,—one must not therefore jump to the conclusion that the value of either is settled for all time or even for any future time. It is only settled for *this* time. In Economics as in Christianity, Now is the accepted time. There is nothing fixed in Values, and never can be from the nature of the case, because Desires are personal to individuals, and Efforts fluctuate with times and persons, and Estimates that wait on these vary from necessity, and the Renderings of to-day may not be the chosen renderings of other persons in the same articles to-morrow. Value is not a quality at all, still less is it a permanent quality, of anything; it is a relation established between two things when these are in the hands of two given persons; but now when these are in the hands of two different persons, whose views are pretty sure to differ from the former, and a new relation is sought to be established between these in the old way of Estimates, is it strange that a new balance is struck, and Value is expressed in quite different terms?

One of the chief charms of Political Economy is the open secret, that it deals not with rigidities and inflexible qualities and mathematical quantities and the unchanging laws of matter, but with the billowy play of desires and estimates and purposes and satisfactions, all of which are mental states, and all of which are subject in the general to ascertainable laws, though laws of a quite different kind from those of Mechanics. Values come and they go. Within certain limits and under certain conditions they may be anticipated and even predicted, but never with the precision of an eclipse or the result of a known chemical combination. There is a useful and fascinating Science of Value, as we shall see indubitably by and by in the present chapter; but it is a science that deals primarily with *persons* and only secondarily with *things*, with mind and not with matter, with the general undulations of the sea and not with the crests of the waves. And all this is so, because Values are relative, because the announcements in the market-place to-day may stand listed differently to-morrow and very differently next year, and because old values may disappear altogether and many new ones come in, all in accordance with the incessant changes in the wants and labors and fashions and projects of men.

We are now in a good place to see once for all the sharp distinction there is between Utility and Value. These two are often confounded to the deep detriment of our Science; and no clear thinking is possible in Economics without drawing this line sharp, and then holding it fast; for the hazard of this confusion is all the greater, because Utility is always connected with Value, although it is a totally different thing from Value. We will see. Utility is the simple capacity of anything to gratify the desire of anybody. This is at once the etymological as well as the popular signification of the word. It is derived from the Latin *utor*, to make use of, a word that is often conjoined in Latin with *fruor*, to enjoy; so much so, that the two verbs are often put together, *utor et fruor*, and also often without the conjunctive, *utor fruor*. Utility, then, is a quality of innumerable things. Anything that is *good for* anything, anything *useful*, anything that has the power to still *the desires* of any person, has Utility. But multitudes of things that have this capacity to gratify human desires are never bought and sold, and therefore can have no Value, since nobody will give anything for them. The air we breathe, the water we refresh ourselves with from spring or brook, the light of the sun and moon and stars, the fragrance of the flowers, the mountain prospect that delights the eye,—all these, and thousands more, possess the highest utility, but no value whatsoever. They are free. They are the bounty of God. They are never bought and sold. They are a vast class of things by themselves, with which Political Economy as such has nothing to do.

Nevertheless the element of Utility comes into every case of Value, because the element of Desire comes into every case of Value, and whatever merely satisfies the Desire of any person is Utility, whether that capacity be the direct gift of God or whether the Efforts of men have been employed to bring it about. It is just here that we see the precise function of our "two efforts" in each case of Value, in distinction from mere Utility in all cases: much of utility is absolutely free, no effort of men having been put forth to secure it, for example, the fragrance of the wild rose; much more of utility is the commingled bounty of Nature and the gratuitous effort of men, for example, the fragrance of the domestic rose brought by the householder himself into his own yard for the gratification of his own family; while by much the most of utility is commingled free gift of God and the compensated efforts of men, for example, the fragrance of the bank of roses cultivated and cared for by the hired gardener. It is important for our purposes to discriminate carefully the three kinds of Utility: (1) what is wholly disconnected from the efforts of men, and comes freely from the hand of God; (2) what is mingled with the unpaid efforts of men, so that the satisfaction of the desire comes partly from Nature and partly from unbought effort; and (3) the compound utility that is partly free gift and partly the result of compensated labor. The last is the only kind of Utility that stands in any connection with Value.

And even this is very different from Value. Utility in all three of its forms—now free, now onerous, now partly bought—is always a quality of one thing by itself, going straight to the satisfaction of some desire, and there an end. It is simplicity itself compared with Value, which is always a resultant of several things, and is specifically a relation of mutual purchase established between two "renderings," each of which expresses the value of the other, in each of which is embodied an "effort" made by each of the two "persons" rendering, and each of which excites a "desire" and an "estimate" before being passed over in ownership to another, and a "satisfaction" afterwards.

The utility in every valuable rendering comes partly from free Nature and partly from compensated effort, but it is remarkable, that a principle, with which we are to become very familiar later on, namely, Competition, eliminates for the most part from all influence upon Value that portion of the Utility that is the free gift of God. The great Father never takes pay for anything, and never authorizes anybody to take pay in his behalf; and, moreover, has arranged things so, that it is exceedingly difficult for any person to extort anything from another person on the strength of anything that God has made, and man has not improved. Take, for example, ten horses of any general grade, brought into the same market by their ten owners for sale. These men did not make these horses, but they have cared for and trained them, or at least have become proprietors by purchase or otherwise of the results of such care and training. The Utility in each horse is compound, consisting partly of what God has done for him and partly of what man has done for him,—the two parts inextricably interwoven,—and all ten are offered now for sale. Each of the owners would indeed be glad to get something for his horse on the ground of what God has done to make him sound and strong and fleet, in addition to a fair compensation for what he (and his predecessors) has done in raising and breaking him; but the cupidity of all is likely to be thwarted by the ultimate willingness of some to sell their horses for a price covering the element of human "efforts" involved, and the action of these tends to fix a general rate for the whole ten, and thus the gratuitous element is eliminated from influence on Value. Even if the ten owners should combine for a higher price, there are doubtless a plenty of horses of that general grade elsewhere, some of whose owners are content to get back an equivalent for their own and others' "efforts" expended on their horses; and so the action of these tends to fix the general price for horses of that kind for that time and place at a point not above a fair estimate of the onerous human elements involved; thus throwing out by the action of competition all effect of natural Utility upon the Value of horses then and there. So of all other products of that kind.

It is true, that in certain unique cases, in which competition has little or no play, because there is only one or a very few owners of such unique products, one cannot certainly say that free Utility may *not* influence the Value to lift it above the gauge of human efforts involved; but such cases are rare, and relatively unimportant; and the tendency is immensely strong, under the natural and beneficial condition of things, for Values to graduate themselves through the reciprocal estimates and renderings of commerce, down to the actual and onerous contribution of *men* to that Utility that underlies Value.

Thus we are brought again and again from differing points of view to the "two renderings" as central and determinative in Value, and also more specifically to the "two efforts" of persons rather than any free contribution of Nature as constituting that portion of the compound Utility, whose function it is to gratify the "two desires" that precede the realization of Value,—that portion of the utility in any rendering that must be *compensated for* by the other rendering. Now in order to reach in a moment more our final definition of "Value," a definition, it is believed, that will cover all the cases and take the life out of endless disputes, we need a scientific term to carry easily and exactly the meaning of any economic *rendering*. Let that word be SERVICE. We must have it in its generalized meaning, to cover the renderings of all the three kinds, in distinction from the term "personal services," which we have already used and shall continue to use to designate one class only of things exchanged, in contradistinction to "commodities" and to "credits," the other two classes.

VALUE IS THE RELATION OF MUTUAL PURCHASE ESTABLISHED BETWEEN TWO SERVICES BY THEIR EXCHANGE.

We offer this definition of "Value" to our readers in much confidence, that they will find it exact and adequate and altogether trustworthy. No one of them, however, is precluded from attempts to improve it in breadth and brevity and beauty; and all are invited to pick logical flaws in it, whether of ambiguity or superfluity or deficiency. Many minds and many hands in many lands have left their impress on parts of this definition, for example,

Aristotle in Greece and Bastiat in France and Macleod in Great Britain; the present writer thinks, that he has bettered the definition of Bastiat, namely, "*Value is the relation of two services exchanged*," by precisely *defining* the relation as one of mutual purchase; and he is sure, that he has improved the definition of Macleod, namely, "*The value of any economic quantity is any other economic quantity for which it can be exchanged*," by making his definition at once more abstract and more general and more definite, and also by escaping the slight implication in the word, "quantity," that only material things are exchanged in economics.

The immense importance of securing *first* a clear and correct Definition of "Value," which is the foundation-word and the circumference-word of Political Economy, and *then* of using that term and all other scientific terms in the Science in their defined senses only, will certainly be appreciated by those who have wandered in the wide wilderness of the discussions on the undefinable word, "Wealth," and especially by those who have reflected most upon the vast and illimitable significance of economic Exchanges on the welfare of mankind. Associate Justice Miller of the Supreme Court of the United States, not an Economist in the technical sense, referred in 1888, in words that are worth remembering, to "*the philosophical maxim of modern times, that of all the agencies of civilization and progress of the human race commerce is the most efficient.*" In August of that year John Sherman of Ohio, a man far enough from being a technical Economist, said in the Senate of the United States, that "*it is almost a crime against civilization*" to maintain commercial barriers between Canada and the United States.

There were tokens a plenty in the year of Grace just referred to, that the Science of Value in all the lands of the civilized world, and particularly in the United States, was drawing to itself a new and more popular esteem. It was seen more clearly and felt more deeply than ever before, that this science has a weighty word for every man and woman and child in the world; that there are certain Rights in every one inherent and inalienable to buy and sell for his own advantage; that most if not all of the Governments, under the lead of comparatively few selfish and powerful men, were infringing upon these Rights, and robbing under the forms of Law the masses of their citizens to immense amounts for the special benefit of these very men; that the only sure defences of the people against these abuses of all kinds were in the maintenance and diffusion of the scientific and consequently disinterested principles and maxims of a sound Political Economy; that such a science was only friendly to the broadest rights, to universal gains, to illimitable increase in human comforts and powers, to international fellowship, to peace on earth and good-will among men; that, accordingly, a science of such scope and tendencies must be encouraged and cultivated and improved; that what had been crude in it, and narrow, and merely national, must be sloughed off; that the English and insular and special speculations of a century ago, which regarded "Wealth" as consisting of material things only, excepting however considerable portions of Adam Smith's immortal book, were antiquated and unusable; that the Science had really moved into a broader and still a well-circumscribed field, new and more permanent foundations were being laid, and fresh contributions from all countries should be welcomed; and that the time had fully come, when the accepted truths of this Science, like those of the other developed sciences, should be practically and steadily applied to the betterment of mankind. Under these broadening and inspiriting and uplifting conditions Political Economy, as never before, thanked God and took courage.

3. Having now a satisfactory definition of Value, and knowing accordingly just what Valuables are in clear distinction from all other things in the world, we must examine with some care two or three of the most general facts and laws and limits of Value, before we pass in the next following chapters to study in detail each of the three kinds of Valuables, namely, material Commodities, personal Services, commercial Credits.

(a) Since Value in general is the relation of mutual purchase between two Services, and consequently the specific value of either can only be expressed by the other,—one Valuable being always measured by the Valuable exchanged against it,—it follows as a matter of course that such a thing as a general Rise or Fall of Valuables is an impossibility. The rise of one valuable involves of necessity a fall in the other, as the fall of one implies the rise of the other. If the articles exchanged be bushels of wheat and dollars of silver, and if a bushel buys a dollar to-day, then wheat is worth a dollar a bushel; but if wheat rises next week, so that a dollar will not buy a full bushel, that is precisely the same thing as saying, that the dollar has fallen in its purchasing-power as compared with the wheat. Such specific changes in the purchasing-power of one Valuable over another are incessant throughout the commercial world, and a merchant's sagacity consists in anticipating these so far as possible and in availing himself of them alertly and prudently; but each one of us must needs see clearly and hold firmly in mind, that each fall in the purchasing-power of a Valuable means a corresponding rise of power in the other Valuable,—if the first buys more of the second than before, then the second must buy less than before of the first; and, consequently, a general rise of Valuables is a contradiction in terms, and so of course is a general fall of Valuables.

This brings us to *Price*. Price is Value reckoned in money; and this is the only difference in the meaning of the two terms. When one valuable is sold against another, even when one of the two is money, each is the *Value* of the other: Value is the general and universal term in Economics. When any other valuable is sold against money, the amount of money it buys is called its *Price*. Price is a specific and restricted term in Economics. Since we shall study Money thoroughly in a later chapter, and there explain the origin and extent of its functions throughout, it is only in order to remark here, that it is for convenience' sake, that is, to make easy the comparison of valuables one with another, that Value in commerce is commonly reduced to Price. Money becomes a sort of measure, by means of which to compare all other valuables with each other. In order to ascertain the Price of a Valuable, it only needs to be sold once against money; but in order to ascertain the Value of a Valuable, it would need to be sold once against all other valuables whatsoever. This last is clearly impracticable; and so Value for practical purposes is reduced to Price. The General is made Particular for convenience. Hence we have "Prices current," but never Values current.

Now it will be plain to all, how there may easily be and often is a general rise or fall of Prices while a rise or fall of Values is impossible. Price is a relative word as much as Value is, but it does not relate to so many things. Price is specific, and Value universal. Both equally involve buying and selling, but one sale of a single valuable against money leads to Price, while ten thousand sales of the same valuable against other than money would not conduct to complete Value. That would require a sale of this valuable against all other valuables in the world, and a complete statement of the comparative results.

General, or at least universal, changes of Prices in rise or fall in any given country are due to general and great changes in the Money current there. Subordinate changes in other valuables, money being supposed to remain uniform, will of course vary their Prices; but it is impossible that such changes should affect equally or even generally all the various and numberless valuables of a whole country; while some are coming easier, others are coming harder, while some are more desired than formerly others are less desired, and this will bring in of course altered prices, some higher and some lower; but a general rise of all prices, or a general fall in the same, can only come about by great changes of some kind in the circulating medium, that is, the money, of the country. For example, in the United States, between 1862 and 1878 inclusive, a government paper promise, called *greenbacks*, was the current money of the country; owing to its excessive issue, and to some doubt in the minds of the people whether the paper would ever be redeemed in gold, it soon became depreciated as compared with gold, the premium on which over the paper money varied at different times from 1 to 185 *per centum*; as all other valuables were then sold against greenback money, which had declined, their prices naturally rose in some sort of proportion as the medium fell; general *values* remained much as before, but general *prices* were much enhanced; and when, after the resumption of specie payments in January, 1879, gold became again the standard medium, general prices declined in full accordance with the same universal principle reversed.

(b) Prices, as we have now seen, are only a subordinate form of Values: the universal law that regulates all the variations of them both, within certain fixed limits to be examined shortly, is called the LAW OF SUPPLY AND DEMAND. This is perhaps the most comprehensive and beautiful law in Political Economy. We shall look at it now only in outline: the filling in will be the pastime and profit of all that is to come.

"Demand" is a technical term in Economics, and accordingly needs to be defined, and then always used in its defined sense. So is "Supply." *Demand is the "desire" of a "person" for something in the hands of another person, coupled with the possession of something else capable of buying that something.* Mere desire has no function in Political Economy: hungry and penniless children passing by the stalls of a great market, have no influence on the prices or values of the viands, on which they cast their eager glances: only desires accompanied by "efforts" competent to excite the desires and to pay for the efforts of another are a Demand. Supply is the same thing as Demand looked at from the other side. Supply is the correlative of Demand. The Supplyer is a person, who has in his possession something desired by the Demander, and who in turn desires something in the hands of the Demander, when both are willing to exchange their "renderings." There is no economical difference in the position of the Demander and the Supplyer. Each is equally a Demand and a Supply with reference to the other. It is the old and ever-recurring case of Value, the propositions being here stated in their most universal terms.

For simplicity's sake, however, and for convenience, without altering the substance of the definitions a particle, the valuables when looked at as a Demand are practically reduced in all markets to their equivalent in Money, so that Money offered or ready to be offered against any other exchangeable thing constitutes what is called in commercial language a Demand; and this is sufficiently accurate as well as current, although it must always be remembered that each valuable in any market in reality constitutes a Demand for another, and is equally a Supply in reference to that other. *Supply is any exchangeable thing offered for sale against any other exchangeable thing.* For example, corn in any market is at bottom a Demand and a Supply at once for every valuable offered in that market at that time, say, ploughs for one thing; but in the talk of the market, the presence of corn there, or its being ready to be immediately brought there and offered in exchange for money, constitutes what is called a Supply of corn; money offered, or ready to be offered, in exchange for corn, constitutes what is called a Demand.

On this account Money seems to play a much more important part in trade than it actually does play; the corn is sold in the terms of money, that is, for dollars and cents as denominations of Value; convenience dictates such a reduction of general Value to this particular form of it, because this is found to make easier the ultimate exchange; but there is not one chance in a hundred, as trade runs nowadays in the larger markets, that this seller of corn will take his pay for it in actual money whether metallic or paper; money is never an ultimate product, but only an intermediate one; this seller of corn wants perhaps a plough or some other farming implement, and ten to one he will take for his corn a bill or order in some form on the seller of ploughs, and it will be corn for a plough, each becoming a Demand and a Supply for the other, though money or rather its denominations has acted as an agent in bringing about the final trade; the details of all this in manner and result will be as plain as day when we come to study "Money" and "Credits" in following chapters; while the essential point to be noted here is, that all Valuables are a Demand and Supply as towards one another. In other words, the world over, A MARKET FOR PRODUCTS IS PRODUCTS IN MARKET.

What, then, is Market-Value returned in the terms of Money? And what is the universal Law of it?

Market-value is the present rate of exchange between dollars and cents and any other valuable, that can be fairly graded in a class made up of valuables similar to itself; and the law of market-value is the equation of Supply and Demand, that is, the current rate is adjusted when money enough is offered to take off within the usual times the valuables on hand and offered for sale. If Demand for any reason become quickened, and the Supply be not increased, there is competition among buyers for the stock in market, and the market-rate rises or tends to rise. If, on the other hand, Demand become sluggish, the Supply remaining the same, there is a like competition among the sellers to dispose of their stock, and market-value sinks or tends to sink. So far it is the simple action on Value of the element of one "desire" expressing itself through a money-demand, the elements of "desire" and of "efforts" expressing themselves through Supply being supposed to remain stable, and the pulsations in the market-rate follow accordingly.

How far can this simple action go? Demand increasing, Supply remaining as before, market-rate rises: how far can it rise from this cause? Here we must remember that Demand not only acts upon Value, but also Value reacts upon Demand. As Value rises, the number of those whose means or inclinations enable them to purchase at the new rate is constantly diminished: there are ten persons who may wish an article at one dollar, of whom not over four will wish it at two dollars, and perhaps only one at three dollars. Every rise in market-rate then, under the impulse of enlarged Demand, tends to cut off a part of that Demand, that is, to lessen the number of those who will purchase at the increased price; and the rate consequently can only rise to that point, whatever it be, where an equalization takes place between the Supply and Demand, between the quantity of flour, for example, offered at the enhanced rate, and the quantity of money in the hands of those willing to exchange it for flour at the higher rate.

Just so in the reverse way, when Demand is slackened, Supply continuing as before, the market-rate is sure to decline; but declining rates tend strongly in turn to increase the demand by bringing the article within the range of a larger number of purchasers; Society is like a pyramid, each lower stratum is broader than the one above; and so the decline of rates under a weaker Demand is arrested by a stronger Demand coming from a wider circle of buyers, and a new market-rate is determined at the point of equalization between the new Demand and the old Supply. Thus every rise or fall of Demand tends to check itself, and will check itself in all the great classes of valuables, even without any variations in the Supply; everything oscillates under the variations of Demand; while the point of stable equilibrium, if we may use the expression of anything so unstable as Market-value, is always the equation of Supply and Demand.

But all considerable variations of market-rate are commonly checked at an earlier point than the one just indicated by variations in the Supply. A sharper Demand carries up the market-rate, and a higher market-rate commonly acts upon Supply to enlarge it, and an increased Supply too checks the rise of market-rate. *Per contra*, a slacker Demand lowers market-rates, and lowered rates often lessen the Supply by the action of holders and speculators,—holders withdrawing their stock for a better market, and speculators buying now when the article is cheap to store away until it shall be dearer. Thus rise of market-rate from Demand growing stronger is checked doubly; first, by curtailing the number of would-be buyers, and second, by enlarging the Supply: the fall of market-rate from Demand growing weaker is checked doubly; first, by increasing the number of consumers of a now cheaper article, and second, by a diminution of Supply by the action of holders and speculators. This double and harmonious working of the law of the Equalization of Demand and Supply is one of the most comprehensive and beautiful laws in Political Economy.

Besides this, we must note the effect on Value of conditions in Supply only, Demand being supposed to continue steady. There are three classes of valuables in respect to the law of their Supply. (1) When the Supply is scant, and cannot be increased at all, as is the case with choice antiques and certain gems and paintings by the old masters, their value may rise to any point under the action of Demand, there is and can be in such cases no market-rate, and the individual value will be struck at the point of equalization of the demand then existing with the supply there offered. For instance, the French Government paid, in 1852, 615,300 francs for a painting by Murillo, which had belonged to Marshal Soult. The genuine Murillos are comparatively few, and their number cannot be increased, and their merit causes a strong "desire" to possess them, and their value rises in connection with the limitation of Supply to a point beyond which no one purchaser can be found. When this painting was offered in Paris for sale, many "persons" of course were anxious to buy it, there was but one painting, there could be but one purchaser, value rose under the influence of a sharp Demand, the rise could not be checked by any duplication of the Supply, and the equation was complete and the value for that sale determined when one party distanced all other competitors and offered a sum greater than any one else would give. The same principle controls all sales of this sort, and is practically the principle of the *Auction*, whose very name indicates its nature in this regard, that Demand becomes restricted to one party, and that the highest bidder.

(2) When the Supply, instead of being absolutely limited, can only be increased with difficulty or after the lapse of time, similar but less extreme results will be observed. Let us suppose, that pianos are selling in some rural community at $300 each, that there are twenty persons in the place who want a piano immediately, that there are but fifteen pianos on hand, and that the number cannot be increased for half a year. The market-rate will certainly rise above $300. How much above? To that point, at which only fifteen of the twenty will be willing to purchase at the new rate. The equation of Supply and Demand will be reached by a rising rate which cuts off five competitors. This is the principle, working only roughly in practice through the estimates and good judgment of dealers and purchasers. A better illustration of this second class of cases is, perhaps, the Grains and other agricultural products. When these have been gathered, there is no more home supply for a year; and any deficiency in the crops will raise their market-rate, not at all in the ratio of the deficiency, but according to the relations of the diminished Supply to a new Demand. Since the abolition of the Corn-Laws in England in 1846, and the resulting ease of grain-imports from abroad, a deficiency of home crops has no such effect on the price of cereals as it had before that time; when, according to Tooke's History of Prices, an expected falling-off of one third in the crops often doubled and sometimes quadrupled the usual prices; which shows that the world ought to become one country in respect to all food supplies, as indeed happily it is now for the most part, each country allowing them to be distributed freely everywhere in accordance with this law of Demand and Supply. Speculation is more busy in grain, in cotton, and in such things

generally, because a new Supply can only be had once a year; early information is eagerly sought at the trade centres in regard to the prospects of the growing crops, and has its influence one way or the other on current prices; but the world is so wide and all the parts of it now so closely connected together by steamship and telegraph, that the prices of the great food staples are remarkably uniform over the earth, and Speculation has not the chance it once had to count and "corner."

(3) In the only remaining and by far most comprehensive class of cases, in which the Supply of Commodities and Services and Credits can be readily and indefinitely increased to meet enhanced Demand, and easily withdrawn from market and stored when Demand declines, each rise and fall of market-rate tends to be speedily checked through the mere action of Supply; and the doubly and harmoniously working Law but just now referred to keeps Value in this class of cases comparatively steady all over the world.

(c) It only remains in this branch of the general discussion on Value, to indicate the Limits, within which all oscillations of Value are contained. These extreme limits are specially to be found in the element of Value which we have called "Efforts." We have clearly seen already, that "efforts" (or Labor) are not, as has been often asserted, the cause of Value, but only one of several constituent causes; if Labor be asserted to be the sole cause of Value, the inquiry becomes instantly pertinent, what is the cause of the value of Labor; yet we know, that "efforts" always stand in preconnection with value, and, the mutual "desires" being presupposed, there must always be Limitations of Value lying partly in the efforts made by the person serving and partly in the efforts saved to the person served. In every valuable transaction, each of the parties is reciprocally serving and served, and it is clear, that the two would not exchange "renderings" unless the service which each renders to the other is less onerous than the "efforts" which each would have to make if each served himself directly. For example, it takes a certain effort for me to bring water from the spring for the use of my family; I am willing to pay a neighbor for bringing it for me, but I should not be willing to make a greater effort for him in return than the effort is to bring it myself; neither should I be willing to make an effort for him in return which I regarded just as onerous as the bringing the water myself; and unless there is some service which he will accept less onerous to me than that, I shall continue to bring the water. On the other hand, he will surely not render the service to me of bringing the water, unless it be less onerous to him to do so than the doing that for himself which I am ready to do for him.

This principle, applicable to all exchanges whatsoever, draws on the one side the outermost line, beyond which Value never can pass. It may be asserted with confidence, that no person will ever knowingly make a greater effort to satisfy a desire through exchange, than the effort needful to satisfy it without an exchange. Therefore, it follows, that all exchanges lessen onerous efforts among men relatively to the satisfaction of their desires, and tend to lessen these more and more as exchanges multiply in number and variety, otherwise the exchanges would not take place.

Moreover, within this outermost Limit of Value, which is made by the comparative onerousness of the respective "efforts," there is a second limitation of a similar kind to be found specially in the element which we have called "estimates." The estimate of each exchanger is based at once on his own effort about to be rendered and on his desire for the return service offered: the element of effort in the case of both being considered for the time as fixed, Value will vary according to the varying desire of each for the return service of the other, affecting of course the "estimate" of each, and furnishing also a secondary Limit of Value. To pursue the same illustration, suppose I regard the effort required to bring the water myself as 10; that there are several persons, who would be glad to do that service for me at a return service which I consider as 8; that there are two persons, who are willing to do it for something which I estimate at 6; and that there is only one person, who will do it for a return service which I regard as 5. It is evident, that the extreme limits of that service to me are 10 and 5. Higher than 10 it cannot go, lower than 5 it cannot sink. But why have I before me three possible classes of renderers? Because the persons in each class, while estimating their own efforts alike in the proposed rendering to me, have varying "desires" as towards a possible rendering from me to them, and consequently put differing "estimates" upon the possible transactions. The man who will bring the water for 5 has for some reason (no matter what) a stronger desire for the return than anybody else, and I should of course employ him so long as he would serve me on those terms; if he decline the exchange, I fall back on one of the two persons in the class above him, and Value rises now from 5 to 6, and will be steadier there than it was before; if each of these in turn should give out, I should fall back upon the larger class ready to serve me at 8, and Value would be very steady at that rate, because there are numerous competitors; and by no possibility could it rise above 10. Between 10 and 5 the value may fluctuate, but it cannot overpass these Limits in either direction under existing circumstances.

Therefore we may conclude, that the *maximum* Value of any Service in exchange will be struck at the point where the recipient will prefer to serve himself, or go without the satisfaction, rather than make the exchange; and the *minimum* Value of any Service in exchange is struck at the point below which the recipient cannot get himself served even by him who most highly estimates the return service offered.

(4) We come now to the last and most important Inquiry in this initial chapter, namely this, *Can there be, and is there, a strict Science of Buying and Selling? Is there a Science by itself, clear and certain, that covers and controls Valuables?*

Here we must go slowly, if we would go surely. We must first find out exactly what a Science is in general, and then ascertain in particular whether Political Economy bears all the marks and stands all the tests of the other genuine Sciences. What is a Science?

A Science is the body of exact definitions and sound principles educed from and applied to a single class of facts or phenomena.

The very first condition, accordingly, of any science is, that there be a single class of facts, objective or subjective, that can be separated from all other classes of facts, in the mind by a generalization and in words by a definition, and that such generalization and definition be clearly made and held; the second condition is, that the class of facts so circumscribed and defined be open to some or all of the logical processes of construction, of which the most important are Induction and Deduction; the third condition is, that the subordinate definitions and working principles within the inchoate Science be all educed from and applied to these circumscribed facts in strict accordance with these well-known logical processes; and the last condition is, that these definitions and principles have gradually become "*a body*," in which there is an organic arrangement of parts, all being placed in a just order and mutual interdependence. There is no old Science, and there can be no new Science, in which these four conditions do not meet and become blended; and the beauty of it is, that this Definition applies to any Science in all stages of its growth. No one of all the Sciences is as yet completed; but just so soon as any correct definitions and principles are drawn from and applied to any *class* of things clearly circumscribed as such, and these definitions and principles are orderly arranged in a *body*, there is an incipient Science; and its progress towards perfection will proceed in precisely the same manner in which its foundations have been laid; new facts and principles and definitions will gradually be discovered, and these when reapplied to the class of things out of which they have sprung, will lead to corrections and adjustments and enlargements of the Science; and no matter how far these logical processes may be carried, the general Definition with which we start will also be found ample at the end of the journey.

All of the Sciences without exception have been developed into their present position in just this manner; and they fall easily into three great classes, namely, the Exact, the Physical, and the Moral Sciences. The ground of this triple classification is partly the distinct subject-matter in the three classes of Sciences, and partly the distinctive prominence of one or more of the logical processes of construction in each.

Thus, the class of the Exact Sciences consists only of the formal Logic, and pure Mathematics. These two are distinct from all other sciences, because their logical method of procedure is wholly Deductive. Deduction is the process of the mind, by which we pass from a *general* truth to a *particular* case under it, that is to say, from *more* to *less* inclusive propositions. Stuart Mill argues at much length in his book on Logic, that even the axioms of pure Mathematics are originally gained by Induction, while others claim that the truth of these axioms is perceived *intuitively*, but no matter how this point is decided, the construction process of the Pure Mathematics is from the General to the Particular. So it is also with the Aristotelian logic, whose Major Premise, whether only *supposed* to be true or intuitively *perceived* or inductively *proved* is always General in its terms. This is the form of Aristotle's Syllogism:—All sinners deserve to be punished; John is a sinner; and therefore, John deserves punishment.

Physical Sciences are those concerned with the classifications and laws of action belonging to material substances. There are a great circle of these, of which Astronomy, Botany, and Chemistry, may serve as examples. They have been mostly developed since the time, and in accordance with the methods, of Lord Bacon; who, in strong reaction against the Deductive logic of Aristotle, exalted Induction or the mode of generalizing from *particulars*, as the true way of building up Sciences; and, as the subject-matter of each of the physical sciences is well open to observation and experiment, to Induction and Deduction, and to corrective verifications, both inductive and deductive, the new method proved remarkably pregnant and successful. Each of these sciences has a distinct *Class* of objects or phenomena to which its attention is directed; the class is circumscribed by the scientific Conception and Definition; its devotees as a rule are skilled in using the Baconian tools; and consequently, its conclusions receive the confidence and control the action of men. All of the Physical Sciences are constantly enlarging "the body of exact definitions and sound principles" connected with their several classes "of facts or phenomena."

Moral Sciences are those concerned with the classifications and laws of action belonging to beings having Thoughts and Desires and Will. The most developed of these sciences at present are Metaphysics, Ethics, and Economics. Each of these is concerned with a single class of phenomena, which may be exactly conceived of and defined, and is open to the logical processes by which alone Sciences can be built up. But Induction cannot march up with quite so sure a stride, nor Deduction descend with so large degrees of certainty, in relation to *persons* endowed with free-will, as in relation to physical substances held firm in the grip of unvaried law. Still, the doubt always attaches far more to the actions of an *individual* than to the actions of the *masses* of men. It is much easier to know human nature in general, than one man in particular, because many Inductions guided by observation and History make it almost certain how masses of men will act under a given set of conditions, while any one *may* act in a contrary way. Deduction, accordingly, cannot hold quite the same place in the Moral Sciences so far as individuals are concerned, as it holds in the Physical and Exact Sciences; but this lack is perhaps more than made up by other advantages. *Experience* in the moral sciences corresponds to *Experiments* in the physical sciences. Then there is the great advantage of *Introspection*; since each man has within himself the means of interpreting and testing the inductions of Metaphysics, Ethics, and Economics. Then also there is the great resource of *Feigned Cases*, which, provided only they be cases possible to occur, open up to Reasoning a new means of proving and correcting. Besides these, which it enjoys in common with them, Economics, as we shall soon see, possesses one other great advantage over and above the rest of the Moral Sciences.

Since, then, Political Economy deals primarily with Persons, and only quite secondarily with Things, it is, under the definition and on every ground, a "moral science"; yet it must not be confounded in the least with what is sometimes called the science of Morals, or Ethics. There is one word that marks and circumscribes the field of Ethics, and that word is *Ought*; there is one word also that marks and circumscribes the field of Economics, and that word is *Value*. Now, the idea of *obligation*, on which ethical science is founded, and the idea of *gainful exchange*, on which economical science is founded, are totally distinct ideas. The imperatives of ethical obligation rest upon the consciences of men, and Duty is to be done at all hazards; guilt is incurred if it be neglected; while pecuniary gains and losses, however large, do not, or at least ought not, weigh a feather against an intuition of Right and Wrong. Economics, on the other hand, does not aspire to place its feet upon this lofty ethical ground; no man is ever under any moral obligation to make a trade; he properly makes it or not, according to his present sense of its gainfulness to himself; and so economic science finds a solid and adequate footing upon the expedient and the useful. Ethics appeals only to an enlightened conscience, and certain conduct is approved because it is Right, and for no other reason; Economics appeals only to an enlightened self-interest, and exchanges are made because they are mutually Advantageous, and for no other reason; each of the two Sciences, therefore, has a basis and sphere of its own, and the grounds of the two are not only independent, but also incommensurable.

We will now apply *seriatim* to Political Economy the four fundamental conditions belonging to all recognized Sciences, and so determine for ourselves whether it be not a strict science, and thus worthy in its leading propositions of all acceptation.

(a) Every science must have to begin with a definite Class of facts, which lie in an easily circumscribable field, and which are not likely to be confounded with other facts of a differing nature. Economy has such a class of facts, that lie in such a field, and that cut themselves off by sharp lines from all other things. *Valuables* is its class of things. It has nothing to do with any other class of things. Its field is Value, or Sales, or Exchanges. This field is perfectly definite. Sales are never confounded with gifts, and are never confounded with thefts. They have a distinctive character of their own. They have always been in the world, will always be in the world in ever-multiplying volume, and no one ever mistakes their main features for anything else. Anything whatsoever that is salable, or is about to be made so, comes within the view of Economics, and scientifically it cares for nothing else. While it finds its field definite, it also finds it broad. It has no wish to encroach on other sciences, nor will it tolerate any encroachments on its own. Before anything is sold, or is being made ready to sell, it cares nothing what other science employs itself upon that thing; after the thing is sold, Economy loses its interest in it, and other sciences may take it up if they choose. Valuableness is the one quality that constitutes the Class of things with which the Science is conversant, and it claims complete jurisdiction over all things just so far forth as they have this one quality, and no farther. Now there *is* in the actual world such a Class of things; its exterior boundaries have been exactly ascertained by a long series of Inductions and Deductions, tentative, corrective, and confirmatory; and accordingly, Political Economy has now in full possession the first grand condition of a Science.

(b) This great class of facts, thus reached by logical Generalization and grasped and held by a mental Conception and fixed by an adequate verbal Definition, is remarkably open to all the logical processes of reasoning, by which alone sciences are constructed, and thus possesses in full measure the second grand condition of the Sciences. Not one logical resource is denied to the economists: all the tools of the scientific workshop are at their hands. Let us now catalogue these in their order.

(1) *Induction.* This is the logical and universal process, by which the mind naturally passes up from a certain number of observed cases, in which a certain quality appears, to a Generalization, which is a conception of the mind followed by a statement in words to the effect, that *all possible cases* of that kind will exhibit the quality already observed in *the few cases*. It has as its basis a confidence in the resemblances and uniformities of Nature; it proceeds upon the axiom that Nature throughout is consistent with herself; and this confidence has been ten thousand times justified in the issue, when

it is found that Nature preordained the Sciences by causing grand analogies to run through each department of her works, including man and his works. The structure of the human mind corresponds with these objective resemblances; it seizes upon them, and delights in them, and naturally and joyfully infers and concludes that what has been observed of *a part* may be safely affirmed of *the whole* of that kind; accordingly, the world over, when certain things are found to be true in a considerable number of cases, the mind leaps over space and time to a whole class, and frames for itself a general rule or principle, which binds all the cases into one bundle, and thereafter confidently affirms what is known to be true of some to be probably true of all. This is inductive Generalization; and the strength and the joy of it is well expressed by Descartes: "*I have thought that I could take as a just generalization that which I very clearly and vividly conceived to be true.*"

Experience in Economics corresponds to Experiment in the Physical Sciences, and furnishes to Induction all the fuel it can ask for to feed its logical furnace and to forge the chains that bind the Cases to the Classes. Personal experience in buying and selling, local experience in buying and selling, and national experience in buying and selling, with all that belongs to these, the records of which are full to overflowing, afford to the inductive inquirer in Economics an inexhaustible supply of material. Instances abound. Particulars may be gathered up one by one on every hand and linked into the inductive chain. If any doubt be felt about the strength of any one of these chains, another one may at once be linked in terms drawn from another field of Experience with a view to test the strength of the first. Most fortunate from this point of view is the United States, because here there are States with substantive powers of control over most matters of trade within their borders, as well as a Nation with sovereign powers of control over some points of trade within the country as a whole. This feature has given birth to commercial experiments as well as commercial experience of all kinds; and Induction rejoices in all these abundant materials for generalization thus furnished free of cost to Science, though unfortunately not free of cost to the People.

(2) *Deduction.* This is a logical process exactly the reverse of the first, in that it descends from a generalized statement reached by the inductive process to some particular, or subordinate class of particulars, ostensibly covered by the general maxim. Induction examines a number of particulars, and then makes a leap, it may be a long leap, over all intervening particulars, to its Generalization clamping them. The main use of Deduction is to make sure of any one of these overleaped particulars, which may come into importance, and thus confirm the generalization, or correct it. It is not strictly true, what is often alleged against deductive reasoning, that there is nothing *new* in its result, that the Induction had already passed through that

particular in rising to its Generalization, and therefore to descend to any particular link to examine that, is something useless. The exact truth is, that it *is* useless to examine again deductively the very particulars that were carefully studied inductively, but on the other hand there is always much actually untraversed territory between these already examined particulars and the inductive generalization, and Deduction is often very useful in carrying us down to questionable points in this territory. Even Lord Bacon, who scorned the syllogism, admits this: "*Axioms duly and orderly formed from particulars easily discover the way to new particulars, and thus render sciences active.*"

We will illustrate this by a reference to Franklin's famous induction to prove the identity of lightning with electricity. Only one experiment, and that a very rude one, was needful in this case; although usually many experiments, or the careful observation of many particulars, are necessary in inductions; but the generalization having been gained, Deduction had a chance to try its hand; it had long been observed that electricity could be conducted from point to point, and if electricity and lightning be identical, then lightning can be so conducted; therefore, deduced Franklin, a pointed iron rod elevated above buildings will harmlessly conduct lightning from the clouds into the ground. Deduction gave mankind the lightning-rod, and so made one point of science "*active*," as Bacon phrased it; and it is noticeable, that Turgot's felicitous epigram turns on the deductive rather than the inductive side of Franklin's experiment: *Eripuit cœlo fulmen sceptrumque tyrannis.*

Let us catch up another illustration from the science of Botany, to show how Deduction may strengthen and sharpen an inductive result. The botanists say, that apple-tree blossoms are always five-petaled, because blossoms from a large number of apple-trees in various localities have been observed to have just five petals to the blossom; so far, they affirm inductively, and indeed securely; but they have also reached by means of another induction a much broader law of plant-life, namely, that outside-growers, when they have petaled flowers at all, always have them five-fold; now apple-trees are outside-growers; and therefore, deductively also, and conclusively beyond shadow of question, apple-tree blossoms are five-petaled.

Political Economy is just as open to Deduction as it is to Induction, and the two continually are reaching each other the hands of economical reasoning, not always indeed pursuing each a separate and distinct path to the end, as in the botanical instance just adduced; because in practice the two processes mingle constantly, and neither is carried out in full and due form, since premises used by the mind are often dropped in the statement, and shortened forms of expression take the place of long-drawn-out formulas. But all good reasoning in Economics, as in all other sciences, is analyzable into one or other of these two processes, both based alike on the uniformities of Nature and the structure of the human mind.

Deduction has not quite the same scope and certainty in Economics as in the Physical Sciences, because any one *may* act contrary to the vastly probable action of many individuals; still, it is a safe and potent process in economics, since it may descend securely from the larger masses to the smaller, even though perchance the individual escape, because of the simplicity and universality and certainty of the impulses that lead men to exchange. John Bascom gives the reason well, why both Induction and Deduction have so firm a grasp upon this science: "*Between one dollar and two dollars a man has no choice, he must take the greater; between one day and two days of labor he must take the less; between the present and the future he must take the present. This is not a sphere of caprice, nor scarcely even of liberty; the actions themselves present no alternative, and, if an alternative giving an opportunity for choice does arise, it arises from some partial or individual impulse, from some one of those transitory and foreign influences, which, while rippling the surface, neither belong to nor affect the current of the stream.*"

(3) *Introspection.* Everybody buys and sells, and almost everybody watches the action of his own mind enough to see what are his *motives* in buying and selling, and soon comes to know also that the other party has corresponding motives. Even the child knows perfectly, that it takes two to make a bargain, that each party renders something to the other, that each is glad to part with something for the sake of receiving something from the other, and that this higher esteem put by each on what is taken from the other makes for each the gain of the trade. A very little introspection tells anybody, that were this higher esteem wanting in the minds of either of the two, the trade would not take place at all. Everybody within the pale of *compos mentis* knows, that, were his own desire for the rendering of another to increase, he himself would offer more of his own rendering rather than forego the trade; and he rightly infers, that what is true of himself is true of all other men; and so, every seller rightly tries to display his wares in such a way as to increase the desire of buyers for them; knowing full well from his own experience in buying that, other things being equal, they will be willing to render him more for them in consequence.

The phrase above, "rightly infers," is based upon the truth, that all men are remarkably alike in certain great departments of action; and that, in no department are they so nearly alike as in this of buying and selling. Introspection, therefore, an easy self-knowledge open to all persons alike, and a personal experience in these matters that everybody gains, give most trustworthy answers to Inductive inquiry along these lines. Trade is natural and gainful, as any person can see, who stops to ask himself why he has made, or is about to make, a given trade; and if natural and gainful to *him*, equally so for precisely the same reasons to the party of the other part; hence no law or encouragement is needed to induce any persons to enter upon traffic; and any law, or artificial obstacle, that hinders any two persons from trading, who would otherwise trade, not only interferes with an inalienable right that belongs to both, but also destroys an inevitable gain that would otherwise accrue to both. Political economy is very fortunate, accordingly, in being able to make its appeal to the common sense of all men, giving sound starting-points through self-knowledge possessed by all men, guiding to safe steps by means of Induction all who like to generalize and prove, and especially breaking up current fallacies by asking the potent question, "How would you like it yourself?"

(4) *Feigned Cases.* There are two kinds of these, namely, those which might be realized in actual fact, and those which never can be so realized. The acute mind of the Greeks marked in their flexible language a decided difference between the class of suppositions that might possibly become facts, and another class of suppositions impossible to become facts, by developing a distinct form of expression for each. This distinction must always be borne in mind by those who use or note in economical discussions the expedient of Feigned Cases. Reasoning is always legitimate and often pregnant from suppositions, whenever these are such as might readily become facts of experience, because in that case the argument proceeds upon recognized and inductive resemblances; but otherwise, no inference at all can be drawn from them, because it is an universal truth in Nature and in Logic, *ex nihilo nihil fit*, out of nothing nothing can come. In plausible suppositions impossible to become facts is a nest of logical fallacies, that need to be watched. A good illustration may be found in the Monetary Conference at Paris in 1881. Delegates were there from all the nations of Europe, from the United States, and even the distant India. Some of these in their eagerness for a factitious ratio of value between gold and silver forgot the important distinction now in hand, and argued of the good results to flow from the realization of a supposition, *which in fact never could be realized.* Mr. Evarts voiced the French and American delegates in this declaration: "*Any ratio now or of late in use by any commercial nation, if adopted by an important group of states, could be maintained; but the adoption of a ratio of 15½ silver to 1 of gold would accomplish the principal object with less disturbance in the monetary systems to be affected by it than any other ratio.*" The fallacy in this passage is in the words, "could be maintained," which are a supposition, and what is much worse, a supposition contrary to fact, from which all arguing is nugatory. Why it is contrary to fact will be seen at length in the following chapter on Money.

On the other hand, a supposition that may clearly become a fact is a substantive thing, and logical inferences may be drawn from it, just as geometrical inferences may be drawn from a *supposed* circle: the circle on the page is not a *perfect* circle—no such circle was ever drawn—but *suppose* it perfect, as it might possibly be, and argument becomes at once valid. Let us take another Monetary Conference at Paris in 1867 as an illustration: its judgment as voiced by Mr. Ruggles of New York was taken with logical propriety, when the great benefits of an international coinage of gold alone were argued and announced, because, while that was then a mere conjectural project, it was possible any day by mutual agreement among the nations to become a reality. An international coinage of gold is a simple question of equivalence of *weights* in the coins of different countries: an equivalence of *values* as between gold and silver coins for any great length of time is neither simple nor possible.

(5) *Results measurable in numbers.* The four preceding logical processes of proof and construction Political Economy is glad to share with the other Moral Sciences, but this fifth and last one it has to itself alone, and this is its chief scientific advantage over them, and is consequently the main reason why it is already more advanced and more symmetrically developed than any of them. In common with them it has important subjective elements, such as Desires, Estimates, and Satisfactions; in marked advantage over them it has also objective elements, that can be weighed and measured and even hardened into statistics. Economics has an ever ready objective test, which mere mental and ethical and other moral processes never can have from their very nature. The *result* of each and of all economic transactions may be measured by money, and put down in a ledger, and published to the world in the form of statistics. An economic blunder, whether in legislation or in private action, pretty soon proves itself to be such by the lessened gains of somebody, and these losses can be stated arithmetically; and similarly, an economic improvement evidences itself at once by increased gains coming to somebody; while it may take years and years to work out the results of an ethical mistake, and even then their amount can only be guessed at.

Theories in metaphysics can only be tested by the *Reason* of men, and reasonable men without apparent bias of motive take opposite views of Sensations and Intuitions and Volitions; while theories in economics, which can be even better tested by the *Reason*, have an additional and almost immediate and constantly recurring test through men's pockets and the tables of the Census. The people indeed sometimes deceive themselves, and are also too often deceived by others, in these matters of buying and selling; but it is none the less of the utmost consequence to this Science, that all the results of good and bad practice in Economics work themselves at last into a definite shape, into facts and figures that cannot lie. It is not, as in Ethics and Metaphysics, that tendencies and potencies only are ascertained, but everything speedily drifts into results measurable in numbers, which stand out like landmarks against the sky. It is just for this reason, as both the schools of the Roman lawyers admitted, namely, that we have in all cases the Return-Service as the outward expression and measure of the Desire and Effort of him who renders the service, and because it makes no difference which of two services exchanged be regarded as the return-service, that our Science is reared on the firm ground of objective realities, notwithstanding the strong subjective elements that have a constant part in it.

(c) The third condition of a recognized Science is, that the logical processes appropriate to its class of facts have been already carefully applied to them and a certain number of "exact definitions and sound principles" have been already "educed from and applied to" them. We do not hesitate a moment to claim, that this condition also is fairly and fully met by Political Economy, and that this is a "Science" under the definition from every point of view, and particularly from this third point of view; and a few examples will now be given as a specimen merely of the logical work already achieved in Economics. First, Induction more or less busy for two thousand years has given at last an exact and acceptable definition of the Science, and impliedly an exact description of the class of facts with which it is conversant, namely, the Science of Sales, or what is exactly equivalent, the Science of Value; and Deduction at all points along this slow road has helped to correct and to broaden successive imperfect inductions, which an inquisitive and tentative and cautious spirit—the mainspring of Constructive Science—has instituted from time to time.

Second, precisely the same processes often repeated have ascertained beyond question, that there are only three classes of Valuables and the exact differences between them, and that, consequently, only six cases of Value are possible to happen.

Third, so many nations at different times in all ages have lowered the standard of their Money under a misapprehension of its nature and in a vain hope of profit, and a general scale of rising prices following each attempt of this kind having been several times observed and no instance to the contrary, Economists came by Induction to assert the proposition, that falling Moneys cause rising Prices; the proposition stood secure on inductive grounds alone; but so soon as a perfect definition of Money, namely, a Measure of Services, had at last been reached both inductively and deductively, it became at once a safe Deduction from the definition, that rising Prices must succeed a falling Measure. Thus assurance became doubly sure.

Fourth, Introspection gives each buyer and seller such firm possession of *his own motive* in buying and selling, that he naturally and inductively concludes on the ground that men are substantially alike, that the *motive is similar* in the party of the other part; each further step of experience in traffic assures him of this beyond a doubt,—each wants to get and does get something from the other of more consequence to him than what he gives; every attempted deviation from rectitude in trade so far forth throws the trader out from opportunity to trade; opportunity to trade is nothing in the world but *a market*; a market is nothing in the world but men with products in their hands, desiring to buy other products with these; the more men anywhere with the more products in their hands of all sorts to buy with, the better market everywhere for other men (the more the better) with other products of all kinds to buy with; all the appropriate logical processes in action and reaction, all the commercial experience of all men everywhere, and all the true statistics of traffic ever gathered, do but assure the inductive assent to one of the best and broadest of all the   Generalizations in Economics, namely this: *A market for products is products in market.*

(d) Are the definitions and principles already logically educed from and applied to the great class of Valuables orderly arranged in "*a body*"? This is the only inquiry that remains, in order to determine whether Political Economy is already a "Science" in the strictest sense of that term. It is admitted, that a jumble of even just definitions and principles do not constitute a science, but only these when placed in a just order and interdependence. A "body" implies an organic arrangement of parts. It has been well said of the human body, that all its parts are reciprocally means and ends; the same may be said of every living organic body, whether vegetable or animal; and the same may be said in the way of analogy of every developed and recognized Science. All the definitions and propositions and illustrations in any science should be so arranged, as to show the mutual relations and reciprocal dependence of all the parts, and as to display the whole in harmony and symmetry.

It is as certain as anything in the future can be in science, that new principles will be discovered in Economics as Time and Inquiry go on, and that these will find their place little by little in a fuller and more rounded "body" than is at present possible; while it is also as certain as anything in the future of science can be, that the Outline of economics is already perfectly drawn, that the great class of Valuables will never be enlarged nor be better described, that the category of Commodities, Services, Credits, is completed for all time, and that the analysis of each act of trade into two Desires and two Efforts and two Estimates and two Renderings and two Satisfactions will never yield additional elements. Political Economy is already a body of exact definitions and sound principles educed from and applied to a single class of facts. This body will indeed be enlarged by a future and finer scientific construction, the arrangement and interdependence of its parts will be better exhibited, the form and filling up of the Science within the outline already determined is sure to become more compact, more robust, and more beautiful, as the decades and centuries go by; while, as in the human body throughout all the changes of its growth and mature life, that future body of economic science in all its stages towards perfection will be but the continuation and fuller development of the present "body" of Political Economy.

CHAPTER II.
MATERIAL COMMODITIES.

Valuables fall naturally and exactly into three classes, Commodities, Services, and Credits. The reasons are obvious at first glance, why articles falling in the first class occupied the thoughts and the efforts of men almost exclusively for the first thousand years of recorded history. Commodities appealed to the senses of men: they are visible, tangible, weighable. Some form of personal slavery existed everywhere, and largely withdrew attention from personal services bought and sold; and there was not apparently sufficient personal confidence between man and man in the earlier ages to allow much development of credits, whose ground is personal trust and whose sphere is future time. Commodities, on the other hand, fitted by the efforts of some men to satisfy the immediate wants of other men, all ready for delivery, to be exchanged against other commodities similarly fitted and at hand, took the field apparently in the earliest ages of recorded Time, gradually became very large in volume, opened new routes of travel and transportation, and served to connect in a rough and ready way neighboring tribes and even neighboring nations.

Commodities are the class of Valuables comprising material things, organic and inorganic, fitted by human efforts to satisfy human desires. Cattle were probably among the first things to become valuable, that is, salable; and it is certain, that they became very early in many quarters of the world a sort of Money or standard of comparison among other things exchangeable, and indeed they continue to be such in some quarters to this day. Near the middle of the sixth book of the Iliad occur these lines:—

"Then did the son of Saturn take awayThe judging mind of Glaucus, when he gaveHis arms of gold away for arms of brassWorn by Tydides Diomed,—*the worthOf fivescore oxen for the worth of nine.*"

Gold and silver also became valuable in the ordinary way in very early times, and later became Money or a medium in exchanging other things; and much later other metals came into use as commodities and then too as money; for the Latin word for money, *pecunia*, derived from *pecus*, cattle, seems to imply some original equivalence in value between the bronze stamped with the image of cattle and the cattle themselves. Parcels of land subdued and improved by human hands were probably bought and sold in some portions of the world as early as anything was,—at any rate very early. Land-parcels are a commodity under the definition. Another passage from

Homer, towards the end of the seventh book of the Iliad, displays some of the commodities in common use during the heroic age in Greece:—

"But the long-haired GreeksBought for themselves their wines; some gave their brass,And others shining steel; some bought with hides,And some with steers, and some with slaves, and thusPrepared an ample banquet."

The earliest detailed record of a commercial transaction in commodities, is the purchase by Abraham of the field and cave in Hebron, more than 2000 years before Christ. It is narrated at length in Genesis xxiii. Long before this purchase, however, it is said of Abraham that he "went up out of Egypt very rich in cattle, in silver, and in gold." This formal sale to him in Hebron of the field and cave of Machpelah is in all its parts instructive to us, and full of signs of the drift of those times. It was "*in the audience of the sons of Heth, before all that went in at the gate of his city, that the field and the cave were made sure unto him for a possession. And Abraham weighed unto Ephron the silver which he had named in the audience of the sons of Heth, four hundred shekels of silver, current money with the merchant.*" In the lack of written and recorded deeds to land-parcels, as we have them now, the sale of them was "*made sure*" before the faces of living men, who would tell the truth and pass on the word. The market-place in those days was "*at the gate of the city*," where the judges also used to hold their courts, the place most frequented of all, and sales were made "*before all that went in*" thither; "*in the audience of the sons of Heth*" was the silver weighed out, and the field made sure in exchange. Then there were "merchants" as a class; silver passed by weight rather than by tale, although it had already passed beyond a mere commodity and had become money, "*current money with the merchant*"; and even at this day the Bank of England takes in and pays out gold and silver by balance rather than by count, though they be in coined money: it is the more accurate method.

The author of the book of Job, believed to be of great antiquity, and certainly true to nature and to fact in its essential parts, knew very well the modes in which the ancient mines were wrought, and the worth of the commodities extracted:—

"Truly there is a vein for silver,And a place for gold, which men refine. Iron is obtained from earth,And stone is melted into copper.Man putteth an end to darkness;He searcheth to the lowest depthsFor the stone of darkness and the shadow of death.From the place where they dwell they open a shaft;Forgotten by the feet,They hang down, they swing away from men.The earth, out of which cometh bread,Is torn up underneath, as it were by fire.Her stones are the place of sapphires,And she hath clods of gold for man.The path thereto no bird knoweth,And the vulture's eye hath not seen it;The fierce wild beast hath not trodden it;The lion hath not passed over it.Man layeth his hand upon the rock;He upturneth mountains from their roots;He cleaveth out streams in the rocks,And his eye seeth every precious thing;He bindeth up the streams, that they trickle not,And bringeth hidden things to light."

The prophet Ezekiel, who wrote in the sixth century before Christ, incidentally described in his chapter xxvii the commerce in commodities, that then centered in the city of Tyre on the eastern Mediterranean. "*All the ships of the sea with their mariners were in thee to traffic in thy merchandise: many islands were at hand to thee for trade: with silver, iron, tin, and lead, they traded in thy fairs: they brought thee for payment horns of ivory and ebony-wood.*" Among the commodities besides these exchanged in that market, are mentioned by the prophet horses and mules and lambs and rams and goats, wine of Helbon and white wool, fine linen and embroidered work, and riding cloths and mantles of blue and chests of damask and thread, wheat and pastry and syrup and oil and balm, precious spices and cassia and sweet reed, and gold and carbuncles and corals and rubies. These old Phœnicians of Tyre colonized Carthage, and thus bore a vast trade in commodities to the West, going overland into the heart of Africa for dates and salt and gold-dust and slaves, and by sea through the Pillars of Hercules northward to the British Isles for the sake of the trade in tin.

The amount of transactions in commodities, the first class of Valuables, has been constantly increasing, under natural impulses which we shall have shortly to describe, from the dawn of authentic History down to the present moment; and figures are baffled in expressing to our minds the sum of these transactions even in a single country, still more their aggregate in the commercial world. The foreign trade of every country is almost exclusively in commodities, and is only a small fraction of its domestic trade in the same; and so, when we remember that the foreign trade of the United States, for example, under a commercial system designed and adapted to curtail such trade, amounted in 1889 to about $1,600,000,000, and the foreign trade by Great Britain the same year to about 4,000,000,000, we gain a glimpse, we touch as it were the hem of the garment, of the gigantic traffic of the world in commodities alone.

The Production of Commodities is the getting them ready to sell and the selling them.

1. We must look first at the REQUISITES of such production. They are three, *Natural Agents, Human Efforts, Reserved Capital.* The following lines of Whittier touch incidentally on these three requisites, and may serve us as a general introduction to them:—

"Speed on the ship!—But let her bearNo merchandise of sin,No groaning cargo of despairHer roomy hold within.

"No Lethean drug for Eastern lands, No poison-draught for ours: But honest fruits of toiling hands, And Nature's sun and showers!"

Natural Agents include not only "Nature's sun and showers," but also all the forces and fertilities and materials of free Nature, that men may and do avail themselves of in preparing commodities to exchange with the commodities of other men. Of higher rank in Production than these natural agencies are the Efforts of men in molding them so as to answer other men's Desires, of which efforts the "toiling hands" of the poet are a symbol. They include also the inventive brains and eloquent tongues and the skilful manipulations of every name. The poet's "ship" is an instance of capital, which is always a result of previous toil reserved to help on some future sales. These three elements, Nature, Labor, Capital, conspire in all production of commodities. Nature comes first with her free forces and materials; and then present toil aided by the results of past toil in the form of capital does all the rest in getting commodities ready to sell and selling them. Let us now note each of these three a little more closely.

(a) Natural Agents. The most important point about these is, that they are the free gifts of God, and continue so throughout the complications and transformations wrought on them and through them by Labor and Capital, until the material commodity of whatever kind is finally sold, and so passes out of the purview of our Science. Many of the gifts of God, like the air we breathe and the light in which we recreate ourselves and the water of refreshment drunk from spring or brook, do not connect themselves in any way with commodities bought and sold, and nobody ever thinks of them as salable at all; but it has seemed and still seems to many, as if the natural fertility in a land-parcel, the water-fall along the course of river or stream, the timber-growth which the hand of man planted not, the deposit of gold or coal in the bowels of the earth, and other such-like cases in which natural gifts *do* connect themselves with human services and then are sold, lifted the Value of the things sold above the point to which the mere human efforts, whether past or present, would raise it. In point of fact, this seeming is not a reality, as will fully appear in the sequel. God is a Giver, and never a Seller; and he has arranged it so in his great world of gifts, that, however much shrewd men may try to monopolize these gifts and then dole them out to other men for pay, they are always practically thwarted in the attempt. God himself never takes pay for anything, and has never authorized anybody to take pay in his behalf; and when this role of Seller of free gifts, which have cost him nothing and which he has not improved, is taken up by any one, he is shortly crowded off the stage in shame by other actors true to Nature.

This is the place for a grand induction. When we study in detail the free gifts of God to this world and its inhabitants, we find they come and keep coming *in great classes*. This is one of the uniformities of Nature, on whose solid ground men tread and stride in safe inductive reasoning. Can a farmer get pay in the price of his grain for the original fertility of his field, which neither he nor his fathers nor his neighbors have bettered or made more available? Doubtless he would be *glad* to do so, doubtless he *would* do so, were it not for the primary fact, that such fertilities as his are in a *class* of fields, that other men in more or less proximity to him raise grain on other fields, whose original fertility is equal to that in his field; and some of these other men in common competition with the rest as sellers will be willing to part with *their* grain for a price which will be a fair equivalent for the onerous human services rendered in getting their grain ready to sell and selling it; and the free action of *these* men as sellers will tend to fix a general market-rate for grain then and there, at which rate *all* must sell whether they will or nill; and where now is the effect on price of God's free gift? It is still free.

Here is a fine water-fall on the bounding river, the banks are low at this point, just the place for mill and factory, the weight of God's free water will turn the wheels, a hamlet will grow up around them—perhaps a city,—can the riparian owner charge a fancy price for site of dam and mill? He might under some circumstances; but the same river doubtless, above, below, rolling over similar geological strata, leaps and falls at other points also; there are other owners of mill-privileges within hail; besides, there are other streams and tributaries in the region round about; and water has a knack of dropping to the lower levels. God's gifts are broad in classes; competition naturally has free play; natural agents are an essential factor in commodities; so and more so are human efforts; but Values tend perpetually and powerfully under natural competition between men as sellers to proportion themselves to the onerous human efforts involved, and to eliminate completely from all influence on themselves the broad and bountiful gifts of Providence.

What has been observed to be true in respect to two or three or more of the classes of God's free gifts *to* men, or *in* men, may almost certainly be inferred to be true of all such classes. Therefore, inductively, *such free gifts have no effect on Values to lift them, their influence being eliminated by human competition.* Of course, if there be unique cases of remarkable gifts, falling in no class, subject consequently to no competition, one cannot say confidently that the free element in conjunction with the onerous element may not make the return-service greater than it would be otherwise. It may, or it may not, make it greater. There is no living principle at work in such cases, that makes it certain, that the return-service will *not* be greater.

Still, unique cases, if they exist, are of little or no consequence in Economics. They are most remarkably few, at all events. Where come in the solitary gifts, that may later be connected with Valuables, on the round earth as God fashioned it? Gold, silver, diamonds, copper, coal, tin, amber, spice-shrubs, chinchona-trees, and all such things, have been scattered too widely and liberally for individuals to monopolize them, or even combinations of men unless they be assisted by law. Where even are the unique cases of God-given talent or genius in men themselves, such as may become connected with Valuables of the second class? Daniel Webster had his competitors in the Court-room and in the Senate, Ben Jonson did not let Shakspeare have it all his own way on the stage, and even "Milton's starry splendor" did not make Paradise Lost sell well.

We must just note here in passing the supreme importance in an economical point of view of untrammelled competition in the sale of commodities. It is the divinely-appointed means, and the only possible means, of preventing wide-spread injustice through Monopoly. Nothing else in the world can be made effective to estop men from robbing their fellow-men through exchanges artificially restricted; from charging more in the market for their wares than a just compensation for their own efforts; from enriching themselves by impoverishing their neighbors; from worsening the quality of their wares offered for sale; and from relying upon the artificial restrictions put on their competitors, rather than on their own skill and enterprise and the goodness of their goods, for a market. The Common Law of England holds monopolies to be illegal, and the reasons given (11 Coke, 84) are, first, because the price of the commodity will be raised; second, because the quality of the commodity will not be so good and merchantable as it was before; and third, because they are apt to throw many working people out of employment. It is nothing less than a crime against Civilization, than a sin against the clear ordinance of God, than an artificial obstruction to individual and national Progress, to put up bars and barriers by law for the purpose of cutting off competition, whether domestic or foreign, either by putting disabilities in the path of any or through monopoly tariff-taxes, in the buying and selling of useful commodities anywhere.

(b) Human Efforts. Every way unlike the free forces and materials of Nature, indispensable as these are in the production of commodities, is the second requisite in such productions, namely, the onerous efforts of men. Persons are very different from things, from powers, from lifeless materials. Persons act from motives only. Minds lie back of bodily exertions, impelling and guiding them. Such efforts as are needful to mold materials into commodities are only put forth in view of, and for the sake of, a remunerative return; and only rational beings, acting under motives whose goal is in the future, capable of foresight and of adapting means to ends, can put forth such efforts. No degree of training can make even the most intelligent animals capable in any degree of that kind of exertion, which we call *Labor*; and there is no improvement whatever in the methods of animals in reaching their instinctive ends,—the beaver builds his dam and the bee gathers and deposits the honey exactly as bees and beavers did ages ago.

In the strictest sense, accordingly, there is no such thing as physical labor, because the mental must coöperate with the physical even in the lowest forms of human exertion; and in the same sense there can be no such thing as exclusively mental labor, for the bodily powers conspire more or less in the highest intellectual efforts that are ever sold. Nevertheless, both the phrases, physical labor and mental labor, are convenient and not harmful, whenever on the one side the bodily powers seem to be predominant in the effort, and on the other the intellectual.

It is now to be noticed, that all that men can do, when they labor physically, is *to move something*. When a man works with his hands or his feet or his whole body, all that he does or can do, is to begin a series of motions or resistances to motion, for this good reason, human muscles in their very structure are capable only of starting motion and stopping motion. All the marvellous results of physical effort in all the world have flowed from so simple a matter as the contraction and expansion of muscle; and the world of materials is so cunningly constructed, that, when these are moved into right position by human hands, or by some form of capital itself the result of previous human handling, the free powers of Nature do all the rest, and valuable commodities are the good outcome. For one example, when the woodman fells a tree for sale, he brings a series of motions (*labor*) to bear upon the trunk, by means of his sharp axe (*capital*), and then the power of gravitation (*nature*) seizes the tree and brings it crashing to the earth. For a second illustration, wool and cotton have by nature a certain tenacity of fibre, and what is more to the point, a certain *kinkiness* of fibre easily interlinking one with another indefinitely in length; men move these separate fibres in certain relations to each other by an instrument (*capital*) called a spindle, and the result is thread; then other men move these threads into relations with each other by means of an implement (*capital*) called a shuttle, and the outcome is a web of cloth; lastly, the tailor moves his shears through the cloth, and then his needles, and the issue is a coat, a commodity, the valuable for which all these processes were gone through with, and by the sale of which all the onerous factors therein are compensated.

Now, since human muscles are soon wearied in action, and since motion is the only thing required of men in the production of commodities, they naturally look around for outside help in this matter; and the first help they lighted on for moving things was the domestic animals, the ox and ass and horse, doubtless domesticated in the very beginnings of society; and as these can be used in so many different places, and for such a variety of purposes, and are so cheaply reared, they are exceedingly useful as a motive power, and will probably never be superseded as such. Inanimate auxiliaries in moving things into right position for the production of commodities, such as the water-wheel and wind-mill, were undoubtedly brought into use much later; and much later still, steam and electricity and other more subtle and recondite natural agents. All of these helps, whether animate or inanimate, do but cause simple motions of the same kind as those caused by the human hand. The most ponderous engine merely reduplicates that which the arm of a child is capable of; while in point of delicacy and firmness of touch, perhaps no machinery can subdivide and apply this motion so skilfully as the human fingers can. It is said that some of the lace made wholly by hand is finer and more delicate than any yet woven by machinery, although the introduction of machinery into lace-making has cheapened lace products in general to a small fraction of their former cost.

What we commonly call *"Power,"* then, by whatever instrumentality furnished, is simple auxiliary motion, additional to that of physical human Labor. Commodities are produced in unlimited quantity and variety by such labor, assisted by the free forces of nature applied by means of animals and implements, which are capital. But such labor is irksome as well as wearisome, and is never expended except in view of a reward, which is secured only from the sale of the finished commodity.

(c) Reserved Capital. We must examine the nature of Capital with care, and follow its varied forms without confusion, because it is the only other factor besides labor in the production of commodities, that has to be paid for out of their sale.

Simplest cases are always the best in economical discussions. Let us take for illustration a recently observed case from the gold hills of North Carolina. All the methods are strongly primitive, but all the elements of production are present. A negro woman is the laborer, the bits of gold scattered in the soil are the free gift of nature, a bored log to divert the water from the mountain stream, and a tin pan in which to gather and wash the sand and gravel, are two crude forms of capital; free gravitation also brings the water through the log, and free gravity carries down the particles of gold to the bottom of the washing-pan, and many other agencies of free nature coöperate in this very simple case of production; and besides the log and the pan, there are doubtless some other forms of capital, at least the whittled plug to stop at need the flow of water through the log. The chief factor in these processes of production is still the laborer, the motions of her hands in stirring the sand and picking out the precious bits at the bottom of the pan are the chief motions, the labor is both physical and mental,—no animal could be trained to adopt means to ends like this negro woman.

It is her capital that now engages our attention. *Any Valuable outside of man himself reserved to assist in the production of further valuables is Capital.* The idea of growth and increase inheres in the very word, which is derived from the Latin noun, *caput*, a head, a source, and gives intimation in its etymology of its scientific meaning. The word, *caput*, is often used in classical Latin for a sum of money put out at interest, and its derivative, *capitale*, is also used in the same sense, at least in mediæval Latin; and from this form of the word have come into English not only *Capital*, but also by corruption *Cattle* and *Chattels*. Flocks and herds were at one time the principal riches of our Saxon ancestors, and also the principal means of *increasing* their riches, and in process of time the same root-word came to be spelled differently as applied to animate or inanimate things of value; while the notion implied in the Latin *caput*, and in the English *source*, came along in all three of these words; and hence the careful definition of Capital above given.

It makes no difference whether the colored woman bored her own log by means of an item of capital already existing, namely, an auger, or hired another person to bore it for her, or bought the log already perforated, it is an article of Capital, a valuable kept to increase future valuables; she might doubtless sell it for something to a new-comer wishing to operate other sand in the neighborhood, but she keeps it to help herself gather more gold for ultimate sale, she practises what we call in Economics *abstinence* and must have her reward for this in the form of *profits* from the ultimate sale of her commodity, gold, as well as a reward for her labor in the form of *wages* from the same source. As one person furnishes both the labor and capital in this case, there is no actual division of the gross return into wages and profits, as there always must be when separate parties furnish the two essential factors, both of which must be remunerated by the sale of the commodity. What is thus true of the log, is equally true of the tin-pan, and even of the plug also, if it be capable of repeated use and cost something of labor and the help of a previous item of capital, namely, the jack-knife. Our negro woman of the South is a small capitalist as well as a rude laborer, and practises *abstinence* as well as puts forth *exertion*, and consequently is entitled to receive *profits* as well as *wages* in the return she gets for her gold-dust when she sells it.

We are now beginning to see what the nature of Capital is, and what the motives are for employing it. In the production of commodities Capital is always something that makes easier to the producers the getting ready to sell and the selling of future commodities. The capital always spares more or less of onerous and irksome human exertion. It always mediates between some free force of Nature and some otherwise more onerous effort of men. The sole motive to employ capital in any one or in all of its multitudinous forms from the simplest to the most complex is to throw off upon the ever-willing shoulders of Nature some part of the irksome effort that would otherwise come to the easily-wearied muscles of men. Nature is "good," to use a commercial term, for all she can be made to carry of men's work, through implements devised and machinery contrived to apply, to commodities in every stage of their transformation and transportation till the last, the ever-present potencies of this physical world. These potencies cost nothing. The implements and machinery cost much in present labor and previously created capital. The ultimate sale of commodities must make return for all the forms of capital employed in their production, in the shape of Profits, the reward of *abstinence*; and for all the forms of direct labor employed in their production, in the shape of Wages, the reward of personal *effort*.

The beaver gnaws down the tree with his teeth from generation to generation in precisely the same manner; but man is a being more nobly endowed than the beaver, and no sooner had he occasion to fell trees, than something of the nature of an axe suggested itself to his ingenuity. It is true, that his earliest attempts at axe-making were probably of the rudest sort, but just as soon as anything was devised, whether of flint or shell or metal, that rendered easier the felling of a tree, Capital made a beginning along that line of obstacles. Our chief interest in studying the implements of the successive so-called Ages of Stone and Bronze and Iron, is to witness the increasing degrees of ingenuity displayed by those pre-historic men. Among the more gifted races, progress in this direction was perhaps more rapid than we are wont to think it was, since Tubal-Cain, the first artificer of record, is said to have "*hammered all kinds of implements out of copper and iron*" (Gen. iv, 22). Lucretius, writing in the century before the Christian era, put down the following lines in vigorous Latin, as translated by Mason Good:—

"Man's earliest arms were fingers, teeth, and nails,And stones, and fragments from the branching woods;Then copper next; and last, as later traced,The tyrant iron."

We are at no loss, then, to explain the origin of Capital and its motives. Tools are invented and employed for no other reason than this, that, by means of their help, the human efforts are lessened relatively to the given satisfactions. Since it requires tools to make tools, the progress of this branch of capital must have been relatively slow at first; but, since every advance in mechanical contrivance makes still further advances easier, there is a natural tendency, which facts abundantly exemplify, to a more and more rapid progression in the number and perfection of all implements of production. The same motive that impelled to the first invention, has impelled to the whole series of inventions since, and will constantly impel to further inventions till the end of time. Every step of this progress gives birth to a larger and still larger proportion of satisfactions relatively to efforts; marks an increasing control on the part of man over the powers of Nature; and gives promise for the time to come of greater advantages still in both of these directions. The powers of Nature, such as those which make the grain grow, bring the tree down, turn the water-wheel, impel the locomotive, and send the message round the world, all stand ready to slave in the service of man; but in order to make their aid available for human purposes, there must be a plough, an axe, a wheel, an engine, an electric machine; and it is because capital brings gratuitous natural forces into service, and the more so as capital progresses, that the Value of those commodities produced by the aid of capital tends constantly to decline as compared with those commodities, in the production of which capital conspires less.

It is already plain, that the class, Capital, is a smaller and a peculiar sub-class under the great class, Valuables; nothing can become Capital until it first become a Valuable, and then be *capitalized* by a distinct act or intention on the part of the owner to reserve it in his own hands as an aid in further production, or transfer it to other hands to be so used, he meanwhile receiving profits as the reward of his abstinence; only a *transferable* valuable, accordingly, can become Capital in any case, that is to say, it must be either a Commodity or a Credit, since personal services, though they may be sold, cannot be put over into the hands of another to be used in production, and therefore cannot become Capital in any case; and the chief peculiarity of this sub-class, Capital, is, unlike the three great classes of Valuables, each of which is utterly distinct from the other two, so that a Commodity can never become a Credit or a personal Service either of the others, that Capital as a class has extremely flexible limits, and consequently certain Commodities and Credits may easily enough be Capital to-day, and fall back to-morrow into their respective classes of mere Valuables and the next day come out from the class Non-Capital into the class Capital again. The same commodities and credits may be capital at one time, and non-capital at another, though they must be valuable all the time, or cease to be commodities and credits. When it is said that a young man's talents and skill are his "capital," the word of course is used in a metaphorical sense, and the meaning is, that skill and talents are *like* capital in some respects. Popular language is not scientific.

Cicero wrote long ago: "Optimum et in privatis familiis et in republica vectigal est parsimonia." *Abstinence is the best means of revenue as well in private families as in the State.* The source of Capital in a distinct act of will saving or sparing from present use (*parsimonia*) a valuable commodity or credit, and the quick nature of Capital as adding to itself (*vectigal*) in profits, are both brought out in this Latin maxim, which is rather an expression of an old and ingrained Roman sentiment than anything original with Cicero. It is the very nature as well as the very name of "Capital" to increase itself by rapid increments. It is as well the Stream as the Source. For example, any sum of money soon doubles itself when put out at compound interest, because the original sum increases day and night until it be repaid. It is of the essence of every form of Capital *to make growth*, because its sole purpose as such is to become an aid to future and further production. A trowel in the hands of a mason, which is capital, pays for itself every day he works with it, and perhaps every hour of the day, in the increased production wrought by means of it. The wheel, which free water turns, though a costly implement, repays that cost a hundred fold in the additional bushels of wheat turned into flour through its aid as capital. So of all implements. So of all machinery. So of all means of transportation: ships, canals, railroads.

There was a strange prejudice in ancient and mediæval times against this natural increase of capital out of its own bowels, as it were, owing probably to this dictum of Aristotle: "*For usury is most reasonably detested, as the increase of our fortune arises from the money itself, and not by employing it for the purpose for which it was intended.*" In 1360, a French bishop, Nicole Oresme, repeats the error of Aristotle under the same rhetorical image: "*It is monstrous and contrary to Nature that a barren stock should give birth, that a thing sterile in its whole being should fructify and be multiplied from itself, and such a thing is money.*" Even Shakspeare catches up the old figure: "*Is your gold and silver ewes and rams?*" Shylock answers: "*I cannot tell; I make it breed as fast.*" In the light of the three requisites of Production, in the light of the purpose and wisdom of God in arranging the active forces of this world, the prejudice in question disappears, and intelligence rejoices in the ever-increasing use of Capital as the handmaid of Labor, in the quick and sure reward of him who practises abstinence, in the production of commodities constantly made easier and cheaper in all directions, in a scale of comforts for the masses of men assuredly rising, in a divinely appointed force lifting like Christianity itself upon the otherwise sagging condition of mankind.

Capital assumes but two economical forms, namely, Circulating Capital and Fixed Capital. *Circulating Capital is all those capitalized products, whether commodities or credits, the returns for the sale or use of which are derived at once and once for all.* All circulating capital will be found in one or other of the following sub-forms: (1) raw materials; (2) wages paid out in view of an ultimate profit; (3) completed products on hand for sale; and (4) products bought and held for the sake of resale. The crucial test of circulating capital is the question, Are the returns to be secured by the single use or single transfer of that particular product? Tools, for example, in the hands of him who has manufactured them for sale is circulating capital. *Fixed Capital is all those capitalized products, which are purchased or held with a view of deriving an income from their delayed and repeated use.* All fixed capital will probably be found in one or other of the sub-forms following: (1) tools and machinery in use; (2) buildings used for productive purposes; (3) permanent improvements in land parcels; (4) investments in aid of locomotion and transportation; (5) products rented or retained for that purpose; and (6) the national money considered as a whole.

2. We will next look at the essential CONDITIONS of the production of Commodities. These are also three, as are the Requisites, namely, *Association, Invention, Freedom.* More or less will men make and sell to one another commodities in any state of society, in which there is permitted any considerable degree of association of men with men locally or commercially, in which is encouraged in any way the universal spirit of invention or the desire to get hard things done easier, and in which some degree of liberty of action and security of property and equality of privileges is guaranteed; but it is very plain, that the production of commodities will increase in all directions and become the greatest in that age and country when and where are allowed the closest ties of human association both in place and in commerce, the freest scope and largest rewards of inventive genius, and the highest possible degree of liberty and security and equality of rights. Let us illustrate from a state of things in the southern half of the United States during the first half of the nineteenth century. For the most part the land owners lived on isolated plantations widely separate from one another, these plantations were cultivated by gangs of slaves, a system that tends to bring all manual labor into contempt, the poor whites scattered in hamlets felt themselves above the slaves and beneath the masters, intercourse between the three classes was little, opportunity to better essentially their condition was denied to all three alike, there were but few cities sprinkled over the vast territory and these relatively small, the only commodity produced on a large scale was raw cotton, the simple device for ginning this had been invented in the decade preceding by a college boy from Connecticut, the agricultural implements were of the rudest kind, even the coarse shoes for the slaves were bought at the North;—in short, the degree of association and invention and freedom was each so low, that the production of commodities was exceedingly small, even as compared with what that production became in one quarter of a century after the abolition of slavery.

(a) Association. If we may continue for purpose of illustration our childhood trust in the story of De Foe, Robinson Crusoe came to lead a very tolerable life upon his desolate island by means of his own industry directed so as to satisfy his own wants by his own efforts. He did everything for himself, and had no opportunity to buy anything or sell anything. The whole course of such an isolated life could never develop the idea of Value, would require no such word as Commodities or suggest their production, and such a man while solitary upon his island could not possess Property in the true sense of that word. Association is the first main condition of Production, because of the natural obstacles interposed between the isolated man and the supply of his various wants. If any one man try to surmount a considerable number of these natural obstacles, he must miserably fail, because his powers are not adequate to the task; and hence it follows, that, in a state of isolation, *men's wants exceed their powers*; but now let the same man devote himself to overcome a single class of obstacles, for instance, those in the way of procuring suitable clothing, and his powers are adequate to this, he soon acquires skill in it, he learns to avail himself of the free help of Nature and the facilitating processes of art, he is able to realize large products along his line, and is now ready to offer his surplus in exchange with other men, who meanwhile have been giving themselves each to another class of obstacles, have concentrated efforts and skill upon them, have succeeded by the help of Nature and art in surmounting them, and are now ready to offer their surplus commodities in exchange for others; and, the exchanges beginning to be made in all directions, men find that they thus obtain vastly greater satisfactions for their various desires than they could possibly get by direct efforts: so that we may even say, that, in a state of society through association, *men's powers tend to overtake their wants.*

Without association with his fellow-men, there is no creature so helpless, so unable to reach his true end, as is man; and therefore it is, that the impulse to association is one of the strongest of our natural impulses. Men come together, as it were by instinct, into society; and, thus associating themselves together, it is soon discovered, not only that there are various desires in the different members of the community, which are now readily met by coöperation and mutual exchange, but also that there are very different powers in the different individuals in relation to those obstacles which are to be surmounted. The tastes and aptitudes of different men are very diverse. There is a great diversity in natural gifts. One man has physical strength, another mechanical ingenuity, a third a philosophical turn, and a fourth a bent and genius for traffic. Now, then, Nature speaks in as loud a voice as she can utter, in favor of such a degree of association and exchange as shall allow a free development of these varying capacities, while they work upon the obstacles to the gratification of men's wants, which lie appropriately opposite to them.

Men must come together either locally or commercially, must learn each other's wants, must compare with each other powers and tastes and opportunities, must come to have some confidence in each other, and then they will begin by rendering mutual services back and forth to experience the better satisfactions and the new strength that exchanges bring. Whatever improves the character of men, and thus leads to greater confidence among them, will enlarge their commerce, and knit closer and wider ties of association and production. Neighborhood associations and productions soon create a surplus to be exchanged for something else with other neighborhoods; parts of single nations however remote from each other find a relative diversity of advantage and an increasing profit in connecting themselves by the ties of trade; and the separate nations learn, though late, that they are only one great family for the grand ends of production and progress. Even within the single nation, there is a strong tendency for particular trades to localize themselves in one spot, as for instance, the manufacture of skin gloves has centered itself for the United States in Gloversville, N. Y.; and so in the great cities that are centres of distribution, for example, the wholesale grocers of St. Paul are on one street, the dry goods houses of Boston are in close proximity, and the booksellers of New York are tending towards each other in place.

Now, this broad association as between persons and nations, instead of detracting at all from the individuality and power of each, is the very thing that brings out the individuality and intensifies the power of each; because it is only thus that full scope is given to the exercise and development of each peculiar power whether of the individual or the nation. Hence the strong tendency everywhere visible in the world of commerce towards Specialties: the old single trades and vocations and professions are constantly breaking themselves up into parts, and each man is taking up that for which he is naturally best fitted and has specially trained himself, and all to the great advantage of individuality and personal power and progress. Mr. Carey is certainly right in his principle (much insisted on in all his books), that the degree of individuality depends on the degree of association, each advancing hand in hand with the other; and he is as certainly wrong in lacking confidence in the natural forces at work tending to the highest degree of association and consequently to the highest degree of individuality. These forces are immensely strong. Men come together as it were by instinct, being conscious of individual feebleness; personal interest is soon seen to follow the bent of social attraction; a just sense of personal dignity and importance in being a substantive part in the ongoings of society enormously strengthens the impulse to association and individuality; the progress of each and all in achievement and elevation still further knits the ties of union; and lastly, a strong feeling of social justice, of what is *due* to others as well as to one's self,—that every man has an inalienable right to his full *opportunity* and all that that implies, to buy and sell and get gain, to life and liberty and the pursuit of happiness. When motives and powers and potencies such as these, proven to be universal by broad and constant inductions, fail as economical forces to secure association and individuality, then it will be time to look around with Mr. Carey for some inferior and factitious force.

(b) Invention. This is the second main condition in the production of commodities; because production is processes, getting something ready to sell and selling it; and Nature stands ever ready with her free agencies to facilitate these processes, just so far as the inventive brain of man can contrive to unite the two. Invention is the marriage of a gratuitous force to an onerous process, and the fruit of that union is an easier way and multiplied utilities. There are some in every considerable community, and more in every community enlarged by the natural association but just now described, who have the knack of contrivance, who find their joy in finding a new power in Nature or some new application of an old power; were it not for unhindered association and free exchange, the individuality of these would be effectually repressed, and they would have to drudge for their daily bread; but the importance of inventors is well understood in every progressive community, and under advanced exchanges their livelihood is guaranteed by those who hope to profit by its results while their work is maturing; and Production rejoices and grows strong and throws out unnumbered hands to make instant use of the new power and the easier processes, in order to multiply commodities in number and variety.

As an illustration of all this, the reader will be interested in a brief account of the series of Inventions made in Great Britain during the last third of the eighteenth century, in consequence of which the Cotton Industry was established in that country in such preëminence as has to this day baffled the attempts of all other countries even to approximate it.

We catch our first glimpse of Cotton in the pages of Herodotus, who wrote more than 400 years B.C. in relation to India as follows: "*There are trees, which grow wild there, the fruit whereof is a wool exceeding in beauty and goodness that of sheep. The natives make their clothes of this tree-wool.*" This passage is interesting, as showing that the first comparison of cotton with wool exhibited their resemblance in whiteness and in *kinkiness*, which latter quality enables them both to be spun into yarn; as showing also, that the Hindoos very early both spun and wove cotton, and then made it into clothes; and as showing lastly, the appropriateness of the original name given to cotton in Europe, namely, "tree-wool," a name by which the

Germans still designate it (Baumwolle). If the extreme East furnishes the first notice of cotton, the extreme West follows it next in order. When the Spaniards discovered Central and Southern America in the first quarter of the sixteenth century, they reported that they found the Mexicans clothed in cotton cloth.

But wool was the staple of England. Parliament and people were jealous of cotton, lest it might prove a rival to wool, and actually prohibited the introduction of printed calicoes (so called from Calicut in India whence they were exported). The taste, however, for calicoes increased in spite of the prohibition, which was afterwards intermitted for a revenue duty on plain cotton, which was then rudely printed on blocks in London, Manchester, and elsewhere; but the prohibition of Parliament against wearing printed calicoes was first repealed in 1736. Fifteen years later the United Kingdom imported only 2,976,610 lbs. of raw cotton, and exported only £45,986 of cotton goods; in one century the import of cotton became 500 times larger than that, and the export of cottons 1300 times larger than that; and this prodigious result was due mainly to three or four inventions occurring within short times of each other, by means of which the free forces of nature took the place of the onerous efforts of men.

John Hargreaves, a poor weaver in the neighborhood of Blackburn in Lancashire, was returning home from a long walk, in which he had been purchasing a further supply of yarn for his own loom. Spinning at that time only admitted of one thread spun at a time by one pair of hands, one of which turned the wheel and thus made the single spindle rapidly revolve, and the other hand pulled gently upon the "roving" attached to the spindle and thus drew it out to the requisite tenuity twisted into yarn. The "carding," then effected by rude instruments called hand-cards, by means of which the fibres of the cotton were disentangled and straightened and laid parallel with each other; and the "roving," a process by which the short fleecy rolls stripped off the hand-cards were applied to the spindle and made into thick threads only slightly twisted, were the two preparatory operations for the spinning. All these operations were slow and clumsy, and the consequent expensiveness of the yarn formed a great obstacle to the establishment of the cotton manufacture in England. The improvements made in the loom of that period by Kay, father and son, had shortly before doubled the power of each weaver, and the spinners could not keep up in furnishing material to the weavers.

As Hargreaves entered his cottage from this excursion to get yarn to keep his loom agoing, his wife, Jenny, accidentally upset the spindle, which, as was her wont, she was diligently using. Her husband noticed that the spindle, which was now thrown into an upright position, continued to revolve just as when horizontal, and that the thread was still spinning in his wife's hands. The idea immediately occurred to him, that it might be possible to connect a considerable number of upright spindles with the revolutions of one wheel, and thus multiply the power of each spinster. "*He contrived a frame in one part of which he placed eight rovings in a row, and in another part a row of eight spindles. The rovings, when extended to the spindles, passed between two horizontal bars of wood, forming a clasp which opened and shut somewhat like a parallel ruler. When pressed together this clasp held the threads fast; a certain portion of roving being extended from the spindles to the wooden clasp, the clasp was closed, and was then drawn along the horizontal frame to a considerable distance from the spindles, by which the threads were lengthened out and reduced to the proper tenuity; this was done with the spinner's left hand, and his right hand at the same time turned a wheel which caused the spindles to revolve rapidly, and thus the roving was spun into yarn. By returning the clasp to its first situation and letting down a piercer wire the yarn was wound upon the spindle.*"

The powers of Hargreaves' machine soon became known among his ignorant neighbors, notwithstanding his strenuous efforts to keep his admirable invention a secret, and these neighbors naturally enough concluded that a contrivance, which enabled one spinster to do the work of eight, would throw many people out of employment. A mob broke into his house and destroyed his machine. Hargreaves retired in disgust to Nottingham, where by means of the friendly assistance of one other person he was enabled to take out a patent for his invention, which he called in compliment to his industrious wife the "*Spinning-Jenny*." This invention gave a new impulse to the cotton manufacture, but had it been unaccompanied by other improvements, no purely cotton goods could have been made in England; because the yarn spun by the new jenny, like that previously spun by hand, was not fine enough nor hard enough to be used as warp, and linen or woollen threads had consequently to be employed for that purpose.

In the very year, however, in which John Hargreaves, the poor weaver, migrated to Nottingham, Richard Arkwright, a poor barber's assistant, took out a patent for his still more celebrated machine for spinning by rollers. In one respect Arkwright was much worse off than Hargreaves: the latter had a helpmate meet for him, the former had a wife who is said to have destroyed the models her husband had made and to have opposed him in every step of his career. But Arkwright was not deterred from his life pursuit by the poverty of his circumstances or the scandalous conduct of his wife. After many years of intense and opposed devotion to the possible application of a simple principle he had conceived in his mind, namely, that of spinning by means of rollers revolving at varying rates of rapidity, he succeeded in contriving and patenting his memorable machine, which, more than any other one invention, localized and concentrated in England the gigantic cotton-industry of the world. Arkwright's idea and achievement was to pass the coarse thread drawn out from the rovings over two pairs of rollers in succession, the first of which revolving slowly fined the thread down evenly and gradually, and then this thread was passed over a second pair of rollers turning with a high velocity and drawing out the line into any requisite tenuity. Thus a cotton thread was spun capable of being used as warp. Cotton cloth as such could now be manufactured in England.

From the circumstance that the mill, at which Arkwright's machinery was first erected, was driven by water power, the machine received the inappropriate name of the "water-frame"; and the thread spun on these rollers was commonly called the "water-twist." The old mode of carding the cotton by hand now furnished the "rovings" too slowly to meet the wants of the new spinning-jenny and the new water-frame; and these great inventions would consequently have proven comparatively useless, had not a more efficient and rapid process of carding the cotton superseded just at the right time the old system of hand-carding. Lewis Paul introduced revolving cylinders for carding the raw cotton into rovings preparatory to spinning, in partial imitation perhaps of Arkwright's principle of spinning the rovings by the rotatory motion of rollers. Paul's machine consisted "*of a horizontal cylinder, covered in its whole circumference with parallel rows of cards with intervening spaces, and turned by a handle. Under the cylinder was a concave frame, lined internally with cards exactly fitting the lower half of the cylinder, so that when the handle was turned, the cards of the cylinder and of the concave frame worked against each other and carded the wool. The cardings were of course only of the length of the cylinder, but an ingenious apparatus was attached for making them into a perpetual carding. Each length was placed on a flat broad riband, which was extended between two short cylinders, and which wound upon one cylinder as it unwound from the other.*"

While the foregoing series of inventions placed an almost unlimited supply of cotton yarn at the disposal of the weaver, the machinery as yet introduced was still incapable of providing yarn fit for the finest grades of cotton cloth. The "water-frame" indeed spun abundant twist for warps, but it could not furnish the finest qualities of yarn, because these were too tenuous to bear safely the pull of the rollers while they wound themselves on the bobbin. Samuel Crompton, a young weaver living near Bolton, possessed the ingenuity needful to remove this difficulty. He succeeded in combining in one machine, which from its nature is happily called the "mule," the several excellences of Hargreaves' spinning-jenny and Arkwright's water-frame. Copying after the latter, the mule has a system of rollers to reduce the roving; copying after the former it has spindles without bobbins to give the twist; and the thread is stretched and spun at the same time by the spindles after the rollers have ceased to give out the rove. "*The distinguishing feature of the mule is that the spindles, instead of being stationary, as in both the other machines, are placed on a movable carriage which is wheeled out to the distance of fifty-four or fifty-six inches from the roller beam, in order to stretch and twist the thread, and wheeled in again to wind it on the spindles. In the jenny, the clasp which held the rovings was drawn back by the hand from the spindles; in the mule, on the contrary, the spindles recede from the clasp, or from the roller-beam which acts as a clasp. The rollers of the mule draw out the roving much less than those of the water-frame, and they act like the clasp of the jenny by stopping and holding fast the rove, after a certain quantity has been given out, whilst the spindles continue to recede for a short distance farther, so that the draught of the thread is in part made by the receding of the spindles. By this arrangement, comprising the advantages both of the roller and the spindles, the thread is stretched now gently and equably, and a much finer quality of yarn can therefore be produced."*

The ingenuity of Hargreaves, Arkwright, and Crompton had been exercised to provide the weaver with yarn, and had now indeed provided him with more yarn than he could use; the spinster had beaten the weaver, just as the weaver had previously beaten the spinster; and the making of cotton cloth seemed likely to continue sluggish, because the yarn could not be woven any faster than a skilled workman could weave it with Kay's improved fly-shuttle. In the summer of 1784, a Kentish clergyman named Edmund Cartwright, being in conversation with some Manchester gentlemen, one of whom observed that, "as soon as Arkwright's patent expired so many mills would be erected and so much cotton spun that hands would never be found to weave it," replied, "Arkwright must then set his wits to work to invent a weaving-mill." Notwithstanding the unanimous opinion expressed by the Manchester gentlemen, that such a weaving-machine was wholly impracticable, the clergyman himself within three years had invented and brought into successful operation the "*power-loom.*" Subsequent inventors improved the idea which Cartwright originated, and before 1834 there were not less than 100,000 power-looms at work in Great Britain alone.

Substantially the same machinery invented for carding and spinning and weaving cotton was very shortly and successfully applied to the carding and spinning and weaving of wool, because the wisdom of Nature imparted to them both the same sort of tenacity of fibre, the same capacity in that fibre to be spun into a thread of indefinite length by means of the little loops or kinks easily interlocking contiguous fibres into a single thread, which two obvious resemblances gave an identical name to the animal and vegetable products otherwise so different from each other.

The spirit of Invention, one of the chief conditions in the production of material commodities, thus simply illustrated along the line of a single manufacture, may serve us for a sample of similar improvements taken and taking place in scores upon scores of other lines of effort and production. The principle is the same in all cases past and present and still to come, namely this, to throw the strain from the mind and muscles of men upon the forces and agencies of free Nature, with which the world around us is crowded in our behalf, and which are waiting to slave in the service of mankind without rest and without fatigue,—without money and without price.

(c) Freedom. By far the most important of all the conditions, under which the production of material commodities goes broadly forward, is liberty of action on the part of the individual; because, wherever such liberty is conceded, association and invention and all other needful conditions follow right along by laws of natural sequence. By liberty of individual action is meant the practical right of every man to employ his own efforts for the satisfaction of his own wants in his own way, whether directly or through exchange. Each man's right of individual freedom is limited of course by every other man's right to equal freedom, which the first man is not at liberty to infringe; and also, in certain few and limited respects, by what is sometimes called the "general good," the judge of the application of which must be the government under which the man lives. With these limitations, which are few in number and never serious in degree when rightly applied, and which limit in common all other rights whatsoever, the right of every man to buy and sell and get gain is just as fully a right as the right of breathing. It stands on the same impregnable ground. It is a natural and self-evident and inalienable right, with which each man has been endowed by his Creator, to put forth efforts for his own well-being and for those dependent upon him, either directly or by means of efforts exchanged with other men equally free; and he is a slave in spirit and position, who tamely submits to have his own rights of buying and selling curtailed, or to stand by and see the rights of his fellow-citizens similarly curtailed, unless such act of interference and curtailment on the part of his Government be justified by a solid proof that some other public or private rights, which are at least as well based as his own, would be endangered by the exercise of his own.

In what cases may a Government properly step in to regulate or prohibit the buying and selling of its citizens? Hundreds of inductions extending through hundreds of years have been carefully and logically conducted in order to reach a just and comprehensive answer to this question; and in all probability the cases have been inductively ascertained for all time, and they are these: *such buying and selling may be controlled and prohibited, as are proven to be contrary* (1) *to the public Morals,* (2) *to the public Health,* (3) *to the public Revenue.* All other buying and selling may be safely assumed to be both profitable to the parties to it, and also useful to the Commonwealth in general; and any interference with it by public authority is a high-handed infringement of natural rights, a blow aimed at the life and source of property. These wrongful strokes at private rights, this restriction on the freedom of individuals to exchange products for their own welfare, is now mostly confined in civilized countries to the region of Taxation. Within this region the wrongs are still frightful. Judge Cooley, in his "Principles of Constitutional Law," states the matter as follows: "*Constitutionally a tax can have no other basis than the raising of revenue for public purposes; and whatever governmental action has not this basis is tyrannical and unlawful. A tax on imports, therefore, the purpose of which is not to raise a revenue, but to discourage and indirectly prohibit some particular import for the sake of some home manufacturer, may well be questioned as being merely colorable, and therefore not warranted by constitutional principle.*"

Formerly, governments interfered almost beyond belief with the freedom of their people in all industrial and commercial action; dictating what should and what should not be grown and manufactured, what should and what should not be exported and imported; decreeing by proclamation or enacting by statute, the number of apprentices each artisan might employ, and the years during which these must serve as such, and the conditions under which they might then work as journeymen; the materials to be used in woven fabrics, and even the widths and other minor features of such fabrics, were prescribed in the foremost of the European nations; in the reign of St. Louis of France, a "Book of Trades" was issued under royal authority and is still extant, which organizes minutely and subjects to cumbersome rules more than one hundred separate industries as then practised; England was the country of the great trading "Companies," and of all of these the same may be said as Adam Smith said of the Turkey Company formed in 1579, namely, it was "a strict and oppressive monopoly"; among others there were the African Company established in 1530, the Russia Company beginning its operations in 1553, the East India Company chartered on the very last day of the seventeenth century and going out of existence in our own time, and the Hudson's Bay Company, chartered in 1670 and so having the sole control in trade of a region forty times larger than all England; while the colonial system prevailing for two centuries in all the countries of Western Europe regulated the commerce and controlled the manufactures in the colonies with a single eye to the benefits of the mother country, as those were conceived of under the wretched Mercantile system.

Happily, since governments have become more enlightened than formerly, they are perceiving for the most part that they have not the least right to interfere in those ways or in any ways with the natural right of their people to make and grow freely all material commodities, and to buy and sell these freely in the best markets wherever these markets are to be found; and they are also perceiving, that by such interference incalculable losses of property and indefinite retardations of progress are caused to their people, as well as weakness to themselves as governments through a more difficult gathering of taxes and a harder maintenance of prestige and power.

The only motive to a mutual exchange of services, whether in one or in all of their three kinds, that is to say, to a free production of commodities and services and credits, is always and everywhere the mutual benefit of the two parties exchanging. After all the processes have been gone through with and the exchanges are consummated, all the parties are richer than before, that is, they have more *satisfactions*, otherwise the processes and exchanges would instantly cease. Therefore, a universally free production benefits everybody, and harms nobody. Moreover, under a system of free production, every man is allowed under the stimulus of self-interest to work away at those obstacles to the gratification of human desires which he feels himself best able to overcome, to follow the bent of his own mind, and to avail himself of all those free helps in his peculiar work which Nature offers to him. Under these circumstances, obstacles give way in all directions; the amount of material products produced is vastly augmented, the number and variety and excellence of personal services proffered are indefinitely increased, and credits compelling the Future to pay tribute to production are multiplied; the diversified and rapidly increasing desires of all persons in such a community are readily met through profitable exchanges; while all peculiar facilities natural and acquired are taken immediate advantage of, the diversities of relative advantage in production become marked in all directions, and a new day of industrial and commercial prosperity is ushered in. Because under freedom all men are sure to dispose of their industrial efforts to the best advantage, they have the strongest possible motives to put them forth; since they can purchase with them what they will and when they will, and where they will. Thus freedom leads to extended association, and also to the invention of machinery and all labor-saving appliances.

3. We are now in position to understand thoroughly the ultimate GROUNDS of the production of material commodities. We have seen, that these commodities have been multiplying in number and variety and excellence ever since the beginnings of history, that they are everywhere multiplying now at a rate hitherto unprecedented and undreamed of, and that improved and improving methods of transportation by land and sea are now carrying these back and forth to the ends of the earth. What is the *principle*, under which these things have been done, are now being done, and are certain to be done in the time to come?

The physical and moral obstacles, that Nature has interposed to the gratification of the multitudinous and constantly increasing desires of men, are so great in all directions, that the powers of the individual man are utterly unable to surmount any considerable number of them; while at the same time, the physical and moral powers, adapted under sufficient motives to overcome these obstacles, are very diverse in the different individuals of mankind. Not only is there a surprising diversity in original gifts, but also the powers acquired by gradual concentration of personal effort upon one set of obstacles become exceedingly diverse, as does moreover familiarity in the use of the gratuitous forces of nature which lend their aid towards overcoming these particular obstacles. As the result of one or two or all of these, one man naturally comes to have a vast advantage over others in his particular branch of business, whatever that may be; each of these others by precisely the same means comes to have a legitimate advantage over the first in his own branch of effort, whatever that may be; and if, as always happens practically, the first has desires which the varied efforts of the others can satisfy, and they too desires which his efforts can satisfy, nothing more is necessary to profitable exchanges between them than this diversity of relative advantage at different points.

It is solely because a given effort irksome in itself put forth for another person, in view of and for the sake of a return-service from him, realizes more of satisfaction to both parties than when put forth for one's self directly, that commercial exchanges ever take place among men. The sole ground of these, the principle underlying them everywhere, is DIVERSITY OF ADVANTAGE BETWEEN DIFFERENT MEN AND BETWEEN DIFFERENT NATIONS IN DIFFERENT RESPECTS. All exchanges whatsoever depend on diversity of relative advantage in the production of commodities or services or credits as between the persons exchanging; and this diversity of relative advantage exists by God's appointment primarily among individual men as such, and only secondarily on the ground of the varied soil and climate and position and natural gifts of different parts of the earth. Reserving these secondary considerations, which are quite secondary in importance also, to a later detailed discussion, it is very clear and of central consequence in our science that a diversity of relative advantage in different things displays itself as between the individuals of every community and country large and small. There is no hamlet in any land in which one man has not an advantage over his neighbors in the making of clothes, another in the making and setting of horse-shoes, a third in the building of houses, a fourth in the curing of diseases, and another in the keeping a school; while each of those neighbors has undoubtedly some advantage or other over each of these in some trade or means of livelihood. As a natural result of this diversity any two of these villagers may profitably exchange their respective efforts with each other, provided of course each has a desire for the product of the other, to the manifest lessening of the effort of each relatively to the satisfaction of each, and the more so as the relative superiority of each to the other in his own trade is the greater.

This point will repay some pains in minute illustration. If the blacksmith can make and set horse-shoes only a trifle better than the tailor could do this if he tried, and the tailor can make coats only a little better than the blacksmith could make one if he chose, there will be but a slight benefit to each in their changing works with one another. For the sake of definiteness, let us say, that the tailor's capacity for making coats is 6, and his capacity in making and setting horse-shoes is 5; and also that the blacksmith's capacity for shoeing horses is 6, and his ability in making coats is 5. Each has a relative superiority to the other of 1 in his own trade; and if they exchange efforts, as they probably would under these circumstances, there is only an advantage of 2 to be divided between them.

Now let us suppose (what might easily become a fact), that the tailor by exclusive and augmented attention to the conditions of his own craft carries up his capacity for making coats to 15, the blacksmith's efficiency in both the trades remaining the same as before. There will now be an increased motive to both the artisans for exchanging products with one another, and a larger gain to each than before as the result of such exchange. The diversity of relative advantage as between the two has now gone up from 2 to 11. The tailor can now make a coat much better and quicker than before; and though the blacksmith owing to his inertness can neither make nor set horse-shoes any better than before, still less make coats any better, he will after all by still trading with the tailor reap a part of the benefit of the latter's increased efficiency in making coats; the new coat is at once better and costs less than the previous one; the tailor is still less inclined than before to leave his new and greater advantage over the blacksmith to set himself to shoeing his own horse; even on the old terms the blacksmith can do that 1 better than he himself can, and rather than forego the trade he will naturally offer the blacksmith somewhat better terms than before, or in other words will feel impelled to share with the blacksmith a part of the proceeds and rewards of his own now superior skill and diligence. The trade began on the sole basis of a relative diversity of advantage as between the two mechanics, each in his own craft; this relative diversity, without which no exchange ever takes place between any two persons, has now gone up as between these two from 2 units of advantage to 11 units of advantage; how will these 11 units be divided in this case? Nobody can tell exactly how they will be divided. Two things about it, however, are *certain* at least in their tendencies and potencies. The blacksmith is sure to get some part of the extra fruit of his neighbor's new push and spirit, while the tailor is sure to get as his own reward by much the larger part of the whole blessed 11.

We must by no means omit to notice the logical inference from this instance, nor fail to make the proper inductive generalization from a sufficient number of similar instances. It is this: no man can make any essential improvement in any of the methods of producing material commodities, without at the same time benefiting other people as well as himself. Under natural law, which is no respecter of persons, he can by no possibility selfishly take to himself the entire fruits of his own growing skill and vigor. The only way in which he can gather in at all the fruits of these is to sell their proceeds in the open market. To broaden his own market for now better and more abundant goods he must offer them to everybody on somewhat better terms than formerly—and the better the terms the broader the market—and he can well afford to do this, because the goods now cost him less of irksome human effort. Every improvement in the production of commodities is precisely of that complexion. The issue of every invention, of every improved process of every kind, is, so far forth, a cheaper product. And this public gain follows, must follow, individual enterprise at single points, even when the great mass of exchangers remain at the old stage of sluggishness. Whatever increases at one point even, and *a fortiori* at two points, the diversity of relative advantage as between any two exchangers, is of benefit to them both, and the greater this relative diversity becomes the greater the benefit to both.

Now let us see how the matter stands, when tailor and blacksmith at the same time feel and obey the impulses to a more skilled and vigorous artisan life. Suppose the blacksmith too carries up his efficiency in his own trade to 15, just as the tailor has done, the potency of each in the trick of the other remaining as before at 5; under these circumstances when the two come to trade with each other, each has a relative superiority over the other of 10, and there is an advantage of 20 points to be divided between the two; the trade is now ten times more profitable to each than it was at the outset, when there was only an aggregate of 2 units for the division between two parties; and accordingly the motive to an exchange and the gain of an exchange as between tailor and blacksmith are ten times greater than they were before. Therefore we lay down the principle, as inductively ascertained and as universally applicable to all exchanges, that the greater the relative superiority at different points as between the parties exchanging, the more beneficial and profitable do the exchanges become to all the participators in them. If this principle be just, and we may well flatter ourselves that it will be found to be just, it follows, that every man who has anything to buy or sell, is directly interested in the highest success of his fellow-exchangers, that every trade finds its own advantage in the success of all other trades, and that all discoveries and inventions by which Nature is made to pay tribute to art is, restrictions apart, so much clear gain to the world at large. In the light of sound and broad principles, what David Hume called the "Jealousy of Trade" is simply silly.

The mainspring that impels all buyers and sellers to quicken their movements and to improve their methods and thus and otherwise to cheapen their costs of production, is the natural press of *competition*. Somebody else is offering this product, or will offer it, for less than we are now selling it for, and we must contrive some way by shortened times or cheaper processes or a quicker zeal not to be beaten in this market-race, is the silent argument ever making itself felt on the mind and hand of the producer. Such natural action always increases the general diversity of relative advantage as among buyers and sellers.

But, on the other hand, whatever lessens or threatens to lessen this natural and most beneficial stress of competition among producers of similar commodities at home or abroad, necessarily lessens the motive on the part of these producers to excellence of quality in their goods and to cheapness of their cost, because it makes less the diversity of relative advantage as between these producers and those producers of other commodities against which the first exchange. The units of advantage that would otherwise be divided between the exchangers are diminished; the motives to trade and the rewards of trade are thus lessened to each pair of parties subject to such diminution of competition, and consequently to the community, or nation, or family of nations, as a whole; and accordingly this is the precise place for us to look into the nature and effects of *Monopoly*, so called, and to perceive once for all, that Monopoly is the enemy of mankind.

Monopoly is a word derived from two Greek words, which mean when combined *selling alone*, that is, the privilege of selling one's commodity free from the competition to which it is naturally subject by other sellers than the privileged one. Monopoly is thus artificial restraint imposed on some buyers and sellers for the supposed benefit of other buyers and sellers. It is wholly unnatural. It is usually enjoyed under the forms of law. Its beneficiaries commonly cajole or extort from Government by hook or by crook the exclusive privilege of selling certain commodities in a designated market. Their motive is purely selfish: it is simply and solely to get for themselves a return-service artificially enhanced by selling commodities in a legally restricted market. The effect in the first instance usually corresponds to their expectations. The public are at their mercy so far as the designated commodities are concerned.

The general story of monopolies is a dreary stretch of record of human greed and wrong on the one hand, and of wide-spread poverty and suffering and slowly-gathering resistance on the other. We will look at only two instances at present in the long account, premising that, the motives of greed and grab are the same in all instances, and the results of wrong and hate on the part of those oppressed by them are the same also in all instances. Let Macaulay (I, 40) tell us something of the first instance selected for illustration. "*But at length the Queen took upon herself to grant patents of monopoly by scores. There was scarcely a family in the realm which did not feel itself aggrieved by the oppression and extortion which this abuse naturally caused. Iron, oil, vinegar, coal, saltpetre, lead, starch, yarn, skins, leather, glass, could be bought only at exorbitant prices. The House of Commons met in an angry mood. It was in vain that a courtly minority blamed the Speaker for suffering the acts of the Queen's Highness to be called in question. The language of the discontented party was high and menacing, and was echoed by the voice of the whole nation. The coach of the chief Minister of the Crown was surrounded by an indignant populace, who cursed the monopolies, and exclaimed that the prerogative should not be suffered to touch the old liberties of England. There seemed for a moment to be some danger that the long and glorious reign of Elisabeth would have a shameful and disastrous end. She, however, with admirable judgment and temper, declined the contest, put herself at the head of the reforming party, redressed the grievance, thanked the Commons in touching and dignified language for their tender care of the general weal, brought back to herself the hearts of the people, and left to her successors a memorable example of the way in which it behooves a ruler to deal with public movements which he has not the means of resisting.*"

Perhaps some one of my readers may suggest, that these are the words of a Whig-Liberal, and may thus exaggerate the cause of the people as against the monopolists. Well, then, let us hear the words of a high Tory-Loyalist, the historian Hume (IV, 335, 350), in relation to the same monopolies. "*The active reign of Elizabeth had enabled many persons to distinguish themselves in civil and military employments; and the Queen, who was not able from her revenue to give them any rewards proportioned to their services, had made use of an expedient which had been employed by her predecessors, but which had never been carried to such an extreme as under her administration. She granted her servants and courtiers patents for monopolies; and those patents they sold to others, who were thereby enabled to raise commodities to what price they pleased, and who put invincible restraints upon all commerce, industry, and emulation in the arts. It is astonishing to consider the number and the importance of those commodities which were thus assigned over to patentees. Currants, salt, iron, powder, cards, calf-skins, felts, pouldavies, ox-skin-bones, train oil, lists of cloth, potashes, anise-seeds, vinegar, seacoals, steel, aquavitæ, brushes, pots, bottles, saltpetre, lead, accidences, oil, calamine stone, oil of blubber, glasses, paper, starch, tin, sulphur, new drapery, dried pilchards, transportation of iron ordnance, of beer, of horn, of leather, importation of Spanish wool, of Irish yarn; these are but a part of the commodities which had been appropriated to monopolists. These monopolists were so exorbitant in their demands, that in some places they raised the price of salt from sixteen pence a bushel to fourteen or fifteen shillings. Such high profits naturally begat intruders upon their commerce; and in order to secure themselves against encroachments, the patentees were armed with high and arbitrary powers from the Council, by which they were enabled to oppress the people at pleasure, and to exact money from such as they thought proper to accuse of interfering with their patent. The patentees of saltpetre, having the power of entering into every house, and of committing what havoc they pleased in stables, cellars, or* wherever they expected saltpetre might be gathered, commonly extorted money from those who desired to free themselves from this damage or trouble. And while all domestic intercourse was restrained, lest any scope should remain for industry, almost every species of foreign commerce was confined to exclusive Companies, who bought and sold at any price that they themselves thought proper to offer or exact."

"The Government of England during that age, however different in other particulars, bore in this respect some resemblance to that of Turkey at present: the Sovereign possessed every power, except that of imposing taxes; and in both countries, this limitation, unsupported by other privileges, appears rather prejudicial to the people. In Turkey, it obliges the Sultan to permit the extortion of the pashas and governors of provinces, from whom he afterwards squeezes presents and takes forfeitures: in England, it engaged the Queen to erect monopolies, and grant patents for exclusive trade; an invention so pernicious, that had she gone on during a tract of years at her own rate, England, the seat of riches, and arts, and commerce, would have contained at present as little industry as Morocco or the coast of Barbary."

But, some one will say, Hume and Macaulay are historians, writing long after these events took place, and may likely have been too favorable in their judgment to freedom of trade domestic and foreign. It is indeed true, that both of them were firmly convinced that freedom of trade is an inalienable right as well as an unspeakable blessing to all men everywhere. So, then, let us go back to contemporaries. Let us hear the eye and ear witnesses of the grievances complained of in 1601. Robert Cecil was then prime minister of Queen Elizabeth. He and his father had had more to do in granting the monopolies than any other persons in the realm except the Queen. Said he from his place in the Commons on the 25th of November: "I say, therefore, there shall be a proclamation general throughout the realm, to notify Her Majesty's resolution in this behalf. And because you may eat your meat more savory than you have done, every man shall have salt as good and cheap as he can buy it or make, freely without danger of that patent which shall be presently revoked. The same benefit shall they have which have cold stomachs, both for aqua vitæ and aqua composita and the like. And they that have weak stomachs, for their satisfaction, shall have vinegar and alegar, and the like, set at liberty. Train oil shall go the same way; oil of blubber shall march in equal rank; brushes and bottles endure the like judgment. Those that desire to go sprucely in their ruffs, may at less charge than accustomed obtain their wish; for the patent for starch, which hath so much been prosecuted, shall now be repealed. The patents for calf-skins and felts, for leather, for cards, for glass, shall also be suspended, and left to the law."

Five days later one hundred and forty members of the House were formally received by Elizabeth in person, the Speaker having been instructed to convey their thanks to her majesty; and, after the Speaker's address, he with the rest knelt down, and the Queen gave her answer as follows: "Mr. Speaker, you give me thanks, but I doubt me, I have more cause to thank you all, than *you me: for had I not received a knowledge from you, I might have fallen into the lap of an error, only for lack of true information. Since I was queen, yet never did I put my pen to any grant, but that upon pretext and semblance made unto me that it was both good and beneficial to the subjects in general, though a private profit to some of my ancient servants who had deserved well; but the contrary being found by experience, I am exceeding beholding to such subjects as would move the same at first. I have ever used to set the last judgment-day before mine eyes, and so to rule as I shall be judged to answer before a higher judge. To whose judgment-seat I do appeal, that never thought was cherished in my heart that tended not to my people's good. And now if my kingly bounty hath been abused, and my grants turned to the hurt of my people, contrary to my will and meaning; or if any in authority under me have neglected or prevented what I have committed to them, I hope God will not lay their culps and offences to my charge. Though you have had, and may have, many princes more mighty and wise, sitting in this seat, yet you never had, or shall have, any that will be more careful and loving."*

These were the last words of Elizabeth to the Commons of England. She died in a little more than a year. In a little less than a year before the death of her successor, the famous Act of Parliament of 1624 declares, that all monopolies, grants, letters patent for the sole buying, selling, and making of goods and manufactures, shall be thereafter wholly null and void. Though this Act, and many others, was violated more or less in the next reign, it effectually secured in the long run the freedom of industry in England; and in the opinion of excellent authorities, has done more to excite the spirit of invention and industry, and to accelerate the progress of commerce in that country, than any other law on the statute book.

Our second instance of Monopolies shall be drawn from the state of things in the United States in this year of Grace, 1890. The monopolies of to-day are secured by means of an instrument called a Tariff, which, later on in these pages, will be fully discussed in its history, inmost nature, and invariable effects. Here it will suffice to say, that a tariff is nothing in the world but a combination of Taxes, which taxes the people of the country, on which the tariff is imposed, are obliged to pay in one form or another. The only word ever uttered by a tariff, the only word a tariff from its own nature can utter, is, *Thou shalt pay*! The ostensible reason for levying these taxes is the constitutional one of getting money into the national Treasury,—"*to pay the debts and provide for the common defence and general welfare of the United States*"; but the real purpose of laying these tariff-taxes at present is only secondarily and remotely the ostensible and constitutional one; because, on the authority of Professor Taussig of Harvard University, there is not a single one of over 4000 items of taxes in this tariff, that is designed primarily to get money into the treasury from the pockets of the people, but every one of them is designed more or less and more rather than less to raise the price of domestic goods to our own people artificially by keeping out of the country by means of these taxes on them the foreign goods, which would otherwise come into a profit. In other words, there is no purely revenue-tax in our immense tariff at present, but every item in the enormous list is a so-called and mis-called "protective"-tax.

By this shutting off from domestic goods the natural competition of corresponding foreign goods by means of such tariff-taxes, a monopoly is created at the instance and for the sole benefit of certain classes of privileged home-producers. They can sell alone (monopoly) just so far as other sellers are kept out by these heavy taxes. The goal of all their striving is to get an artificially-enhanced price for their own products at the cost of their countrymen by means of a market restricted to themselves through obstacles excluding foreign sellers. The end proposed by these shrewd manipulators is realized in fact. Domestic prices are lifted on so-called "protected" goods. This is the first effect of the monopoly. It has often been alleged, and with great vehemence by the late Horace Greely, that competition among the domestic producers of such wares will lower their price again to the natural point; but if this is so, what *motive* have the individual producers to work so assiduously in elections and lobbyings to get on and keep on these tariff-taxes? Again, Mr. Greely, and all others of like association, forgets the admirable generalization of Robert Stephenson,—"*Where combination is possible, competition is impossible.*" Combination among producers to keep up prices is always possible in a market restricted by law. This has been proven on a large scale in the United States during each of the past thirty years: combinations among coal operators to keep up the prices of "protected" coal by restricting the annual output of their collieries; combinations among carpet and other woollen manufacturers to maintain high prices of their fabrics by restricting their workmen to certain hours per day or to certain months per year; have been among the commonest of industrial events in all this interval. Within a very few years past there has come into almost universal vogue among these monopolists a new kind of combination called "*Trusts,*"—again abusing a good word by making it cover an abominable purpose,—which are probably illegal at Common Law, which only become possible under monstrously unjust tariff laws, and which work wide-spread wrong among the masses of the people.

A second effect of this monopoly (as of all monopolies) is to worsen the quality of the goods sold in an artificially restricted market. The historian Gibbon noticed this fact more than a century ago, and said: "*The spirit of monopolists is narrow, lazy and oppressive. Their work is more costly and less productive than that of independent artists; and the new improvements so eagerly grasped by the competition of freedom, are admitted by them with slow and sullen reluctance.*" Alfred Lapoint, United States consul in Peru, warned the State Department at

Washington in 1883 of this poor quality of our manufactures, which were then trying to find a South American market. He wrote: "*It is my duty to indicate that great carelessness prevails with our manufacturers; for instance, I was called upon to purchase in the United States a steam pump and boiler, which I ordered from one of the most famed manufacturers, and when it arrived, not alone was the boiler inadequate for the pump, but actually after two months' work the upper tube sheet split in three parts, a proof of its bad quality and construction.*" As men are, a natural competition among buyers and sellers is just as needful to keep up the quality of goods as to keep down their price. Good quality always costs more of effort and skill and capital than bad quality: why should producers continue to furnish good quality to a market from which a free competition in good qualities is excluded by law? Every tendency of human nature, as well as every relevant fact in history, attests, that poor wares at high rates invariably attends upon tariff-monopolies. Shoddy takes the place of wool. Cheaper crowds out better material. Skilled workmanship is displaced by unskilled. Processes of manufacture are hastened in time, and left incomplete to the damage of the goods in order to save capital. Monopoly is always and everywhere the foe of excellence.

A third effect of tariff-monopoly is to prevent the sale abroad of domestic goods to the same extent and amount as foreign wares are kept out by these monopoly-taxes. This vital and fundamental result is almost always overlooked. If a man or a nation refuse to *buy* of a proffered customer, they cannot by any possibility *sell* to him; because buying and selling are reciprocal and synchronous; because it takes two to make a bargain; because material commodities, for the most part, ultimately, exchange against each other; and because the only motive a foreigner ever has to bring his goods *hither*, is to take in exchange for them our domestic goods at a profit, and carry these *hence*. To forbid entrance to foreign goods is to forbid exit to domestic goods. Monopoly-tariff-taxes, therefore, so far forth, destroy the market for home products, without creating or tending to create, any other market for them. Such taxes, accordingly, cause a dead loss all around,—to the foreign producer who wants to buy our products with his own, to the home producer who wants to sell his own products against those, and even to the government also as a tax-collector, which can get no revenue on foreign goods excluded by monopoly-taxes.

There is a final and deeper point of view, from which all such monopolies are wholly condemnable. *They lessen of necessity,—from their own nature and inexorable operation,—*THE DIVERSITY OF RELATIVE ADVANTAGE AS BETWEEN EXCHANGERS, on which diversity, as we have now seen, the whole fact and gain of exchanges depend. Taxes on raw materials, for example, whether actually paid on them or used to enhance the price of other corresponding materials as in the tariff-taxes, increase the costs of all products into which such taxed materials enter, and so restrict the market of the home-producer by lessening his relative advantage as compared with the relative advantage of the foreigner over him. He cannot sell so well, perhaps cannot sell at all, his cost-enhanced products. Monopoly-taxes on industrial processes of any kind, on the means of transportation, have similar effects on the cost of products; and of course, similar effects in lessening Diversity, in restricting markets, and in destroying the life of Trade.

Before quitting this subject, it may be well for us briefly to classify Monopolies.

(a) Patent Rights. In the great parliamentary Statute of 21 James I, which declared the exclusive privileges to use any and to sell any merchandise to be contrary to the ancient and fundamental laws of the realm, and all grants and dispensations for such monopolies to be of none effect, two exceptions had been made; the first, in favor of Patents for fourteen years to the true and first inventors of new manufactures within the realm; and the second, in favor of the grants by Act of Parliament to any Company for the enlargement of foreign Trade, of which the East India Company chartered on the last day of the last year of the sixteenth century became the most famous and the longest-lived. Open letters or letters *patent*, as they were called, giving to inventors exclusive authority to vend for a limited time any chattel or article of commerce, of which a *model* could be made showing the point and application of what was claimed to be *new*, and Copyrights, which grant an exclusive property also for a limited time to authors and discoverers of something new and useful, of which a model cannot be made, or, as it is phrased in the Constitution of the United States, "*the exclusive right to their respective writings and discoveries*"; are a part of the results among all English-speaking peoples of the two exceptions in this famous and beneficent Act of Parliament.

In the United States a patent lasts for 17 years, and is not reissued except by a special act of Congress; a copyright lasts for 28 years, and may be renewed by the author, his widow, or children, for 14 years longer. In the constitution of the new German Empire of 1871, this protection of intellectual property (*der Schutz des geistigen Eigenthums*) is expressly included in the matters which are to be dealt with by the *Reichstag* or imperial parliament.

Now while patents and copyrights are a monopoly under the definition, they are quite distinct in their purpose and spirit from the monopolies already described. On the whole, Society does well in trying to protect, by law, inventors and thinkers in the sole use and benefit of their respective products for a brief and specified time. There are large difficulties in the way of reaching this end practically, as is proven by the endless and expensive lawsuits in such cases, but the postulate on which it is attempted is sound, namely, that otherwise citizens would have less motive to think and to invent; since in that case only the public-spirited and the rich could or would devote themselves to an important branch of the public progress. A patent or copyright is merely a return service which Society renders for a service received. It violates no man's right of property, as an ordinary monopoly does, but on the other hand is a provision to protect for a time a new right of property created by the thought and efforts of a deserving class of men. The phrase, "intellectual property," used above in translating from the German, is not well chosen, since we have amply learned that anything is property that can be bought and sold, that simple rights of many kinds are constantly on sale in the market, and consequently that patents and copyrights are at once proper and property because they are a technical return-service for other services ready to be rendered to the community.

(b) Revenue Rights. Once at a court ball, Napoleon the First noticed a lady very richly dressed and wearing splendid diamonds, and on asking for her name, ascertained that she was the wife of a tobacco manufacturer of Paris; whereupon it occurred immediately to the quick mind of the French ruler, that the State might just as well have those great profits as an individual; and the sale of tobacco in all its forms became accordingly a State monopoly in the interest of taxation, and so it has continued to this day, and yields now about 400,000,000 francs a year. Other nations have adopted to some small extent this mode of indirect taxation of their people. By legally cutting off the competition of all private dealers in the taxed article, and by preventing to the utmost of their power its being smuggled into the country, Governments are enabled to sell the article at a price enhanced artificially by the monopoly; but all that the people are made to pay *extra* under the monopoly, saving the costs of maintaining it, goes directly into the treasury of the State; and, so far forth, becomes an unobjectionable mode of taxation. Under all forms of taxation, the aim should clearly be, that the Treasury receive all that the People are made to pay, except the cost of an economical collection.

(c) Tariff Monopolies. The United States has never undertaken, like France and Germany, to vend directly and exclusively an article taxed by themselves for the sole purpose of revenue; but unfortunately they have undertaken and still maintain (1890) monopolies a thousand times more unjust and objectionable than any such revenue-monopoly can be; they have laid distinct tariff-taxes upon thousands of foreign articles, not with the design of getting revenue from them, but with an avowed and realized design of *preventing* revenue by means of these taxes, since they have made the taxes so high and onerous as to be in many cases absolutely prohibitory of the entry of the goods, and in all cases more or less prohibitory of such entry. Revenue can only be gotten on goods that come in, while the very intent and result of these taxes is to shut the foreign goods out on which they are levied, so as to give certain domestic producers (who have themselves secured this legislation) the monopoly of the home market in these goods.

This is the very core of public wrong-doing. This is the worst form of monopoly that ever existed in a civilized country. Queen Elizabeth's monopolies, which so roused the ire of the Parliament of 1601, were nothing in enormity as compared with these tariff-taxes. Civilization long ago sloughed off such direct grants of personal privilege as were forbidden forever by the Act of 1624, and accordingly there is no need of mentioning these in the present classification. Tariff-taxes for other ends than pure revenue are the worst monopolies in existence, because (1) they compel the people to pay under ostensible taxes many times more than the Treasury gets from them in actual revenue; (2) they are wholly deceptive in their terms, and their operation is clothed in disguises difficult to strip off; (3) they are always put on at the instance and under the pressure of the man (or men) who expects thereby to raise the price of his own wares at the expense of his countrymen; (4) they create under legal forms however unconstitutional privileged classes in the community; (5) their first effect is invariably to make the rich richer and the poor poorer; (6) their ultimate effect is to impoverish the privileged classes themselves by taking away from them the natural spur of competition and self-dependence, in consequence of which their own goods become poor, and their zeal flags, and they come to lean still more heavily on monopoly-supports; (7) they destroy the market for domestic goods to precisely the same extent as they cut off the market for foreign goods, and (8) their whole retinue of evils is wrapped up in the great fact, that the *Diversity of Relative Advantage* is thereby diminished both as among domestic producers of commodities and as between foreign and domestic producers.

The expression, "natural monopoly," is sometimes used of those, who, under freedom, and using to the utmost their natural gifts and acquired skill, have distanced all local competitors, and may be said to control the market in their own interest, furnishing the best goods at the cheapest rates. This is in no proper sense of the term a "monopoly." Production has no complaint to make of any such pre-eminence in excellence and opportunity. It harms nobody and benefits everybody. Exchange rejoices over every man and woman and child, who so puts his head and heart and hand into his own peculiar product as to outstrip all others in that one line in point of ease and excellence, and so be able to offer a service at once better and cheaper than any one else can offer it then and there; and when all men and women and children, so far as they are employed commercially, come to possess a "natural monopoly" each in his own specialty, then Exchanges become as profitable and progressive as possible then and there, because the ever-blessed diversity of relative advantage has its utmost limit.

4. We come now to consider the natural LIMITS, if any such there be, to the Production of material commodities. This point has been much discussed. For example, Dr. Chalmers, a Scotch clergyman of great intelligence, profoundly moved by the condition of the poor in Glasgow, published in 1822 an interesting but not over-sound treatise entitled "Political Economy," in which the proposition is maintained, that the universal market is strictly limited, and therefore that, were it not for the unproductive consumption of the rich and luxurious, and the equally unproductive consumption of national wars, there would soon be a general glut of material commodities, and consequently Production would have to cease for the lack of a vent for its products. Pretty soon we shall be able to detect the enormous fallacy in this proposition. On the other hand, in 1803, Jean-Baptiste Say, a very competent French economist, in chapter xv of his well-known treatise, fully developed this very important proposition, if true, namely, *that production may go on indefinitely in all directions without ever a fear of reaching a general glut of products.*

What is a market? What is a limited market? What is an illimitable market? A market, as we have already seen in substance, is nothing in the world but certain *persons* somewhere with return-services in their hands desirous to part with these in order to get, that is, to buy, some other services offered in exchange. Each set of services is equally a market in relation to the other set. *A market is always persons having something in their hands to sell.* Buyers and sellers are equally a market in relation to each other. Whenever anybody goes forth to buy, he must of course take with him something with which to pay for what he wants to buy, that is to say, he must become a seller the very instant he becomes a buyer; and whenever anybody wants to sell something, he must of course want something already in the hands of somebody else, in which to take his pay, that is, he becomes a buyer the moment he becomes a seller. This helps us to see perfectly what a market is. Defined in the terms of persons, *a market is two men, each glad to get the product of the other, and to render in return his own product*; defined in the terms of things, *a market for products is products in market.*

Now, what can limit the universal market for material products? Clearly, it can only be limited either in the element of *Desires* or in the element of *Return-Services.* But the desires of all men, even of one man, which the efforts of other men may satisfy, have never yet come to a stand-still. Who ever heard of even one man, who was in possession of all the products of all kinds, that he wanted? Even if there were one such man somewhere, there are millions upon millions of other men, whose desires for products such as the efforts of other men can furnish are unlimited in number and infinite in degree. It is not possible, therefore, that there should be a lack of human desires anywhere, that could put any bound to the production of commodities or hinder in the least its ever-swelling march.

If only two things can limit the universal market, and if there never has been and never can be any lack on the part of some men of Desires which the efforts of other men can satisfy through exchange, can there ever be any lack in the second element of a market, namely, in Return-services? It is not meant to be asserted, that there are not definite limitations at any one time or place, or in the whole world at any given period, in the capacities of men then and there to produce material commodities, with their knowledge of things and powers of invention; but what *is* meant to be asserted is this, that wherever Production is most busy and universal in response to the desires of some men somewhere, *there* will be the greatest plenty of return-services, with which to pay for the services of these "some men somewhere" offered in response to the desires of the first set of producers. Therefore, no general glut of products is possible to occur. The more and the more *kinds* of commodities produced anywhere, the better market *that* for the more and the more kinds of commodities produced somewhere else. The nearer Industry may seem to be about to come to the goal of a limit, the farther off from that goal it is in reality. The aggregate of human industrial powers has indeed a potential limit at any one moment, but the knowledge of things and the power of invention and the means of transportation are enlarging every moment of time; so that, that potential limit never can become an actual limitation. Human industry will go on enlarging and diversifying itself so long as the world shall stand.

Let us put this vastly important argument in other and briefer words: the Desires of men which the Efforts of other men can satisfy through exchange are unlimited in number and indefinite in degree; and therefore, mutual industrial efforts can continue to be put forth in exchange, until these unlimited and indefinite desires of all men are all met,—a goal which clearly never can be reached.

This proposition demolishes at a stroke the fallacy, that pervades Dr. Chalmers' book but just now alluded to; and, what is more to the present point, demolishes equally fallacies current and prevalent in the United States at this hour. What our national industries need and all they need, what they always needed and all they ever will need, is a quick market for their products; products in market is the only market for products; but the United States for 30 years past has been putting vast obstacles in the shape of formidable taxation in the way of the presence of products from abroad in our domestic market, and consequently and inexorably the market for domestic products has been lost in foreign countries, to the immense and irreparable damage of domestic producers as well as to the foreign producers themselves.

No general glut of exchangeable products is possible to take place in this world under natural liberty and just law, because under these the diversity of relative advantage and consequently the profitableness of commercial exchanges is all the time widening everywhere, tending to bring the whole earth into a commercial and blessed union.

On the other hand, while a general glut of products is impossible to occur under a decent freedom, a partial glut in respect to certain commodities in certain places is very common. Through want of foresight as to a prospective demand, or miscalculation as to its probable amount, particular services are sometimes offered in too great abundance or of a kind not now adapted to the chosen market, and in respect to these the market may truly be said to be glutted. This frequently happens with editions of books; more copies are printed than can be sold at paying prices. Also, when the fashion changes, which is after all less capricious than is commonly supposed, the goods that were fashionable but are so no longer, are very apt to be somewhere in excess of the demand for them. Nothing can then hinder a partial or total loss in their value in the hands of their last holders. Precautions, however, may well be taken to avoid losses of this character, through the cultivation of foresight, and by studying as accurately as possible the nature of human desires and the not altogether irregular changes that have been observed to take place in them. This constitutes the art of mercantile sagacity; and the most successful producers in all the departments of exchange are those who best develop this attainable sagacity, who adapt their particular services closest to the existing and to the coming demands; who, to excellence in the substance of their products, add taste and attractiveness to their form; and who, as the result of this, tend rather to lead the fashions of the many than to follow in their wake. It cannot be wrong to repeat here in substance, what has indeed been said already in another connection, that Production as a general rule is no dead level of monotonous exertion,—no going forth and coming back on precisely the same track,—since its sphere is Life with all its wants and Man with all his desires; since there is scope and verge enough for the development of ingenious minds in almost all of its departments; and since its ultimate goal is beyond the ken of man.

5. We must now study with considerable pains the ultimate facts and the essential functions of LANDS in connection with the Production of material commodities. This has always been the most vexed question in our Science; but it is approaching, even if it has not already reached, a satisfactory and

final solution. The present writer believes that his own studies and researches have thrown some original and important light upon the perplexing problem of the Value of lands and of their produce. His present readers are surely entitled to his clearest possible presentation of all the facts and principles of this radical question.

The French "physiocrats" of a hundred years ago, founders of the first School in Political Economy, excellent men for the most part as well as good economists in general, thought, that lands were property in a peculiar and eminent sense, that they were the ultimate source of all values but their own, and that consequently lands should bear the weight of the national taxes. English economists, constituting with their followers in other countries the second School in our Science, while not going to the length of the physiocrats, still maintained that the value of lands and of the produce of lands were distinct in important respects from all other values whatever. In our own time and country, Henry George, though belonging for the most part to the third economic School, is a great stickler for a single tax on lands in lieu of all other taxes. We must, then, concentrate all the lights we can gather on these points of dispute and difficulty.

(a) *The presumption in science is always against the existence of a few outlying cases, whenever the induction has been long and carefully conducted by many persons, and the generalization appears on all other grounds to be sound and comprehensive.* All induction proceeds upon the premise, that Nature is *uniform* in those essential resemblances that constitute a *class* of things in science. Nature has so often justified confidence in her essential resemblances even under the greatest differences in external circumstance and apparent diversity, that the presumption becomes immensely strong in her favor, whenever a generalization patiently gathered from many particulars seems to cover the whole ground concerned except a few obstinate-looking items, that have not yet been closely studied. Two to one these items also will presently fall into their predestined place. We have already seen abundant grounds for believing, that Values arise from human services rendered and received: is it at all likely, considering the nature of scientific generalization and the history of all the more advanced sciences, that in Political Economy, lands and their produce should be found to constitute an outlying exception to the law of all other valuable things?

(b) There is one vital distinction to be made at the outset and held to throughout the discussion, namely, that, between all lands as a *physical thing*, which God made and gave to all men in common without any effort of their own, and some lands now as a *valuable thing*, in all probability made such through the action of human desires and human efforts brought to bear upon what *was* merely physical but what has now *become* valuable. The failure to distinguish between *lands* as such and *valuable lands* as such, has always wrought confusion and mischief in the land problem. The two things are utterly different and incommensurable. There are vast stretches of lands on the surface of the earth, to which no *value* ever attached or ever will attach. They are lands, and that is all. Political Economy has nothing to say of them, and nothing to do with them. Because they are never bought or sold, because they never give birth to "produce," they lie wholly outside the field of Value. Then there are immense areas of lands now valuable, that were once as valueless as the first class. With these Political Economy has a great deal to do, and also with the way in which they passed from valueless to valuable. Then there is a third class of lands, that have not yet been studied as they ought and till recently have not been studied at all, namely, those known to have been valuable at one time, but which have now lost their value either wholly or in large measure. There are such lands as these in every State of our Union, and in every civilized country beneath the sun; and Political Economy has already learned something, and is destined to learn much more, about the processes by which lands pass from out the first great class into the second, and from the second into the third. Valueless, Valuable, Unvalued,—these three words describe to the economist all the lands of the world.

(c) If we may trust the simple record in Genesis, the whole earth was given of God to the whole race, under the direction that they "*replenish and subdue it.*" All the lands were then certainly valueless, although some of them were doubtless possessed of Utility, that is, a capacity to gratify human desires through a direct appropriation, which is a very different thing from Value, which last is the rendering and receiving of equivalents as between two persons. It seems very plain, that under this word, "Subdue," and under the human services implied in that, came in the first idea of ownership in land. When a family or tribe commenced the work of subjugation upon a piece of land, when they enclosed it, settled on it, tilled it, in any way whatever improved it by their own toil, then *could* first the idea of ownership dawn upon their minds, then first began that land to be capable of value, since now that family might reasonably say to another, If you want this field, you must give us an equivalent for what we have expended on it to improve it. If the transfer took place, what was it that was sold? What was it that was paid for by the party of the second part? It could not be the inherent quality of the soil, it could not be anything that the first family had gratuitously entered upon, because similar free land with all its inherent qualities lay open to occupation on every hand, and the second family would surely say, For as much effort as you have put upon your land to better it, we can make other free land as good as yours, consequently we can give you no more at the most than a fair equivalent for your efforts already expended. If the parcel were sold, therefore, the *value* of it must have been determined, not by the *gratuitous* elements involved but the *onerous* elements involved.

The physical thing, land, which cost nothing, has now become the valuable thing, land, through a series of human efforts expended of such kind as call out human desires for the results reached, and justify the rendering of return-services for them; and that which the buyer pays for is never the free *old* but always the onerous *new*; new utilities, that cost something, have been added to and intermixed with old utilities, that cost nothing; and solely in consequence of this expenditure of efforts on the part of some men, answering to the desires and calling out the efforts of other men, do parcels of land pass out from the first great class into the second great class. So far as it can be gathered from the nature of the case, and from the known steps of past experience, this is the simple and rational process by which valueless lands become valuable, and *less* valuable become *more* valuable lands.

(d) This line of proof, strong in itself, is strengthened by observing how land-parcels gradually and practically pass out from the second into the third class of lands,—from the Valuable into the Unvalued. As it is only human Efforts wisely bestowed upon valueless lands or in some connection with them, that ever make these valuable, so it is, that these Efforts intermitted for a time, or less wisely bestowed, or reckoned less in harmony with the present and prospective desires of other men, invariably cause a loss of value in valuable lands; and, if such neglect or unwisdom of effort continue long enough, nothing is more certain, than that lands so treated will lose their value altogether, nobody will give anything for them, they will drop out from the second class into the third by the same path (only in inverse order), by which they crept at first from valueless to valuable. Under the writer's own observation in different parts of New England, whole tiers of farms once valuable and productive have lost that character either wholly or for the most part, taxes can no longer be collected from them, nobody will really give anything for them in exchange, they are abandoned of their former owners, they are left to lie waste or to grow up into forest again. It follows from all this beyond a doubt, and the logical issue is one of vast consequence to mankind, that Value is no attribute of matter, no inherent quality of lands as such wherever situated, but it comes and goes, it is a relation of mutual purchase between human services rendered and received.

(e) Land-parcels becoming valuable in the way but just now indicated, and so long as they continue valuable, that is, salable, are technically *Commodities*, according to our triple division of all Valuables. They belong in this grand division, that we are specially studying in this chapter, for the same reason as a horse does or a steam-engine does. Men did not originally make the land as a congeries of matter, neither do men make horses, nor do they make the iron ore out of which most parts of the steam-engine is made; but men do modify bits of the land as God made it, they subdue it, they improve it in manifold ways, they make it *desirable* in the eyes of other men, and thus or otherwise they come into possession of it, gain for themselves a right to sell it, prepare it to be sold and sell it, on the same principle as men raise and break and train horses and prepare them to be sold and sell them, and just as men by many processes transform the iron ore into a steam-engine and sell that. Ricardo, in his famous doctrine of Rent, says a good deal about "the original and indestructible powers of the soil"; but as a matter of fact, *there are no such powers,* since the elements and properties that constitute land are all the time changing under chemical and other action; and even if there were such powers, it would still be impossible to separate what God did for the land from what men have done in order to fit it to be sold; and what men have ever been authorized to take pay from other men for what God did in the creation of the world? The simple truth is, that Value is never of God's creation but only of men's exertion. There never was any land anywhere fit for cultivation and sale without more or less expenditure of human labor and reserved capital upon it; and the "powers" of the land, whatever they are, instead of being "indestructible," are in a constant process of wearing out, and require a constant application of labor and capital to keep up their fertility. Valuable pieces of land, accordingly, like all other commodities, derive their *utility* partly from the free contribution of Nature, and partly from the onerous contribution of men; but, on the other hand, they derive their *value*, whether the value be then increasing or diminishing, wholly from human desires and corresponding efforts.

(f) It is but a step from this impregnable position to another, namely, that Henry George is wholly wrong in his view, that there is Value in lands as God made them and gave them to men in common; and consequently, wholly wrong in his doctrine, that a single tax on land values would be just and equal to land owners, and might well be made to take the place of all other taxes on all other persons. He says: "*If we are all here by the equal permission of the Creator, we are all here with an equal title to the enjoyments of his bounty.*" What bounty? If he means the original utility which God put into all lands in common, and which certain men have done nothing to better, there is nobody to dispute his proposition. But he does not mean that, because there is nothing of any significance that could come out of that. What he means is, that it is God and not man who makes lands valuable. He makes no distinction between Utility and Value in lands. He lumps the two together in one, and calls the aggregate the Creator's "bounty." He goes on to say: "*There is on earth no power which can rightfully make a grant of exclusive ownership in land.*" Well! Is there any power on earth which can rightfully deny to any man or family the proprietorship of his own exclusive *efforts*, nobody's else rights being infringed thereby? Or can deny to him or them the *results* of such efforts, however embodied? When valueless lands are made valuable by human efforts expended to that end, does not the "value" belong to those who made it? When valuable lands have been made more valuable than they were by the efforts and foresight of their owners, the rights of others untouched, does not the "increment" belong to those who have created it? The truth is, if Henry George's powers of radical analysis had been at all equal to his remarkable power of rhetorical presentation, the world would never have been treated to his popular and imposing land-fallacies. Prudhon's "Property is theft," and George's "Single tax on land," rest on the same basis of socialism.

(g) All valuable land-parcels are material Commodities, made to be such by onerous human efforts of some sort expended upon or in some connection with the free Utilities furnished by Nature; the utilities are one thing in origin and function, and the values are a very different thing both in origin and function; and the present point is, that nearly all valuable lands everywhere are Capital also, that is to say, products reserved to aid in a further and future production. Capital is a relatively small class under the immensely large class Values. Capital is by no means coincident with Commodities, since vast lines of the latter are consumed with no reference to a further production by means of their use. But capital is always either commodities or claims, and valuable bits of land are always commodities and nearly always capital; because all tillage and pasture lands, all forests grown for wood and timber, and lands of all sorts rented or held for resale at a higher price, are capital under the definition, are "*products reserved as an aid to further production.*" The peculiarity of all farming lands is this, they are themselves commodities, in whose creation God's free gifts and men's onerous labors have conspired; and they are held in reserve by their owners as capital, for the sake of producing by their means with the help of more of God's free gifts further valuable commodities, such as grain, and fruit and timber. Farms in their highest reach of previous culture still need for crops the sun and the rain. Indeed the sun is the most useful and powerful force in the world. Oh! how it warms and lifts and quickens! Give it and the rain and the dew but a fair chance on lands properly prepared for them, and endless fields blossom like the rose and are white to the harvest!

Agriculture always has been and always will be the vocation of the masses of mankind. Under a fair freedom, and a decent law, and a reasonable industry, Agriculture is always profitable; because it is natural, that is, designed by God for the welfare of mankind; because it lies at the basis of all other industries,—most of the food of mankind, most of the raw material of all manufactures, most of the subject-matter of all national and international commerce,—come out of the farms of the world; because it has been ordered so in the nature of things, that, under a tolerable freedom, a given amount of agricultural products tends constantly to buy, that is, to pay for, more and more of almost all kinds of manufactured products, for a reason to be explained shortly, thus tending strongly to uplift the farming masses in a scale of comforts; and because there is no other main line of human activities so constantly and so prodigiously and so gratuitously assisted by Natural Agents as is Agriculture. As Milton has profoundly expressed it in the "Hymn to the Nativity," the Sun is indeed to Mother Earth *"her lusty paramour."* But at this very time of writing a wail is coming up in ever deepening tones from Italy and France and Germany and Russia and especially the United States, that a colossal blunder in legislation common to all these countries now, say rather a colossal crime of the powerful few against the humble many, in the shape of tariff-monopolies, neutralizes in large part these natural advantages of agriculture, makes farming unprofitable and farmers unable to pay their taxes, diverts young men in increasing numbers from the farms to the towns, plasters the lands over with mortgages, shuts out from their natural markets the products of the land, thus depressing their price, and shuts off from farmers by outrageous taxes their natural supplies, thus augmenting their price. Farmers in all these countries are revolving between the upper and the nether millstones. Count Giusso, ex-Mayor of Naples, and now a deputy from that city, has just made a speech in the Italian Parliament, which sets forth in strong terms the great depression in Agriculture, and the critical condition of the public finances, brought about by the new policy of protectionism there. He says: *"The Utopian idea of creating an industrial Italy on the ruins of an agricultural Italy, has been a colossal error big with disastrous results. We have preferred the shop to the land; we have preferred the coal we do not possess to our Italian sun; we have preferred the motive force of steam to the most powerful motive force in the universe, the sun; and we are naturally suffering the sad consequences."* Exports increased in Italy in 1888 by $24,000,000, and imports by $42,000,000; and the Count quotes the cry coming up from one end of the Peninsula to the other: *"Give us the means of selling our products, and we will pay the taxes."* England is the only considerable country in the world, whose customs-revenue increased in the fiscal year 1888-89 over the year before; this English increase was over 5 *per centum*, which means an increase both in imports and exports, whose movements are almost absolutely free so far as England is concerned; while in all the countries mentioned above, which are under a different system in that respect, there was a *deficit* of revenue from tariff-taxes as compared with the year before, and a *decrease* in both exports and imports.

(h) If nearly all bits of valuable lands be capital, as we have just seen strong grounds for believing, then it follows of course, *that the Rent of leased lands whether for buildings or harvests is the same in nature with the Interest on money loaned, and is the measure of the service rendered by the owners to the actual users of the Capital.*

This proposition, seen in its radical proofs and in its logical corollaries, takes the very life out of Henry George's land-theories, and out of the popular remedies thereto annexed. The writer firmly believes also, that this proposition in the grounds of it and in the inferences from it might have been used by Mr. Gladstone and his followers with telling effect in the animated discussions of the Irish land-question in the British Parliament during the decade 1880-90. In the debates on the Irish Land Bill passed in 1881, the representatives of the land-owners in Ireland held to their right to take all the rent they could extort by the help of the law; on the other hand the representatives of the Irish rent-payers held to their right as cultivators and maintainers to withhold rent in large part or altogether; and Mr. Gladstone, as representative of the nation, while insisting on the right of the owners to certain rents, insisted equally on the right of the cultivators to certain important privileges in the soil. Our present proposition with those that spring out of it, though it was not used by Gladstone, as it might well have been to smooth his pathway through the roughness of that legislation, yet justifies at one and the same time the discontent of the Irish rent-payer, the claim of the Irish land-holder to an assured rent of some sort, and the fundamental principle of the Irish Land Bill of 1881. That bill gives a certain modified ownership and control to the actual cultivators and maintainers of the soil. That is right.

The principle of land-values herewith enunciated, their uprise and increase and frequent decay also in all land-parcels, justifies completely the concessions to tenants in that bill; while the old and still commonly accepted English principles of land, and the false yet famous doctrine of Rent promulgated by Ricardo at the beginning of the century, are wholly against Gladstone and his concessions in that bill. Let us now see whither simple analysis and logical processes will quickly bring us in this whole matter. Valuable land was once valueless, and always remained so, until, by virtue of human efforts expended upon it or in some direct connection with it, coupled with the desires of certain other men for that land or its produce, accompanied with a readiness on the part of these men to render some equivalent for it or its use, first imparted value to that particular patch; moreover, it has been found in practice ten thousand times, just as one would expect, knowing the origin of value in general, that, unless human efforts are further and constantly expended on or in connection with that piece, and unless desires of other men continue to turn towards it in the way of exchange, its value will silently and inevitably escape from it; therefore, whoever has come into possession of that valuable piece of land by purchase or inheritance, and foregoes the use of it in favor of another as a tenant, is morally and commercially entitled to the stipulated return for that use, *which is rent*; but also, if that other, aside from the current use which is always a wearing-out process, contributes in any way to the continuance and increase of the value and fertility of the land, then and so far he gains rights in the land and becomes a sort of joint owner of it, since what he has done in the way of maintenance and improvement is inextricably mingled with what the other owners or users have done, and is of the same nature with that; and, therefore, the modified ownership of certain tenants recognized in Gladstone's bill is in strict accordance with ultimate justice, as it is also in strict accord with right, that the legal owner should continue to receive a return in the shape of rent for all the fertility and opportunity actually contributed by him, and no more. The discontent of the Irish peasantry has largely come from an instinct or intelligence more unerring than the economics of the land-owners, namely, that they are called on to pay rent for what they themselves have *contributed* in addition to the rent for what they have *received*. The true origin of value in land, and the only way in which value in land is kept up, seems to have penetrated deeper into the minds of Irish tenants than into the minds of many British statesmen.

(i) If the bulk of all valuable land-parcels be capital, as it is, then one might expect beforehand to find *a law of diminishing returns* from such lands, agricultural labor and skill remaining the same; because, all capital is tools made such by the expenditure of human efforts on changeable material, and then by the practice of *abstinence*, and tools from their very nature are always wearing out. Increase of efforts in connection with any form of capital unimproved by new inventions and uninvigorated by fresh skill, though they may indeed increase the aggregate return, cannot, for the reason just given, *secure an increase proportioned to the increase of the efforts*. The English writers generally, and Mr. Ricardo in particular, justly lay much stress on this proposition, although they have not taken lands to be capital, and have proven the law of diminishing returns in a different way from ours, and consequently have not set the propositions of land in their best and most ultimate relations. Their method of proving the law, however, is short and conclusive: If by doubling the efforts upon a piece of land, double the produce could be secured, and by quadrupling it, quadruple, and so on, there would be no reason why any man should ever cultivate more than a square acre, or even a square rod. He has a strong motive to confine his culture to a small space, just so long as the amount of produce is in the ratio of the efforts expended, because there is less locomotion of tools and fertilizers and crops. The fact that he extends his culture from one acre to another, and then to distant acres, notwithstanding the inconvenience and expense of transportation, is an irrefragable proof of the proposition in question. Increase of agricultural efforts and expenditures on a given space of land will secure a larger amount of produce, but as a general law, *the increased amount will not be proportioned to the increased expenditure.*

It is through this law of diminishing returns, that the Creator has secured the gradual occupation, by men, of almost the whole earth. There is a strong and natural tendency to leave the old acres to advance upon new, the old countries to emigrate to new, whenever the returns begin to bear a more unfavorable ratio to the labors bestowed. The farmer will advance from the first to the second acre as soon as he thinks that more produce can be obtained from it by a given amount of efforts than can be gotten by a like expenditure of additional efforts upon the first acre, allowance being made for the increased inconvenience; and so, cultivation has gradually extended itself and men have become dispersed over the whole earth. Other principles leading to dispersion have undoubtedly co-operated, but this is the fundamental one, operative at all times, changing the course of population, and consequently of empire.

(j) It follows from the points already made, *that all permanent improvements in agriculture retard the operation of the law of diminishing returns.* The recent introduction of the silo, for example, upon the long-used and wearing-out farms of New England promises, if the public law would quit throwing in obstacles, to help restore the fertility of many of them. The discovery of new and more available fertilizers, the invention of better agricultural implements, the light thrown by chemistry upon agriculture, the consequent adoption of better methods of culture and rotation of crops, the more perfect adaptation to the various soils of the kinds of produce sought to be raised from them,—all these and similar improvements tend to increase the ratio of produce to the labor, and to disguise the law just established. The lands that are now under cultivation may be made, under more skilful modes of culture to yield indefinitely more than at present, and the vast still uncultivated lands of the world may come to render an incalculable quantity of food to the world's population; but yet, as improvements are naturally less continuous in this than in most other departments of production, as invention has much less play, as there is less opportunity for the division and co-operation of laborers, *as nothing can materially shorten the time during which the fruits of the earth must ripen,* it is certain that possible improvements will never override the law of diminishing returns; and, consequently, *that the value of agricultural produce tends constantly to rise relatively to manufactured products generally.*

(k) The last point to be made under the general topic we are now discussing, is, *that the best tenure of lands in the interest of the production of material commodities is the fee simple in the hands of the actual cultivators.* This is the old Teutonic holding; but special circumstances in the British Islands have gradually changed these small holdings once cultivated by the hands of their free owners into large estates, the parts of which are leased out at will or for a term of years to tenants or "farmers" as they are there called, who, in turn, being small capitalists, as the land-owners are large capitalists, furnish the stock and hire the laborers and thus become the actual cultivators, and even often sublet parts of their own leased holdings to tenants of the next degree below, who can furnish less stock and can hire fewer laborers. The word "farmer" as used in the United States has a quite different meaning from that it bears in Great Britain; it means here a man cultivating his own fields with his own funds in his own way, and it means there a man cultivating another's fields with his own funds in a way and on terms made a matter of contract between the two; and these two modes of culture are so distinct that they are not likely to lie alongside of each other to any great extent for a very long time in the same country. Since her great Revolution, and under the action of the law requiring the equal partition of every man's landed estate among all his children, France has had for the most part the small holding tilled by the owner's own hands, instead of the great estates of the old *régime*, the average being about 14 acres to each owner, and nearly one fourth of the entire population being proprietors of land either in town or country; in the United States the plough is guided almost wholly by the man who owns the soil he tills; while in Great Britain the original peasant proprietor has almost entirely disappeared. Each system has its advocates and arguments.

The question at bottom is, whether capital in the form of tillable land is more *effective* when held in large masses and loaned out to men, who possess small capitals in another form than land, and are willing to apply these for a return upon that land, or when held in small masses and used as capital by the owners themselves, who also own some capital in another form than land and are willing to apply this to their own profit upon their land. We hold, that the latter method is better than the former, both for the maintenance and improvement of the land itself as capital and also for the current production of commodities from it, because, (1) when one owns the farm he works, from the very nature of permanent ownership he takes a greater interest in it, perhaps he has inherited it from his fathers, perhaps he has bought it and paid for it at the hardest, at any rate it is his own, and as all men work from *motives* and the energy of the work is proportioned to the constant press of the motives, then must the owner of the capital, whose abstinence *makes* it capital, be under the strongest possible motive at once to improve his capital and also to make the current produce from it as great as possible, since the capital itself and all it yields is his own; moreover, (2) ownership improves the moral *character* of the cultivators, it tends to make them industrious, thrifty, frugal, independent, hopeful of the future, anxious to give their children better privileges than they themselves had, and it would seem as if the masses of men are educated by nothing so much, at least by nothing more, as and than by the *ownership* of land, wherever such tenure is possible and easy to the masses; and (3) the outward testimony is abundant from many lands, that the peasant proprietor *is* a happier and more virtuous man, a more productive and progressive one, than the mere tenant and farm-laborer, while there is much perhaps less conclusive testimony that leased lands are inferior in point of improvements and productiveness to the same lands when cultivated by their owners and to contiguous or at least similar lands still so cultivated.

It is a cognate point yet worthy of separate mention, that a general division of lands into farms only moderately large and approximately equal is most favorable to the largest aggregate production. Such a division takes place of itself wherever the lands are held in fee simple, and the cost of land-transfers is slight, and there are no such obstacles as slavery or primogeniture, as has happened practically in New England and in the Middle and Western States, and as is now happening of its own accord more or less at the South. The Greek writer, Aristotle, quoted some centuries before Christ from "the African," probably some Carthaginian writer on agriculture, the now familiar saying, "*the best manure for the land is the foot of the owner.*" This homely word long attributed to Dr. Franklin, who stole it for his "Poor Richard's Almanack" more than a century ago, is based on the sound principle, that personal supervision to be most effective must be limited in its sphere, and that the best agricultural skill becomes weak when it attempts to exhibit itself on too broad a surface. Because a man can cultivate 100 acres better than any of his neighbors, it does not prove that he will cultivate 50 acres additional to them better than a neighbor of inferior skill, who is the owner of these 50 and no more. When the freeholds are small and nearly equal a wide competition among the farmers comes naturally into play, success is seen to depend upon personal efforts of intelligence and will, and interest and hope become the motives to the most productive cultivation. There is a high pleasure in possession and in self-guided exertion, and an impulse is broadly felt over the whole region to get as much as possible out of the land and at the same time to keep good and ever improve its condition. To protect and advance his own interests, to attend upon the seasons, to watch and wait, to foresee and plan and labor,—all this develops the farmer, and gives him energy and independence; and wherever there is a broad basis of such independent yeomanry to lean back upon, when heavy taxes are to be raised and strong blows of battle are to be struck, the national safety and position are assured.

6. We come now in the last place to consider the *Costs of Production* of material commodities of all sorts. Valuable patches of land, all prepared for Production in its several kinds, are the most important Commodities in the world, and the largest also in volume of Value. What did it cost "*to subdue*" the present tillable lands of this country? How much did it cost to get ready

for grazing the broad pastures? To make accessible the forests that yield the timber? To open up the mines also and bring them into "touch" with the population? These questions are of great consequence, not that the actual past cost of any class of these more permanent "commodities" in the commercial world will be any safe guide to their present value, since cheaper and cheaper means of subduing the rugged forms of Nature are all the while coming into play, and all things that did cost more once tend pitilessly to fall to what similar things cost now; and since also it is never "efforts" alone that determine the value of anything, but efforts in conjunction with the "desires" of other men. Still, the *amount* of efforts expended at any given time upon these more stable commodities to make them productive, that is, their cost of production, is always gauged in general by an *estimate* of what the "desires" for them will be when completed; and this makes their cost of production a sort of loose measure of their value at the time. The main reason, however, why the cost of production of these primal commodities, namely, valuable land-patches, whatever may be expected to be produced from them afterwards, is so important, is, that as a general rule, the less the cost of any commodity meeting a universal want *the wider and surer is its market.* The larger the circle of the buyers of anything the more certain its sale; because, the world over, the men of small incomes are manifold larger in number than the men of large incomes. Society is like a pyramid: the lowest course of masonry is the longest and widest,—has the most stones or bricks in it,—and ever fewer towards the top.

If we reckon valuable lands as the *primary* commodities, then the *secondary* commodities will be of two classes, namely, (1) the *produce* of these valuable lands, whether animal or vegetable or mineral, such as cattle and cereals and coal; and (2) vendible material products obtained by human efforts from non-valuable land and sea, such as furs and fish. This division of material commodities into primary and secondary, and the distinction among secondary commodities according as their source is costly and costless, has never before been drawn in Political Economy; and it is fully believed, that the thoughtful reader and student will pretty soon perceive its advantages in helping clear up one of the most confused and perplexing sections of our Science, namely, that which relates to the causes and measures of *Rent.* We are now to inquire into the elements of the *cost of production* of each of these three classes of commodities; and we may find ourselves surprised at the simplicity and certainty of these elements.

1. We will now look into the Cost of Production of valuable land-patches themselves, the first and most important class of commodities. Here, as everywhere else in Valuables, we discover certain free gifts of Nature, without whose presence indeed the value could never come into being, but which are not *constituents* of the value, because they are gratuitous, given of God, and because the natural competition among buyers and sellers inevitably flings out from all effect on value of the otherwise possible action of these free and bountiful gifts, as have been already fully illustrated in chapter first. No piece of land ever yet had one particle of Value until human efforts of some sort had been expended on it or in some connection with it, for two excellent reasons, first, no man would ever even *think* of saying to another in reference to such a piece of land "Give me something for it and I will pass it over to you," and second, even if he did think of such an absurdity the other would reply "Why should I give you anything for something to which you have not the least claim, especially as I can take for nothing just such pieces all around here?" It must be remembered, not only that God gave the whole earth to all mankind without distinction, but also that his bountiful hand scattered all peculiar kinds of patches in great number upon each of the Continents. There is a plenty of Utility (gratuitous) in land-parcels just as God made them, but no possibility of Value (onerous) till other hands than His have touched and benefited them.

What, then, are the onerous elements that enter into the value of land-parcels and constitute their Cost of Production? There are only two such elements, namely, *Cost of Labor and Cost of Capital.* To find out exactly what "Labor" is, and what there is in it entitling and assuring its reward in "Wages," will be the task and perhaps also the pleasure of the next chapter; but it will suffice for the present discussion to say, that Labor is human exertion put forth for the sake of a commercial return. Lands can by no possibility be brought out of a state of nature into a state of value without the expenditure of Labor; and the actual or estimated cost of this labor, accordingly, is the first constituent of the Cost of Production of valuable lands considered as Commodities. Labor, however, can not apply itself to free lands in order to make them valuable without the co-operation of another onerous element, namely, Capital, in some of its many forms. For example, if forest lands are to be made tillable, the trees must first be cut down, and this will require besides the muscular exertion of the laborer something in the way of an axe, which is capital, the result of previous labor reserved to assist in further production: if native prairie is to be subdued to a valuable commodity, something of the nature of a plough must be employed in the process, and horses or a steam engine to propel it, and a plough and horses are capital, and still require fresh labor to make them useful in production. But capital always costs something; and, therefore, the cost of the Capital enters in as a second constituent into the cost of production of Land-Commodities. But these two costs are all. We shall search in vain for any other onerous element in the cost of producing commodities. There are two variables only in the Cost of Production, which itself is the sum of the two subordinate costs.

(a) And now let us analyze first the Cost of Labor in this connection, and then second the Cost of Capital, and we shall soon reach radical and unchangeable ground, and find in the sum of these two an aggregate Cost of Production, and also all of the variables that can ever enter into such Cost. It is plain to reason, that only by Labor non-valuable land-pieces ever did or ever can become valuable. Captain John Smith understood this in 1607 at Jamestown as well as anybody understands it now: there were 48 gentlemen, and only 12 tillers of the soil, among the 105 colonists, who originally landed there: "*nothing is to be expected hence,*" he wrote of the new country, *but by* "*labor.*" new supplies of laborers, aided by a wise allotment of land-parcels to each colonist, secured after five years of struggle the lasting fortunes of Virginia: "*men fell to building houses and planting corn*": the very streets of Jamestown were sown with tobacco; and in fifteen years the colony numbered 5000 souls.

Now the cost of Labor is analyzable into three variables only, namely, (1) the *efficiency* of the labor; (2) the *rate* of nominal wages paid; (3) the cost to the employer of *that valuable,* in which the wages are paid. Let us see: what an employer wants *is to get things done*; consequently, if an employer hire two men to work for him at the same rate of wages, and if one be twice as efficient a laborer as the other, the *cost* of the labor of the first is only one half the cost of the labor of the second: therefore, a *high rate of wages* does not mean *a high cost of labor* whenever and wherever the laborers are very efficient. As a rule, it is found, that the cost of labor in reference to a given product is *the least* in those countries, like the United States and Great Britain, in which the rates of nominal wages are *the highest*; because, it is found also, that a high *efficiency* of laborers accompanies both as a cause and as an effect high rates of wages.

Secondly, there are striking differences in the rates of nominal wages paid for a day's work in the same general employment in different parts of the same country, and especially in different countries. The agricultural laborer in the west of England, say in Wiltshire, gets about 10*s.* per week, while in the north of England, say Nottinghamshire, laborers at the same general work get about 16*s.* per week. Walker in his Wages-Question gathers from the best authorities many such statements as these: "On the Grand Trunk Railway in Canada the French-Canadian laborers received 3*s.* 6*d.* a day, while the Englishmen received from 5*s.* to 6*s.* a day, but it was found that the English did the greatest amount of work for the money." "In the quarry at Bonnieres, in which Frenchmen, Irishmen, and Englishmen were employed side by side, the Frenchmen received 3, the Irishmen 4, and the Englishmen 6, francs a day; and at those different rates the Englishman was found to be the most advantageous workman of the three." "The statistics of the iron industry in France show, that on the average 42 men are employed to do the same work in smelting pig iron as is done by 25 men on the Tees." "In India, although the cost of daily labor ranges from 4½d. to 6d. a day, mile for mile, the cost of railway work is about the same as in England." Thus it is plain, that a *high rate of wages* does not import a *high cost of labor*, but rather the reverse. A vast mass of current fallacies are disposed of in a moment by this truth seen in its grounds. The United States have shown in the past the highest rates of nominal wages in the world, and at the same time have shown the lowest costs of labor to the employers, because as a rule the laborers here have been more efficient than elsewhere. England has the highest rates of wages and the lowest costs of labor in Europe for the same reason. The degree of *efficiency* shown by different laborers is the second variable in a cost of labor.

Thirdly, if that valuable, whether money or other, in which wages are paid, varies in cost to the employer, then the cost of the labor paid for by that valuable, efficiency of the laborers, and nominal rate of pay remaining the same, will of course be varied thereby. We shall learn hereafter in the chapter under that title, that the value of "Money" is by no means invariable even in one country, just as we have already learned the variable nature of all other values; and, too, wages are not always paid in money, though they are commonly reckoned in the terms of money; and accordingly, the third and last variable in a cost of labor is the cost to the employer of that valuable, whatever it be, in which the wages are paid. Assuming, as we may, that given wages are paid in money, then any country that has for any reason a more abundant money than another may clearly pay higher rates of nominal wages than that other without making its costs of labor any higher than in that. The United States, for example, has usually had a very abundant money (not always of the best kind), which of course has tended to make higher the current prices of all commodities, and this has enabled capitalist-employers to pay higher nominal rates of wages, without at all enhancing relatively the costs of labor, and also without really benefiting the laborers.

(b) We will now analyze second the Cost of Capital in this connection, as the only other element of cost in the Cost of Production of Commodities in general, and particularly now in the cost of making worthless land-pieces valuable so as to be used in further production. Here too we find three variables, no one of which can be safely neglected any more than the other three in the reckoning that has for its object a prospective cost of production. These are, first, *the current rate per centum*; second, *the time for which the capital is advanced*; and third, *the liability of that form of capital to slow or rapid wearing out*. For instance, under the first variable, the rate per centum of capital, if the rate at Amsterdam be 3 and that at New York be 7, if the cost of labor be equal in the two cities, if the time of advance be one year, and if there be no liability of the capital to wear out; then any commodity made at Amsterdam with an outlay of $100 may be sold at a profit for $103, while a similar commodity made at New York with the same outlay cannot be sold for less than $107. All other things being equal, a *low rate per centum* of capital in any country gives that country an advantage in the markets of the world for selling its commodities over other countries offering similar commodities where the rate is higher, because its cost of their production is less. Of course also such a country can subjugate its wild lands and make them valuable at less cost than the other countries.

To illustrate the operation of the second variable, the time for which the capital is advanced, let the same suppositions be continued, except that the *time of advance* at New York be extended to four years. Then the commodity may be sold at and from Amsterdam, as before, at $103, but the corresponding commodity at and from New York for not less than $131, so far as mere cost of production determines the prices. This point is also well shown up in the case of wine, which, to reach its perfection, requires to be kept a number of years, for, if it be genuine and ripe, its cost of production has been by so much enhanced by its delay in reaching the market. If the time of advance be long, and the rate *per centum* high at the same time, the cost of capital from the two causes combined multiplies the cost of the product; and consequently, only countries in which the *rates* are low can successfully engage in enterprises requiring a large capital to be invested for *long periods* before returns are realized. One million of Dutch capital at 3% a year, expecting to realize returns only after 20 years, may be remunerated by products selling for $1,806,111; but American capital under like circumstances, except that the rate here is 7%, must have a return of $3,869,685, or lose by the operation.

To illustrate the action of the third and last variable, we must observe, that all forms of capital wear out, but some forms much faster than others, and that this makes a difference in the sinking-funds that must be reserved out of the gross profits of the capital in order to replace the principal whole. This difference will at once affect the cost of capital, and so of production, and so indirectly the ultimate value of the product. Suppose there are two commodities, which we will call A and B, produced in two different establishments, in each of which is invested a capital of $11,000, in one of which is used a machine that costs $1000 and is wholly worn out by one year's use, and in the other a machine costing the same sum, which will last, however, for ten years. Suppose further, that the rate *per centum* of profit be 10, and the time consumed in completing each of the two products be one year. Now there is a marked difference in the Cost of Capital in the two establishments, and this difference will indirectly but immediately appear in the Value of the respective products. For, to A must be charged not only $1100, the interest on the whole capital at the current rate, but also another $1000, wherewith to replace the machine already worn out by a single year's use. A, accordingly, cannot be sold without loss for less than $2100. B, however, will cost less and can be sold for less at the usual profit. Because, to it must be charged, as before, $1100, current rate of profit on the capital invested, and only $100 (really less than that for an obvious reason) to replace the durable machine after ten years' use. The capitalist, therefore, can sell B for $1200, and make something over the current rate of profit.

Since the cost of capital invariably resolves itself into these three variables, every capitalist in order to become successful as such must give strict attention to all three of these points. To any one who projects the making of valueless into valuable land, or valuable into more valuable land, by the expenditure of capital upon them for that purpose, it becomes a matter of prime importance for him to inquire how long a time the whole process will take, how much he must allow *per annum* for the cost of all the implements employed, and especially how complete in action and duration are these costly implements. The *durability of machinery*, whatever the name it bear and whatsoever the work it do, is at once the most significant and the most neglected point in the actual and prospective Production of our time and country; and no condemnation can be too severe upon a policy of public law, such as now prevails, whose whole tendency and actual effect is to worsen the quality and lessen the durability of all commercial implements whatsoever, from the needle to the locomotive. The same abominable public policy increases the cost and decreases the durability of all agricultural implements, like the axe and the plough, designed and adapted to transform valueless and non-productive into valuable and food-producing lands.

2. Now, having fully seen the elements of the cost of reducing land itself from a natural into a valuable and productive form, what next are the elements of the cost of production of those material commodities produced for sale *by the aid* of these subdued and now productive lands? Commodities so produced constitute the second class in the law of their Cost of Production. And a vastly important class it is. The food of the world, so far as that food is purchased as the product, whether animal or vegetable, of valuable lands; the fuel of the world, so far as that fuel is bought from owned and accessible forests and mines; the clothing of the world, so far as the fabrics come from the cultivated cotton and flax and wool and skins offered for sale; the shelter of the world, so far as the wood and brick and stones and lime are drawn from valuable lands and quarries; and the warehouses and the temples and the theatres of the world, built, as

they are, out of the products of costly and rentful lands: these all, and many more like these, constitute a class of commodities immense in their volume, whose cost of production has in it an element peculiar and additional to that of the first class already analyzed, and to that of the third class also soon to be considered.

This peculiar and additional element in the cost of production of these things, class second of commodities, is called RENT. Interminable have been and still are, especially in the British Islands, the definitions and discussions upon Rent: they have boxed the compass of economical nomenclature: they have run up and down the entire gamut of possible expression on such a theme. David Ricardo, the Anglo-Jewish Banker, formerly announced, near the beginning of this century, that "*Rent is that portion of the produce of the earth, which is paid to the landlord for the use of the original and indestructible powers of the soil.*" Two objections lie with fatal weight against this definition and all that is involved in it: first, there *are* no "indestructible powers of the soil," either "original" or acquired, since the universal verdict of all agriculture has been and still is, that the "powers" of all soils are continually wearing out, and need to be constantly renovated by fertilizers and manipulations of all sorts; and second, even if there were such "original and indestructible powers," it would be impossible to separate them from the additional "powers" acquired by means of the capital expended to bring that land from the state of nature to its present state, and the landlord has had nothing to do with any "powers" of the land except those conferred by his own labor and capital upon it, and can by no possibility put himself into a position where he can *enforce* any claim of his own for a return from any "original powers" of any land-parcel whatever. The simple truth is, and it illumines the whole subject of agriculture and its products, that the value of land-parcels and also the value of the transient use of them, or *Rent*, hang wholly on the onerous human efforts involved in them, and not at all on original and gratuitous utilities. Science has only to unfold the plan of God and its actual and beneficent workings. "*In the sweat of thy face shalt thou eat bread.*" All that God furnishes to men in order to get a living and in order even to get rich is Opportunity. The opportunity is ample. The call to a partnership in Effort as between God and men is loud and constant. The world with all its powers, free lands with all their utilities, the change of seasons, the blessed sun and the blessed dew and rain, the constant disintegration of rocks beneath the soil and the gradual clothing with lichens and moss and verdure of the rocks above in preparation for a new soil, and the wonderful chemistry of the vast laboratory of Nature, all work night and day without fee or reward in the service of mankind. But men themselves must not intermit their labor. All values are of *their* creation and maintenance. If they cease or relax their labor upon land-pieces so only made valuable and rentful, then will the value and the rent begin to slip away inexorably, and no prayers and no regrets will avail to call them back.

Now, then, since commodities of the second class in the cost of their production must respond not only to the *current* cost of Labor and Capital in bringing them to market, but also something additional in the way of Rent to the *past* cost of the implement, the land-parcel, without whose contributing agency present results could not be gained; *Rent is the Rendering for the present use of a Valuable made such by past Labor and Capital.* Land-parcels leased for agriculture; mines and the access to them leased for the production of metals and minerals; and forests whose growth has been permitted by the past *abstinence* of their owners; all properly yield a rent; because these forms of capital, whose existence is due to past labor and capital, are present contributors to products, whose sale must compensate not only present labor and the use of current capital, but also the use of these more permanent forms of capital long ago created.

A competent authority estimated in 1881, that the land-parcels of the United Kingdom of Great Britain were worth £3,000,000,000; and there were at the same time 6,000,000 of inhabited houses, excluding factories and business premises and tenements renting for £20 and under. Most of these lands and houses are rented by their owners to the actual occupiers on the just principle explained above, inasmuch as the lease-system is the prevailing one in that country. According to the Census of 1880, there were 4,008,907 so-called farms in the United States in that year. Most of these are held in fee simple, and are tilled by their owners; but just so far as land-patches and forests and mines are leased in this country, their products must provide in their price of sale for current rents, as well as current costs of present production. This is just as it should be, and just as it must be, if Capital is to take this form of assisting the processes of future production.

But this form of Capital, as well as all other forms of the same, is perpetually wearing out, that is to say, is gradually losing its power to contribute as at first to the present and future processes of production. This loss is in the very nature of things,—in the very nature of all Capital. The great Father never intended that His children should cease from work. He has ordered all things so, that they cannot cease from work, and continue to live in any comfort and progress. Value, as we have already thoroughly learned, is not a quality that can be put into anything *to stay there*: it is a recurring relation of mutual services between man and man; and each of these services of the three kinds involves recurring Efforts. Capital is a form of Value; and, consequently, it cannot possibly take on a shape not subject to the *law of diminishing returns.* This is deductive proof. And precisely the same result is reached by Induction. Men have noticed and recorded the fact at all times, and have made provision for it in their pecuniary calculations, that tools and machinery need to be repaired and then replaced, that the current interest on moneyed capital tends to decline from generation to generation in all progressive countries, and also that lands and other forms of real estate so lose their productive and rental power unless cared for in renovation that men migrate and emigrate in consequence.

How much Rent shall the tenant pay to the landlord for the present use of the latter's old lands? Or in other words, how much shall be added to the going price of the product on account of the diminishing return due for the use of the old landed capital? This is a hard question to answer: probably the hardest question that is ever asked in practical Economics. Mr. Gladstone wrestled with it as complicated with a larger political question in passing the Irish Land Bill of 1881. Another honest athlete, Mr. Parnell, wrestled with it upon the same parliamentary arena. Scores of able and practical statesmen in Great Britain, and elsewhere, have struggled to reach a practical answer to this question; and scores of able and theoretical economists in all countries have striven to reach a theoretical answer to it. Most of these answers have been inharmonious, and many of them contradictory, with each other. The Land Bill of 1881 created a parliamentary Commission, whose duty and authority it was, to visit the Irish counties in person, to gain information in detail, to take sworn testimony of all the parties concerned, and then to lift or lower rents according to their discretion. The discontent of the Irish tenants in general was considerably mollified by the action of this Commission; while the debates and wrangles of the parliamentary session of 1889, and the persistent agitations for Home Rule (an agitation at once political and economical), show that the results of the work of that Commission were not wholly satisfactory.

(a) It is easy enough to see why the solution of this general problem is so extremely difficult. The new is mixed in with the old. The result of the old labor and capital is a productive piece of land; the current labor and capital is expended upon the same piece to make it more productive; the same sort of thing is done now that was done then, and the results of the two are now thoroughly intermixed; there were original free utilities in soil and growths and deposits, but these had and have no value and can never yield rent; the old labor and capital improved the soil by clearing and drainage and fertilizers, and made the growths and deposits more valuable and accessible, so that even the old onerous was more or less transformed into the original gratuitous; and now the new onerous, the fresh cultivation and fertilization and betterments generally, in soils and roads and buildings, are inextricably commingled with former betterments of the same general kind and with the original free gifts of Nature. No wonder the Commission of 1881 found difficulty in determining what was what and which was which! No wonder that Irish tenants on long leases quarrel with their landlords about the betterments, how much is new, how much is old! It is clear, that when the lease is ended, the landlord ought to compensate the tenant for all that portion of the latter's betterments, which is not already worn out; it is equally clear, that the tenant ought to be willing to pay a fair rent for the use of the unexpended betterments of the landlord and his predecessors; while there is room and verge enough for endless disputes between them as to the respective amounts of these, and consequently as to the amounts of rent and of its remissions.

These difficulties and intricacies do not belong to the *principles* of the Science of buying and selling, which are in the main clear and certain in their action, but are incidents of determining in certain cases *what that is*, which is bought and sold. Parties in interest in all kinds of buying and selling are sometimes compelled to go to the courts in order to have the Law decide what their respective rights are as buyers and sellers; but this is no fault of Political Economy as a science, or of trading as an art; two men in all cases make their own bargain, according to their own estimate of the respective rendering and receiving of each; if the uncertainties of language, the misconception on the part of one or both of the terms agreed upon, and the misapprehension of some of the circumstances of the case, breed confusion and litigation, all this cannot be justly charged to the science of Political Economy.

Nevertheless, it is into these incidental intricacies and uncertainties, that Henry George's now famous theory of landed rents and the taxation of them, strikes its roots. Instead of building his structure upon firm and open ground, so that thoughtful men can see that his basis is solid and scientific, Mr. George dashes at once into a thicket and lays his foundations with quickness and assurance where all is dark and doubtful, or at best where all is rather incidental than fundamental and demonstrable, and pretty soon displays a superstructure that appears attractive both without and within, through whose airy halls he knows how to conduct to their delight the credulous and discontented, and on whose walls hang plausible pictures calculated to invite and hold the attention of the masses. Let the perfect integrity and rhetorical ability of Mr. George be freely conceded; let it be freely conceded also, that he teaches in his books and lectures a great deal of vastly important industrial truth in a popular way so as to accomplish great good, such, for example, as the imperative need of greater simplicity in taxation, and the indisputable right of the people to their liberty in buying and selling; yet it must at the same time be owned, that he has never yet found out exactly what *Value* is in general, consequently what are the causes of value in lands, and what are the nature and grounds of Rent. Something more of patient and radical analysis at the outset, and of logical and scientific unfolding afterwards, would have made Henry George one of the chief benefactors of his age.

(b) It is also very easy to see, that the current price of produce, that is, what is gotten in return for the sale of what is gotten out of the land-parcels, must have a dominant influence upon what can be paid as rent for the use of the parcels. Unless the return from the produce be sufficient to reward at current rates the present labor and capital employed upon the parcel, the parcel will not continue to be cultivated at all, otherwise men would act without a motive for action, which they never do; unless, therefore, the price of produce be more than high enough to repay current wages and profits, there will be nothing left for Rent; and, consequently, the amount of the rent that can continue to be paid for lands will be *the difference between the going price of what is produced from them and the current expenses of cultivating them*. Here, as everywhere else within the domain of Exchange, Competition exerts its beneficent action. If one dealer, or ten, endeavors to put a price upon the produce more than enough to pay current wages and profits with a fair margin for the diminishing rate of rent, there are a plenty of others, dealers in the same grade of produce, who will be content with a fair return for present and past expenditure of labor and capital; and the action of these will effectually debar the others from exorbitant rates. The price of produce, accordingly, under free competition, is the divinely appointed regulator of landed rents. It regulates also, though more indirectly, the current rates of wages and profits in agriculture.

Very different from this is Ricardo's doctrine of Rent. He makes everything turn on the Cost of Production of the Produce, which is Effort, ignoring the ever-varying demands for the produce, which is Desire. His doctrine, too famous and too long received for us to pass by in this connection, though now superannuated, was for substance, this: there are some lands in every country whose produce just repays the expenses of cultivation, and consequently yields no margin for rent; and the cost of production on these rentless and poorest lands under cultivation, will determine the price of the produce; and as there can be but one price in the same market, the produce raised on more fertile land will be sold for the same price, and this price, besides paying the cost of cultivation, will yield a rent rising higher according as the land is more fertile; so that the rent paid on any land is always a measure of the excess of productiveness of that land over the least productive land under paying cultivation; and therefore, an increased demand for food in consequence of increased population, and the higher price resulting, will force cultivation down upon still poorer soils, or compel a higher culture for less remunerative returns on the old soils, according to the law of diminishing returns, which in either case will raise the rents on all the soils above that grade that just repays the expenses of cultivation; so that it is the sole interest of landlords, as such, that population should be dense and food high, their interest being directly antagonistic to that of the other classes of the community.

(c) Finally, in this connection, it is easy enough to see, what were the motives on the part of the landlords, and what were the results on the part of the masses, of Great Britain, in putting on and keeping on the infamous Corn Laws, so-called, which were repealed forever in 1846. The Corn Laws forbade the importation of foreign cereals under heavy pecuniary penalties. The simple purpose of the landlords then governing England was to raise the price of their grain by shutting off Competition of foreigners by means of these prohibitory tariff-taxes. It was Protectionism pure and simple. It was designed to raise the price of bread to the masses of their countrymen, and often did raise it to the point of their starvation. But we have just seen, that the higher the price of the produce, the wider the margin for Rent for the lands that produce it. The Corn Laws of England enriched the landlords at the expense of all other classes and to the starvation of many of the poor. As has been well said, this was the most successful of all the many expedients that have been tried, "*to fertilize the rich man's land by the sweat of the poor man's brow.*" The words of Daniel O'Connell, spoken Sept. 28, 1843, in his parliamentary fight against the high-tariff Corn Laws, were surfeited with truth and righteousness: "*But what is the meaning of 'Protection'? It means an additional sixpence for each loaf; that is the Irish of it. If the landlord had not the protection, the loaf would sell for a shilling, but if he has protection, it will sell for one and sixpence. Protection is the English for sixpence; and what is more, it is the English for an extorted sixpence. The real meaning of 'Protection,' therefore, is robbery,—robbery of the poor by the rich.*"

At the present moment and for twenty-five years past, the public laws of the United States ostensibly relating to Taxes, have had an immense influence upon the value and rents of the agricultural lands of the country to depress them; because these laws have put up nearly or wholly impassable barriers to the coming in of those foreign goods, against which the farmers would naturally and profitably and inevitably have sold their surplus agricultural produce; by destroying the foreign market for farm products, these laws do in effect destroy a large part of the value of the farms of the country, and of what would otherwise be the rentals of a part of them; the Constitution of the country expressly forbids any taxation whatever of Exports, but these laws have precisely the same effect on the value of farm products if they were themselves forbidden to be exported, because those goods for which these would be otherwise exchanged for a profit are forbidden to be imported. *A market for products is products in market.* Thus these wretched laws lower the price of farm products, and consequently the value of farms and of their rents, and impoverish the farmers who are nearly one-half of the entire population of the country.

While these paragraphs are being written, comes the intelligence of the formation of the "North American Salt Company," whose purpose is in their own language "*to unify and systematize the salt interests of the United States and Canada,*" and to this end "*arrangements have been completed for the purchase and control of nearly all the existing salt properties of the North American continent.*" As this is a fair instance out of some thousands, in which a tariff-tax has the designed effect to lift or lower values which deeply concern the people, let us look at it for a moment. On the average of the past twenty-five years the tariff-tax on salt has in general doubled the cost of that necessary of life to the whole people of the United States. When Canada had no such tax, American makers of it sold salt sometimes to the Canadians 40% less than they would sell it to their own countrymen. On the basis of this United States tariff-tax (it would never have been dreamed of without it) this new company comes forward with a scheme of international monopoly to control in their own interest the price of a prime necessity of life. They propose to issue stock and bonds to the amount of $15,000,000, with which to buy up "the existing salt properties"; and they frankly avow in the prospectus from which we are quoting, that profits of $2,000,000 a year on their capital are justified by the present outlook. Whence are these immense profits to come? Out of the pockets of the masses of the American people bound hand and foot in the meshes of a legal monopoly, which they themselves allow themselves to be ensnared in! In a similar but more outrageous way, are bound up at the present moment in the secret so-called "Trusts" about forty more of the necessaries of life; each one of which, unless it be the "Standard Oil Trust," has its footing in a so-called "protective" tariff-tax, and would collapse instantly on the repeal of that!

It was necessary in order to complete our study of the second class of material commodities, namely, those produced from valuable and rentful lands, to glance in passing at the frequently disturbing effect on these, aside from their cost of production, of sinister laws plausibly imposed upon an unsuspicious people in the interest and at the instance of a privileged few.

3. It only remains in this chapter, devoted to the discussion of material Commodities in their three economic classes, to conclude with a glance at the third class, namely, those material valuables that are obtained from free and unowned sources, such as masts cut in the wilds of America on both oceans two and three hundred years ago, and fish caught on the Banks of Newfoundland, and furs gathered to such profit in the north by the Hudson's Bay Company, and salt evaporated in the tropics by a free sun from old ocean's brine.

These, and all such things as these, have a cost of production determined only by the cost of present labor and capital, and consequently a grade of value determined only by present Demand and Supply, unentangled for the most part by questions of rent and prior claim and taxation and nationality. All these things, accordingly, are relatively cheap, except as the element of Scarcity, and on that account of strong Desire, may sometimes come in to enhance the value. No man can tell the time exactly when French fishermen from the coasts of Brittany ventured over to the Banks of Newfoundland in their frail barks for the abundant cod in those waters, and went back home again at the close of the season freighted with plenty of a free and cheap food for their families and countrymen; or when it was that rude men calling themselves English followed these in their western track for the same general purposes, to become thereby hardy seamen on deeper seas, such as those who gained long afterwards the naval victories of Nelson; and we have all read in the fascinating pages of Irving the ventures and adventures of John Jacob Astor, the attraction of free furs in the Northwest of America, the hazards and the history incident to obtaining them, and the immense profits gained by their sale in the markets of the old world.

CHAPTER III.
PERSONAL SERVICES.

There are three kinds of things only ever bought and sold in this good world of ours. In the preceding chapter we have conned carefully the first kind, material commodities, in their three subdivisions of land-parcels and products of such parcels and products of free land and sea. In the present chapter we come to study the second kind of valuable things, personal services, which we shall also find subdivisible into three classes. We have treated of Commodities first, because their value in its grounds and changes is more easily understood than that of the other two kinds, while in point of *time* Services might well enough have been considered first, since it is these that manipulate into value the originally rude forms of Nature. The main difference between the two is this: in Commodities the attention is naturally drawn to tangible *things* offered for sale, such as lands and wheat and fish; while in Services the attention is strongly drawn to *persons* offering them for sale, such as the common laborer and the skilled artisan and the professional artist. This distinction, though obvious and useful as between commodities and services, is not after all radical; because Economics is a science of Persons from beginning to end; inasmuch as the services precede and are merged in the commodities, and inasmuch as the Desires (personal) of some men for the renderings of other men antedate and underlie all exchanges whatsoever.

Personal Services are technically named *Labor* in the science of Political Economy. This nomenclature is old and familiar, and will probably always persist on that account, but it is not of itself of the happiest, and it gives birth to some ambiguities and many fallacies. Let us look at these for a moment, before we pass to the definition and discussion of what is commonly called Labor, but what is better described by the term, Personal Services.

Contrast will help us a little here. Commodities can always be measured by some *Standard* outside of themselves: for example, land-parcels are measured into acres and fractions thereof by a surveyor's compass and chain; metals and cereals are weighed into centners and parts thereof by scales of some sort; and sugar is not only weighed at the custom-house, but tested as to other qualities by the polariscope. Now land, wheat, sugar, and all other commodities, have an existence separate from the standards that measure them, and whether they are bought or not they continue for a time essentially the same. They exist *per se*. They were indeed brought into existence on purpose to be sold, and if they cannot be sold, similar things additional will not then and there be brought into the market, but these things themselves are there separate from the seller and separate from the buyer. Not so with personal services. They do not exist *per se*. They are not separate from the seller, and they cannot come into existence without a buyer. *Skill* is something the artisan cannot part with, nor can he sell the service to which the skill gives rise till the buyer be present with the return-service in his hands. The Laborer of any class cannot put his "service" on exhibition, and then wait for a buyer, as the commercial drummer sells goods by sample. The doctor, for example, must have his *patient* before he can show his skill. The buying and selling of personal services, accordingly, is more intimate and ultimate than the buying and selling of commodities: it brings people more closely together: it depends much more on traits of *character* and on acquired *skill*.

Right here we may see clearly the main objection to the term, "Labor," as commonly used, and the bad fallacy to which it gives birth. "Labor" is indeed in form and origin an *abstract* term as much as "service" is, with this difference, that the word "service" radically implies the person serving and another person served at the same instant; but the term "Labor" has long been taking on itself in the mouths of men a *concrete* meaning, as if it might be something separate from the laborers, as in the common phrase "Labor and Capital," which has already done a world of mischief and is likely to do a good deal more, because it seems to imply, that the two are alike in independent self-existence, and that they stand over against each other on equal terms for a fair bargain or for a free fight. This is not the case, as we shall see more fully later; since capital is something separable from the capitalist, always a commodity or a claim, always transferable, always valuable or else it will not be "Capital." Some of the German economists, and particularly John Conrad of Halle, have avoided this difficulty by a clean nomenclature. They say "*Labor-givers*" and "*Labor-takers*," instead of Laborers and Capitalists, and especially instead of "Labor and Capital," thus emphasizing the personal element in both terms, and also leaving themselves free to define and use the term "Capital" as distinct from any particular capitalist, while the term "Labor" cannot be defined and used as distinct from any given laborer. This precise point, though probably new, is of very considerable consequence in the true doctrine of Wages.

We are compelled by the exigencies of the English language and the still stronger fetters of economical custom to continue to use the terms "Labor" and "Laborers" in their technical sense, and in connection with the scientific terms "Capital" and "Capitalist"; but we shall always use each of these words in the same meaning, and free them as far as possible from the fungous accretions that have fastened upon them in the course of time.

Personal effort of any kind put forth for another in view of a return-service and for the sake of it is labor.

Laborers are persons rendering their peculiar services to other persons for a commercial reward.

The valuable received by a laborer for his service rendered is Wages.

These definitions exclude from our circle of view all Efforts of anybody put forth for other than commercial reasons; and they include all Efforts of everybody, from the President to the scrub, put forth under the inducement of a return-service or Wages. No good end seems to be reached by trying to distinguish, as Francis Walker does in his "Wages-Question," between the "Wages-class" and the "Salary-class," because there appears to be no scientific or other economical difference between Wages and Salary. Each is a return-service for another service rendered, and that is all there is to it. The whole class of Laborers, accordingly, in any civilized and progressive country, is immensely large and becoming constantly larger. Excluding, of course, from this class all persons in so far as they render so-called moral services to others, which are in their very nature *free*, such as those that spring from duty and courtesy and benevolence, and these happily are also an immense and fast-augmenting class, though our Science has nothing to do with them directly, the number of those persons in every community and in every rank of every community, who sell personal services of some sort in distinction from commodities and credits, is pretty nearly as large as the *per capita* population of adults and competents within that circuit. It must be borne in mind, that the same persons whose primary business it may be to sell commodities or credits, often sell services also in some subordinate or incidental way; and also, that the same persons, who are dispensing on the one hand their gifts and moral renderings freely, are frequently of the busiest in selling on the other hand their personal services for pay. In other words, the sellers of Services cannot be discriminated *as to their persons* from other sellers, or even from downright *givers*; but the *action* itself, and the law of it, is quite distinct in the three cases of selling, and utterly diverse in the one case of giving.

Now, can we sub-classify within this vast class of service-sellers, so as to help us understand better the class as a whole, and so especially as to help us understand better the Law of Wages within the entire class? We have just criticised Walker in a friendly spirit for attempting to draw lines of demarcation within this wide field: can we draw any useful ones ourselves less open to criticism than his, and such as rest back upon fair differences in nature and form? Walker makes his distinctions turn on certain peculiarities in the return-services: can we make ours turn better and clearer on certain peculiarities in the services themselves? We can at least try. Hard and fast lines cannot be drawn here, we admit. The exterior lines around Commodities and around Services and around Credits are each sharp and firm; and so is the deep-fixed circle that includes all three of these alike as Valuables; but *within* the smaller circles the lines of needful division are somewhat more shadowy, though we leave with confidence to competent Economists the triple lines but just now drawn within the sphere of material Commodities.

A rude classification among "Laborers," then, yet one useful and indeed indispensable, may be made into (1) Common Laborers, (2) Skilled Laborers, and (3) Professional Laborers.

Common Laborers are those, whose services may be acceptably rendered by an ordinarily competent person after a little patient practice and instruction, without anything corresponding to an *apprenticeship* as a preliminary to their selling their service. Farm hands, teamsters, porters, waiters, miners, 'longshoremen, railroad laborers, and many more belong to this first class. Owing to the ease with which this class can be recruited at any time from growing boys and emigrating foreigners and from those who may have essayed the class above and fallen back, the Supply here is kept constantly large relatively to the Demand for such services, and consequently Wages are always the lowest and steadiest in this lowest class of Laborers.

Skilled Laborers are those, who have had to pass through something equivalent to an apprenticeship in order to be able to offer their services for sale. These, as a class, present some considerable points of difference from common laborers. Their numbers are fewer, for the reason, that relatively few parents can afford to give their children the time and money needful for them to learn a trade, or to become skilful in any art requiring prolonged education; as a result of this lessened press of competition among themselves, and because being intelligent and consequently mobile they are able to insist better on their claims and distribute themselves to points where their services are in more demand; and because they are likely to be subject to a stronger Demand than common laborers, on account of the close connection of their services with special accumulations of Capital; the Wages of skilled laborers will infallibly rule higher than those of common laborers. Artisans in general constitute this second class of laborers.

Professional Laborers are those, who have received a technical education,—something more than an apprenticeship,—expressly to fit them to render difficult and delicate services to their fellow-men for pay, and who possess besides the requisite character and talents and genius to enable them to succeed. Clergymen, physicians, lawyers, literary men, artists, actors, and many more, render professional services loosely so-called. The obstacles at the entrance of this path occasioned by the lack (1) of appropriate natural gifts, or (2) of the requisite industry and character, or (3) of the means of suitable education and training, practically exclude so many persons, that the competition in the higher walks of professional life is not such as to prevent a very large remuneration for services rendered. The demand for these is often peculiarly intense, as well as the supply peculiarly limited. When great interests of property, of reputation, of life, are at stake, it is felt that the best men to secure these must be had at almost any price. Fees and rewards for services of great delicacy, of great difficulty, of great danger, are paid by individuals and corporations and nations without grudging. Comparatively few men reach the highest points of excellence in their respective professions, and they have in consequence a natural monopoly in these fields of effort, and receive for their labor a very high rate of Wages. For example, Daniel Webster often took a fee of $1000 for a single plea in court; Paganini, a like sum for an hour's playing on a violin; and Jenny Lind, at least as much for an evening's singing in a concert, because there was in each case a strong demand for a peculiar service and only one person in the world who could render that service in the circumstances to the same perfection. But the objections which lie with such force against artificial monopolies, cannot be urged at all against a natural monopoly; for, if the road to excellence be open to all, and no artificial obstructions thrown in the way of any, there is no blame but rather praise for him who distances all competitors, and asks and receives for services of peculiar excellence a large remuneration. Exchange rejoices in all diversities of advantage that are the birth of freedom, but reprobates with all her force advantage that is gained by artificial restrictions, because artificial restrictions always infringe on somebody's right to render services for a return; and the right to render services for a return is the fundamental conception in the Right of Property.

Is it open for us, to gain a somewhat deeper and clearer sense of *what that is exactly* that is rendered in these three classes of personal Services, before we pass to the considerations which determine in all cases their Value? It is plain, that what common Laborers sell for the most part, if not exclusively, is *muscular exertion* of some kind, guided by the mind as trained in habit, and aided by appropriate implements, all designed to meet the desire and so call forth the return-service of the purchaser; it is equally plain, that skilled Laborers with scarcely any more exceptions than before sell the same sort of physical exertions, or motions, this time guided by mental action of a higher grade and wider scope, and aided also by more elaborate tools working towards the desires and consequent returns of a set of buyers more scrupulous and exacting than the first set; and it is plain enough, that some of the highest professional services, for instance the surgeon's, though not by any means the mass of such services, are essentially of the same kind as the two former, namely, muscular motions, guided by the most intimate and exact knowledge of things, and aided too by instruments the most scientific and expensive. In many of the professional services the physical element sinks to a minimum, while the intellectual and moral factors come to the front and take up the chief attention; it will be found, however, that the physical factor is always present in some degree, as, for example, in the counsel's plea before the court, and in the physician's visit on his patient; and in almost all cases, if not in all, some implement or other plays its part in the process of professional service before it ends, as Cicero used a pitch-pipe or tuning-fork to gauge his voice in his great pleas for Roman clients.

Precisely what is rendered, then, in all cases of Personal Services in each of their three loose kinds, is *muscular motion conjoined with mental effort and both these assisted by habit and by some form of what we call Capital.* The Services are therefore *Personal* in the highest sense. The Mind and Body of the Laborer conspire to render them. The most sagacious animal can never be trained to render one of them. They are wholly *human.* Nevertheless the muscular part in the rendering—motion and resistance to motion—is just what tools and machinery can be made to take the place of in large measure but never in whole measure, because tools may not be taught *to think.* It may seem sometimes as if machinery were about to take the place of human hands in some classes of Production; but it will be found in the ultimate issue, as it has been found in every stage of the process, that human hands and human minds in action are absolutely essential at every point of the Exchanges among men. Men are so made and Society is so organized, that they need increasingly for their comfort and progress the personal services of their fellow-men, and can render their own in exchange for these; and consequently, there never can fail (under freedom) a MARKET for Personal Services of the three kinds.

Having now seen as closely as possible what that is which is rendered in personal services, let us pass to the principles which determine their remuneration. That is, we will now inquire carefully into the Value of personal services. We have learned already, that Demand and Supply in their action and reaction upon each other determine in all cases the value of Commodities for the time being; and we shall find it to be equally the dictate of all reason, and the outcome of all experience, that Demand and Supply decide too in all cases on the value of all Services and all Credits then and there. Shall we look first at the considerations that issue in the Demand for personal services, and then at those other considerations that limit the Supply of them?

1. Demand is never the mere desire for anything, but desire coupled with the ability to pay for it at rates satisfactory to the present holder. The

Demand for Services, therefore, is made by the prospective purchasers of them; and the purchasers, of course, are those who desire them and are willing to pay for them at current rates. It will be easiest and surest for us to study the Demand for Services in each of the three classes of them in succession.

(1) The Demand for Common Laborers has several points of difference from that for Skilled, and from that for Professional, Laborers. It is scarcely ever intense. It is mostly disconnected from large accumulations of Capital. The desire is usually for immediate gratification, without any other end in view. It is frequently for such a service, as, if a renderer may not be conveniently and cheaply found, one is inclined to do for himself. For instances: if the barber be not accessible and reasonable and tolerably skilful, a man will certainly shave himself, provided he have not yet attained the independence and the luxury of wearing a full beard; and the ordinary housewife, if the cleanly and tractable domestic does not come into sight, will do her own work with casual assistance. It is this important fact, that common services among men and women in common life may in many cases be dispensed with altogether, and in many other cases substitutes be found for them, in connection with the other important fact, that common laborers learn their art quickly and easily, and consequently are present everywhere in large numbers, that makes the Wages of such laborers uniformly low. The Demand is moderate and the Supply is large.

(2) The Demand for Skilled Laborers is steadier and stronger than for Common, because in general the desire for these is not for immediate gratification, but for an ultimate satisfaction to arise from the commercial coöperation of these laborers with their employers, who are capitalists, in connection with accumulations of capital, the end in view being the production of commodities for sale at a profit. Here comes in a new motive on the part of capitalists to buy the personal services of laborers. The motive is simple and intelligible and commendable, but its nature and operation is popularly and grossly misapprehended.

Capital is the result of Abstinence from the present use of a Valuable in gratification, for the sake of a future increase of it through Production. But Abstinence is always irksome in itself. It must have its prospective reward in an increase, a profit, or it will never transform itself from a mere valuable into a capitalized product. Now, the owner of the valuable, having transformed it into capital from this motive, is under a commercial necessity to hire laborers, in order by their help to make his capital yield a profit. Capital lying idle decreases in *value* even, to say nothing of its yielding no increase to itself; and the motive of the capital-owner, accordingly, is strong and constant to buy the services of laborers, to marry these services with his own capitalized products, and thus to produce commodities for sale, whose value shall be greater than the present value of the capital and the services combined. Here we reach in the minds and motives of a large class of men an ultimate Demand for laborers, and specially for skilled laborers, which is as true and constant to its legitimate end of Profit as the needle is true and constant to the pole.

At this point it is very evident, that, if the fair expectation of the capitalists be realized in a steady profit, and the larger the circle of capitalists and the more of capitalized products to each the better for all concerned, the Demand for laborers will become steady, and will be likely to steadily increase, because there will then be a constant motive on the part of all capitalists as such to put back a part or all of their yearly profits into capitalized products, and thus the Demand for laborers will become more intense, and the rates of Wages so far forth must be enhanced. The steady Demand for the services of the laborers hinges upon the steady Profits of the capitalists, and there is no antagonism between the interests of these two classes of buyers and sellers, but rather a complete identity of interest between them.

We are looking now solely at what constitutes the Demand for laborers of the second class. As always, so here, there is Desire first and then a ready Return-service. The Desire of employers of this class is for a Profit on their capital, and the return-service for the laborers is present as a part of these capitalized products. This part of the capital we call Wages-Portion. It is already in hand or provided to be in hand when the wages fall due. Of course it is expected, that the current wages will ultimately come out of the current joint-production of the laborers upon the capitalized products set apart for that purpose by the capitalist. But if the profits fail to the capitalists at the end of that industrial-cycle, whether it be two months or twenty-four, then Desire will fail or be weakened to hire laborers for the next cycle, and the return-services or Wages-Portion with which to pay them for another cycle will be lessened of necessity. Both elements in Demand are curtailed by the falling-off of Profits. There is at the same instant less desire to buy services and less ability to pay for them. It is of the very nature of capitalized products to wear out in the process of production; if there be not net profits at the end of the cycle for the capitalists, it shall go hard but there will be less wages for the laborers during the next cycle. This is not a matter of sentiment or of philanthropy, but of eternal law, which God has ordained and the devices of men cannot frustrate. Capitalists and laborers are joint partners in the same concern. Under industrial and commercial freedom their interests are identical. Both are buyers and sellers to each other at the same instant; and, as always when both parties are alike benefited and satisfied with a trade, both will cheerfully and profitably continue the connection. The Demand of each class for the product of the other will continue unabated. Profits and wages reciprocally beget each other.

But still it is not altogether true, what has sometimes been stated by economists, that capitalists are under the same sort of pressure to buy their services as the laborers are to sell them. Capital is a Valuable already created by the mutual desires and efforts of two persons, and is now the exclusive property of one of them, and has also been set apart by him through an act of will to be thereafter an aid to some future production under the motive of a new value to accrue thereby. The capital has now become secondary to and separated from the person who owns it. He very seldom understands the real nature and operation of it. He commonly imparts to it in his imagination a more substantive and persistent existence than it actually possesses. He is frequently more or less stuck up as towards his neighbors and employees in consequence of his possession of it. The very fact that he has capitalized it for future operations shows that he is independent of it as a means of present livelihood. The personal services of the laborers, on the other hand, stand in very different relations to *them*. Their personal services may indeed be *valuable*, but they cannot be *capitalized*. As laborers they have nothing else to sell. Unless they sell their services now, these have no existence even, still less can they have any value. It is only by a mischievous figure of speech, that the skill of laborers is sometimes spoken of as their "Capital." Therefore, the laborers are under a certain remote yet inherent disadvantage as sellers of their personal services, when compared with the capitalists as buyers of them. This disadvantage, however, though apparent in the nature of things, and under certain circumstances disastrous to the laborers, may disappear practically under another and natural state of things; and it is every way to be desired by both classes alike that it should disappear in practice.

Whenever there is a broad and constant and profitable market for all the commodities the capitalists and the laborers can jointly produce,—that is to say, whenever profits are steady and remunerative and wages are high and growing in their purchasing-power,—the Demand for skilled laborers must always be such as puts the laborers on a footing of equality as over against the capitalists, because under such circumstances the purchasers of services are many and eager, two bosses will be likely to be bidding for one skilled laborer, and then wages are always growing in dollars and each dollar growing in effective purchasing-power.

It is of the last importance in this connection to notice, that everything in Profits and Wages turns in the last resort upon the breadth and freedom of MARKETS. It is out of the return-service received from the *sale* of the commodities produced jointly by the capitalists and laborers, that both wages and profits must ultimately be paid. There is no other possible source of them. When the Market fails, everything fails that leads up to a market. Particularly fails the Demand for laborers for the next industrial cycle, and of course drops also the prospective wages for that cycle. The public folly and universal loss of shutting off foreign markets for our own commodities by lofty tariff-barriers, as has been conspicuously done by the United States for thirty years past, follows of course from this radical truth; and the Wages of laborers, instead of being lifted by tariff-taxes, as has been so often falsely and wickedly asserted, are inevitably *depressed* by them, because they effectually forbid to capitalists and laborers their best and freely chosen *markets* for the sale of their joint products.

Another vastly important matter, constantly affecting the Demand for laborers of the second class, is the Competency or otherwise of the practical managers of the Capital invested in industrial enterprises. Capital cannot manage itself. It is of itself wholly inert. It is always either a Commodity or a Credit. Conscious of their inability to handle wisely their own bits of Capital, or else taught it through a bitter experience, by far the larger number of individual owners of it loan it to others to manage; they invest it in some industrial corporation, in a bank or a mill or a railroad. Some one person, or at least a small body of persons, must practically manage now all specific accumulations of capital. It is they in their capacity of manipulating-capitalists, who constitute in large measure the Demand for laborers. But such managers, who are at once skilful and long-headed and honest, do not grow upon a chance bush. They are rare. Most of them in this country at least have been those, who started in a small way in the control of their own earned or small-inherited properties, and rose through practice and knowledge and conscience to the ability to handle profitably to all concerned large masses of Capital. In the hands of such men, given a tolerable chance by public law and private circumstances, both Profits and Wages are sure to come in satisfactorily. They are Captains of Industry. They are an honor to human nature. They are a blessing to the whole community. They have no need and no will to ask to be bolstered up in their business by unjust taxes enforced upon a whole people.

Such men sometimes have sons or *protégés*, who possess similar capacities and similar integrity, and these by experience become able to carry on the business to similar successful issues. This is happy, but it is unusual. More commonly, in the second, and pretty certainly in the third, generation, the line of royal succession fails. There comes in a lieutenant rather than a captain of Industry. Likely enough he mistakes the nature of capital, and thinks that it will go along of itself without that eternal vigilance that is the one price of its maintenance and increase; likely enough he lacks the touch and rule of men, and his laborers become demoralized and refractory; more likely still he thinks he sees other operators around him getting quicker rich by speculating in enterprises outside the legitimate business, and takes some of his own and of what is not his own and throws it out of its proper channels; and, as the result of one or all of these, things soon go wrong, profits and wages fall off, poor work is done and finds slow sale, and Demand for laborers (which is their life-blood) slackens or goes out in that establishment. No wonder the Paper-makers in their annual gathering at Saratoga of 1889, resolved as the main outcome of their meeting, that they would bring up their sons (or somebody's sons) to succeed them in their business by a thorough practical training in the paper-mill itself, beginning early and continuing long. Industrial higher education in this or some other form is the secondary hope of manufacturing business in the United States, the primary hope being in a decent commercial liberty to buy their supplies and to sell their products in the best markets wherever these are to be found.

There is one other important item that bears directly upon the Demand for laborers of the second class, and consequently upon their Wages, namely, the constant introduction of more and better Machinery. At first blush it would seem, and it has often been stated so, that the use of machinery takes just so much work from human hands, reduces by so much the Demand for laborers, and tends to lessen by so much their wages. All this is the opposite of the truth; but before we explain *why* it is the opposite of the truth, let us attend carefully to the truth itself, as stated in 1889 by the highest living authority on these special points, Sir Edwin Chadwick, the octogenarian pioneer in sanitary and economic reforms. Fifty-six years ago Chadwick joined with his colleagues of the English Factory Inspection Board in recommending reduced hours of labor and other improvements which have now become general in England. In a paper recently read before the Political Economy Club, he calls attention to the greatly increased production which follows improved machinery and shortened hours.

He says: "*Spinning machines which formerly turned 8000 in a minute, now turn 11,000; and in Lancashire not more than half the hands are now employed to produce the same amount with new machinery as were employed on the machinery of 1833. As an example of the extent of the reduction of hands by these improvements, it may be mentioned that one large family of cotton spinners in Manchester, which 40 years ago employed 11,000 hands, could not now muster one half that number.* YET THE MILL POPULATION HAS INCREASED, AS WELL AS THE GENERAL POPULATION, THE HANDS DISCHARGED BEING ABSORBED IN OTHER EMPLOYMENTS. *At the beginning of the century the cost of spinning a pound of yarn was a shilling. The pound of that same yarn is now spun for a half-penny by hands earning double wages for their increased energetic attention and skill. It is now found, however, that the strain of the increased responsible attention cannot be so long sustained as the slow, semi-automatic pace by the old working of the old mills with the long hours. Hence there is a tendency to a further voluntary reduction of the working hours in the best mills, first to nine hours. In one mill, in which 2000 men are employed a voluntary reduction has been effected to about eight hours with a more equable production; and I have heard of other examples. As showing the cost of working with inferior hands and loose regulations, a recent report from the Manchester Chamber of Commerce states that 20s. worth of bundled yarn may be produced at a cost of from 2d. to 3d. per pound less in Manchester than in Bombay, notwithstanding the hours of working are 80 hours per week, while in Manchester they are only 50. At the present time Lancashire, with its short hours, will meet Germany or any other country, in neutral markets, in the world. In Germany the spinners and weavers still work 13 hours a day as they once did in England; France has only come down to 12 hours; whereas the English rate has long been 10 hours, and may soon be 9 or even 8. And this reduction improves the health of the wage-workers, while the reduced cost of production allows them higher wages; yet Germany with its long hours and high tariff maintains a system* OF LOW PAY, DEAR PRODUCTION, HIGH COST OF DISTRIBUTION, AND LIMITED SALES."

The accuracy of these important statements of fact is confirmed on every hand. Committees of British spinners and weavers have repeatedly visited the United States, and then reported to their fellows at home, that wages, all things considered, were equal for spinners and weavers in Great Britain and the United States, and in some cases and respects higher in the former. Many times before his late lamented death, John Bright publicly testified that wages in England during his parliamentary life had risen in general 50%, and in some of the manufacturing lines 100%. A few months before these statements of Chadwick were made, Sir Richard Temple reported to his section of the British Association, "*That the average earnings per head in the United Kingdom, taking the whole population without division into classes, is £35, 4s., and exceeds the average of the United States, which is £27, 4s., and of Canada, which is £26, 18s., and of the Continent, which is £18, 1s.; while it falls below that of Australia, which is £43, 4s. per head.*"

According to this, the average earnings in Great Britain per head of the population are 30% higher than in the United States, and 81% higher than on the Continent of Europe. Truly, Britain is a prosperous and profitable country so far as average earnings of the whole people by the year is concerned. Sir Richard goes on in the same statistical paper to show, that the average annual profit on British Capital is 14%, and that Capital yields about the same rate for the United States.

Now, can we easily give the grounds on which the introduction of more and better machinery, instead of displacing laborers, tends to lift and actually does lift the wages of those concerned, who continue to work with their hands and heads? We will try it.

(a) It takes the hands and heads of laborers to invent and construct and keep in repair the machinery itself, that is often supposed to displace laborers, and so far forth opens a vent for the more profitable employment of some of the laborers, who before performed the cruder and more repetitive and automatic parts of the processes, which parts alone machinery can be made to perform.

(b) Machinery always lessens the cost of a given amount of production, otherwise there would be no motive for its introduction. But, other things being equal, the lessened cost of a commodity broadens the market for its sale. The cheaper a useful commodity is offered, the more the buyers of it the world over. The more and the better the machinery brought in, the more and the cheaper the commodities produced and the broader and better the markets to be supplied; and, therefore, the more and the more skilful the hands needed to tend the machinery and to market the products.

(c) The more commodities thus created by men and machines, and the wider the markets found for them over the earth, the more laborers are required to extract and prepare and transport the raw materials for the now augmenting commodities, and also to ship and distribute the finished products. As Chadwick says, notwithstanding the strictly *factory* hands have diminished one half in one place, "yet the *mill* population has increased, as well as the general population, the hands discharged being absorbed in other employments."

(d) These improvements in machinery, and the consequent refinements in the skill of the laborers, cheapen also of course the commodities consumed by the laborers themselves, and therefore a given rate of wages, to say nothing of a rate sure to enlarge under these circumstances, now secures for the laborers a higher grade of comforts.

More and better and more durable machinery, consequently, so far forth, tends at once to enhance the rate of laborers' wages and increase the purchasing power of the unit in which wages are paid.

To return now to the main line of discussion under the present head, we have shown by proof positive that there is nothing either in new machinery introduced, or in higher wages paid in connection with such machinery, or in shortened hours made possible by these two, to lessen the Demand of Capitalists for the personal services of Laborers; because, there is nothing in all these, commercial and industrial freedom being presupposed, to lessen the Profits of the Capitalists, which profits are the sole motive actuating them as such. That high wages and short hours are rather an advantage to Profits in connection with skilled laborers and fine machinery, than a disadvantage when compared with long hours and low pay and poor implements, is clearly shown by Chadwick in the passage quoted comparing

England with English Bombay, where the working hours are 60% more and the wages greatly less and the cost of the machinery very little; "twenty shillings' worth of bundled yarn may be produced at a cost of from 2d. to 3d. less in Manchester than in Bombay"; call it 2½d. less; that is, it costs the Bombay spinner more than 1% per pound of yarn more to spin it than it costs the Manchester spinner! For truth and decency's sake, then, let us have done with the gabble in this country about the advantages of "pauper labor" over skilled, of low wages over high, of cheap machinery over dear!

The penetrating reader will perceive, that the root of this whole matter lies in the breadth and quickness of the *Markets*, in which the commodities produced by the laborers and capitalists may be sold against other commodities, and against Services and Credits; if the markets of the world are free to all to buy in and to sell in, which seemingly two things are precisely one and the same thing, then the Demand of Capitalists for the services of laborers to create and market salable commodities wherever these may be wanted, can apparently never slacken on the whole; because, the desires of men which the efforts of other men may satisfy commercially, are indefinite in number and unlimited in degree; and, therefore, the Wages of the skilled laborers, the commercial freedom of the nations being presupposed, are likely to be on the whole on a steady rise throughout the world; and the amount and excellence of the machinery on a similar rise, since Capitalists can always under these circumstances see their Profits looming up ahead of them,—the profits of an endlessly diversified and marketable Production.

The chief reason at any rate, and almost the only reason in common sight, why little England has surpassed in commercial prosperity of every sort every other nation on the globe during the past forty years, as evidenced by these statistics of Sir Richard Temple and other abounding proofs on sea and land, is in the fact, that her statesmen of the last generation came to perceive clearly, and then helped the people to see, that a market for products is products in market; that her traditional tariff-barriers to keep foreign goods out kept in equally domestic goods that wanted to get out for a profit, and so down went the tariff-barriers little by little, accursed alike by God and Englishmen, never to be set up again around the shores of the land of Cobden and Bright and Elliott; and to-day we read, that the average annual Earnings per head of the entire population of the United Kingdom, men and women and children, English and Irish and Scotch, are $176, while the annual average Profits of Capital within the three kingdoms is 14%.

(3) In the last place here, we must now look at the Demand for the personal services of Professional laborers. These are persons, who have done something more with reference to their life-work than serve an

apprenticeship to a trade, or acquire some mechanical skill in connection with some kind of machinery. An Education rather than an Apprenticeship is implied in Professional laborers. Knowledge of the bodies and of the minds of men; acquaintance with some one section at least of the general laws that pervade the universe; some confidence (the more the better) in God, who created and governs the world; are all requisite to a reasonable success on the part of Professional laborers. The Demand for their services, and of course also the Return made to them for such services, will largely depend on such superior knowledge and confidence acquired by such persons, and involved in their services. Clergymen, physicians, lawyers, statesmen, literators, actors, teachers, and scientific experts, may serve as our chief examples of Professional laborers.

(a) "All that a man hath will he give for his life." When men fall sick, or those fall sick who are dear to them, they send for the doctor. Scarcely any trait of human nature is more universal than this. And the trait puts honor on human nature, because it implies a relatively high estimate of the worth of life in the mind of the patient, and also a relatively high confidence in a certain class of one's fellow-men. As Society progresses, and as Christianity deepens the sense of the worth of the individual life, and knits a stronger tie of confidence between man and man, a change is slowly coming over the relations between physicians and their patients; people do not wait to fall sick before they send for the doctor, so much as they formerly did; some individuals and families are establishing connections with a medical adviser, who studies their constitutions and habits of life beforehand, guides them in general sanitation, and thus both he and they are better ready for curatives in times of illness. Gladstone has long had such an attendant, with the best of results as he thinks, and strongly commended such action to John Bright, but too late to save the latter from what was thought to be premature death in consequence of imprudent and ill-advised handling of his health. In a few cases in England and the United States an annual salary is paid a physician for general care of the family's health, whether sickness befall or not, instead of the more usual fees on consultation and attendance. Dr. Munn of New York receives such an annual salary from Mr. Jay Gould. But in whatever way medical services are paid for, the Demand for them is constant and intense. The motive to buy them is immediate and personal, not mediate and remote, as in the case of capitalists and laborers of the second class.

It is to be noticed further in respect to physicians, and indeed in respect to all professional laborers much more than in respect to other laborers, that much knowledge has been gained by them for its own sake, out of pure love for it, rather than for the sake of merely selling their services as laborers; while this does not diminish in the least the commercial character of their services, it tends to beget on the part of the buyers of them a stronger confidence in the men who render them, so that the Demand for such services and consequently the pay for them is enhanced by the trust reposed in the laborers on the ground of something acquired by them for other than selling purposes, and which indeed *cannot be sold*; and superior *character* also, as well as superior knowledge, which is wholly *moral* in its basis and not mercantile at all, affects the Demand for the services of the possessor of it to increase it, on the ground of a naturally stronger trust in him as a professional laborer, and at the same time tends to increase his Wages by limiting the circle of those who can offer in competition such services on the background of such superior knowledge and character.

(b) Lawyers do not meet such a universal Demand in the nature of things as do physicians. Said Jonathan Smith of Lanesborough in the Massachusetts Convention of 1788: "We have no lawyer in our town, and we do well enough without." Still, one hundred years after that time there were about 70,000 lawyers in the United States, and Lanesborough itself had had in the meantime at least three distinguished ones. The interests of property and of reputation, and the constitutional rights of individuals as over against the claims of Government, so far as these may be conserved through the agency of lawyers, are by no means so constant and imperative as are the interests of life and health. Yet lawyers are in legitimate request in all civilized countries. A Latin legal maxim announces the obvious truth: *It is the interest of the Commonwealth that there should be an end of disputes and litigations.* Beyond question courts and counsel are wholesome on the whole for the individual and for the commonwealth. But the extremely complicated and unsatisfactory condition of American Law at present, owing to the fact that we have a none too simple United States Law with its three grades of courts and judges, and considerably divergent bodies of Law in each of 42 States, and owing also to the fact that our law in general is drawn almost at random from two pretty distinct Sources, the Common Law of England and the Civil Law of Rome, multiplies the number of lawyers relatively to the population out of all proportion to such ratio in other countries, and tends to make the lawyers as a class too conservative of old and drawn-out processes to the extent of opposing obvious betterments and simplifications. Said David Dudley Field, President of the American Bar Association, in August, 1889, at Chicago: "*So far as I am aware, there is no other country calling itself civilized where it takes so long to punish a criminal, and so many years to get a final decision between man and man. Truly we may say, that Justice passes through the land on leaden sandals. One of our most trustworthy journalists asserts that more murderers are hung by mobs every year than are executed in course of law. And yet we have, it is computed, nearly 70,000 lawyers in the country. The proportion of the legal element is, in France, 1:4762; in Germany, 1:6423; in the United States, 1:909. Now turn from the performers to the performance. It appears that the average length of a lawsuit varies very much in the different States; the greatest being about 6 years, and the least 1½. Very few States finish a litigation in this shorter period. Taking all these figures together, is it any wonder that a cynic should say that we American lawyers talk more and speed less than any other equal number of men known to history?"*

Mr. Field then repeated his well-known argument for Codification, ascribing the law's delays to the chaotic condition of the law, and maintaining that it is the first duty of a government to bring the laws to the knowledge of the People. *"You must, of course, be true to your clients and the courts, but you must also give speedy justice to your fellow-citizens, more speedy than you have yet given, and you must give them a chance to know their laws."*

Owing to the immense difficulties in the way of any one person mastering the various branches of the law in this country, it is falling more and more into specialties, and lawyers are devoting themselves to some one of its many branches, the main division line being between "Law" and "Equity" technically so-called; and whenever one becomes eminent along any line, his compensation is apt to be very large owing at once to a large Demand and to a small Supply at that point, while the average compensation of the lawyers as a whole class is meagre enough, because there are too many of them, and the people have become very suspicious of the law's meshes and delays.

(c) The grounds for the unabating Demand in Christian countries for religious teachers and preachers, let us rather say, for spiritual guides, lie deep down in the nature of man. If there be one proposition about men more incontestable than another, it may be this, that men are made in the image of God, and that there is among men in general an irrepressible striving to maintain and deepen this image. The touch between man and man and between man and God is such at this point, that men can help each other in this striving, and that they *feel* that they can help each other. This is the chief reason why some men are constantly consecrating themselves to the Christian ministry, and other men as constantly soliciting these to become their pastors and teachers. Those more enlightened in divine things and more spiritually minded offer themselves, as it were, not commercially but morally, to the unenlightened and less advanced as guides and helpers. It is, as it was with Wolfe and his men at the Heights of Abraham: those who got first to the top tarried a little to help those up who came after. And the most striking thing about it is, that the masses of men at bottom are as desirous to be uplifted as the choicer spirits among them are desirous to help the work forward. Ministers are still, and always will be (human nature is unchangeable), eagerly called; chapels and churches and cathedrals are still going up all over the earth; worship and petition and aspiration are ever ascending on the great world's altar stairs towards

heaven, guided and inflamed by the chosen and choosing men of God,—
"*when priests on grand cathedral altars praise!*"

It is a monstrous perversion of language to maintain, that a clergyman in rendering such services as these is selling his religion. It is true, that he is selling under Demand services to the appropriate rendering of which his own personal piety contributes one large element, and thorough confidence in him on the part of his people as a good and earnest man contributes another large element; but the piety and the spiritual power and the worthy example are not nourished for the sake of selling the services, but for their own sake in personal worth and worthiness, and these things must not be confounded with the services that are sold. Accordingly, while the clergyman's vocation is sacred, and belongs to the sphere of religion, his salary belongs to the sphere of exchange, and its determination, in harmony of course with the higher impulses, is a business transaction. This distinction ought to be better understood than it is; and both clergymen and people need to be reminded that the spiritual things belong to one sphere, and the temporal things to another. The amount of a minister's salary, and the time and mode of its payment, are matters of pure business; and the minister himself is to be blamed if he does not attend to them, and insist on them, on business principles.

In the professions generally, and particularly in the ministerial profession, while, if we confine our attention to those persons who both have the requisite gifts of Nature and have been also thoroughly trained, we shall find a high rate of compensation on the two grounds of a strong Demand and a limited Supply, we must bear in mind too the counter-working influences which tend to increase the competition and thus decrease the compensation, namely, the respectability which attends them, the desire of knowledge for its own sake which is gained in connection with them, the instruction wholly or in part gratuitously offered to those in course of preparation for them, and the desire to do good without regard to pecuniary reward which actuates many who enter upon them.

(d) Physicians and lawyers and clergymen serve primarily individuals, or at most relatively small groups of individuals, and of course look for their pay to those whom they have served. It is different with Statesmen, the fourth class of professional laborers that we need to look at in an economic view. Statesmen worthy of the name serve at least a whole nation, and to the nation as such must they turn for their pecuniary rewards. And such men have never turned in vain to those whom they have benefited as a whole. Bismarck is the best modern instance of a Statesman, who has received from a grateful country immense money-measured remunerations for immense political services rendered. The Demand for the services of Statesmen rests in the deep consciousness of men organized politically into a Nation, that they need, especially in trying times, a Man of the highest natural gifts, and of the broadest attainments and of the loftiest political integrity to plan and act for them in emergencies, as they are conscious that they cannot plan and act for themselves organically. This does not mean, that the one ever knows essentials better than the many: he does not. This does not mean, that the true objective of a nation's march is ever discerned more clearly, or rather *felt after* more eagerly, by one man than by the many men concerned: it is not. Still less does it mean "*a man on horseback.*" But it does mean this: a Nation (as the very name implies) is made up of the thoughts and hopes and throbbings and dim forecastings and half-formed purposes of multitudes constituting a unit (born together for one destiny on earth); and the true Statesman is one of themselves, sharing with them at once the traditions of the past and the perspectives of the future; one, with the instinct and the intellect to gather up and embody the general feeling and the general will; one, who has gained in some way the confidence of the masses who are willing for the time being to entrust to him the guidance of their affairs, and to empower him to plan and act for them as their champion and deliverer; and one, who (because he *is* one) can better seize the propitious moments for declaration and negotiation and public action, yet who never forgets that he is nothing but an *agent* for others, and is as ready to lay down responsibility at the public will as to assume it at the public will.

Washington was such a statesman, and Lincoln. Even Bismarck, under monarchical and later imperial environment, disclaims anything substantive and original in his own action: he did what he could not help doing: he followed the instincts of Prussia, and his own; and became the means of fulfilling as they gradually ripened the longings of the other German people for unity and order. Such a statesman was Chatham in England, and Cavour in Italy. Now, such services as these, done for a whole people, always deserve and usually receive, though not expressly bargained for beforehand, yet implied in the public devotion of one party and the general *consensus* of the other, extraordinary honors and emoluments. This is right, even on purely Economic principles. The services of great statesmen to their country in great epochs and emergencies are at once a gift and a sale, they are both patriotic and economic, there is equally a national Demand for them and a grateful recognition of them, the Supply is always exceedingly rare and the reward often exceedingly great; and it is to be put down to the lasting credit of the science of Economics, that its peculiar motives and results may mingle in and harmonize with the motives and results of the higher moral impulses, such as those of Patriotism and Religion, as in the cases of the Soldier and Statesman and Clergyman. There was no rational ground for the hesitation of Garibaldi to receive from the Parliament of Italy in 1875 an annual pension of 50,000 lire.

(e) There is a single class more of Professional laborers, loosely so-named, which should be noted before we dismiss the subject of Demand for laborers to pass to consider the Supply of them, namely, Literators and Artists and Actors of the highest rank. Statesmen primarily serve the individual nation that selects and rewards them, though their influence may indirectly uplift other nations also; but the great Writers and Painters and Actors, whatever may be their local habitation and name at first, soon come to belong to the world at large and to derive their revenue from many lands, because the highest Art is cosmopolitan in its own nature, and the best characterization of men as such cannot but be the property of Mankind. Shakspeare is no longer English, nor Angelo Italian, nor Mozart German, nor even Bernhardt French. Deep as are the scars and the sea that separate nation from nation, there is something deeper still in the innate recognition by man of man as depicted by the great Masters in immortal lines. There is, accordingly, a sort of Demand in the inmost soul of Humanity as such for these living and lofty touches and delineations of itself, whencesoever they may come. There is not indeed nor can there be, as in most other cases of sale, a bargain made beforehand between these preordained sellers of the rarest services and their silent yet waiting purchasers, yet there is after all an antecedent and an assured understanding between them. They are in touch even across the sea. The master strikes his chord, and the audience, fit, though few and scattered, listens and applauds *and makes return.*

Is the principle of "International Copyright," so-called, correct? Let us look narrowly before we pronounce. At present this good country of ours makes itself a mocking and a by-word even to its own intelligent and art-loving citizens by putting a tariff-tax of 30% on paintings and statuary by foreign artists, not at all to get revenue thereby, but to "protect" domestic artists in their inferior work by artificially lifting the price of their wares. So far is carried this jealousy of foreign works of art, that when the artists generously loan them for exhibition on our national occasions, they are put under bonds *not to sell them on this side* without previously paying the tariff-tax, which is graciously intermitted during the Exposition. This is Restriction. This is Protectionism pure and simple. This is legally excluding the Better in order to give a forced currency to the Worse. Now, domestic Copyright restricts the sale of any book to one publisher in his interest and in that of the author. The book now in the reader's hand is thus copyrighted. This legal arrangement between authors and publishers and their public may be perhaps logically defended, it may even be for the public weal on the whole, though in many cases it doubtless raises the price of good books, which would have been published without any such artificial encouragement. The copyright, however, like all patent-rights also, soon expires by limitation of time, and the public thereafter have the unrestricted use of what is really their own.

For what is sometimes called "literary property" is not property in the strict sense of the word. A book is not like a plough or a house. Its contents even when most original have been but colored, as it were, and rearranged and reinforced by the author's individual mind. Its substance always comes out of the common stock. It cannot be the author's own, as the bushel of wheat is the farmer's, who sowed the seed on his own land and threshed it in his own barn and carried it to market in his own wagon. The rights of the individual and the rights of the Community commingle more or less in private property of every kind, at least to the extent that the latter may tax the property if needful for the common wellbeing, as it is bound also legally to secure it to the owner when threatened by others; it is no part of the purpose of the present book to draw the wavering line in general between the rights of individuals and the rights of their Government as towards them; but the distinction between common property and copyrighted property is plain enough to everybody, and the Law puts emphasis on the distinction by making the one quickly terminable and the other continual. So then, when the Government under which the author resides, has given him a limited copyright within its own jurisdiction, it would seem as if the individual right in the premises had been sufficiently recognized alongside of the undoubted right of the Whole to the ultimate use of the labors of their own citizen.

When, however, it comes to International Copyright, which is an attempt to secure to authors of one country artificial privileges under restriction in selling their wares in all other countries, the argument breaks down. Even for the one country, in which the author lives and is taxable, the argument is not very strong, and hardly binds advanced public opinion either as to the grounds of it or even the practical benefits of it on the whole. By the attempted extension of it to all countries, its reasonableness disappears. Taxation cannot extend beyond the jurisdiction of the country taxing; and it certainly seems as if a legal privilege, beyond common law privileges, ought not by extension through the formal action of other countries to exempt from taxation (in case it were needful) the results of the original privilege. The purpose of International Copyright is not the blessed one as announced to the world by James Smithson, "*the increase and diffusion of knowledge among mankind*," but directly and artificially by means of legal restrictions the "increase" of the prices of books and of other "knowledge" to the masses of "mankind," and the "diffusion" of these extra prices as between authors and publishers. Protectionism does not seem to be one whit more respectable in this form than in the form of tariff-taxes on foreign works of art.

2. We have already seen in our first chapter the proofs of the proposition, that the Value of anything whatsoever bought and sold is determined by the Demand for it and the Supply of it then and there present. Also we have now seen at considerable length the main phases and grounds of the Demand for each of the three classes of Personal services bought and sold among men. The next topic in order is the Supply of personal services in the various markets. Here it will not be necessary to distinguish particularly the three classes of Services, inasmuch as the circumstances governing the Supply in each are substantially similar.

In Economics generally we have to deal chiefly with Persons, and only subordinately with Things; when we come to the Supply of personal services, answering to the Demand for them on the part of other persons, this point becomes conspicuous; and it is here, if anywhere, within the realm of our science, that we need to devote a word to a singular doctrine, that has been famous for nearly a century under the term of *Malthusianism*. Thomas Robert Malthus, 1766-1836, was an English clergyman and teacher, a wide traveller and keen observer of men, one who divided his time during a long life between cure and chair and the libraries of the Universities, published in 1798 his "*Essay on the Principles of Population as it affects the Future Improvement of Society*"; in this and in subsequent editions enlarged and enriched, he brought out with its proofs the core of his startling pronouncement, that the human race is found to increase in numbers in something like geometrical progression, while the means of subsistence for them on any given area of agriculture can only increase in something like arithmetical proportion; the United States was then doubling its population in 25 years, and he calculated that, at this rate, the inhabitants of any country in five centuries would increase to above a million times their present number, which would give England in that time more than twenty million millions of people, or more than could even get standing-room there; for this natural tendency of the law of human fecundity to outstrip the results of the law of returns from land, he saw no remedy except in checks to population, which he divided into *the positive* and *the preventive*, the first of which, such as war and famine and disease, increase the annual number of deaths; and the second of which, such as prudence in contracting marriage and temperance after marriage, diminish the number of births; and Malthus and his followers, among whom the famous Thomas Chalmers was prominent, were at great pains to inculcate upon the laboring classes the duty of later marriages and fewer children, as an indispensable condition of their rise in comforts, and of "the future improvement of Society."

These discussions have attracted great attention almost to the present day, and have been supposed to be very pertinent to the subject of wages, and thus to be an important part of Political Economy; but when one looks more closely, the force of that spring of population which the Creator has coiled up in the nature of man, as contrasted with the weakness of that power by which the earth brings forth sustenance for man, is seen to be a topic in Physiology and not in Political Economy at all. Political Economy presupposes the existence of Persons able and willing to make exchanges with each other, before it even begins its inquiries and generalizations. How they come into existence, the rate of their natural increase, and the ratio of this increase to the increase of food, however interesting as physiological questions, have clearly nothing to do with our Science. Each adult human being is as much constituted by Nature to receive personal services as to render them, in Economics each without exception receives when and because he renders, and all alike are naturally able to become capitalists also; economical laws present no obstacles, that we can see, to all men becoming *rich*, as we use that term; the town or city in which many people are growing rich simultaneously, is the best place in the world for other people to go to get rich in, and not at all towns in which other people are getting poorer; most men are unwilling, some perhaps may be unable, to fulfil the moral conditions of growing rich; while, we may depend upon it, the famines of the world have been caused more by the indolence and want of foresight of individuals, and especially by the monstrous maladministrations of Governments, than by any law of the increase of population.

Experience too has shown, that the strong impulse in mankind towards procreation is not too strong for the purpose intended by the Creator; that HE who is the author of the impulses is author also of natural counterworkings of them; that, as men under moral and religious training come more and more under the influence of reason and affection, the preventive checks to population come silently and effectually into operation; and that, taking the world at large, food and comforts have more than kept pace with the stride of population, since its inhabitants as a whole were plainly never so well fed and clothed and housed as now. The abstract antagonism of the law of the increase of population with the law of the increase of food, or what we prefer to call the law of diminishing returns from Land, may be admitted, if one chooses to insist on it; but any practical *tendency* of these to come into collision, as the world is and is to be, is confidently denied. When Malthus wrote, and long afterwards, England was under the dominance of Protectionism; the wretched Corn-laws forbidding the importations of foreign grain, in order that the domestic growers might sell to their countrymen at artificial prices, and thus grow the richer as bread became the dearer, were only repealed in 1846; and the demonstrated ability of Great Britain under free trade to draw on the fertility of the whole world for the steadily and increasingly cheap maintenance of her people, demonstrates the irrelevancy of Malthusianism to the Science of Economics.

The Supply of personal services at any time or place in answer to the Demand for them, is affected by several important circumstances, which we shall now proceed to consider in their order.

(a) The *agreeableness* or disagreeableness of rendering a given set of services will affect the Supply of laborers at that point, and help to determine the rate of Wages paid to them; because the more agreeable employment will attract the larger number of laborers, will experience in consequence the press of competition, and the rate of wages then and there will be lessened thereby. The more disagreeable employment will feel less the pressure of numbers, and will secure, other things being equal, a higher rate of remuneration in consequence. Among the elements which, in spite of diversity of tastes, make any employment agreeable or disagreeable to the laborers, are (1) the less or greater exertion of physical strength required, (2) the healthfulness or unhealthfulness of the service, (3) its cleanliness or dirtiness, (4) the degree of liberty or confinement in it, (5) the safety or hazard of the employment, (6) the esteem or disrepute of it in public opinion. To illustrate each of these in order, the stone-mason, the glass-blower, the scavenger, the factory operative, the worker in a powder-mill, the smuggler, will each receive a larger compensation owing to the peculiar element of disagreeableness involved in his own personal service; and he will be able to demand and secure the higher rate through the action of this disagreeableness upon the Supply of such laborers. Of all these elements, public opinion is perhaps the most operative; and if this be favorable to an employment, and some social consideration be attached to it, and only common qualifications be required for it, the wages in it will infallibly be low. This is doubtless the main reason why so many young women prefer to teach, rather than be employed in mills or shops or offices, and why the wages of female teachers have been so remarkably low; although each of the elements of agreeableness specified above may also contribute something towards the same result. If a business be decidedly opposed to public opinion, it must hold out the inducement of a large reward, or nobody will engage in it. This explains the abnormal gains of the slave-trade, the liquor-business, of gambling-houses, and of lotteries.

(b) The *easiness* or difficulty of learning to render acceptably a given set of personal services, will have a quick and constant influence on the Supply of these services, and of course also on the rate of the return paid for them. The elements of this Difficulty in general are time, expense, lack of natural gifts, want of foresight on the part of those concerned, and lack of push and persistency on the part of the learner himself. To put a boy apprentice to a trade, for example, requires on the part of the parents a foresight, an ability to get on without his immediate help, and sometimes also an amount of money for his board and clothes which all parents do not possess; many boys too, who must acquire their skill to sell personal services when they are young, if at all, find on trial that they do not like the trade, or have not the requisite gifts, or fail in the appropriate patience and propulsion; and the consequence is, that the Supply of laborers along that particular line is lessened, and the right to demand and the ability to secure a higher rate of wages than is accorded to common laborers accompany the small supply, through the reduction of numbers which these obstacles at the entrance occasion and the consequent weakness of competition. This is one principal ground of the difference in the wages of skilled and unskilled laborers; the other being, as we have seen, the stronger and more constant Demand for the former, owing to the impulse imparted by Capital. All these points of difficulty at the outset apply still more strongly in the case of professional laborers, serving more effectually to thin out the ranks of these, and pushing upward still higher the gauge of compensation for the successful competitors.

(c) The *constancy* or inconstancy of prospective employment in a given business, is a consideration that affects the Supply within it, and then the wages. If the services be of such a character, that they can only be carried on during nine months of the year, the wages of the renderers will be greater by the day or the month than they would be, provided the services were in order during all the twelve months. The laborer is apt to look at the aggregate earnings of the year, and will hardly take up a trade which affords employment but a part of the time, unless some compensation can be found in the higher wages for that time. This is the chief reason why the wages of the mason and house-painter, in this climate at least, are higher than those of the blacksmith and carpenter. The coachman, also, may stand by his horses half the day or night with no call for his services, and must have, therefore, a proportionably higher fare from those whom he does transport. In general, it is found that men prefer a constant rendering with a lower rate of pay, than an inconstant one with a prospect of larger wages for the particular jobs actually done; and because the many prefer that, those who take up with the other are able to secure a higher relative rate of pay in their less eligible vocation. It must be noticed, however, as counterworking this, that some men have desire for intervals of leisure in their business, and for opportunity to make these intervals subservient to some avocation or other means of livelihood.

(d) The *probability of success* or the opposite in any line of personal services, is a circumstance that has some influence on the rate of wages paid in it, through the action of this probability on the numbers of those who enter upon it. If ultimate success be doubtful, fewer persons will naturally engage in such a business, and those who dare in it and succeed, will probably reap a very high reward. So, also, those who take jobs by the contract, and therein assume more or less of risk, are commonly paid at a higher rate for their services than those who do similar work by the day. It is true, that this is owing partly to the fact that the contractor usually puts in his own capital more or less, and must therefore be paid profits as well as wages, and also that the wages of superintendence are due to him in addition to ordinary wages; still, there is a residuum of difference, which can only be accounted for by the risk he runs of a successful issue of his contract. The general variation in Supply and wages from this fourth cause, would certainly be greater than it is, were it not for the overweening confidence which men in all generations seem to have in their own good luck. This excess of worldly faith is always seen in the rush which is made for newly discovered mining regions. It was seen to perfection in 1889 in the uncontrollable advance of thousands *into*, and their almost immediate exit *out of*, the then just opened territory of Oklahoma. The facility with which lottery tickets are sold even yet in many countries proves the prevalence of this over-confidence. It is demonstrable beforehand on the doctrine of Chances, that no person can rationally buy *any* lottery ticket at its advertised price, because if that person should buy all the tickets advertised he would certainly lose money, since the sum of the prizes is always less than the sum of the prices. Otherwise the projectors of the lottery would always lose money.

(e) The *mobility* or immobility of laborers as a class acts powerfully upon the Supply of them at any one time and place, and consequently upon the rates of wages then and there. In some countries, notably in the United States, laborers as a class move from place to place with considerable facility under the action of Demand for personal services. According to the Census of 1870, 7,500,000 of the native population dwelt in other States than those in which they were born. Many of these, doubtless, had left their native region to obtain more fertile land, and many also to obtain more remunerative employment as laborers. The native American, more than most other persons, is not only willing to move from place to place in the hope of bettering his condition, but is also willing to change his occupation from time to time in the same hope. There is more freedom of movement locally, and less fixedness of occupation on the part of laborers and others, in this country than in any other industrial country. Even foreign immigrants here,—factory operatives, miners, and other laborers,—seem to catch after a while the spirit of the country in both these respects. There is one considerable advantage in all this, namely, competition becomes more uniform in all places, an unusual demand for laborers at any one point is easily met, and wages neither rise so high nor fall so low at special points as they otherwise would. But there are considerable disadvantages in all this too, chiefly these, the services of laborers floating locally or changing the kind of their labor can never become so excellent as service more *steady* in place and time; and, especially, thorough apprenticeships, or whatever may be equivalent to these, are held in too little esteem by public opinion, and are too little requisite in order to obtain transient employment. To meet the obvious pressure of these disadvantages, an admirable device is now being hit on, namely, to introduce into our public schools something in the way of "manual training" for the various trades. Public institutions also, some of them on a great scale, as the Cooper Union in New York and a more recent munificent foundation in Philadelphia, have been established on purpose to train boys and girls both in eye and hand to render skilfully those artisan services of the various kinds which will always be in demand among men, and which have certainly deteriorated among us owing in part to the disuse of the old apprenticeship-system.

In Europe, on the other hand, the laborers as a class are far less mobile than here; and in Asia still less so. There is said to be no country in Europe in which the proportion of foreigners to the native population exceeds *three per centum*. In England, which is a small country, the difference in Wages between the northern and southern counties is very remarkable. Professor Fawcett is authority for the statement, that an ordinary agricultural laborer in Yorkshire during the winter months earns 13 shillings a week, while a Wiltshire or Dorsetshire laborer doing similar work during the same number of hours earns but 9 shillings. The contrast in general between the Wages of English agricultural laborers and those paid in mills and mines and furnaces is still more striking. And so more or less, in respect to the Value of Commodities: competition is yet by no means perfect in distributing these so as to make their price uniform in the same country or even in the same county; but the immobility of laborers for an obvious reason is much greater than the immobility of goods. While laborers should certainly be free to go wherever their services may be in greater Demand, the natural reluctance of most men to leave their native haunts, enables each of the nations to work out its freely chosen ends without wholesale interference from abroad. If China should precipitate itself upon the United States, or India upon England, as the mere *economical* impulse might indicate, it would be disastrous to the western nations; but men are everywhere under other influences besides the economical one, although this is strong and distinct and pervasive; Political Economy deals with men as they *are* all things considered, and with Buying and Selling as this actually takes place over the world, or rather as it would take place if factitious economical restraints were removed; and Providence has other great ends in view besides commercial prosperity, vital as that is to all other progress, and often holds one impulse in check by a stronger one.

(f) *Custom*, with its cognates Prejudice and Fashion, has still a good deal to do with the Supply of laborers in certain departments of effort, and of course with the rates of wages in them. In former times in this country and in the older countries particularly, Custom and decree were dominant in determining, for example, the current fees of lawyers and doctors, competition coming in to decide how many such fees a professional laborer should get, rather than the amount of each particular fee. The shares of the produce going respectively to the agricultural tenant and to the landowner, were specially under the dominion of Custom; as the mode (now decadent) of taking farms "*at the halves*," once universally prevalent in New England, sufficiently shows. In certain other matters relating to land and trade, Custom has long been gradually hardening into express law, as, for instance, the famous "Ulster Right" in Ireland. Prejudice, which is only another name for Custom, has some voice still in adjusting rates of wages, as may be seen in women's wages crowded down apparently to a point unreasonably low as compared with the wages of men; and also in the rate of John Chinaman's wages in those parts of the United States where he ventures to offer his services in the teeth of public opinion and hostile legislation. It may be spoken with general truth and satisfaction, that competition seems now to be breaking down mere custom and prejudice in all directions, and may perhaps in the good time coming reign supreme over the economic field; while Fashion, which bears indeed on one side of its shield the motto "custom," carries too on the other the bold word "competition," and this second side is likely to be presented to the public mostly in the future, because, they who lead the styles in any department whatsoever will always offer their services to Society at an advantage to themselves, that being one form of competition, and their rate of compensation will be legitimately higher than the average rate of their fellows, of which a good instance was the marked worldly prosperity during the decade of the Eighties of Worth, the man-dressmaker of Paris.

(g) *Legal Restrictions* are another cause acting on wages, by acting directly on the Supply of laborers. Laws inhibiting or promoting immigration; laws appointing the fees and salaries of officials; tariff-taxes, whether prohibitory or only restrictive; laws creating privileged classes of any kind, which is only another designation for laws restricting the rights of the masses; unequal modes of taxation, whether adopted in ignorance or by design; all have a direct and powerful agency upon the distribution of laborers, upon the supply of them at given points, and upon the rates of their wages. Governments are coming, however, much more freely than formerly, but never through their natural choice and drift as governments, only by the gradual and oft-disappointed compulsion of their citizens, to leave all these matters Economical except the wages of their own servants and those commodities which they choose to tax, to the simple and safe action of Supply and Demand.

(h) *Voluntary Associations* for that avowed purpose were a mediæval, and have come to be again a modern, agency in adjusting the Supply of laborers to their respective markets, and in regulating the wages of various classes of them. The Guilds of the Middle Ages, and particularly the old guilds of London, had a remarkable history, upon which we can not here even touch. Their local importance is sufficiently attested by the fact, that the City Hall of London is to this day the "Guildhall." King Edward III. humored the civic feeling of his time by becoming himself a member of the Guild of Armorers. "A seven years' apprenticeship formed the necessary prelude to full membership of any trade-guild. Their regulations were of the minutest character; the quality and value of work was rigidly prescribed, the hours of toil fixed from daybreak to curfew, and strict provision made against competition in labor. At each meeting of these guilds their members gathered round the Craft-box, which contained the rules of their Society, and stood with bared heads as it was opened. The warden and a quorum of guild-brothers formed a court which enforced the ordinances of the guild, inspected all work done by its members, confiscated unlawful tools or unworthy goods; and disobedience to their orders was punished by fines, or in the last resort by expulsion, which involved the loss of right to trade. A common fund was raised by contributions among the members, which not only provided for the trade objects of the guild, but sufficed to found chantries and masses, and set up painted windows in the church of their patron saint. Even at the present day the arms of the craft-guild may often be seen blazoned in cathedrals, side by side with those of prelates and kings."

The Trades-Unions and Brotherhoods of the present day cannot plead the provocations and justifications of their mediæval predecessors. It cannot be denied, however, that they have some provocations and justifications in the bad example set before them by the various combinations (implied or explicit) of the Wages-payers as a class. If the Wages-payers combine, then the Wages-takers would seem to have no resource but in combination. Both alike are wrong in this. Both alike oppose in this the spirit of Political Economy, which is ever the spirit of Freedom, and is ever against such factitious associations for such purposes, because they tend to destroy the independence of personal action on the part of both payers and takers of wages, and tend also to bring all the workmen of any one general grade down to one level of effort and reward.

(i) Lastly, we must note the influence of *Casual Events* upon wages, as these events affect the Supply of laborers. For example, in 1348, a terrible plague, called the Black Death, invaded England and swept away more than one-half of its population. "Even when the first burst of panic was over, the sudden rise of wages consequent on the enormous diminution in the supply of free labor, though accompanied by a corresponding rise in the price of food, rudely disturbed the course of industrial employments; harvests rotted on the ground, and fields were left untilled, not merely from scarcity of hands, but from the strife which now for the first time revealed itself between Capital and Labor" (Green). The landowners of the country districts, and the craftsmen of the towns, not understanding the law of Wages as an invariable resultant of the Demand and Supply of laborers, were scandalized by what seemed to them the extravagant demands of the new labor-class. Parliament equally ignorant with the People of the natural economic law, enacted as follows: "*Every man or woman of whatsoever condition, free or bond, able in body, and within the age of threescore years, and not having of his own whereof he may live, nor land of his own about the tillage of which he may occupy himself, and not serving any other, shall be bound to serve the employer who shall require him to do so, and shall take only the wages which were accustomed to be taken in the neighborhood where he is bound to serve two years before the plague began.*" Afterwards, the runaway laborer was ordered by Parliamentary enactment to be branded in the forehead by a hot iron, and the harboring of the country serfs in the towns, in which under their civic rules a serf keeping himself a year and a day was thereafter free, was rigorously forbidden. These acts of Parliament, and many more of the same kind, were powerless to keep down wages to the old standard, but were powerful to keep up ill-blood and social discontent. They prepared the way for agitators like John Ball, for the poet-agitator Piers Ploughman, and for the great Peasant Revolt of 1381. John Ball's famous rhyme condensed the scorn for the nobles, the longing for just rule, and the resentment at oppression, of the peasants of that time and of all times:—

"When Adam delved and Eve span,Who was then the gentleman?"

A hundred years after the Black Death the wages of a common English laborer—we have the highest authority for the statement—commanded twice the amount of the necessaries of life which could have been obtained for the wages paid under Edward III.

3. Having now seen fully the varied action of Supply and Demand upon the Value of personal services in their three kinds, we come at length to the most important general point in this chapter, namely, that in the second class of Services, those purchased in connection with the use of *Capital,* WAGES ARE ALL THE TIME ENLARGING RELATIVELY TO PROFITS. We have seen clearly already, that Cost of Labor and Cost of Capital are the only onerous elements in the cost of Commodities; because, while Natural Agents are all the time assisting and assisting more and more effectively in

such production, they work without weariness or decay and without fee or reward. The reward of laborers is Wages, and the reward of capitalists is Profits; and we are now to demonstrate, that the part of their joint products falling to laborers as wages is all the while increasing as compared with the remaining part falling to capitalists as profits. This truth is of the deepest significance, and of the most cheering character; because men are more important in the universe than things; and because the number of men who sell their services as laborers is vastly greater than the number of men who sell their services as capitalists.

It is another indisputable and exhilarating truth for the masses of mankind, that the Value of each item or article of those products created by the joint action of laborers and capitalists is ever becoming less and less as measured by any relatively fixed standard as Money; so that, while wages as thus measured becomes a larger and larger aggregate as compared with the aggregate of profits, and is shared of course by a much larger number of people, those commodities looked at as a collection of items for which the wages of these many is usually expended for their own comforts, are becoming all the time cheaper and cheaper to everybody, owing to the ever-enlarging and wholly gratuitous action of natural forces.

For the sake of simplicity in the argument on this great point, we will first look at what the facts are through recent illustrations gathered by other parties for a wholly different purpose, and then give in detail the economical grounds for these patent and universal facts. Take for example, from Poor's Railroad Manual for 1889 a table showing in a graphic way the steady reduction in freight charges per ton per mile from 1865 to 1888 of seven representative Eastern trunk railroad lines, namely, the Pennsylvania, Fort Wayne and Chicago, New York Central, Michigan Central, Lake Shore, Boston and Albany, and Lake Erie and Western; and of six leading Western roads, namely, the Illinois Central, St. Paul, Burlington and Quincy, Chicago and Northwestern, Rock Island, and Chicago and Alton. The following are the figures:—

RATE CHARGES PER TON PER MILE (IN CENTS).

Year.	Eastern.	Western.	Year.	Eastern.	Western.
1865	2.900	3.642	1877	.971	1.664
1866	2.503	3.459	1878	.898	1.476
1867	2.305	3.175	1879	.764	1.279
1868	2.132	3.151	1880	.869	1.389

1869	1.860	3.026	1881	.763	1.405
1870	1.593	2.423	1882	.756	1.364
1871	1.478	2.509	1883	.829	1.310
1872	1.504	2.324	1884	.740	1.220
1873	1.476	2.188	1885	.636	1.158
1874	1.332	2.160	1886	.711	1.111
1875	1.161	1.979	1887	.718	1.014
1876	.985	1.877	1888	.609	.934

This reduction of rates in the case of the group of Eastern roads has amounted to 79 *per centum*, and in the Western group to 73 *per centum*, in the twenty-four years. Not less remarkable than the extent of this decline in freight charges per mile is its uniformity. Both groups show a wonderful steadiness in the progress of rate reductions. Starting at quite different points as to territorial development, they have yet travelled at a nearly equal pace in the same direction. This shows the operation of causes at once steady and universal. Statistics can never of themselves yield us *causes*; but they guide the way to them; at any rate, they prevent any radical misinterpretation of them. The great and overshadowing cause here of the cheaper freights per ton, as everywhere else of cheaper rates at the junction of efforts by capitalists and laborers, is of course the perpetual and augmenting and ever-gratuitous assistance of natural forces at every point.

While the rates of freight per ton have decreased more than three-quarters in less than one-quarter of a century in the case of these 13 railroads on the whole average, the entire cost of the operation of these roads in this interval of time has not been diminished to any appreciable extent, as also stated by the same Manual. The main item in all the operation-expenses of railroads is the wages paid to the laborers of all grades; and the laborers are quite as well paid now on these 13 roads as they were in 1865, proper allowances being made for the changed and changing standards in the national Money. If, on a broad view, railroad employees of all grades have lost nothing as such in their wages in this interval; and the general public, including these laborers and also the capitalists concerned, have greatly gained, how can we account for the immensely lessened freight-charges while the whole operation-expenses continue substantially as before?

There is only one rational account to be given of this. And it is trustworthy. All known facts jump with it, and nothing substantial can be urged against it. The gains to the masses including the capitalists and the laborers *have come out of the capitalists as such*. This is apparent as well as real. Cost of Labor and Cost of Capital is the whole cost. If the whole cost of moving one ton of freight from Boston to Chicago is ¾ less than it was ¼ of a century ago, the cost of the labor being the same at the two points of time, then the conclusion is inevitable, that the *cost of the capital* at the second point is less than it was at the first point. With this conclusion all facts agree. All the laborers connected with a railroad from highest to lowest must be paid at any rate, or else the trains will certainly cease to move, whether the stockholders receive any dividend or not on their capital invested. The original *stock*—the capital that built the roads—of many if not of most the railroads in the country, has been annihilated, a new indebtedness in another form called *bonds* having taken the place of it. Even the nominal dividends of dividend-paying roads have declined in the interval from 10 or 8 to 5 or 4 *per centum* in the general, that is, 50 *per centum*. It is perfectly evident on every hand, that there is something in the nature and progress of things, that makes for wages as contrasted with profits: wages hold on and relatively enlarge, profits decline or go out altogether.

Fortunately we are not left to generalities here, however plain and certain these may be. One of the 13 railroads specified above, the Illinois Central, made a remarkable exhibit in its own annual Report of 1887, showing the cost of its locomotive service for each year of the thirty years preceding. This cost per mile run had fallen from 26.52 cents in 1857 to 13.93 cents in 1886. This reduction had been effected wholly on the *Capital* side of the account, by inventions and improvements of all sorts in the *machinery* of locomotion; while the wages of the engineers and firemen had risen in the period from 4.51 cents to 5.52 cents per mile run. The cost of the labor had risen both relatively and absolutely while the cost of the capital had declined both absolutely and relatively. In 1857 the engineers and firemen had received as wages 17% of the entire cost of the locomotive service, but in 1886 they had received 39% of that total cost. The table is as follows: —

I. C. R. R. CO.

PERFORMANCE OF LOCOMOTIVES. RELATION OF WAGES TO TOTAL COST PER MILE RUN.

Years.	Cost of wages of engineers and firemen per mile run.	Total cost per mile run.	Years.	Cost of wages of engineers and firemen per mile run.	Total cost per mile run.

		Cents.	Cents.				Cents.	Cents.
1857		4.51	26.22	1872			5.77	21.76
1858		3.97	19.81	1873			5.84	21.10
1859	Gold.	3.81	20.78	1874			6.02	19.57
1860		3.96	20.17	1875	Currency.		6.03	19.57
1861		3.84	18.92	1876			5.79	18.81
1862		3.85	17.42	1877			5.54	17.21
1863		3.93	22.28	1878			5.46	15.29
1864		5.56	33.52	1879			5.41	14.15
1865		5.65	37.44	1880			5.41	14.95
1866		5.78	32.67	1881			5.54	16.58
1867	Currency.	6.18	29.62	1882			5.09	15.82
1868		6.11	27.57	1883	Gold.		5.35	15.57
1869		5.88	25.49	1884			5.28	14.45
1870		5.95	25.15	1885			5.49	15.02
1871		5.72	21.50	1886			5.52	13.93

In 1857 the engineers and firemen received 17 $^{201}/_{1000}$ per cent. of total cost.
In 1865 the engineers and firemen received 15 $^{91}/_{1000}$ per cent. of total cost.
In 1867 the engineers and firemen received 20 $^{865}/_{1000}$ per cent. of total cost.
In 1886 the engineers and firemen received 39 $^{627}/_{1000}$ per cent. of total cost.

These illustrations from the railroads are plainly indicative of a general truth of the utmost importance in Political Economy, namely, *that all increase of Capital and all inventions and improvements in its practical application, while it redounds to the benefit of capitalists as a class, redounds in a still higher degree to the benefit of laborers as a class.* Let us now attend for a moment to the convincing Proof of this truth in two phases of such proof, and also to a cheering conclusion that follows it.

(a) As any country grows older in time and richer through abstinence, and as the whole world thus grows older and richer, the tendency there and everywhere towards a general decline in the rate *per centum* for the use of capital becomes patent and universal. The rate of interest on money loaned, and the rate of profits on capital used, tend all the while to go down as and because capital accumulates. No one will dispute this as a simple fact of history. And no economist will dispute, that this is just what we might expect beforehand as a corollary from the admitted proposition, that, other things being equal, an increased Supply of anything means a lessened Value for any specific part of it. Three centuries ago in England the legal rate of interest was 10%, while now the current rate is about 4% in that country, and has been considerably lower than that in Holland, although in both countries and everywhere else there are temporary interruptions and reactions in the constant tendency now being considered. During the first years of mining operations in California, from 8% to 15% per month with security of real estate was paid for the use of money, which enormous rates long ago declined to rates not much higher than those paid in the States along the Mississippi River, and in these also the rates are all the while approximating those current in the older Eastern States, whose own rates too are slowly declining. But, while there is a less rate of profit or interest on each 100 invested, there are many more hundreds capitalized; consequently, there is an absolute gain to capitalists as a class, at once in the aggregate amount of the capital and in the aggregate sum of the profits from it, since no capitalist would have a motive to capitalize further under the smaller rates of profit, unless the aggregate of profits under the new conditions were greater than under the old condition of higher rates; and, as much of this accumulating capital in order to become productive must now be offered to laborers in the form of wages, we might almost pronounce beforehand, that it would prove both an absolute and also a *relative* gain to laborers as a class. And so it is.

(b) Let us take to figures. An hypothesis or supposed case, whenever it may easily become an overt fact, may be reasoned from just as logically and securely as the overt fact itself. Let $100,000,000, while the rate of profit is 6%, and $500,000,000, when the rate has fallen to 4%, be expended in payment of simple wages. So far forth as that one element of cost goes, the value of the products to be divided yearly between capitalists and laborers will become respectively $106,000,000 and $520,000,000. In the first case, $6,000,000 is profits and $100,000,000 is wages; in the second case,

$20,000,000 is profits and $500,000,000 is wages. Here is an absolute gain to the capitalists, since profits have gone up from $6,000,000 to $20,000,000, and so are more than *three* times as great as before. But wages have gone up both absolutely and relatively to the rise of profits. They have risen from $100,000,000 to $500,000,000, and are *five* times as great as before. Profits have risen as in the ratio 1:3+, but wages in the ratio of 1:5. This arithmetical example is put for the sake of illustration merely, but the principle of it holds good in every case, in which the rate *per centum* goes down in consequence of the increase of capital in business; and, therefore, the advantages of ever-enlarging Capital are even greater to laborers as a class than to the capitalists themselves. Most assuredly, if the capitalists take less out of each hundred of the swelling hundreds now than before, the laborers must take more out of each hundred than before. Profits and Wages are reciprocally the *leavings* of each other, because the aggregate products created by the joint agency of Capitalist and Laborer are wholly to be divided between the two. There can be no other *claimant* even.

(c) This demonstration is extremely important in Political Economy, and consequently in Social Life; for it proves beyond the possibility of a cavil, the Value of personal services tends constantly to rise, not only as compared with the Value of the material commodities which by the aid of capital they help to create (a truth we have seen before), but also as compared with the Value of the use of its co-partner capital itself; and therefore, that there is inwrought into the very substance of things in this world a tendency towards an equality of economical condition among men. God has ordered it, and men cannot radically alter it. Self-interest is indeed the mainspring of movement in the economic world; but the beauty of it and the wonder of it is, that no man can labor intelligently and productively under the influence of self-interest without at the same time benefiting the masses of men. His fair exchanges benefit the parties of the other part as much as they benefit himself. His very savings productively employed are poor men's livings. Only under the blessed freedom of universal Buying and Selling, subject only to the taxation of a good Government for public purposes purely, can these broad benefits designed by a wise Providence be fully realized in action; and the power of individual greed and corporate privilege and governmental perversion to thwart the beneficent though complicated workings of these laws of Capital and Labor towards the common weal and universal progress of mankind is shortlived and soon punished.

4. How comes it about, then, if these laws of mutual inter-dependence between capitalists and laborers are so well-placed and Providentially balanced, that there always have been and are still so many misunderstandings and ill-feelings and actual collisions between employers

and skilled laborers, whose interests are at bottom one and whose relations ought to be so cordial? This is the last topic in our Chapter on Personal Services. Here we must look around narrowly and tread carefully. But there is a path. We can find it if we will. It leads through many short-comings in men's characters and through much ignorance of plain economical truths and past unreasoning jealousies and aggregated action on the part of both classes, and over the needful distinctions between impulsive selfishness and a true self-interest back to the same old laws of God laid down at once in the constitution of things and in the constitution of men.

Labor-troubles are almost as old as Civilization. The Greek poet Euripides in his play of the "Supplicants" both indicates facts as they were then, and points out a future hope in which we may share, that these middle classes by a better harmony preordained and mutually beneficial may yet "save the State":—

"In each StateAre marked three classes: of the public goodThe rich are listless, all their thoughts to moreAspiring; they that struggle with their wants,Short of the means of life, are clamorous, rude,To envy much addicted, 'gainst the richAiming their bitter shafts, and led awayBy the false glosses of their wily leaders.'Twixt these extremes there are who save the State,Guardians of order, and their country's laws."

At Rome and in the Roman Empire, instead of the usual voluntary union of capitalists and laborers for the mutual advantage of each other, the laborer was owned by the capitalist, and the true relations between the two were thoroughly disguised and wretchedly distorted. Business in all its branches came to be carried on by means of slaves; the lands were tilled by slaves; slaves became the artisans of the country; the money-lenders and bankers of the centre scattered branch-banks in the towns under the direction of their slaves and freedmen; the Company that leased on speculation the Customs-Taxes from the State had their slaves and freedmen levy these taxes at each custom-house; the contractor for buildings bought architect-slaves; and the merchant imported his goods in ships of his own manned by his slaves or freedmen, and then sold the same at wholesale or retail by the same means. In this way a gigantic system of unnatural traffic was built up and extended. In this way the very name "laborer" became tainted by the vile system of slavery of which he was a part, and the distinction itself between capitalist and laborer was obliterated. "Roman mercantile transactions fully kept pace with the contemporary development of political power, and were no less grand of their kind." "The Roman *denarius* followed up closely the Roman legions." "It is very possible that, compared with the suffering of the Roman slaves, the sum of all negro suffering is but a drop" (Mommsen).

We want now to examine critically the CAUSES of these constantly recurring labor-troubles, the true economical REMEDIES for them, and in connection with these the futility of the remedies popularly recommended for low Wages and the disputes between employers and employed of the second class.

(1) There is an extremely common misapprehension on the part of both labor-givers and labor-takers as to the real *nature* of the transaction between them. Both parties forget, or rather neither party is ever fully instructed, that it is a case of pure Buying and Selling. There is never any *obligation* of the moral sort between buyers and sellers. The relation itself is purely economical. Moral considerations indeed cover this relation from above, just as they cover all other relations between man and man in human Society; and any two individuals standing over against one another as buyer and seller, also stand over against each other in higher and broader relations as man and man; but it works confusion and mischief as between both, whenever relations differing in their nature and operation and reward are not separated from each other in the mind of each relator, and whenever each does not act in the particular relation according to the nature and rules of that relation alone. When A hires B to work in his factory, this new relation is economical not moral; there were moral relations between the two before this relation was knit, and will be again after this has been broken, and indeed are while this continues; but the economical relation is one thing, and the others a very different thing; they are so different, that they cannot be blended in mind or motive to any advantage to either individual or to either set of relations; and any degree of confusion as between the relations has always wrought mischief as between the individuals, because instead of seeing either set of relations in its own clear light, they now see both in a commingled twilight.

What is the economical relation? This. A desires the personal service of B in his factory purely for his pecuniary benefit, and assumes his own ability to make all the calculations requisite for determining how much he can (profitably to himself) offer B for his service; and B, who knows all about his own skill, how it was acquired and how much it has cost, wants to sell his service to A for the sake of the pecuniary return or wages. There is no obligation resting upon either. Man to man, each in his own right. There is no benevolence in the heart of either, so far as this matter goes. Benevolence is now an impertinence. It is a question of honest gain in broad daylight. Benevolence is blessed in its own sphere, but there is no call for it here and now. If it comes in an unbidden guest, it comes in to mar and to distort. It is an incongruity. "*I never knew a Jew converted but it spoilt him,*" was the word of one deeply versed in human nature and in Christian experience. Conversion is good, and its field is broad; but the Jew *as such* is incongruous with it. Good is benevolence and wide its field, but Buying and Selling does not need it. Its own motives are independent of it, and sufficient without it.

A clouded understanding of this vital distinction has always played its part in Labor-troubles. Buyers and Sellers of personal services are always on a plane of perfect equality as such exchangers, and no one can be more independent than either of them except the hermit in his cell. Which must look out for the interest of the other beyond the terms implied in the trade itself? Which is the superior party? Which should take off his hat, the other remaining covered? The truth is, and all experience and all analysis brings us up abreast of it, that the two parties to a trade of any kind stand on a footing of absolute equality towards each other then and there in the economical relation about to be knit, and any conception in the mind of either that he has the other "at his mercy" in either the good or bad sense of that phrase, disturbs and destroys the proper conditions and balances of the exchange in hand; and, what is more to the point, it implies that each party has *not* all he can do to fulfil in the letter and in the spirit what is always implied in the terms of a trade deliberately entered upon by two parties. When B agrees to work for A at skilled labor in his factory for a year at $15 per week, he makes a good deal of a contract; and virtually pledges to A not only the motions of his hands for that period of time, but also the vigorous attention of his mind to that service and to the general interests of his employer so far as these come under his own eye and supervision. Nor is this all: he virtually pledges himself to B to coöperate with the least possible friction in all plans for betterment in his division of the work, and to cordially coalesce with all other employees for the general ends of the business without too much of self-assertion and without too little of courtesy to others. To fulfil this contract in all its spirit rounds up the circle of B's economical obligations to A. He will practically have all he can do, so far as A is concerned, and in consistency with all his various duties to others, to make good to him at all points his simple business pledges. Benevolence, the interests of a common citizenship, and the reciprocal ties of religion, lie wholly outside.

A will practically have all he can do, so far as B is concerned, to fulfil in the letter and in the spirit his economical obligations to him, without troubling himself to see whether B is going to vote the same party ticket that he himself votes, and without confounding either B's poverty or prosperity with his own obligation to be polite to him at all times and to pay him promptly his weekly stipend. So long as B renders in letter and in spirit what he has agreed to render, and A returns in the same way what he has promised to return, the less either thinks and talks and acts about the other in all the other relations of life, the better hope of good success to both in this relation. Church relations and social relations and political relations are all of consequence in themselves; but when any of these begin to get mixed up with labor-relations, there is soon a muss and a mess. Incongruous things, things no way vitally connected with that, often come in to disturb and destroy a simple matter of mutual renderings.

(a) The first practical remedy for difficulties arising under this first head, is a clearer separation in the mind of both parties to a trade of what really belongs to Buying and Selling from what belongs to all other departments of activity. More common sense is needed at this point, more simple analysis, more daylight, more personal independence, more introspection as to motives, more power in making distinctions, and a more practical separation of what is clear and fixed from what is complex and obscure in human relations. Metaphysics may yet lie in cloud-land, Ethics may not yet have drawn its outer and interior lines so strong and deep as it will, Sociology also is a vast field of complexities, but truth to tell Economics has no mysteries to speak of. I buy and sell for my own advantage, which proves in the nature of things to be for the equal advantage of my compeer. It is my business and my compeer's business and every other man's business who buys and sells, to pick that action out in its motive and result from the great mass of dubious actions, and to set it up in its own light, to rejoice in it as the clearest thing in social action, to claim it as God's own plan so far forth for our comfort and progress, and then to see to it that no preposterous hand mixes it up with perplexities or theologies or other abominations—muddying with a tentative pole the stream of our clear brook! In this country at least, in its ignorance of common things and common science, the pulpit often fulminates against the gains of exchange as "materialism," and mixes up buying and selling with "worldliness," and only half permits its deluded hearers the privileges of the market, and illustrates again in modern times such teaching as is denounced to St. Timothy,—"*some swerving turned aside to vain babbling, desiring to be teachers of the Law, understanding neither what they say, nor whereof they affirm.*" "Let every shoemaker stick to his last." Those who have looked into it with any care have found, that Exchange in all its natural outgoings is not answerable to these pulpit charges, nor is contrary to the letter or spirit of the biblical precepts, but on the other hand is in full harmony with the claims of Conscience and with all the inbreathings and aspirations of Christianity.

(b) The second practical remedy for the labor-difficulties arising from the want of thorough understanding by both parties of the real nature of hired renderings of the second class, is fair *common honesty*. More of an easily accessible intelligence, more of penetration and separation as to social relations in general, meets the first point; but quite as needful as this simple intellectual process, is the still simpler moral habit of doing just what one has agreed to do, without evasions and without diminutions. Labor difficulties take their origin more often, perhaps, in some clouded moral action of one of the parties, than in a clouded mental apprehension. Men are too conscious as men of their own temptations, to be lax in their pledged renderings and of their own shortcomings at this point, not to be suspicious of each other as buyers and sellers, for fear the party of the other part is about to withdraw something either in quantity or quality of what he has promised to render; there is almost always something or other to give color to such a suspicion, and it grows by what it feeds on; frank explanations are not had at the outset, and a good understanding is not come to, as it doubtless might be in nine cases out of ten; and the little cloud, at first no bigger than a man's hand, by and by becomes black and threatening, and bursts at last in a strike or lock-out of large proportions. An open honesty that is such and seems such, that is not beyond the aim and reach of common men, that is taught in scores of forms in "Poor Richard's Almanack," and that each man ever likes to meet with and so ought ever to put forth, is in fact a preventive of conflicts between laborers and employers, and would if properly manifested have prevented multitudes of such actual conflicts. Here is the main, almost the sole, point of contact between strict Ethics and the Economics. What buyers and sellers, that is to say, the whole practical world, needs, is not disquisitions on Morals from Press or Pulpit, but an inner ear to hear the true click of Conscience, and the quick and open answer in honest action.

(2) A second general cause of the Labor-troubles of the past and present has been a strong tendency to neglect the special *preparation* for their peculiar functions by both capitalists and laborers. A successful employer of laborers year in and year out to their advantage and his own is always one who has been *trained* to that function by special preparations. He is a living man with all the limitations of living men: he has to deal with many living men with all their imperfections: he has to deal also, and constantly, with what is in its own nature dead, namely, Capital, always either a commodity or a claim: to animate and invigorate these dead forms of value, to put them into vital connection with living men who shall enhance their value, and thus to become a leader to living men as towards swelling interests, demands unusual native gifts and a special long-continued training. When one looks from without upon such an establishment as this in full action, it seems automatic, it seems as if almost anybody with a clear head could continue to direct it; and when this "captain of industry" departs this life, perhaps his son or some previous subordinate, without the proper gifts and at least without the peculiar training, assumes the post of direction. For a little everything seems to go on as before. As sure as fate, however, a friction will soon develop here, and a misunderstanding there, there will be whisperings among the men, some breath of suspicion will be

likely to cloud the borrowing-power, opening difficulties of any kind such as loss of credit or a weakening of the usual markets are apt to throw a new operator more or less off his base, and gathering labor-troubles of any sort commonly find such a man unprepared for lack of suitable training and experience to ward them off or to make timely concessions to the men or to minimize the evil results when these become inevitable.

Also labor-troubles are quite as likely to arise from the want of character and training and considerateness of the employees towards the capitalists. The relations are reciprocal and they are also in their very nature delicate. One poor workman however good his disposition, one unfaithful overseer no matter how great his possible skill, may mar the current product in such a way as to lose it the market and cost the establishment the present profit. The strength of a chain is the strength of its weakest link. It is a matter of immense difficulty at any time, and emphatically so at the present time to organize a working force in factory from top to bottom so as to have it go forward as a unit as towards the marketing of the product, without bad workmanship at some point and unskilful supervision at another; because the laborers as a rule have not given themselves time to learn thoroughly their special parts, because they are not content to remain steady at one thing and at one place, and because they do not practically recognize even if they perceive it that their own permanent interests are exactly coincident with the permanent interests of their employers. Just now in this country the public Law robs the manufacturers (at their own behest) of their best markets at home and abroad, makes it difficult or impossible for them through wanton taxation of their raw materials to create a good quality of goods for any market, and so multiplies frictions and failures and losses along the whole line of production. The lack of what may be called Apprenticeship on the part of skilled laborers, the consequent difficulty of rising from one gradation of effort to a higher and better-paid one, the restlessness of native laborers under such disabilities, the rapid admixture of foreigners, the lack of coherence throughout in point of intelligence and apparent identity of interests, together with the instability and haphazardness of the resources and personal training of the employers as a class, gives birth to Labor-troubles which are at the same time Capital-troubles, to read the daily record of which makes one sick at heart.

(a) The only possible and practicable remedy for this state of things, so far as the employers are concerned, is in a more conservative attitude of capitalists as a class about passing over their resources to the hands of men who have not proven their ability to handle them wisely by a full course of training in the management of practical affairs. By a wretched policy in this country at present Capital is prohibited from building and from buying ships, with which to navigate the oceans; from selling domestic manufactures in foreign markets; and also from a profitable agriculture, which may sell its products abroad and take its pay back. Consequently Capital, eager in its own nature to be invested to a profit somehow somewhere, has rushed without due circumspection into the hands of domestic operators, who have not been half fitted for their task, who have knitted relations with laborers without being able to secure their permanent respect or to control their services, and who have lost to their owners in multitudes of cases the entire capital intrusted to them. If capitalists had had during the last quarter of a century one-half of their natural and proper chance to invest their money to a profit, there would not have been such a reckless investment through incompetent hands in building mills and foundries in this interval of time, and such wholesale losses in connection with them. When capital comes to be at liberty to turn right or left according to its own will in view of a prospective profit, factory companies and projectors cannot draw resources from the public for their operations, without demonstrating to the owners the trained and tried capacity of the practical operators, who will buy the materials and hire the laborers and market the products.

(b) The practical remedy for the inexperience and instability and unskilfulness of laborers as tending towards labor-troubles of all kinds and degrees, is only to be found in a want of market for such services. In a natural and wholesome state of things, such as would exist in the United States were it not for national laws tampering with Trade and with Money, the questions asked an applicant for skilled work by any labor-taker would be, "*What have you learned to do? How long and for what pay do you want to do it? What do you want to reach next, when the present job is done?*" When employment turns on good answers to such questions as these, and when the questions themselves are put in good faith, there will be an end of Strikes and Lockouts. Untrained and restless hands will get nothing to do in mills and factories. Apprenticeship in its various forms will come back into vogue, and will probably be made a part of the course in public schools. The division and gradation of laborers will be carried out further than it ever yet has been. Laborers will then be *organized* in the best sense of that word, and to the best advantage of capitalists. The permanent Supply of skilled laborers will be constantly adjusting itself to a permanent and increasing Demand for them. And it requires no millennium for such a state of things to come in. It requires nothing but an ordinary and enlightened and beneficent selfishness on the part of capitalists to adjust itself to the ordinary selfishness of laborers sure to become enlightened and beneficent to the best and ever-growing interests of both parties. This is not the spoken word of Morality, still less is it the divine word of Religion, it is only the common programme of a common-sense Political Economy.

(3) The third and last general cause of misunderstandings and embittered disputes as between laborers and capitalists is partly economical and partly moral, and consequently the remedy for it is partly moral and partly economical. The Past projects itself down into the Present partly with blessings and partly with curses. In the old times under Slavery and Feudalism the laborer always came forward to his task with a taint upon him. Sometimes the taint attached to his birth, and at all times it attached to his calling. Slavery in all its forms always makes manual labor degrading. The courtly Cicero *apologizes* in a letter to his friend for his open sorrow over the death of his favorite slave; and in several passages of his treatise on Morals he follows his Greek teachers, Plato and Aristotle, and declaims in a pitiful way against the noble rights of laborers. "*All artisans are engaged in a degrading profession.*" Again, "*there can be nothing ingenuous in a workshop.*" When trade and commerce are carried on on a small scale, "*they are to be regarded as disgraceful*"; when on a large scale, "*they must not be greatly condemned—non admodum vituperanda!*" (I, 42.)

Serfdom once existed in England, and threw its shade over free laborers there long after itself had disappeared. A class of indented servants pervaded all the New England Colonies, and a clause of the New England Confederation of 1643 provided for their forced rendition from Colony to Colony, and passed over almost verbally into the Constitution of the United States of 1787 as applicable to the slaves of the South. In this way in all parts of this country manual laborers came to be more or less off color, and this has continued in a continually lessened degree till this time. When those who work with their hands are looked down upon by those who do not, two sets of feelings are apt to be engendered equally unfortunate to the two classes that entertain them. The non-manual workers, the employers, are more or less puffed up with pride and a sense of superiority (there are beautiful exceptions) as towards their laborers, and the latter in their turn are apt to develop alongside an unmanly servility and an apparent deference, a sort of secret breasting up of hostility and defiance, which is sure to manifest itself when labor troubles come on even when it has not helped to brood these troubles into life. The parties then are not well placed as towards each other to negotiate and to compromise and to coalesce in a future harmony. The party of the first part is too proud to yield to their inferiors, and the party of the second part is too bitter to be sweetened. Who is sufficient for these things? And what is the remedy for them?

(a) So far as employers are concerned, their natural though unreasonable and provoking arrogance may well be reduced by the economical reflection, that the laborers are exactly as necessary to production as the capitalists are, that the two stand on a precise level so far as the product goes, that each is one blade of the shears and the other the other and that it takes both blades to cut anything, that while the laborers are sellers in the open market the capitalists are likewise sellers and that the same ultimate purchaser furnishes the market for both sets of sellers, that as sellers they are only equal in position, that buying and selling is a levelling as well as an uplifting process the world over, and that as such co-equal partners in one indivisible operation all haughtiness on one side and all undue humility on the other is nothing but obstacle as towards the common end; and also by the moral and social reflection, that their laborers are just such men as themselves in motive and action, that the two are very likely to exchange places with each other before very long, that riches are extremely liable to take to themselves wings and fly away, that Christianity is no respecter of persons, that humanity deems nothing human alien from itself, that morality puts the golden rule upon the fore-front of its precepts, and that whatever may unite any body of men in a legitimate purpose of achievement along any line of human action multiplies the power of each individual and exalts his standing and responsibility as such individual and thus reduplicates the reward of his individual action.

(b) So far as the employees are concerned, in any temporary sense of dependence or even of injustice, there is open to them the economical reflection (and it will do them good to bring it home) that their best route to the respect and favor and feeling of equality of their employers is through the excellence of the service they render them and the courtesy (not servility) with which they render it, that as every capitalist becomes such by means of abstinence they may themselves by saving become capitalists, that there is nothing in the nature of their work or its relations to capital to cause them to hang down their heads, that handsome is that handsome does, that the opportune offer of the present capital to work on gives them a chance to exhibit their skill and to earn a living, that the capitalists are just as dependent on them as they upon those, and that as single sellers of a valuable personal service they daily confront on a footing of equality the sellers of a valuable product so created; and there is open to them also the moral and social reflection fortified by constant observation and experience, that no matter where a man begins it is the end that crowns his work, that life to all is a series of stepping-stones, that manly qualities are appreciated everywhere, that character tells in the lowest position however high and low are reckoned, that the poor gain and hold friends quite as well as the rich, that there was a certain poor wise man that saved the city by his wisdom and gained a lasting record in consequence, that the poor and the rich are constantly changing places in this world, and that there is no respect of persons with God.

We may see now what we are to think of some popular remedies constantly recommended for low Wages. A brief discussion of what is false will give us a stronger hold of what is true. The chapter will close with relevant reference to three current remedies.

1. It is being dinned into the ears of the present generation, that Government has large functions in the ongoings of business, that it ought sometimes to interfere to better the rate of Wages, at least to designate a minimum below which they shall not go, and that Government should hold itself ready to undertake directly to carry on certain branches of business under certain circumstances. This scheme goes under the high-sounding name of *Nationalism*. Richard T. Ely, Professor of Political Economy in Johns Hopkins University, is one of the most prominent representatives at present of this school of thought. In his Introduction to Political Economy just published (1889), he lays down this principle: "*When for any class of business it becomes necessary to abandon the principle of freedom in the establishment of enterprises, this business should be entirely turned over to Government, either local, state, or federal, according to the nature of the undertaking.*" He begins his book by attempting to hammer in the "lesson" that as Civilization improves, coöperation takes the place of individualism. The golden age of individualism, he says, is among the wild tribes of Australia. They never coöperate with each other in their economic efforts, or in anything else. No one expects anything from his neighbor, and every one does unto others as he thinks they would do to him. The life there is one prolonged scene of selfishness and fear. But as civilization comes in, he says, individualism goes out, and coöperation takes its place. The fine old Bentham principle of *laissez faire*, which most English thinkers for a century past have regarded as established forever in the nature of man and in God's plans of providence and government, is gently tossed by Dr. Ely into the wilds of Australian barbarism.

There are some propositions that are *certainly* true, and one of them is, that no man can write like that, who ever analyzed into their elements either Economics or Politics, who ever gained a clear conception of the sphere of either science in its relation to the other, or who ever saw distinctly the relations of either to the nature of Man. The sole motive in Buying and Selling is the gain of the individual, each for and by himself. That always was the motive, is now, and always will be. No complications of modern business, no complexities of credit, no combinations of capitalists or laborers, ever altered or ever can alter one particle the motives of men in buying and selling. In a natural and progressive state of things, Individualism, instead of going out, comes more and more into play, through the Division of Labor and the falling of all sorts of services more and more into specialties. To talk glibly, as Professor Ely does, about

Government taking up easily and carrying on in a better way and to better ends branches of pure business as they are dropped or forced from the hands of Individuals, is ignorance at once and alike of the real nature of Government and of Business. Let us look at a few of the native incongruities and logical fallacies of this nationalistic position.

(1) What is human Government? Is there anything substantive and continuous in its *personnel* and purposes, as there is in the government of God? Is government anything more, can it be anything more, than a transient Committee of the citizens charged and changed to do in certain few particulars the changing will of a Majority? Government is indeed a necessity, as men are, to restrain the lawless, and to shape the ends of the law-abiding; but it has to be administered, if at all, by precisely the same kind of men as the rest are, chosen for brief periods, their duties sharply prescribed by constitution or custom, and impeachments or other punishments provided for them when they transgress. One President of the United States and one Judge of its Supreme Court have already been solemnly impeached by the sovereign people themselves.

Government, then, is an *Agent*, and nothing more. Even nationalists will not contend for the divine right of kings. And the duties of every decent government on earth are *political* in their character. The agents are chosen and dismissed with a direct reference to that kind of action. Politics has a sphere wholly distinct from Economics. The true and only end of politics is the greatest good of the greatest number, so far as that end can be mediated by governmental agents of the people. Individualism as such does indeed sink out of sight under a true Politics, and the inalienable rights of one are maintained for the sake of and in consistency with the greater rights of all. But Economics is all individuals from beginning to end. "*It takes two to make a bargain.*" Only two. Each of the two has his own motive, estimates for himself, gives and takes for himself, and enjoys alone his own gain. All this is involved in the very idea of *Property*, which is derived from *proprius*, and which means *one's own*. How illogical, then, and incongruous, to suppose, that a set of limited human agents briefly trained to purely *political* action, and liable to be turned out of office by every change in party administration, can be competent at the same time and in addition to perform *economical* functions for the people!

Notice, too, that governmental agents in all good countries are already *overburdened* with their mere political duties. Work is behindhand in every portfolio, on every court calendar, and in every legislative body, in Christendom. How absurd it is, therefore, to talk about throwing upon shoulders, already overburdened, additional loads of a different kind, for which shoulders and heads are wholly unfitted!

Why not, then, inquires our nationalist innovator, organize new bureaus to undertake in their behalf the buying and selling of the people? Ah! Who pays the taxes needful for the support of the present *political* bureaus? And who would have to pay the taxes needful for the support of the new *economical* bureaus? Besides not having any substantive existence of its own Government has not one cent of money, except what the people voluntarily pay in taxes out of their own personal gains, in order to maintain their own agents to do certain political things for them, which they cannot do as well for themselves directly; and when it comes to the cold question for the people themselves to answer, whether they will organize a new set of hired men to do their trading for them, and pay them for doing this out of aggregate gains certainly to be vastly diminished by the process, our nationalistic leaders will perhaps find out that the people have common sense, whether the said leaders have it or not.

But the damning difficulty with this governmental business association is, after all, in the inevitable *lack of motive* on the part of the hired men doing the buying and selling. It is an honor to human nature, that hired men never have and never can have the zeal and enterprise of principals and owners to forecast and to perform and to lay up; because it shows that man is a rational animal, made in the image of his Maker, always acting under the pressure of personal motives, and always estimating what is his own more highly than what belongs to another. Business motives act in their fulness only on the individual, whose is the effort and whose is the return. Any policy whatever on the part of Government, which lessens the number and the eagerness of individual operators in favor of great artificial combinations resting in the shadow of the Law, lessens of necessity the gains of exchanges, and the progress of the nation, because it lessens of necessity the press of motive on the many to work and save.

Government, accordingly, is quite too far off in every respect from the business, that is to say, from the buying and selling of the people, to undertake any branch of it when "it becomes necessary to abandon the principle of freedom in the establishment of enterprises." It will then be high time to "abandon" the "enterprises" themselves. If the "principle of freedom" cannot compass the "establishment of enterprises," is it likely that the "principle" of secondary and irresponsible agents can do it? To show the people how to make their bargains, how to buy and sell and save and spend, is a function government is not fitted for, was not established to perform, and never undertook without making a botch of it.

In the Preamble of the Constitution of the United States there is a careful and complete and elegant enumeration of the purposes, which the body of the instrument was designed to attain. These purposes are six. No one of them contains even a hint of any purpose to enter upon the "establishment of enterprises," still less of any necessity "to abandon the principle of freedom." The last of these six purposes is phrased: "AND TO SECURE THE BLESSINGS OF LIBERTY TO OURSELVES AND OUR POSTERITY." The liberty to buy and sell freely was precisely that "liberty" of the Colonies which was most threatened and infringed by the British Government, to vindicate that special "liberty" was the chief cause of the American Revolution, and "to secure the blessings" of that and other forms of similar "liberty" was the final purpose of the Constitution of the United States.

It is true indeed that the Constitution empowers Congress, a creature of the People, "*to establish Post Offices and Post Roads*"; but the purpose of this was *political*, and not pecuniary; it was to bind all the States together in one Union of intelligence and intercourse; it was to keep the outlying and distant parts in touch with the central and seaboard; it is not in any sense a "business" enterprise; the department of the mails is not now and never has been, for any length of time, self-supporting; and it illustrates through and through in its "Star route frauds" and other contracts, in its appointment and removal of postmasters, and in the sickening dependence of primal Service of the people on partisan and corrupting impulses, many of them inherent evils of the much-vaunted Nationalism.

But besides all these vital and political objections to the assumption on the part of government of any direct industrial functions whatever, there remains two other fundamental objections, of which the first is, that our national government has received no powers to any such end, and is emphatically prohibited in the Constitution itself from exercising them:— "THE POWERS NOT DELEGATED TO THE UNITED STATES BY THE CONSTITUTION, NOR PROHIBITED BY IT TO THE STATES, ARE RESERVED TO THE STATES RESPECTIVELY OR TO THE PEOPLE."

(2) The second remaining objection is, that such proposed action of government could have no tendency at all either to enlarge the Wages-portion, or to increase the industrial efficiency of the laborers, or to diminish the number of competitors at any one point of the wages-scale. As a matter of fact, such governmental action would have precisely the opposite effect at each of these three vital points of wages: employers would have less motive to swell the wages-portion, laborers less motive to improve their capacity, and more motive to congregate locally. Suppose, that at some given point in the scale of wages, free and intelligent competition has been had on both sides, and that the average rate of wages as thus determined proves one dollar per day for each laborer. Suppose further, that everybody outside the employers thinks this is quite too little, and that government accordingly issues a decree that wages at that point must be thereafter one dollar and a half per day. That decree can have no tendency at all to enlarge the *wages-portion* of those particular employers,

because *that* has already been determined for the next industrial cycle by the general productiveness of the cycle last past, and by the last division under free competition between wages and profits; if, therefore, the decree were carried out, as it never practically could be, the result would be that only two-thirds of the laborers previously employed could be employed then at all, and the remaining third would certainly be worse off than before; and besides the Division of Labor being necessarily lessened, production would be less profitable to the employers, and the next wages-portion would certainly be less than the one before, and thus the outcome of the *remedy* would be worse than the *disease*. Now let alone the artificial interference of government, and all natural accessions to Capital at that point, all investment of profits in an enlarged business, all saving from expenditure for the sake of further production, tend strongly of their own accord to enlarge the wages-portion, and thus, the number and intelligence of the laborers continuing as before, are sure to raise the rate of wages. Or, if there be no accessions to Capital, or other influence swelling the wages-portion, and the number of laborers be diminished at that point, as by migration to new fields of effort or enlistment in armies, the competition of wages-givers for laborers will be quickened, and the rate of wages will rise. Reversed conditions will of course give reversed results.

2. A second popular remedy for low Wages, not only proposed, but also for a long time brought into practical action, is Labor-Unions in their various forms and with their manifold methods of operation upon employers. It is important to note here and to remember, that the Guilds of the mediæval times, from which the modern Trades-Unions have borrowed something of form and much of nomenclature, were in substance extremely different from their modern imitators. Those were combinations of Masters with their journeymen and apprentices and dependents in order to control the entire manufacture and sale of a certain class of products, from the name of which the Guild usually took its own name, as "Cloth-workers' guild," "Shoemakers' guild," and so on. Whittier, himself a shoemaker in his boyhood, apostrophizes the latter guild in words which more or less describe them all: —

"Ho! workers of the old time styledThe gentle Craft of Leather!Young brothers of the ancient guild,Stand forth once more together!Call out again your long array,In the olden merry manner!Once more on gay St. Crispin's day,Fling out your blazoned banner!"

These masters thus organized with their laborers were the capitalists of their time, and in this vital matter differed from the Unions of to-day, which are made up of laborers as such organized to confront, and if need be, to antagonize, capitalists. A royal charter was indispensable to the legal existence of those craftsmen. It took money for them to start their guilds, and in progress of time most of them became very rich. "A common fund was raised by contributions among the members, which not only provided for the trade objects of the guild; but sufficed to found chantries and masses, and set up painted windows in the church of their patron saint. Even at the present day the arms of the craft-guild may often be seen blazoned in cathedrals side by side with those of prelates and kings." This radical difference between the two must always be borne in mind in all arguments and inferences drawn over from the mediæval "unions" to those of the present day.

Two points may be freely conceded to these labor-organizations before we pass to the economic objections to them. In the first place, the employers *set the example* for the employees in a tacit if not open combination as against the employees in their own interest and emolument. The so-called "protective" tariff, for instance, is nothing in the world but a strongly-linked combination of certain rich capitalists to extort from the masses (their own laborers included) artificially lifted prices for the necessaries of life; and the certain result of shutting out imports by tariff-taxes is the shutting in of would-be exports, to the certain lowering of general wages in a country, because there is a lessened demand for laborers in consequence. For a second good instance of combinations as against employees on the part of employers, take the well-known understanding among manufacturers of the same sort of goods in the same general locality, that laborers discharged from one establishment shall not be hired in any of the rest; and that if the general voice call for a "shut down," or for three-fourths time or less, all in that line of goods shall comply. How can laborers be blamed for organizations in their own behalf when they find themselves confronted as individuals with an organization of employers?

Then, too, it must be acknowledged, that, had it not been for united action of some sort on the part of the laborers, the unreasonable hours of fifty years ago in mills and factories would probably not have been shortened to this day. Capitalists as a class are conservative of methods, as well as of ends. The cotton and woollen manufacturers of Berkshire County, for example, who may doubtless be taken as a fair sample of the manufacturers of New England, stiffly refused the demands of their work-people that the hours might be reduced from an average of 14 throughout the year to an average of 11. When the late Civil War was going on, and the manufacturing became extremely profitable, and the mills were more or less depleted by enlistment, and the remaining hands felt more independent from the consequent rise of wages, the combined demand in one mill for fewer hours was reinforced by simultaneous demands for the same in other mills in the neighborhood (the time and manner having been agreed upon beforehand), and visits in force by the work-people from mill to mill completed the desired reform. The mill-owners were sullen and indignant, and submitted of necessity. The work-men were right. The reform was imperative. Credit must be given to them for the good they have done acting as a body on this and other occasions.

On the other hand, all this is not *business*. All this is contrary to the very old, and the very good adage, that it takes *two* to make a bargain. If we express this adage in the language of our science, it will take some such form as this: When two men have mutual services to exchange, let them come to a fair agreement as to the terms on which they will exchange. Certainly, let each make the best terms he can, but let the bargain always be free. If one party, who happens to have the power to do it, uses anything like compulsion upon the other, it ceases so far forth to be a bargain at all, and becomes a sort of robbery, of which in some cases courts will take cognizance. Now, workmen bring a certain valuable service to the market, just such a service as the capitalist wants, and he has to offer just such a service as they want, namely, wages: let the two parties come to a free and fair agreement on the terms of their exchange; let each workman by all means make the very best terms he can, insisting to the last penny on all he can get elsewhere, for the value of his service is determined, as other values are determined, by what it will bring: let the employer do just the same on his side, and so let a fair bargain for the time present be struck. This is a very good kind of *striking*, and the more intelligence and skill and self-respect a workman has, the better prepared he is to strike the bargain and secure his just due by and for himself alone; and this gives a good chance for every man who has any peculiar gift, who may have surpassed his fellows in diligence and skill, to secure a proportionate reward now and to go on higher in future; all this gives opportunity for *diversity of relative advantage*, which, as we have seen, lies at the basis of all exchange, which itself starts in individualism and naturally proceeds in a still higher individualism to the end. This is the only way for a laborer of talent and diligence to secure fully what belongs to *him* as a man and a workman. If he cannot get from a given employer what he thinks he ought to get, what he thinks the service is worth in another market, let him exercise his perfect right to quit and go elsewhere. All this is fair and aboveboard and individual and progressive.

Everybody knows that there is a kind of *striking* now in vogue wholly different from this, in that it brings a sort of compulsion into play. *A fair bargain should be broken, if at all, just as it was made, with the two parties face to face, and everybody else aloof; and a new bargain should be made, just as the old one was, with the two parties face to face, and everybody else aloof.* But a combination among workmen to leave an employer in the lurch, and especially a combination which forces into its ranks by cajoling or menaces those who are unwilling to join it, as is so commonly the case in Strikes, is not only contrary to the inmost nature of a bargain, but is also of itself a sort of confession of the injustice of the claim. If the claim be just so far as *all* the individuals are concerned, there is no occasion to extort it. If the value of the service rendered by each be equal to the sum demanded, and especially if this can be obtained elsewhere, which is the only gauge of the value of any service anywhere, there is no need of conference and combination and conspiracy. Of course, this radical argument against Strikes implies that employers of that grade have not entered into a combination not to hire dissatisfied laborers from other establishments; if they have, then the agreement can be turned with equal force against the employers themselves, for *they* are resorting to means outside the nature of a bargain, means of the same nature as a Strike. Let, then, each workman tell his employer the present facts just as they are, and if this appeal prove ineffective to secure his commercial right, let him go quickly where he can get the most for his service. That this is not done, that means of the nature of a threat are brought to bear upon the employer, that the justice of the claim is not relied on in a case where more than anywhere else justice can enforce itself, that free and full explanations are not had, that no notice is given, that great damage is expected by their action to accrue to the employer,—all this seems to forget that the transaction between employers and employed is a case of pure exchange, a simple bargain of one service against another service.

The above is the universal and fundamental objection to Strikes. *The remedy for economical evils, real or supposed, must ever be found in economical considerations.* The strong but foolish tendency of the times is to mix up things that are quite distinct; to try to apply to the evils of Trade the rules of Morals, which is a useless task; to appeal to Politics in matters of pure Bargain; and to resort to Force to cure the evils that flow from the wholly voluntary action of individuals. This is like the doctor who would cure bodily ailments by mental and spiritual recipes. It has all the absurdities of the late famous "Mind-cure." The mind is indeed higher than the body, but bodily maladies must be treated as such, or the patient will die; the imperatives of Ethics are certainly superior to the profitables of Economics, but the latter are well able to take care of themselves on their own ground; Religion is loftier than Morals, but it becomes a very poor substitute for morals in the daily routine of life. *Similia similibus curantur.* Economical evils can only be removed by a better Economics better applied. Strikes are an outside and irrelevant remedy for low Wages.

A bad principle works badly in practice of course; the principle that underlies strikes is so opposed to the fundamental nature of exchange, that we might know beforehand that it would work badly; and as a matter of fact, it does work badly enough both upon employers and employed, because strikes are certain to embitter the relations between the two classes, which ought always to be cordial and free, and especially, because strikes must work on the minds of the capitalist to lessen the Wages-Portion for the next industrial cycle. Fortunately, we possess authentic statistics gathered about Strikes by the Massachusetts Bureau of Statistics of Labor, and published in detail in the Report of December, 1888. The information given is exact in relation to five principal States, and approximate in relation to the other parts of the United States. We will copy first the table exhibiting the Losses in six years on account of Strikes of both Employers and Employees, and the outside assistance received by the latter:—

EMPLOYEES' LOSS AND ASSISTANCE AND EMPLOYERS' LOSS IN THE FIVE PRINCIPAL STATES ON ACCOUNT OF STRIKES AND LOCK-OUTS FOR 1881-1886.

STATES.	Employees' Loss.	Employees' Assistance.	Employers' Loss.
Strikes.			
Illinois,	$6,636,208	$238,452	$5,251,829
Massachusetts,	4,200,489	266,708	1,970,881
New York,	8,581,784	726,696	5,966,421
Ohio,	6,378,757	415,568	2,793,427
Pennsylvania,	12,890,346	781,338	3,897,757
Other parts of the United States,	13,127,139	895,795	10,821,238
THE UNITED STATES,	$51,814,723	$3,324,557	$30,701,553

The large percentage of establishments represented in this table, in which the strikes were ordered by labor-organizations, is particularly noticeable. In New York 94.26% of the establishments had strikes which were ordered, in Illinois 83.96%, in Massachusetts 81.91%, and in the United States 82.24%. The "walking-delegate" so-called became the principal personage in all these strikes; he brought the orders to the men from the "central-union" of their special organization, and became in most cases the sole means of communication between the two. "*You are the strike,*" exclaimed the Lord Mayor of London the other day to Mr. Burns, the walking delegate of the dock-laborers now on strike in that city. That the daily bread and home comforts of tens of thousands of men depend on the secret and irresponsible decision of a little knot of agitators, sending out their verbal and often ambiguous written orders by a walking-delegate or two, is one of the monstrosities of Strikes often witnessed in the United States. The laborers sometimes do not know even the causes of the strike. There has been great want and suffering for three months past among the striking coal-miners in the State of Illinois; and a brief editorial in the "Springfield Republican" of Aug. 24, 1889, describes the state of things so justly, that we quote it:—

"Ex-Congressman William L. Scott, who owns coal mines at Spring Valley, Ill., has offered to pay 75 cents a ton for mining to the strikers who in their destitution have been subsisting for some time on public charity. This is $2\frac{1}{2}$ cents a ton more than the miners have asked for, but it is coupled with the condition that each man must seek work individually and not through some outside union committee. Although the men have been reduced to a state of abject want it is said the conditions imposed will prevent a settlement. In that case we may conclude that a few well-fed walking delegates are acting for the men and not they for themselves. It is a strange time to quibble over such a matter. The worst and most oppressive enemy of labor is the parasite who lives upon its distresses."

A strike is a state of war, and like war, there are two parties to it, and it cannot be expected that the party of the other part should not strike back. The "*lock-out*" is the counter-stroke of the capitalist to the "*strike*" of the laborer. Lock-outs, however, are comparatively infrequent. Capitalists, as a rule, are conservative and forbearing. Massachusetts took the statistics of lock-outs as carefully as those of strikes, and the following is the table:—

STATES.	Employees' Loss.	Employees' Assistance.	Employers' Loss.
Lock-outs.			
Illinois,	$533,497	$5,374	$347,065
Massachusetts,	952,310	136,626	550,675
New York,	3,150,123	392,316	845,262

Ohio,	848,829	231,870	493,100
Pennsylvania,	712,956	77,038	237,735
Other parts of the United States,	1,960,002	262,814	988,424
THE UNITED STATES,	$8,157,717	$1,106,038	$3,462,261

Like war too, strikes and lock-outs are wasteful and demoralizing to both parties. Why should there be a resort to force to settle an industrial dispute any more than to settle any other private dispute? Will such a resort be long tolerated by public opinion in civilized countries? The Legislature of Massachusetts in 1886 provided for a State Board of Arbitration for the settlement of differences between employers and employees. The statute was crude in some respects, and the basis of it not very firmly fixed in the nature of things, but the Bureau of Labor reports that it has been justified by the results in its practical application during the short time of its operation. The broad truth is, that the value of Commodities and the value of Credits is now left to the safe action of Demand and Supply under free competition in every country in Christendom: why should not the value of Services be left to the same safe and inexorable action? Governments gave up long ago all idea of regulating directly or indirectly the prices of merchandise and the prices of commercial claims of all kinds: will they not shortly give up also all idea of regulating directly or indirectly the rates of Wages? They will. The three kinds of things bought and sold are on an exact level in the nature of things, so far as Government is concerned. Wages are abundantly able to take care of themselves in the ordinary way, as goods do, and stocks and bonds; and an enlightened Public Opinion is fast coming to see, that a man's personal service rendered needs no more the oversight of the State in its sale than his horse, or note of hand at interest. Strikes, and lock-outs, and all extraordinary courts or boards to settle quarrels between a labor-giver and a labor-taker as such, since it is a case of ordinary buying and selling, are foredoomed to pass out in the good time coming.

Towards this good end works strongly the common *futility* of strikes and lock-outs. Carroll D. Wright, chief of the Bureau of Labor in Massachusetts, now the head of the National Bureau of Labor, in his State Report for 1880, gave a succinct account of all strikes in that State from their beginning in 1830. They were 159 in all, of which 109 were unsuccessful, 18 apparently successful, 16 compromised, 6 partly successful, and 10 "result unknown." In Great Britain during the year 1878, there occurred 277 strikes, of which 256 were failures, 17 were compromised, and only 4 were successful. The following table taken from the Massachusetts Report of 1888, gives on a broad scale the results of Strikes in the United States for six years:—

GENERAL SUMMARY OF STRIKES IN FIVE PRINCIPAL STATES FOR 1881-1886.

Percentages.

CLASSIFICATIONS.	Illinois.	Massachusetts.	New York.	Ohio.	Pennsylvania.	Other Parts of the United States.	THE UNITED STATES.
Strikes.							
Ordered by labor organizations,	83.96	81.91	94.26	71.21	61.59	73.06	82.24
Establishments closed,	70.70	79.10	51.01	81.21	70.11	57.57	60.13
Causes:							
Against reduction of wages,	5.35	6.23	2.50	20.73	22.65	8.61	7.77
For change of hour of beginning work,	-	-	3.86	-	-	0.05	1.61
For increase of wages,	41.54	35.28	39.09	52.42	46.97	45.01	42.32
For increase of wages and reduction of hours,	17.85	0.50	9.37	1.85	1.06	4.96	7.59
For reduction of hours,	18.35	42.71	24.31	5.32	5.32	17.23	19.48
For reduction of hours and against being compelled to board with employer,	-	-	7.32	-	-	2.19	3.59
Other causes,	16.91	15.28	13.55	19.68	24.00	21.95	17.64

Results:

Succeeded,	54.16		35.28	*51.05	49.44		32.60	42.69	*46.52
Succeeded partly,	10.33		45.93	*8.14	8.87		17.57	17.27	*13.47
Failed,	35.51		18.79	*40.65	41.69		49.83	40.04	*39.95

    * In 15 establishments the results were not ascertained.

3. The third popular remedy for low Wages, which has at least the merit of being in the line of economical considerations, as the other two are not, is "Co-operation." The interest in this proposed remedy is much less both in Europe and in the United States than formerly, owing to the failures that have mostly attended the attempts to put the scheme into practice, although there have been some remarkable successes also, particularly in England. The idea of Co-operation is this, namely, that certain laborers within given classes combine of their own accord, (1) *either to purchase their necessaries in common and at wholesale, hence at cheaper rates because avoiding all profits of the middlemen; or (2), more especially to engage in the joint production of the commodities they are familiar with, the laborers furnishing the capital also from their little hoards or borrowing it on the strength of their individual or associated credit, managing the business themselves, all being co-partners, and of course all sharing pro rata the entire profits of the concern.*

All this is well; and in countries where laborers have been under traditional disabilities, it may be in some cases very promotive of their self-respect, activity, frugality, and general welfare; but any one can see that no new economic principle is involved in the plan. As in all other production, so here, there must be (1) capital from some source, (2) steady and skilful labor, and (3) superintendence or management of the business. It is at the third point that schemes of co-operation have mostly broken down. The faculty of good management is rare; the organizing and executive ability needful to carry through any scheme of co-operation will not come upon call; if any of the co-operators chance to possess it, the scheme may succeed, although he who is conscious of having it will prefer to use it for his own gain in his own way, to say nothing of the practical impossibility of any man's working with the same spirit when the gain or loss is to be largely another's as when it is to be wholly his own; moreover, it has been well said, "it is impossible *to hire* commercial genius or the instincts of a skilful trader"; so that, while there is no trouble about the workmen uniting the character of capitalist and laborer in their own persons, and no doubt that they will work harder and more skilfully while sharing profits as well as receiving wages, it is still true, that the difficulty of securing a real "captain of industry," and thus a perfect organization and management of the whole business, puts the scheme of co-operation out of the question as a means of raising wages, or promoting the general welfare of laborers.

In this country, where there is nothing to hinder any laborer from becoming a capitalist, where the savings-banks are open to the smallest gains, where nothing is more common than for two or more workmen to organize a firm to carry on some branch of business, where most of the present capitalists proper were formerly laborers proper, and where the shares of most of the joint-stock companies are open to everybody who has the means to buy them, there is only one consideration that seems to justify any special jealousy of laborers as such towards capitalists as such; and that is the fact, that Legislation, every now and then, sometimes on a small scale and then on a gigantic one, now by means of corporate charters and then by other means more indirect and effective, *does confer certain extraordinary privileges upon capitalists.* So long as capitalists and laborers rest upon their natural rights and positions, neither can get any undue advantage of the other; and just so far as each recognizes their identity of economic interest and the consequent reciprocity of obligation and effort, the prosperity of each will help build up the other; but, on the other hand, so far forth as any advantages are given to capitalists by special laws, either of State or Nation, these become necessarily unjust to laborers, and ultimately also injurious to capitalists; and in this case, the laborers, seeing just what it is that hurts them, *ought to combine together and to strike, not capital (their best friend), but a piece of perverted legislation (their worst enemy).*

CHAPTER IV.
COMMERCIAL CREDITS.

Political Economy is the Science of Sales; and because it *is* the science of sales, its definitions and principles must cover equally all cases of sales actually occurring or possible to occur. We have seen repeatedly, that only three kinds of things are ever bought and sold, or ever will be, and these are Commodities and Services and Claims. The first two kinds have been fully elucidated already in the two preceding chapters, and it belongs to the present chapter to explain and illustrate clearly the peculiarities of the third kind of things salable. Ours is the only science that has to do with the motives and facts and economic results of all sales as such.

The discussions of the present chapter will proceed orderly through the following topics:—

- *The Nature of Credit.*

- *The Forms of Credit.*

- *The Advantages of Credit.*

- *The Disadvantages of Credit.*

1. Certain things are essential in every sale of anything, and of course are common to all sales of everything, such as two persons and two desires and two estimates and two renderings; while there are certain *peculiarities* in the sale of things belonging to each of the three special classes of things salable; for example, in the sale of a commodity there is a rendering of a tangible object that has been prepared for sale in past time, and in the sale of a service a rendering of an intangible something wholly in the present time; while in the sale of a credit there are likewise two peculiarities, one of them relating to future time and the other to a special trust felt in a person by some other person. We must now study these two peculiarities with care; and, mastering these, we shall be master of the Nature of Credit.

a. Some sales are consummated at once, the things exchanged and the ownership in them are mutually passed over then and there, the reciprocal satisfactions are entered upon immediately, and there is at once an economical end.

For example, one neighbor sells another a peck of green peas and takes in pay a peck of new potatoes, both vegetables may be cooked for dinner in the respective families the same day, and the commercial transaction is all over. But there are other exchanges, an immense class of them, different from these in this respect, that though the transaction considered as a mere case of value created and measured is then and there ended, yet considered as to the nature of that preliminary exchange which implies and requires another future exchange to consummate it, it is not then and there ultimately closed, but one (or both) of the parties then exchanging relies on the good faith of some one else to fulfil in the future a pledge expressly or impliedly made in the prior exchange. Commonly some external evidence of the pledge is created and passed at the time, but this is not essential to the validity of the pledge itself. For example, A buys 50 bushels of wheat of B, and B takes in pay for it A's note of hand at six months for $75. The note is not the pledge, but it is a legal and convenient proof of it. As a case in Value, the wheat is sold for the pledge and the pledge is the equivalent of the wheat. Each party rendered the other then and there satisfactory equivalents. All our definitions apply here perfectly.

Still a further and future exchange was contemplated by both parties at the time of making this exchange, and as a silent part of it. A takes what is now his own wheat, and B takes as an equivalent for what was his wheat a right to demand of A in six months an equivalent for the present equivalent (the pledge) for the sake of which B rendered the wheat. The note of hand is the evidence of this pledge, and it belongs absolutely to B. It is his property. He may keep it till maturity and then sell it to A for its face, or he may sell it at once to a bank for its face less the discount for six months. Discount is the difference between the face and the present price of a note of hand. The first peculiarity, then, of Credit is, that it always involves the element of future time. But it involves this secondarily, and not primarily. In other words, a present equivalent is always rendered by both parties in every commercial transaction; but the present equivalent in the case of a credit transaction is the right to demand something of somebody sometime in the future. This distinction is very important, as we shall see clearly when we come to treat of Banking, though it is generally ill-understood at present. Valuables, when they exchange at all, exchange once for all. But there is one kind of valuables, namely, claims, which, when subject to exchange, imply and require another and a future exchange, not necessarily between the parties to the first exchange, but between *some* two parties; and not, speaking strictly, to *consummate* the first exchange, because that took and gave its own satisfactory equivalents; but, as involving both time and trust, the credit sale must in the nature of things be followed by another sale of one of the three kinds.

We see, accordingly, that in Credit our science of Economics takes partial possession of future time for certain purposes of its own. Exchange sets its throne and reigns pre-eminently in present time; but its sceptre extends also over past time, so far as all capital is concerned, and so far as all material commodities (the result of past work) are exposed for sale in the present; and its right hand of rule goes forth also to grasp the future, under limitations indeed both as to the stretch of time covered and as to the character of the persons concerned, but still there is there a fair domain and a broad domain, and a realm on the whole winning a wider and wider circuit. It is one of the proud boasts of Political Economy as a science, as it is too one of the exalted traits of human nature, that the lordly impulse to buy and sell does not confine itself to what the Past offers in all its accumulated valuables, nor to what the Present unfolds in the unlimited desires and efforts of congregated men, but reaches out also into the Future, and makes that pay tribute more and more into the vast treasury of its Gains. And this too is legitimate. Man is at once and all the time actor and historian and prophet. The future is not wholly unknown. Given the one assumption, that Earth and Men go on as heretofore, Exchange knows well enough, and better and better, whom of the coming men to trust and for how long a time. The doctrine of averages and of probabilities comes along to guide and to enhearten the investor. Any thoroughly established government of to-day can borrow all the money that it wants on its public pledge to repay the principal fifty years hence. England has borrowed millions of pounds sterling, giving no day certain in the future for its repayment. These funds are called "Consolidated Annuities": the interest on them is paid on a day nominated in the bond: the principal is to be paid when the borrower chooses, or never.

b. The other and final peculiarity of Credit is, that it always involves on the part of one person a commercial confidence in some person *as such*. The term, Credit, is derived from the Latin CREDO, *I believe*, and the corresponding term, Debt, from DEBEO, *I owe*. Thus the personal element and the future element are wrapt up in the very origin of the words. There is no credit without debt, and no debt without credit. The very words imply a *belief* of one of the two parties in a commercial promise made by the other, and also an *obligation* acknowledged by this party as due to the first. There is a basis for credit in human nature. Faith in each other to a certain extent is natural to men. Whatever enlarges the intellectual foresight, and especially the moral character of men, opens a broader and surer field for Credits. Civilization, so-called, and Christianity certainly, deepens and broadens the natural trust of man in man. Despite all the instances of broken faith, and they are too many; despite the shocks and cautions that come every now and then to every man who trusts much in his fellow-men; experience itself justifies and rewards an ever-growing commercial trust. It is one of the noble things in international commerce, as we shall see, that men trust each other across the oceans, and lay millions of value upon the faith of a single firm. As the core of the Christian religion is confidence in a

Person, so the very substance of credits is a natural and in general well-grounded faith in *persons as such*.

A Credit, then, may be defined to be *a Right to demand something of somebody*; and a Debt to be *an Obligation to pay something to somebody*. What always lies, accordingly, between creditors and debtors, are Rights coupled with Obligations; and these are *Property*, just as much as anything is and for the same reason, since they always may be, and usually are, bought and sold by other parties as well as the original parties. In these Rights or Claims, therefore, arises a commerce, domestic and foreign, immense in extent and amount, and the Rights themselves take their undisputed place on an equality with tangible Commodities and personal Services.

Having thus reached an ultimate and satisfactory definition of Credit, we must still pursue a little further our present object, namely, to obtain a clear conception of the *nature* of this great class of Valuables, by drawing two or three distinctions between Credit-Rights and some other rights very apt to be confounded with them.

(1) The distinction between credit-rights and other rights is well rooted in the Latin language and in the Roman law, while the corresponding English terms are quite ambiguous and need to be used with great caution. In Latin, a true debt is called a *Mutuum*, because it lies between two persons, a creditor, and a debtor, and is a credit-right independent of the question of fact whether the debtor has now the thing rendered to him or not, indeed whether he has anything at all to pay with or not; on the other hand, a thing merely lent, when the very thing lent is to be returned to its owner, who has not in the meantime parted with his property to the other, is called in Latin a *Commodatum*. The English tongue has but the one word, *Loan*, for the two very distinct operations: for the loan of a book, for instance, which is to be returned after use, and which may be legally reclaimed by the owner if he chance to find it anywhere, that is, the Latin *commodatum*; and for the loan of money, or other such measurable thing, which is to be returned *in kind* only, and which may *not* legally be reclaimed except through some action of the borrower, since the ownership of that thing rendered has passed over to him completely, that is, the Latin *mutuum*. The same ambiguity of course inheres in the corresponding English word, *Borrow*. The English language is relatively poor in words expressing nice legal distinctions.

Now, as a true debt is a claim on a *person* and never on a *thing*, the Roman Law is true to the nature of things and to the vital distinctions of our science, when it names the right to which a *mutuum* gives birth as a *jus in personam*, that is to say, a right against the person; while it names the legal obligation arising out of a *commodatum* as a *jus in re*, that is to say, a right to the very thing. So strongly is this doctrine, namely, that the security of a true debt lies against persons and not against things, intrenched in the Roman Law, that debts or credits are even termed "*nomina*," *names*, in that law, as when Ulpian says, "*Nomina eorum qui sub conditione vel in diem debent et emere et vendere solemus*": We are accustomed to buy and sell DEBTS payable on a certain day and at a certain event. The fundamental law of the present national banks of the United States explicitly recognizes this old and good distinction by requiring the banks to loan money on *personal* security only, that is to say, no tangible things, not even real estate, may be taken as *original* security for any loan.

(2) Henry Dunning Macleod, who has cast fresh light on the nature of Credit, draws another distinction that lies on the threshold of the subject, namely, that between paper documents conveying titles to *specific things*, such as a bill of lading, for example, and those conveying *credit-rights*, such as a bank-note, for example. Bills of lading describe the goods, go out with the goods, are a title to the goods, and have no value separate from the goods; bank-notes have nothing to do with any specific pieces of property anywhere, are in no proper sense a title to anything whatever, but a general *claim* for something upon some person somewhere that awaits his action for its validity and realization. For instance, a grain-dealer in Chicago sells 1,000 bushels of No. 2 wheat to a party in New York, and ships the grain to that point by rail: two kinds of paper documents arise in connection with this transaction, which are quite diverse in their nature and course of operation: one is a *bill of lading*, that goes along with the wheat, and gives the person named in the bill a complete title to 1,000 bushels of wheat of a certain description, and the holder of the bill takes the wheat and asks no favors of anybody; and the other is a *bill of exchange*, drawn by the grain-dealer in Chicago on the consignee of the wheat in New York, which bill of exchange is sold at once by the creditor in Chicago to a banker there, provided the banker has commercial confidence in the two names on the bill and a sufficient motive in the shape of a discount for buying it: thus the bill of lading has in it neither element of Credit, neither Time nor Trust, while the bill of exchange has both of these elements in it.

(3) Attention should be called to a third distinction of the same general nature, as between relations very different in themselves and yet extremely liable to be confounded with each other. Let us take a common instance: a customer of a bank takes a package of valuables of any kind to his banker, such as bonds and bills payable and jewels and plate, and asks him to take care of it for the present in his vault, subject of course to a return to him or any one else to his order at any time: no property in these valuables passes over to the banker, it is not a deposit in the ordinary banking sense, the relation of debtor and creditor does not arise as between banker and depositor, the banker becomes Trustee or Bailee of the package, and is

bound to exercise common vigilance in the care of it, but if it be burned or stolen extraordinarily the loss is the customer's and not the banker's. But now, on the other hand, when a customer deposits in the banking sense money or bills payable with his banker, the property in the money and bills passes over to the banker instantly, the relation of debtor and creditor arises, the depositor receives a credit on the banker's books in return for the money and bills rendered, the exchange as a mere case of value is consummated to the profit of both parties, but the return-service to the depositor is *the right to demand equivalents of the banker at some future time.* In other words, it is a case in Credit.

(4) As this general distinction is vital, we shall lose nothing in the end if we make even a fourth exemplification of it. The United States Treasury receives silver dollars of its own minting from any person who chooses to place them there, and gives out in token what are called "Silver certificates" to the same amount, entitling the bearer to take out the dollars again at will, and thus the certificates being more convenient than the dollars and just as valuable become a part of the money of the country. The Treasury is bound to exercise due care in the keeping of these silver coins, and to return them to the holders of certificates on demand, just as the elevator and railroad companies are under legal obligations to show diligence in keeping and transporting the wheat of our former example; but the United States is not *debtor* to the holders of these certificates any more than the elevator company is *debtor* to the wheat shipper, and consequently there is no element of Credit in these certificates. Just so of the later gold certificate. On the other hand, the so-called greenbacks issued by the United States are also a part of the money of the country, but they are *credit*-money, inasmuch as they are a *promise* to pay to the bearer some time in the future so many dollars. The Treasury has never kept up any special fund of gold and silver, with which to redeem the greenbacks. They rest back for their value on the good faith of the country. The United States is *debtor* to the bearers, and these in turn are *creditors*, and the legal-tender quality of the greenbacks does not alter their character as a form of pure credit. Both the elements of good faith and future time inhere in the greenbacks, as they do also in the bonds of the United States, while in the certificates neither of these elements appears.

However, circumstances easily conceivable and which were actually realized in the case of the famous Bank of Amsterdam, founded in 1609, might make the United States a debtor and the holders of the silver certificates creditors in the commercial sense of those terms. The Directors of the Bank of Amsterdam, towards the close of the second century of its beneficent existence, loaned out to the Dutch East India Company and to the City of Amsterdam large parts of the bullion, on which its certificates ("bank money") were based, unknown to the public, which felt unlimited confidence in the bank, and the result was in 1795, when the French invaded Holland and the facts became known, that bank money which had previously borne a premium of 5% fell at once to a discount of 16%, although the bullion that remained and the debts due the Bank were fully equal to redeem the certificates and were used for that purpose. So, if the United States should use, clandestinely or otherwise, the silver dollars for other purposes than to redeem the certificates on demand, the latter would undoubtedly both in law and fact be transformed from mere token-money (as now) into credit-money valid as against the United States as debtor, like the greenbacks at present.

Have we now compassed our first object? Do we fully understand, from the foregoing descriptions and distinctions, the *Nature* of Credit? If so, we are prepared to look narrowly into its *Forms*.

2. Credit-rights are commonly, but not always, recorded upon paper; but it is important to observe, that the paper-document is the mere evidence of the right, and not the right itself, which lies back of the paper as substance to shadow, and persists intact even were the paper lost or destroyed. These paper instruments of Credit are commonly contemplated as of two kinds, Promises to pay and Orders to pay, but there is not at bottom any radical difference between these, the Right as between two persons is not affected by this superficial difference, as we shall see, and the present enumeration of credit-forms will proceed independently of it.

a. Book Accounts. A charge in a trader's books is both a current and a legal evidence that the person charged has received a certain service, and has virtually promised to render the sum charged as a return-service. Book accounts are the most common of the forms of credit; and if the person charged fails of his own accord to complete the exchange thus commenced, the law, in the absence of any proof to make the charge suspicious, collects it, if possible, and forcibly completes the exchange. The convenience of this form of credit is so great, that it is not likely ever to be disused; and as between people who deal much with each other is very useful, inasmuch as their respective book accounts are set against each other in settlement, and only balances are required to be cancelled in money. It is for the benefit of both creditors and debtors, however, even when the same parties are both creditor and debtor, that such credits should be short in time and such settlements frequent, since in book accounts there is no interest on charges however long they run, and since in this way only can the creditor realize the full gain of the exchange, and the debtor keep fair his mercantile name. If it be difficult or impossible to follow strictly the excellent financial maxim, "Pay as you go," the next best thing to that is, "Go and pay." The gains of an exchange are lessened, or its terms become more onerous, just in proportion as delay in its completion is experienced or expected. Book accounts are subject also to this disadvantage as compared with other forms of credit, that their number and amount as against any person are less likely to become publicly known, and therefore he is more likely to be trusted in this form by others beyond the point of his solvency and their safety.

b. Promissory Notes. These differ from Book accounts in that they are always either expressly or virtually on interest, and are consequently negotiable. They are issued by individuals, corporations, and Nations. If the principal be deemed secure, that is, if there be a thorough trust on the part of the holder in the maker of the note, the time of the payment of the principal becomes a matter of comparative indifference, because the interest is compensation for delay, and is often the motive on the part of the holder for rendering that service of which the note is evidence. Indeed a long obligation, other things being equal, is commonly preferred to a short one, and bears a higher price. When a note is sold (negotiated) by the original holder it becomes payable to the purchaser, or to each subsequent purchaser in turn, and thus may run a devious round, may play a part in many commercial transactions, may be set off by the transient holder against a debt owed by him and thus cancel that, and when itself is cancelled by ultimate set-off or by any other mode of payment the last holder takes the return for the service originally rendered by the first holder. The promissory notes of individuals are frequently discounted by Banks in a manner to be presently explained. These are always for short times, and are debts bought by banks on the personal security of the names upon the notes. The notes are founded on the relation of debtor and creditor, which is always a personal relation, and so differ in their nature from a *mortgage*, which is a qualified *title* to a specific piece of property, usually real estate. A note secured by a mortgage is, as it were, absorbed into the mortgage, and becomes another thing from a common promissory note, or *commercial paper*, as it is called. A mortgage rests therefore on other grounds than a commercial trust in the good faith of a *person*.

Corporations also issue promissory notes, and as such issuers become in a sense *moral persons* entitled to confidence according to the character and purposes of the individual corporators and the financial means and methods of the corporation itself. It is an old saying, that "corporations have no souls"; economists as such have no need to pronounce on that proposition; the fact is enough for them, that the short notes of corporations are often discounted by bankers on the same ground as the notes of individuals are discounted; and that their long-time obligations, commonly called *Bonds*, are all the time bought and sold in the market like commodities. Many of the Railroad bonds, of which immense quantities are in the markets of the world, rest back also for their security upon *Mortgages* of the real estate of the corporations made over to Trustees to hold for the assurance of the holders of the bonds. The personal obligation of the corporators is thus reinforced, much as a common mortgage reinforces the note or bond, to secure which the mortgage is executed. Whenever *all* the real estate of a railroad company becomes subject to a mortgage, when there are previous partial mortgages or liens, these latter take precedence in due order of any subsequent pledges or bonds secured by what is properly called the *consolidated mortgage*. Such a mortgage has recently been executed by the Northern Pacific Railroad Company for $160,000,000. Railroad Bonds so fortified in proper and legal terms possess the highest possible credit-security to their holders. When no such consolidated or "blanket" mortgage has been put on the property, first and second and third mortgages sometimes support bonds of primary and secondary and tertiary validity; and sometimes so-called *Income-bonds* are issued, with or without mortgages behind them, for the payment of the interest on which bonds the net earnings of the corporations are specifically pledged. Frequently also simple long-time bonds resting on corporation security only are negotiated without difficulty.

It must be constantly borne in mind, that certificates of Stock in railroad and all other similar corporations are not credit-documents at all, but are mere evidences of so much proportional *ownership* in the corporate property. They are not interest-bearing documents at all, although they may draw interest or rather dividends, if the property be prosperous. They are somewhat like deeds to land, in which no element of credit inheres.

Nations too are moral persons in the same loose though binding sense as corporations, and as such often issue promissory notes on interest, commonly called in this country Bonds, in Great Britain Funds, and in some countries Stocks. These are always pure credit. Nations give no mortgages. Yet they often borrow at a less rate of interest than the most solvent individuals or corporations can, as is seen by the fact, that British consols carry but 3%, and yet bear a premium in the present market. The term, "consols," is a popular contraction of "consolidated annuities," the Act to create which at 3%, out of a then confused mass of public debts at various rates of interest passed Parliament in 1757. The maximum of the British debt was $4,500,000,000 in 1815, and has now decreased to $3,467,787,960.

The United States also sold its bonds at 3% for a small premium in 1882. It had borrowed of its own citizens in 1862-65, both inclusive, about $2,500,000,000 on its bonds at different rates of interest and at different times of repayment: some of these bore gold interest at 6% annually, Government reserving the right to pay the principal in five years and pledging itself to pay it twenty years from date, and so these bonds were called "Five-twenties"; others bore gold interest at 5%, becoming payable at ten and demandable at forty years, and so were called "Ten-forties"; and still others bore greenback interest at $7\,{}^{30}/_{100}\%$, the principal payable in greenbacks at three years, or fundable in gold sixes, at the option of the holders, and these were named "Seven-thirties." Over $90,000,000 of this last kind of bonds were subscribed for by the American people in the course of a single week in the spring of 1865. The whole of our national debt issued prior to 1865 was made payable on a day certain; the so-called "consols" of 1865 and 1867 and 1868 were payable *not more* than forty years from date; while all the bonds authorized from 1870 to 1882 were Consols proper, whose peculiarity is, that they never fall due so as to become a claim for the principal against the Government, but after a day fixed or on a condition fixed are payable "at the pleasure of the United States."

The separate States of our Union, as sovereign in their own sphere quite as much as the national Government is sovereign in its sphere, have unlimited power to contract debts for State purposes through their regularly constituted authorities; and consequently to issue promissory notes or bonds to liquidate such debts. New York commenced in this way in 1817 the magnificent enterprise of the Erie Canal, to connect the great Lakes with the city of New York by an inland water-way for commerce, and the completion of this in 1825 made the State the "Empire State," and the city the undisputed commercial metropolis of the Union. In a similar way Massachusetts undertook in 1862 the completion of the Hoosac Tunnel for a railway lengthwise of the State; and although the process became unduly expensive, and great abuses sprang up in connection with it, no one now questions that the pecuniary and moral resources of the State have been augmented, on the whole, by contracting the debt and providing by taxation for the liquidation of both interest and principal. The credit of Massachusetts, that is, the ability to borrow money at low rates of interest, has been at times greater than that of the United States; mainly because the State in 1862 and onwards refused to avail itself of a depreciated national paper-money (greenbacks) made legal tender for all debts, with which to pay the interest on its then existing State debt, but persisted throughout (alone of the States) to pay that interest so soon as due in gold coin. On the other hand, several of the States of the Union at different times, and under more or less of provocation and justification, have made a partial or entire repudiation of certain portions of their public debts, justly damaging to their individual credit, and even to the good name abroad of the whole people of the United States.

Counties and cities and towns may also issue interest-bearing bonds for public improvements, which have a *quasi* governmental character, but only under conditions and to a maximum amount prescribed by a law of the State.

c. Bank Bills. These are a form of promissory notes not on interest, and thus differ from the notes of ordinary corporations, and from the bonds of nations and states and municipalities; but the issuing Bank offers, as a sort of compensation for the privilege of circulating notes not on interest, to convert them into coin, that is, to pay them instantly on the demand of any holder. It is this proffered and immediate convertibility into coin that enables the promissory notes of a bank to circulate as money, while the notes of other corporations and individuals equally solid and solvent do not circulate as money. It must be borne in mind, however, that this offer to convert them into the legal and ultimate coin-money does not essentially alter the nature of Bank Bills; they are a form of commercial credit; and although they are commonly issued against another form of such credit, namely, against the interest-bearing promissory notes of individuals and corporations who resort to the bank for discount, this only complicates the exchange without changing its nature. It is a common instance of exchanging one form of credit for another form which happens to have a greater currency or validity than the first, and for this superiority of the bank credit the individual credit pays an interest, in other words, is discounted; and such exchanges of one form of paper credit for another, with or without a premium, may go on indefinitely; especially as *credit-money* in the form of bank bills, such paper may serve as a medium in many exchanges; but ultimately, and before the entire series of transactions is closed, such bank bills are to be redeemed in coin, or taken in by the banker in payment of some debt due to him, in both which cases they are extinguished as an instrument of Credit.

The Bank of England keeps out in circulation on the average £25,000,000 in bank bills. It has been computed, that the average length of life of a Bank of England bill between its issue and redemption is about three days; and no bill once redeemed or received back over the counters of the Bank is ever issued again. It is then placed on file for record only. The joint-stock and private banks of England and Wales circulate on the average rather more than £4,000,000 of bank bills of their own; and no bank bill of any kind is legal in England and Wales of a less denomination than £5. The ten Scotch banks and their branches keep out in bills about £5,000,000; six out of the nine Irish banks and their branches issue on the average not far from £10,000,000; but both the Scotch and Irish banks are allowed to put out £1 bills.

Bank bills, as a form of paper credit not on interest, but ostensibly redeemable in coin on demand of the holder, have been issued in the United States by more parties and to a larger extent and with more recklessness as to redemption than in any other country. Omitting all reference to Colonial issues, and confining the outlook to the first century under the Constitution, let us note, that when the present national government went into operation in 1789, the "Bank of North America" in Philadelphia and the "Bank of New York" in New York and the "Bank of Massachusetts" in Boston had been opened for business, and all three were State banks issuing bills convertible into coin, though each confined its business mostly to the city in which it was located. Two years later under the auspices of Alexander Hamilton, then Secretary of the Treasury, the first "United States Bank" went into operation at Philadelphia under a charter from Congress that was to run twenty years with a capital stock of $10,000,000. At first no bills were issued by this bank of a less denomination than $10; the money was popular and was converted on demand; the Bank was prosperous, and paid dividends to stockholders never falling below 8% and frequently rising to 10% annually; as the time approached for the charter to expire, the stockholders were anxious for a renewal of their privileges; but the opposition to them in Congress was now strong, owing mainly to the increase in the number of State banks from 3 to 88; and accordingly the recharter was defeated in the House by one vote, and in the Senate also, by the casting vote of the Vice-President, and the Bank was obliged to wind up its affairs in 1811.

Then came in a sort of mania for the creation of new State banks, under the hope that these, now there was no National Bank, might obtain the Custody and temporary use of the national funds, and especially might furnish the country with paper money in the shape of State bank bills. The number of banks went up to 246 in 1816. So many bank bills were put out, and became so much distrusted, and so many were presented for redemption, that the banks could not respond in coin, and in the fall of 1814, there was a general stoppage of specie payment in all the banks of the Country excepting those in New England. General resumption of specie payment by the banks did not take place till 1819. New York bank bills went down to 90%, those of Philadelphia to 82%, those of Baltimore to 80%, and those of Pittsburg to 75%.

Under these circumstances the Second Bank of the United States went into operation in January, 1817, also with a charter to run twenty years, with a capital stock of $35,000,000, of which the national Government subscribed one-fifth. The new Bank helped indeed the State banks to resume specie payments, as was a part of the purpose, but it pushed its own bills into circulation with such eagerness, that it is thought $100,000,000 of them were in the hands of the people, before the first year was out. In this way the Bank fell into difficulties. Its bills were distrusted. Coin came to bear a premium over them of 10%. President Jackson began his famous contest with the Bank seven years before its charter was to expire, and took care that it went out of being the same year that he went out of office, in 1837, namely.

The next year the State banks increased in number to 675, and continued to increase till 1862, when there were over 1500 of them, and when the issue of the "Greenbacks" by the national Government interfered with what had been their exclusive issuing of the paper money after 1837. In 1857, before the commercial panic of that year, the aggregate of their bills stood at $214,000,000, the largest it ever reached. These bills were nominally convertible into coin at the will of the holders, but they were never actually so convertible for any great length of time. The ratio of their volume to the specie reserved to redeem it was always a very high ratio. For instance, the average for the whole country in January, 1863, was 4:1; in Rhode Island 12:1; and in Vermont 28:1. Such a paper money can be called convertible only by a stretch of courtesy.

It was wisely determined by the People to abandon this loose form of paper money, and in 1863 went into operation the present national banking system, under which originally $300,000,000 of bank bills were authorized to be issued in the aggregate, but this limit was extended in 1870 to $354,000,000, and the Act of 1875 removed all restrictions on the total amount, while there have always been restrictions on the amount that can be issued by any *one* bank in the system. By the law of 1882, national banks may withdraw their bills by depositing lawful money in the Treasury to take them up, and then take back the proportionate amount of the bonds held for the security of the bills. There were outstanding Dec. 26, 1883, $341,320,256 of these national bank bills, but their volume declined under the law of 1882 to $151,702,809 on Oct. 4, 1888. These bills were from the first redeemable in greenbacks, which were themselves, however, irredeemable in gold and silver till New Year's, 1879, since which time till the present all the paper money of the United States of both kinds has been convertible into coin at the will of the holder.

d. Bank Deposits. We are studying in order the forms of commercial Credits, and we have now come to that one which is central in the operations of Banking, and accordingly this is the place for us to understand clearly what a Bank is, who a Banker is, and what are the motives actuating at once the Banker and his Customers. A BANK IS AN INSTITUTION FOR THE CREATION, MANAGEMENT, AND EXTINCTION OF CREDITS. Money of any kind plays a very subordinate part in the general operations of banks, which live and move and have their being in the sphere of pure Credits. *Bankers are buyers and sellers of credits.* As merchants are dealers in commodities, so bankers are dealers in credits, buying (1) some credits with other credits, (2) some credits with money, and (3) money also with credits. Before unfolding these three operations of bankers in their motives and profits, a glance backward to the origin of banks would be a help to us in grasping their nature and benefits.

The word "bank" meant originally a mass or pile or ridge of earth, as we still say, a *sand-bank*, and the *banks* of a river. When first applied to commercial transactions, the word had a different meaning from what it has at present, although the idea of *credit* has inhered in it from the first: in 1171, the Republic of Venice, being at war, ordered a forced loan from its citizens, and promised to pay interest on it at 5%; and certificates were issued for the sums paid in, and public commissioners were appointed to manage the payment of the interest and the transfers of the certificates, which were made negotiable. The Italian word applied to such a public loan is *monte*, but as the Germans were then strong in Italy, the German equivalent word, *bank*, came to be used alongside of it and instead of it. It meant this common contribution of the citizens to the wants of the State, represented by the mass of the certificates, and came to be applied also to the *place* where the commissioners paid the interest and transferred the shares. Two other such loans were contracted there afterwards, and an English writer, in 1646, quoted by Macleod, speaks of the "*three bankes of Venice*," meaning these three public debts, including the evidences of them and the place where they were managed.

The Bank of England also was in its origin in 1694 an incorporation of those persons willing to subscribe to a public loan in time of stress, as "The Governer and Company of the Bank of England." The subscribers to a loan of £1,200,000 became an association, or bank, on the condition that the Government should pay interest to the lenders at 8% annually, and also £4000 a year in addition for the management of the bank, that is, of this debt of £1,200,000 which was the sole capital stock of the new Company, which was authorized to issue an equivalent amount of bank bills to circulate as money. The capital stock was of no use, so far as redeeming these bills was concerned, the stockholders must furnish other money for that purpose besides what they have loaned to the State, but the ownership of so much of the public debt divided among the shareholders, made the Bank respectable, and tended to give public credit to its bills, which at first were paid promptly in coin on demand, and thus the Bank, by increasing the volume of money and by showing confidence in the stability of the State, strengthened the revolutionary position of William and Mary, and consequently the Whigs were the friends and the Jacobites the enemies of the Bank. This function of issuing bills or promissory notes designed to circulate as money, thus begun and still continued by the Bank of England, is much less important in modern banking than the other two functions of receiving Deposits and making Discounts, but it was the function on which the turn began to be made from the older to the newer modes of Banking. All that is needful to be said on this tertiary or money-issuing function of Banks has been already urged under the last head.

The two Banks of the United States in succession, as they were more or less modelled after the Bank of England, gave the same prominence to the function of issuing paper money, under the belief that government bonds afford the best security for the redemption of bank bills, an idea that underlies our present system of National Banks also; and, moreover, those two great banks began to teach the people of the United States something of the mysteries of *Deposit-banking*, the point that we have now in hand. One-fifth of the capital stock of the first Bank, $2,000,000 out of $10,000,000, was subscribed by the national Government; and besides, the proceeds of the national taxes as they were paid in were passed over to the Bank as *Deposits*, that is to say, the Bank bought this money of the Government, paying for it with a Credit; and then properly used the money as its own in paying expenses and in discounting paper. Bank deposits do not belong to the depositors, but to the bank; which has thus bought money with credit; and when Andrew Jackson suddenly removed from the second Bank of the United States the national moneys deposited there, and placed them "in the custody," as he expressed it, of certain selected State banks, these amounted at the moment to $10,000,000, and the discount line resting in part on these deposits was at the time over $60,000,000, he removed them under a strong misapprehension *of the nature of such deposits*; and their *removal* affected credit, and disarranged business to a remarkable degree, and caused intense excitement all over the Union. Depositing those national moneys with the Bank was a *trade* between the Government and the Bank for the time being. The Government took in return for the moneys a Right to demand of the Bank in future by cheque or otherwise sums at its convenience to the aggregate of the sums deposited; the moneys became the property of the Bank to be used at its discretion in its ordinary business; the Government took its return-service for the moneys in a Credit, that is, a right to draw out at its convenience in the future corresponding sums; there was a commercial understanding in that case between the Government and the Bank underlying the buying and selling involved in the Deposit, as there always is between depositors and their banks; the banks are always bound to order their business in such a way as to be able to respond to every depositor's call for money, when it comes; but banks in general find practically that a cash reserve of one-third of their Deposits is ample to answer the current demands of their depositors, and the remaining two-thirds may be safely used in discounting short-time commercial paper to their own profit; Deposits, accordingly, are not placed "in the custody" of the banks receiving them; they are really bought by the banks of their customers, who receive in return certain privileges and credits that they prefer to the "custody" of their own moneys; and under these general motives on both sides, there has grown up in all commercial countries an immense line of Bank Deposits so-called, and perhaps we may say that the principal function of banks at present is to buy these deposits with their Credit, and then to handle them in further operations to the convenience of their customers and to their own gain.

Under our present national banking system the Government is still a depositor of public moneys in some of the banks designated as "depositaries." At the close of the fiscal year, 1888, there were 290 of such depositary national banks, and the Treasurer held United States bonds of the face value of $56,128,000 and the market value of $68,668,182 in trust for these banks to secure public moneys lodged with them. This system of national deposit with the banks began in 1864. The total held by the banks June 30, 1888, was $58,712,511, an increase during the year of $35,395,633.

But our concern is especially with the Bank Deposits of individuals, with their motives in making these, and with the motives and the methods of the bankers in handling them. In order to draw the confidence of the people in its locality, a bank must not only be, but also *seem* to be, well-to-do and prosperous. Most bankers find it to their account to become known owners of public stocks; and in many cases, as in the present national banks of this country, are required by law to own such stocks, and this gives them a kind of credit and public standing scarcely to be reached by the ownership of ordinary property. Thus the Bank of England held at the outset £1,200,000, and now holds £15,000,000 of securities, mostly of the public debt of England. As merchants begin by laying in stocks of goods of the kinds they purpose to deal in and offering them for sale, so bankers begin by bringing together money and credits of their own in order to attract to themselves in the way of buying and selling the money and credits of other people. In order to deal successfully in credits the banker must have *credit*, that is, he must have the reputation of having property of his own, and of being an honest and careful manager of his own affairs and of the affairs of others so far as they are intrusted to him. Each of our present national banks, now (1890) 3150 in number, must have by law a paid-up capital of not less than $100,000, and in cities of 50,000 people their capital must not be less than $200,000 each, except that in places having less than 6000 inhabitants banks with not less than $50,000 capital *may be* organized at the discretion of the Secretary of the Treasury. The main purpose of all this is to secure strong financial organizations fitted to draw the confidence of the communities in which they are placed, and in this manner and by means also of constant national supervision to attract the Deposits of the people to the banks.

Now, as was said a little while ago, perhaps the central function in banking is for the banker to receive his customer's money and also his credits falling due, and to render to him in return for these *a credit*, that is, a right to demand from himself an equal sum at a future time or times. The evidence of this right is entered on the banker's books, and usually too on the customer's passbook, and thus becomes what is called a DEPOSIT. The ownership of the money and of the credits deposited passes over completely from the customer to the banker. It is a complete case of buying and selling to the mutual profit of the parties. The banker has the right to do just what he pleases with his deposits, and the customer has a right to draw cheques on his credit as and when he pleases; only the banker's entry of the transaction on his books is a virtual and a legal *promise* to pay that amount to his customer, and therefore he must be ready to respond to his customer's call, whenever the latter demands, not his own money, but so much of his banker's money. *A deposit, accordingly, is not the very thing deposited, but a credit.* It is the banker's promise and the depositor's property. It is in this way that a banker buys ready money with a credit.

The motive, then, that leads the depositor to intrust his money to the banker is the desire, not to have that specific money kept safely for him, for he lost possession of it absolutely when it passed the counter, he *sold* it and took his pay in something else, but rather to have the unquestioned right to call on the banker for such sums (not to exceed the deposit in the aggregate) and at such times as may suit his own convenience. He has such confidence in the integrity and solvency of the banker, finds it so practically convenient to have dealings with him, and comes to have certain minor privileges at the bank in other relations over non-depositors, that he quite prefers a credit on the banker to the possession of the money itself.

The corresponding motive of the banker to receive his customer's funds on these terms is that he finds by experience (his own and others'), that he can safely use a large portion of these moneys deposited in other operations in credit profitable to himself, and at the same time be practically sure of meeting all his customer's calls for money as they are made. Every good banker finds out, that many of his customers wish always to leave a balance in his hands; that while some of them are constantly drawing cheques on him for cash, others of them are as constantly depositing with him in cash; and that consequently he can properly and safely use a large part of the money he has purchased with his credit to purchase other credits with. Deposit-banking, therefore, is not only convenient and profitable for the depositor, but also excellent and profitable for the banker.

Besides these two parties benefited, there is a gain, too, for the community at large in deposit-banking; inasmuch as a new capital as such has been thereby created, a series of new values, which would not otherwise have existed at all. Were there no deposit-bank in that locality, every man now a customer of it would of course keep his own reserves for himself for prospective contingencies: now, all these little reserves are aggregated in the bank, the convenience of them for each customer's contingencies is just as great as if he kept his own in his own safe or wallet, but the banker finds that he can use, say two-thirds of the whole, and still answer each customer's call. Here is a new capital. Here are scattered valuables brought together to be loaned out to a profit, which were otherwise barren and useless for the time being. Industry is quickened in a wide circle, products are created and brought to market, wages are paid and profits are gained, in direct consequence of bringing together under favorable auspices for safe loaning the little hoards and driblets of many individuals, which were practically useless in isolated hands.

It may easily be objected at this point, that it is entirely possible that any banker might be called upon to pay off all his deposit-liabilities at once in money, which, if it happened, would break him of course; so it is abstractly possible that all the lives insured in a Life Insurance Company might terminate in one day, in which case no Company in the world could meet its obligations; and so it is abstractly possible that all the houses insured in a Fire Insurance Company might be burned up in a single night, which, if it happened, would cause the collapse of the soundest company; but in all these cases of possibility there is a *certainty* that the possibility will not become a fact. *Ex nihilo nihil fit.* A supposition practically impossible to become a fact can yield no logical inference whatever. The Greek language has a special grammatical form for a hypothesis impossible to be realized in fact: would that the English had also such a form of speech! It would save us a mess of bad reasoning. If, however, any banker may have misjudged for his locality at any time the proper ratio of reserves kept to deposits received, and be crowded in consequence, he must sell some of the securities bought with the excess, or borrow money on them.

Surprisingly large is the amount of bank deposits in all the leading commercial nations of the world. The average public and private deposits of the Bank of England, on which no current interest is paid by the Bank, amounts to about £40,000,000 all the time. The ten joint-stock banks of London carry about £80,000,000 in private deposits, of which those to remain some time *draw* an interest, but those lodged on current accounts and on call *draw* none. Scotland has carried deposit-banking further and to greater advantage than any other country in the world. There are now no private banks in Scotland, but the ten joint-stock banks with their numerous branches scattered to every village in the land hold constantly about £70,000,000 as individual deposits, on which current interest is allowed, and so the habit of keeping one's account with a banker has become universal with the people. No one thinks of keeping money to any amount in his house or about his person, and consequently house-breaking and highway robbery have almost ceased. Bankers even attend all the great fairs in the country to receive deposits and to pay off cheques. Credit in this form and in another form soon to be described treads its utmost verge in Scotland. Although in the United States the custom of keeping deposits with bankers and drawing cheques against them has not gone nearly so far as in Scotland, and not nearly so far as it will go in the immediate future, yet the aggregate of individual deposits in the national banks alone, Oct. 4, 1888, was $1,350,320,861, an increase in just seven years of 26%.

e. Bank Discounts. The credits that are discounted by bankers may be either the promissory notes of individuals and corporations already characterized, or the Bills of Exchange soon to be characterized, but the entire function of discount is so peculiar, that the paper subjected to it ought to be enumerated in a classification of the instruments of Credit. The discounting of commercial paper is the second essential function of banking, as the buying and handling of deposits is the first; and it is more in accordance with genuine *banking* to pass the price of the paper discounted to the seller's credit in the form of a deposit, that is, to buy one credit by creating another, than to pay the money over the counter at once, and thus to buy credits with money. Those who do the latter are called *bill-discounters* rather than bankers, but most of our bankers do both, though there is a tendency towards the separation of the two in this country also.

Manufacturers and wholesale merchants usually sell their goods *on time*, as it is called, say three or six months. Debts are thus created, or to say the same thing in other words, Credits are thus given. The manufacturer or wholesaler is creditor and the jobber or retailer is debtor. But a debt is property; and the creditor in this case wishes to avail himself of his property at once for further production; so he either takes a Promissory Note from his debtor, or draws a Bill of Exchange upon him, and this piece of property is ready for sale. Neither piece mentions *interest* expressly, but the face sum virtually covers it as contemplating discount. Banks have been organized for the express purpose of buying for their own profit and for the convenience of business such pieces of property; some banker, accordingly, buys this particular piece, that is to say, this creditor passes over to this banker the commercial right to demand payment from this debtor at the end of three months, and receives in return from the banker either money direct or so much of the banker's credit, that is, a deposit in favor of the creditor on the banker's books. For furnishing this creditor either with ready money or a more available credit in lieu of his mercantile paper, the banker charges of course *a percentage*. This is *Discount. Discount is the difference between the face and the price of the paper.* This percentage called discount is the chief source of profit in ordinary banking. It is virtually compound interest on the sum advanced till the maturity of the paper, when the banker realizes from the debtor its full face.

The following is a common form of a bankable note:—

> $1,000WILLIAMSTOWN, Mass., Nov. 10, 1889.

> Three months after date I promise to pay to the order of JOSHUA SWAN, one thousand dollars, payable at the Williamstown National Bank, value received.

> Due Feb. $^{10}/_{13}$. LEANDER ALLEN.

When Swan has put his name on the back of this note, that is in bank phrase, has *indorsed* it, in token that he thereby at once sells and guarantees it to the bank, it is then discounted on the strength of the two *names*, Allen and Swan. As Allen technically takes the advance from the bank for his own benefit, he is technically expected to take up the note when it matures, and if he do not, the bank falls back on Swan, who is equally bound with Allen to see that it is paid at the proper time. Two names are nearly always, not always, requisite to a note acceptable for discount at a bank; and more names merely strengthen the note, since it is discounted on the combined validity of all the names upon it.

One obvious advantage of discount is, that it tends to make all capital active and thus productive. It enables the banks to sell their credit and make a gain, to use a part of their money deposits to buy mercantile paper with, and so get a bank interest on them; it enables dealers in commodities to realize in cash *minus* the discount the sum of what they have sold *on time*; and by means of *accommodation* notes or bills, which only differ from the others in that there is no *actual* debt between the parties, business men may swell the volume of their business temporarily, and non-business people may borrow small sums for convenience or emergencies. Bankers have not always credit enough or money enough from their depositors to buy in either mode all the good paper that is offered to them, in which case, they raise the rate of discount unless the law forbids, or by easy evasions even when the law forbids; or else accommodate regular customers and large depositors first, or buy of all that are "good" a certain proportion only.

The discount line of 3140 national banks reporting Oct. 4, 1888, was $1,674,886,285.29.

It is thus through the purchase of discountable notes for money, that banks derive their partial character as money-lenders. Also, such reserve sums as they do not wish to invest in negotiable paper, on account of the time involved before such paper matures, banks frequently loan *on call* to those customers who have good collateral securities to pledge for the repayment of such loans. The terms of such a contract give the bank full authority to sell such collateral "*at the Brokers' Board or at public or private sale, or otherwise at said bank's option, on the non-performance of this promise, and without notice.*" So far forth banks become direct money-lenders. It ought also to be added, that promissory notes with a single name (or more) are often discounted by banks partly on the strength of collateral securities deposited to fortify the names upon the notes.

f. Bills of Exchange. A Bill of Exchange is a written instrument designed to secure the payment of a distant debt without the transmission of money, being in effect a setting-off or exchange of one debt against another. It is in form and in several technicalities different from a promissory note, inasmuch as it is an *order to pay* instead of a *promise to pay*, and inasmuch as the maker of a note is always *debtor* and the drawer of a bill of exchange is always *creditor*; but all this makes practically very little difference between the two as instruments of Credit, since nearly all bills of exchange come into banks in the way of ordinary business, either for discount or collection, and as the banks care nothing except for *names*, the *form* of the purchasable paper is a matter of indifference to them. The following is the essential form of an inland bill of exchange:—

> $3,000 PITTSFIELD, Mass., Oct. 16, 1889.
>
> Four months after date pay to the order of JOHN KENT three thousand dollars, value received, and charge the same to account of
>
> To ELI TRIPP, Boston, Mass. DAN STORRS.

In the case of this bill, which may serve as a sample of thousands, Storrs is the *drawer*, who is creditor in relation to Tripp, and Tripp is *drawee*, but Storrs is debtor in relation to Kent, who is the *payee*. A bill of exchange is the sale of a debt, in such a way that two debts are so far forth set off against each other, and both transactions are closed without sending any money at all. Tripp owes Storrs, and Storrs owes Kent, and so Storrs pays Kent by an order on Tripp. As this is a bill at four months, Kent will doubtless send it to Tripp for his *acceptance*, as it is called, that is, his acknowledgment that he owes Storrs to that amount, and that he will pay the sum to the holder of the bill when it becomes due. An acceptance is written on the *face* of a bill, and an indorsement upon the *back* of the note: the initials are sufficient for the name of an acceptor, but the full business name is usual for an indorser.

Thus a bill of exchange is the formal sale of a debt, in order to liquidate thereby another debt, when the parties to the transaction live in different and distant places. Storrs does business in Pittsfield, and Tripp in Boston, and it is a matter of comparative indifference where Kent lives, unless there is trouble at the time of collection, for he will perhaps negotiate this bill again, that is, make use of it to pay some debt that he himself owes. It is not often that the same person, as Tripp, happens to owe another person in a distant town, as Storrs, the same amount as Storrs owes another person somewhere, as Kent; but by two bills of exchange, one drawn by each creditor on his own debtor, and then each set off against the other, through the simple and beautiful expedient of bank balances, substantially the same advantages are reached as if it always happened so. Many bills of exchange are drawn *at sight*, as it is called, in which case the payee presents it for payment to the drawee, there is no acceptance and no discount, and a bill of this kind becomes the same as a cheque.

Time bills, however, are usually discounted: the payee indorses his claim over to a fourth party by name, or, by what is called an indorsement *in blank*, that is, by merely writing his own name on the back of the bill, makes it payable to bearer: when banks buy these bills for discount, it is on the joint credit of acceptor and drawer and payee, and in that order of validity and precedence: a promissory note may be protested by a bank without notice to the maker, but a bill of exchange cannot be without notice to the drawer: a promissory note has two parties to it, a debtor and a creditor; while a bill of exchange has three parties to it, two creditors and a debtor.

Inland bills of exchange, both time bills and sight bills, are very convenient in settling debts between distant places without the costly, and more or less hazardous, transmission of money back and forth; besides this, time bills possess the very useful function of enabling a debt due from one person to avail the creditor as a means of obtaining credit from a third party in discount; and in addition to these two points of benefit, it is plain, that the common use of bills of exchange in all their forms releases from use large amounts of money that would else be needful in trade. The less money in use in any country beyond a certain point, the better, because, if coin, it costs much to mint and maintain it, and if paper, it is difficult to make and sustain it of full value.

Bankers sometimes change what they call "exchange" for settling debts between distant places in the same country; in some cases there may be a sound reason for this, in other cases there is none, but in all cases it adds a little to the profits of the banks for handling the bills of exchange; the principle of charging an "exchange" is this,—when one place as Chicago draws more bills on another place as New York than suffice to cancel the bills drawn at that time by New York on Chicago, the point *at* which the larger indebtedness lies is the point for sending drafts *to* which banks naturally charge a percentage; perhaps the idea, which is actually realized in foreign exchange, that money may have to be sent to liquidate such a balance, may have brought in the custom of charging "exchange" in such cases; and there are instances aside from such a supposed balance, in which there may be an extra cost of collection in some form to the bank, that may justify an "exchange" charge; but there is another principle counterworking and often neutralizing entirely this alleged doctrine of a "balance" of debt as between two distant places, namely, that the chief settling place and commercial centre of a country, such as New York is, draws towards itself from the whole circuit with such force, everybody wanting a balance there and having occasion to send funds thither, that drafts on such a place are apt to bear a premium without any reference to its comparative indebtedness at the time.

Very similar to these inland bills in their nature and course and usefulness are Foreign Bills of Exchange, which, as a vastly important topic, especially in its relations with Foreign Trade, we must now study minutely and completely. Commercial relations between two countries, let us say, for instance, France and England, always give rise to a mutual indebtedness of their merchants; if these reciprocal debts were all to be paid by the actual sending of money to and from, there would have to be a constant and expensive and more or less hazardous outward and inward flow of the precious metals in respect to each country; all which necessity is neatly obviated by the use of reciprocal bills of exchange, and coin is only transmitted to settle the balances on whichever side there may happen an excess of debt at the time. French dealers are always sending goods to England, and English dealers goods to France; and for what they send to England the French merchants draw bills of exchange on the parties to whom the goods are consigned, and the English merchants draw similar bills on their debtors in France; then these bills are bought up by bankers or brokers in either country, and virtually exposed again for sale through new bills drawn against them to any parties who may have debts to pay in the other country. Thus bills on London, in other words, on English debtors, are always for sale in France; and bills on France, that is, on French debtors, are always for sale in London; the reciprocal debtors of the two countries, therefore, instead of sending coin to cancel their debts, buy and transmit these bills.

Let us take a sample instance. Pierre & Co. of Paris send a cargo of wine worth £1000 in English money to John Barclay of London. Barclay thus becomes indebted to the Paris firm to that amount, and Pierre & Co. draw at once, so soon as the cargo is despatched, a bill in francs to the equivalent of £1000. If they themselves have no debt to pay in London, they will sell this bill immediately to a Paris banker or broker (if the exchange be then at par) for its full face *minus* interest for the time it has to run, say two months;

this broker is now ready to sell this bill again, or what is the same, his own bill drawn on the strength of it, to anybody in Paris who may have a debt to pay in London; and the party in London who receives it in liquidation of a French debt to him, presents it at maturity to John Barclay for payment. Thus one bill of exchange serves the ends of two creditors and one debtor: Pierre & Co. get their pay for the wine, the London party gets his pay for goods, and Barclay pays his debt, by means of it. A bill drawn in London for a cargo of hardware sent to Paris is similarly negotiated with a London broker or banker, and finds its way similarly to France in payment of some English debt owed there, and ends its course when it reaches the French firm on which it was originally drawn.

We are now in position to understand clearly what is meant by the *par of Exchange* in its commercial (not coinage) import. The merchants in Paris, who have debts due to them from London, draw bills of exchange for the amount of these debts; and, through the agency of middlemen, go into the market to sell these bills to other Paris dealers who have debts to pay in London. If the former class have a larger amount to sell than the latter have occasion to buy, in other words, if there be a larger amount of debts due from London to Paris than from Paris to London, then the natural competition of the sellers in Paris of the bills on London will lower their price somewhat in that market (Paris), in order, as usual, that the Supply and Demand may be equalized there. In this case the par of exchange is disturbed, a bill on London for £100 in francs may not sell for over £99, and the exchange is then said to be 1% *against* London, or, which is the same thing, 1% *in favor* of Paris.

The *par of Exchange*, accordingly, between two countries, depends on the substantial equality of their commercial debts. In the above example, if the exchange as against London in favor of Paris continue long, and especially if the premium of 1% on bills drawn in London on Paris be sufficient to cover the expense of the transmission of specie from London to Paris, gold will begin to flow from London to Paris, because the debtors there may find it cheaper for themselves to buy and send gold than to pay the high premium on bills; and thus the equilibrium of payments and the commercial par may be restored. Also, this par tends to restore itself, without any sending of specie, in this other perfectly natural and effectual way: if bills on Paris are at a premium in London, for the same reason that they are so will bills on London be at a discount in Paris; therefore, there will be a direct encouragement to the extent of the premium for *exportation* of goods from England to France, because on every cargo thus sent bills can be drawn and sold in London for a premium; while the more bills on Paris thus offered in London, the more the premium disappears of course, and the par will be restored so soon as the bills on Paris substantially equal the bills on London offered in Paris; and at the same time, so long as the discount on London bills continues in Paris, there is a direct *discouragement* to further exportations from France to England, because the bills drawn in virtue of such cargoes can only be sold below par, and this too tends to *restore* the par in the commercial sense of the term.

Here is another instance of a magnificently comprehensive law, by which Nature vindicates her right to reign in the domain of Exchange. It is through this natural and beneficent law of automatic compensations, stimulating exportations on the one side and slackening them on the other, that most of the casual disturbances of the commercial par as between two countries are easily and perfectly rectified.

While this great law is in full possession of our minds, let us note in passing how artificial restrictions by one country on the importation of goods from another, commonly called "Protectionism," affects this commercial par as between those two countries. Besides stopping absolutely a mass of otherwise profitable exportations and importations for both countries, it makes less profitable to the country imposing the restrictions whatever foreign trade *does take place* between them in spite of the restrictions. Suppose England, as is the fact, opens her ports freely to the commodities of France, while France puts restrictions in the shape of heavy taxes upon importations from England; more French goods are likely under these circumstances to seek English ports than English goods to seek French ports, because they are more welcome; consequently, more bills of exchange drawn on London will naturally be offered in Paris than bills on Paris in London, and will so far forth be sold at a discount, while the London bills drawn on Paris will be sold at a premium; in other words, the comparatively few goods that do get out of a "protected" country, realize less to their owners than the natural value, because the bills drawn on them are extremely apt to be sold below par! With this course of things all known facts agree. Since the United States became conspicuously a "protected" country a quarter of a century ago, it has been at rare intervals and for short periods that bills drawn here on London have been at par. They have been usually much below par. The equivalent of £1 sterling in United States money is $4.8665; and when bills on London sell for less per pound sterling than $4.86, they are at a discount in New York or Boston; and exporters here are direct losers to the extent of the discount.

If, however, notwithstanding the beautiful action of this great law of commerce, the disturbance in the commercial par as between two countries continues obstinate, it indicates one of several things as true of the country, whose bills of exchange drawn on another persist in a considerable discount; (1) it has come to be a pretty steady debtor country as towards the other, by sending thither its national or State or corporation bonds, whose interest and ultimately principal also must sooner or later be remitted in exports *extra* to the exports needed to pay for the current imports of goods; (2) it has either naturally or by persistence in a bad public policy little or no shipping of its own, so that freights both ways have to be paid to foreigners in the form of exported goods *extra* to those exported to pay for those imported in transient trade, which of course increases the number and face of the bills drawn *in* the luckless country *on* the lucky country or countries; (3) it has made the vast and fatal mistake of excluding by legal barriers of taxes put on for that purpose the goods of foreigners, whose only motive in coming is to take off corresponding goods of the deluded country's own to the profit of both, and so these last-mentioned goods must seek a foreign market (if at all) at reduced rates, their natural market having been destroyed by national law; and (4) it may have made the national money in which the bills drawn on it are liable to be paid an inferior money, either transiently by mere abundance or permanently by worsened quality, which is well illustrated in the instance of Amsterdam as cited in a preceding chapter, and which can only be remedied by raising the standard of the money to the level of the best.

Very little, if anything, can be inferred as to the prosperity of a country or even as to the real condition of its "exchanges" in this technical sense of the term, by the transient movements of gold to and from the commercial countries, in their present complex relations as gold-producing and non-gold-producing countries and as debt-settling and non-debt-settling centres. Gold moves back and forth in obedience to several other impulses than to settle the balances in an international trade of Commodities. Gold-producing countries of course export gold just as they would any other native product. If for any reason gold becomes relatively more abundant in one country than in other commercial countries around it, general prices will rise in that country in consequence; which means, that gold is then and there the cheapest article that the people of that country can export to pay their commercial debts with. Also, the imports which a nation pays for in gold, or in bills of exchange bought above par, are often bought with a high profit. Creditor nations, nations that have managed to make themselves settling-places for the world's commercial debts, and nations that welcome imports without impediment from every quarter of the earth (and England may serve as a sample for all these three), will largely pay for imports in gold or in bills bearing a premium.

It is a thousand pities, that technical terms which are quite misleading unless one remembers their origin and exact significance, have come to be intrenched in commercial language too strongly to be dislodged at this late day, as the common terms to express the state of the "exchanges" as between two countries. These terms are *"against"* and *"in favor of."* The old

Mercantile system, which has left other unsavory progeny behind it besides this, in order to keep and heap gold and silver in a country, encouraged exports in every way and discouraged imports, in order that the "*balance of trade*," as the phrase ran, that is, the difference in volume between exports and imports, might come back to the country in gold and silver; and this foolish and now thoroughly exploded notion gave rise to the terms in question; exchanges were then said to be "against" a country when the record seemed to show more imports than exports, as if that implied that the imports were too great for a "balance" in gold and silver; and were said to be "in favor of" a country when its export-line was greater than the line of imports, as implying a favorable balance to be met by a specie-import in future. The false "System" is gone forever, but the "terms" still abide in commercial language, and confuse the minds more or less (more rather than less) of everybody who tries to make these terms a vehicle of thought. We have now described the causes and courses of international bills of exchange without resorting to these technicalities, which imply movements of gold and silver which do not actually take place under the conditions supposed; for example, the exchanges were "in favor" of the United States in 1874-77, there being an apparent trade balance of $164,000,000 in 1877 and a still larger in 1876 and a larger one in the two years preceding, but the import of specie was small in all those years, averaging about $25,000,000 a year, and the rest of the excess of exports went to pay interest due to foreigners, freights on the cargoes both ways, and so on. It is difficult to use without abusing the terms "against" and "in favor of" in this connection, and the reader is cautioned not to employ them; although "discount" and "premium" on international bills of exchange are matters extremely important to observe and to know the grounds of. Were there no counterworking principle, bills of exchange drawn *on* capitalist and creditor countries, like Great Britain, whose imports are apt to be strongly in excess of the exports, and whose public policy is wise enough to put no obstacles in the way of the free receipt of imports, would be at a *discount* in countries sending exports thither.

This counterworking principle, already illustrated as to inland exchange in the case of New York, is best seen internationally in connection with London, which is the settling-place of the world's commerce. When the Romans dredged the Thames and made "the pool" just below London Bridge, they took the first steps towards making that town a commercial centre; since a market for products is products in market, the busy exchange of commodities there has quickened in every age the accumulation of capital and the increase of population; previous to the Dock Laborers' Strike in 1889, about 100 vessels entered the port of London every day, which received about one-half of the total customs revenue of the United Kingdom, and sent out about one-fourth of its exports; the business of out-of-the-way and semi-civilized countries has somehow (and it would not be hard to tell why) centered in London, as well as the business of originally British Colonies everywhere and of all other commercial countries; accordingly, debtors and creditors abound there, bills of exchange concentre there, and debts due from everywhere are payable *there*; and therefore, because bills on London are good all over the world, the Demand for them counterworks the natural cheapness of the bills drawn on exports *thither* as compared with the natural dearness of the bills drawn there on exports *thence*.

Another thing must be borne in mind in comparing the merchandise accounts of any country, namely, that whenever the "exchange" is sufficient to cover the cost and risk of the transmission of gold, gold itself is likely to go freely from the country, in which bills drawn on exports are at a premium, or to use for once the old hazardous phrase, "*against*" which the exchanges have turned, and bills will be drawn on that gold, as upon common merchandise, and sold of course for the sake of the premium; or, if a decidedly higher rate of discount prevail in a neighboring country, gold will naturally go thither from the lower-rate lands, because lenders in the latter will desire to realize the higher rate of current interest on money, and bills will be drawn on this gold as well, which will tend to lower the premium on bills there; unless, then, the premium *and* the difference in interest abroad will justify the speculation, the gold will not stir; although, if the difference in interest abroad were very considerable and promised to continue for some time, the bills on the gold might sell at a discount and still leave a profit to the senders; but the home bankers can always stop a drain of gold of this kind by raising their own rates of discount.

This casual mention of bankers leads on to the weighty point, that the whole business of foreign exchange is falling more and more into the hands of the bankers, because bills drawn *by* and *upon* well-known bankers naturally have a better credit than ordinary commercial bills, the names upon which are less widely and favorably known. Accordingly, persons sending cargoes of cotton, say, or of any other valuables, from New York to Liverpool, arrange with their bankers in New York to have the proceeds of the cargoes put to the *bankers'* credit in London, and then these bankers draw bills on the London bankers, which will bring a higher price in New York than a common commercial bill, because many remitters and most travellers prefer bankers' bills, which, though they cost more, pay better and buy better abroad. Commercial bills are still bought and sold in every commercial town, but bankers' bills are more and more taking their place; and the quotations usually give the current price of each.

London is so prominent as the settling-place of the world's transactions by means of bills drawn on and by London bankers, partly on account of the commercial predominance of England, partly from excellent banking customs there, and mainly because an immense mass of cheap loanable capital exists there, which even foreigners may borrow at London rates, provided only that they can get credit there, that is, leave to draw on a London banker, to whom of course remittances must be made as fast as he accepts their bills. Besides, the Bank of England, as the principal bank in Great Britain, and as closely connected with the Government, acts as a bank of support to the public and private Credit of that country. It does a regular business as a bank of deposits and discounts, but it means to keep its rate of discount somewhat above the rate demanded by the other bankers in London, so as not to come into competition with them much in their ordinary business, and be able to act as a bank of support to them and all others in times of pressure. All banks have about so much credit to sell, *and no more*; most banks sell in ordinary times about all the credit they have, because their profits depend on that; but if the Bank of England did this, it would become useless in periods of panic. In point of fact, that Bank just begins to sell its reserve credit, when the credit of the bankers below is exhausted. When they are at the *end* of their rope, there is generally an abundance of slack rope still in the great Institution above.

Now, as gold can be drawn out of the Bank of England by the cheques of depositors as well as by the presentation of its own notes for redemption, the Rate of Discount becomes a matter of prime importance in the management of the Bank. The whole line of deposits is a line of liabilities to pay out gold, if the depositors demand it; and, as deposits come largely through discounts, whenever there is a strong tendency to draw out gold so as to weaken the reserves of the Bank, the directors have an effectual remedy by raising the rate of discount. The higher the *price* the Bank charges for its credit, the fewer, so far forth, will be its customers, and the smaller its line of deposits, and the less likely a continuous drain of gold from its vaults. The Bank of England is managed throughout by so simple a manner as the turning back and forth of this magic screw of Discount.

Besides the use of the term "Par of Exchange" in the broad commercial sense in which we have now been examining it, as indicating the substantial equality of international debts as between two countries by the current prices of bills of exchange, there is another and subordinate sense in which the phrase is employed, namely, as denoting the *relative value* of the coins of one nation in the coins of another. Thus, our present gold dollar contains 23.22 grains of pure gold; the English pound sterling contains 113.001 grains; consequently, there are $4.8665 to the English pound; and this is the "par of exchange" (in the secondary sense) between the United States and Great Britain. Between the United States and France the "par" is $1 to 5.18 francs, since the franc is 19.29 of our cents. An English shilling equals

24.33 of our cents, the new German "mark" is 23.82 cents, and the new Scandinavian "crown" equals 26.78 cents.

g. Bank Cheques. In substance indeed and even in form, Cheques are Bills of Exchange, but the two have such differing legal incidents, and run so different a course towards extinguishment, that for our purposes in this treatise they should be put under a separate discussion. Bills of exchange are expressly drawn "at sight" or for a day certain, when they become payable by the drawee: cheques *say* nothing about "sight" or any future date, though they are *really* drawn at sight, and are payable to bearer on demand: they must, therefore, be presented for payment within the shortest reasonable time (all things considered), in order that the holder may legally claim against the drawer should the banker fail meantime: a cheque is held as the payment of a debt until it be dishonored on presentation: the banker bears the risk of the forgery of the drawer's name, unless his mistake be made easier by the drawer's carelessness in drawing: a cheque is not payable after the drawer's death. The parties to cheques are the Drawer, who is a depositor with some banker; that banker thus becomes the Drawee; and the person named in the cheque is the Payee, who can indorse his own right over to another person by name or in blank to bearer. When a cheque is drawn in this way by one *banker* upon another, it is usually called in this country a *Draft.*

Formerly in England, and in other countries as well, each considerable dealer kept his own strong box, and when he had occasion to make payments, told down the solid cash upon his own counter. Afterwards, the goldsmiths of London solicited the honor of keeping in their vaults the spare cash of the merchants, and these in their payments among each other came to employ orders or cheques drawn on the goldsmiths, and at the shops of the latter the principal payments in coin were effected. The later introduction of Banks brought along with it the custom, now continually widening in commercial countries among all classes of the people, of keeping one's funds with some banker, and making payments by written orders or cheques upon him. When the person making the payment and the person receiving it keep their money with the same banker, there is no need of any money at all passing in the premises, the sum being merely transferred in the banker's books from the credit of the payer to the credit of the receiver. The banker is quite willing usually to do this business for nothing, and even sometimes to allow the depositors a low rate of interest on all balances remaining in his hands, in consideration of the privilege involved of loaning such proportion of the aggregate of these sums as he deems safe to other parties at a higher rate of interest.

In the larger cities, by an arrangement called the "Clearing-house," substantially the same benefits are secured as if all the depositors of the city kept their cash at the same bank; inasmuch as all the cheques drawn on each of the different banks, and passing in the course of the business day into other banks, are assorted before evening at all the banks, and adjusted the next morning through the clearing-house, and the credits and debits of each bank are set off as far as possible against each other, leaving only small balances to be settled in money.

The London Bankers' Clearing-house was established in 1775; in 1864, the Bank of England was admitted to it; and since then, the Clearing-house itself, and all the bankers and firms using it, keep accounts with the Bank of England, and the balances, formerly settled by money, are now adjusted by simple transfers of account on the books of that great Bank. This carries out the grand principle of the Clearing further than it has yet been carried in this Country, although the United States Sub-Treasury not very long ago joined the New York Clearing-house, while the practical details of the Clearing are simpler and better in New York than in London. The average clearings in the London house (and there are besides many other clearing-houses in the United Kingdom) were £5,218,000,000 a year for 1875-80, and the amounts cleared frequently rose to £20,000,000 a day; which, if paid in gold coin, would weigh about 157 tons and require about 80 horses to carry it; and if paid in silver coin would weigh more than 2500 tons and require 1275 horses. This is stated on the excellent authority of the late Professor Jevons.

The total business of the 23 clearing-houses of the United States in 1880 was over $50,000,000,000; the New York Clearing-house did 65% of that business for that year; and the average daily clearings there for the fiscal year 1879 were $76,167,983.

We will now describe mainly from personal observation the New York Clearing-house, which was established in 1853, premising that the principle is the same, though the details may be different, in all other clearing-houses wherever located. Business men in New York, as elsewhere, usually pass in to their bankers as a deposit all the cheques and current credits received in the course of a business day. It is the custom for everybody to draw his own cheque *on* his banker to make payments with, and to pass in *to* his banker the cheques he receives from others. Say there are sixty clearing-banks in New York City. Each of these banks sorts out after business hours every day all the cheques it has received that day drawn on each of the other banks into separate parcels ready for the clearing the next morning. Each bank has, then, fifty-nine parcels *to deliver*, which represent the property of that bank, and are a *claim* upon the other banks; and also *to receive* fifty-nine parcels, which represent the property of the other banks, and are a claim upon *itself.*

Before ten o'clock in the morning sixty messengers, each having fifty-nine parcels to deliver, appear at the clearing-house, each reporting to the manager at once for record the amount of "exchange" he has brought, which is entered of course as *credit* to his bank; and then all take their positions in order in front of the sixty desks, which occupy the floor of the house, behind which sit sixty clerks, each representing one of the banks. Each messenger stands opposite the desk of his own bank, with his fifty-nine parcels already arranged in the exact order of the bank-desks before him. Of course no messenger has anything to deliver to the clerk of his own bank. Each clerk inside his desk has a sheet of paper containing the names of all the other banks arranged in the same order as the desks, with the amounts carried out upon it which his messenger has just brought to each. All these are entered in his credit column. Each messenger carries also a slip of paper ready to be delivered with each parcel to each clerk, on which is entered the amount of the cheques he now brings to each bank. Of course the amount delivered *to* each bank is *debit* to that bank, just as the amount brought *by* each is *credit* to that bank.

A signal from the manager, who stands on a raised platform at one end of the room with his two or more clerks before him, and each messenger steps forward to the next desk in front of him, delivers his parcel and also the slip that goes with it, which latter the clerk signs with his initials and hands back to the messenger as his voucher for the delivery; and then each messenger advances to the next desk,—the whole *cue* moving in order,—at which precisely the same things take place as before, and so on, until the circuit of the room is made, and each comes opposite again the desk of his own bank, having passed to each its "exchange" and taken a receipt for each delivery. This process takes about ten minutes; when each clerk, who had on his sheet to start with the *credit* due to his bank, has now the *data* (fifty-nine items) by which to calculate the *debit* of his bank. The difference between the aggregate of cheques *received* and *brought* by his bank is the balance due *to* or *from* the clearing-house as to that bank.

All the clerks report to the manager the amounts *received* by each, and as his proof-sheets hold already the amounts *brought*, if the two columns add up alike, no mistake has been made, and the general clearing is over. Thirty-five minutes are allowed the clerks to enter, report, and prove their work. Fines are imposed for errors discovered after that time. The Clearing-house gives tickets of debit or credit to all the banks, and the debit ones must pay in lawful money before half-past one, and the credit ones will get their due from the manager immediately after. The largest sum ever cleared in New York in one day was $206,034,920.51 on Nov. 17, 1868, and the smallest $8,357,394.82 on Oct. 30 of the panic year, 1857.

h. Crossed Cheques. About twenty years ago there was instituted in London what is called the Cheque-Bank, which is designed to bring the benefits of the credit-system in the form of cheques more easily to all classes of the people. The cheques issued by this institution are so different in character and in course from common bank-cheques, and are in some respects so new in principle, that we must give to them a separate heading and a full explanation.

The Cheque-Bank is a stock company in London under that style, which has entered into relations with nearly all the banks and bankers of the United Kingdom, and with many Colonial and foreign banks also, by which Cheque-Books are furnished for sale by the Cheque-Bank through these associated banks, which also agree to cash the cheques, every cheque in which books indicates by printed and indelible perforated notices upon the forms what the utmost sum is against which that cheque can be drawn; the aggregate of these perforated sums is the price for which each book is sold less $1\frac{1}{5}$ penny for each cheque in it, of which the penny is for the Government stamp required and the one-fifth for the profits of the Cheque-Bank; and all these cheques in books of different sizes and amounts are drawn in form *on* the Cheque-Bank, and *Crossed*, that is, *only made payable through a banker*. It is one security against fraud that each cheque bears on its face the utmost sum for which it can be used, and another is that it can only be taken up by a banker and thus settled ultimately through the clearing-house. The Crossed Cheques Act of Parliament in 1876 makes any obliteration of the crossing or essential alteration of a cheque *felony* at law.

Cheque-crossing is of two kinds, *special* and *general*; when any particular banker's name is written between two transverse lines, in which form alone crossed cheques differ from ordinary ones, that makes that cheque payable by him only; when the words "*and Company*" or "*and Co.*" are written between these lines, that makes the cheque payable only through *some* banker, that is, the cheque is crossed *generally*; and when two parallel transverse lines simply are drawn across the face of a cheque, with or without the words "not negotiable," that cheque is legally deemed to be *crossed* and crossed *generally*. When a cheque is uncrossed, the lawful holder may cross it either generally or specially; when it is crossed generally, he may at his option cross it specially; and whether crossed generally or specially he may add the words "not negotiable." All this facilitates greatly the *collection* of cheques by set-off through the clearing; and has a direct bearing on the fortunes of the Cheque-Bank.

The Cheque-Bank publicly guarantees the payment of all the cheques in all its cheque-books to the maximum amount for which each cheque may be drawn; and it may well do this, for no cheque-book is sold except for money, and the money is ready in the hands of some banker to pay every cheque when presented; any banker or other person will give cash for them, or take them in payment for goods or other services, or if they are drawn for a sum larger than the debt due will give back the charge to the bearer; and if the cheques be actually drawn for less than the maximum perforated on them, the Bank itself will give additional cheques for the balance. The ultimate payment, then, of these cheques is as sure as anything in the future can be; the buyer of a cheque-book knows, that the money is already in deposit to pay them, and that the government-stamps on them have already been paid for, while the receiver of an ordinary cheque cannot know beforehand that the drawer has money in deposit against it. Moreover, the holder of an ordinary cheque must use due diligence in presenting it for payment as soon as possible, or delay it at his own risk, while the holder of these has no motive whatever for haste,—time does not deteriorate them. All money received for cheque-books is left in the hands of the bankers who sell them, or transferred to other bankers in order to meet the cheques presented elsewhere, and accordingly an interest is paid by the bankers to the Cheque-Bank, on the balance of deposits thus held, and this interest, together with the one-fifth of a penny for each cheque, is the only source of profit to the Cheque-Bank. Of course, the longer these cheques remain out before presentation, the more profitable to the Cheque-Bank; and their average length of life has been heretofore not far from ten days.

Since these cheques are crossed *generally* (not specially) with the words "and Co.," that is to say, since they can ultimately be taken up only by some banker, they have a more *generalized* character than common bank-cheques, they are safer to carry and keep than so much money would be, there is no difficulty in shopping or paying wages by means of them, they are very much the same in their nature as bank bills are, and might easily in certain circumstances become *money* just as bank bills in some circumstances are money. Each of the associated banks keeps an account of course with the Cheque-Bank, but is not obliged to keep a separate account with the purchasers of cheque-books, which is a great relief to the banks. In this way the Cheque-Bank extends the use of cheques in the lieu of money to a great multitude of small transactions, and relieves the other banks from what would otherwise be a great deal of troublesome accounting and collection. The ingenuity and the utility of this comparatively new form of Credit cannot be questioned for one moment; the promoters of the Bank intended that their cheques should be received by the people as a substitute for cash and for Post Office orders, and such has been the effect, many railway and other companies having long ago agreed to receive them as cash, and the people generally regard them as cheaper and more convenient than postal orders and even for many purposes than cash.

i. Cash Credits. As the Cheque-Bank in the sense as just explained has been thus far in the history of Credit peculiar to England, so we have now to look to Scotland only for an exemplification of a form of Credit hitherto confined to that country. It is a national characteristic of the Scotch to be "canny," that is, they *can*, a word from the old Teutonic *können, to be able*; and, as a consequence, Scotch Banking has long been famous the world over; and the one peculiarity of it, with which we are now concerned, goes back certainly to 1729, as we happen to know from a minute of the Directors of the Bank of Scotland under that date. That bank was chartered by the old Scotch Parliament in 1695, one year after the chartering by the English Parliament of the Bank of England, and under substantially the same title as that, namely, "The Governor and Company of the Bank of Scotland." It began to establish branches in different towns of the realm in 1696, and began to issue bank notes for £1 (a privilege denied to the Bank of England) in 1704; and it began also at a very early period to exhibit the two main peculiarities of Scotch banking, namely, (1) to receive deposits *on interest* and (2) *to grant credit on cash accounts*, or, as they have come to be called less properly, Cash Credits.

This second peculiarity, which has proved extremely beneficial to Scotland, is for substance this, to create a drawing account in favor of a deserving customer, who has made as yet no deposits in the bank, but who draws out money and pays it in from time to time just like an ordinary depositor, and instead of receiving interest on the daily balance to his *credit* (old Scotch fashion), he pays interest on the daily balance to his *debit*. These accounts are called Cash Credits. They are not intended to be dead loans, but quick accounts; and they are not granted except to persons in business, or to those who are frequently drawing out and paying in money. The individual who has obtained such a credit is enabled to draw the whole sum, or any part of it, when he pleases, replacing it, or portions of it, when he pleases, according as he finds it convenient, interest being charged only upon such part as he draws out.

David Hume in his Essay of the Balance of Trade, published in 1752, makes this nice point in favor of Cash Credits: "If a man borrows £5000 from a private hand, besides that it is not always to be found when required, he pays interest for it whether he be using it or not. On the other hand, his Cash Credit costs him nothing, except during the moment it is of service to him; and this circumstance is of equal advantage as if he had borrowed money at a much lower rate of interest." The Cash Credit is always for a limited sum, seldom under £100, given upon the customer's own security, and that in addition of two or three individuals approved by the bank, who become sureties for its payment. Of course, only those banks can furnish such credits which possess a surplus of credit more than they can sell in the ordinary way, and these credits are safe and useful only in small communities, in which men are well known to each other. Some friends of the parties thus accommodated always guarantee the bank against loss; but the losses have proved to be insignificant, the gains to be marvellous; and this form of credit issued on the basis of no previous transaction in the way of deposits illustrates better than any other the radical principle, that Credit is Capital.

The Report of a Committee of the House of Lords made in 1826 on Scotch and Irish banking describes very clearly and fully the system of Cash Credits: "There is also one part of their system, which is stated by all the witnesses to have had the best effects upon the people of Scotland, and particularly upon the middling and poorer classes of society, in producing and encouraging habits of frugality and industry. The practice referred to is that of Cash Credits. Any person who applies to a bank for a Cash Credit is called upon to produce two or more competent sureties, who are jointly bound; and after a full inquiry into the character of the applicant, the nature of his business, and the sufficiency of his securities, he is allowed to open a credit, and to draw upon the bank for the whole of its amount, or for such part of it as his daily transactions may require. To the credit of the account he pays in such sums as he may not have occasion to use, and interest is charged or credited upon the daily balance, as the case may be. From the facility which these Cash Credits give to all the small transactions of the country, and from the opportunities which they afford to persons who begin business with little or no capital but their character to employ profitably the minutest products of their industry, it cannot be doubted that the most important advantages are derived to the whole community. The advantage to the banks that give these Cash Credits arises from the call which they continually produce for the issue of their paper, and from the opportunity which they afford for the profitable employment of part of their deposits. The banks are indeed so sensible that, in order to make this part of their business advantageous and secure, it is necessary that their Cash Credits should be operated upon, that they refuse to continue them unless this implied condition be fulfilled. The total amount of their Cash Credits is stated by one witness to be £5,000,000, of which the average amount advanced by the banks may be one-third."

There are only ten Banks doing business in Scotland, and the Bank of Scotland, the oldest of these, had 86 branches in 1875, and the average number of branches of the other nine is very nearly the same with that.

j. Circular Credits. These are a device of bankers to enable travellers and merchants of one country to obtain credit and cash in foreign countries in sums to suit their convenience, not to exceed in the aggregate the limit mentioned in the credits drawn. These credits assume different forms and are called by different names, but they are all at bottom foreign Bills of Exchange. They are Orders to pay. They are drawn by Bankers at home upon Bankers abroad. They are bought by travellers and others, because they are safer to carry than so much money would be, and much more convenient. In nearly all of those forms the credits are available for no one else than the payee, whose name is upon the form as well as the names of the bankers who are the drawees, and so the credits are not liable to be stolen, although they may be temporarily (not ultimately) lost. Purchasers of such credits can obtain money on them in all of the principal cities of the world in just such sums as they need. They have ultimately to pay for no more credit than they actually use, because the drawer will pay back to the payee, in case he has bought and paid for the entire credit drawn, the cash difference; while on the other hand, arrangements can always be made beforehand, by which money need not be deposited with the banker at home any faster than it is actually called for abroad; and while also a good customer of the bank drawing the credit, one who keeps ordinarily a good line of deposits, may pay for whatever credit he has used when he returns from his trip.

There is one kind of these foreign credits that deserves separate mention, since it has come of late years into quite general use, namely, "Circular Notes," as they are called. These are sight bills of exchange, each drawn for a relatively small amount, say £10, and multiplied in number to the requirements of the buyer, and drawn by one domestic banking-house, say Kountze Brothers of New York, on one foreign banking-house, say Union Bank of London, the names of drawer and drawee only being upon the "notes," the payee or buyer being expected to indorse each note in the presence of the Correspondent making the payment. The notes, therefore, are not negotiable except by the signature of the payee himself from time to time as he needs the proceeds. This makes them safer than so much money to carry: if stolen, they could do the thief no possible good. At the same time the drawer of the notes furnishes the payee a circular letter addressed to his banking correspondents all over the world, just as in an ordinary Letter of Credit, containing the name and also the personal signature of the payee, but unlike the ordinary Letter making no reference to the amounts of credit furnished, and there are no indorsements of any kind by the correspondents on this circular letter, which the payee is cautioned in print on the back *to keep separate* from the Circular Notes covered by it. One of these letters runs as follows, the name of the payee being entered in manuscript and also in autograph:—

"TO OUR CORRESPONDENTS,

GENTLEMEN,

THIS LETTER WILL BE PRESENTED TO YOU BY GRACE
PERRY, WHO IS RECOMMENDED TO YOUR KIND
ATTENTION, AND IS SUPPLIED WITH OUR CIRCULAR
NOTES, THE VALUE OF WHICH PLEASE FURNISH AT THE
CURRENT RATE FOR SIGHT BILLS ON LONDON, WITHOUT
ANY EXPENSE TO US. AFTER YOU HAVE EXAMINED THIS
LETTER, PLEASE RETURN IT TO THE BEARER, IN WHOSE
HANDS IT WILL REMAIN UNTIL THE EXPIRATION OF THE
CIRCULAR NOTES."

These Circular Notes approximate in certain respects in kind towards the cheques of the Cheque-Bank of London: both are bought at the outset and paid for in full on the spot; and both are drawn *upon one Bank*, which is the ultimate Drawee and Payer. In two essential respects, however, the notes differ from the cheques: the cheques are payable to Bearer without any indorsement by anybody, and so have a much more *generalized* purchasing-power than the notes, which have to be indorsed by the payee (not named indeed in the notes but in the letter accompanying them), as they are negotiated in a way preliminary to their ultimate payment by the single bank on which they are drawn; and also the notes, like all other foreign bills of exchange, are subject in their value to the fluctuations of International Exchange, while the cheques in their value are independent of commercial exchanges "in favor" or "against" any country, and entitle the bearer to so many pounds sterling in value according to English coinage without any possible discount or premium. These London Cheques, accordingly, approach much nearer to the character of Money than any other form of Credit yet devised, except Bank bills undoubtedly convertible; and already take their place as one of the *media* in the international trade, and are sold in New York by authorized agents of the Cheque-Bank, as they have long been by such agents in all English and Colonial and in many foreign cities.

These *Ten* are the principle instruments in Credit-Exchanges throughout the world; and we pass now, as proposed, to the next section of our subject, namely, the Advantages of Credit.

3. As introducing these advantages and also as illustrating them, we call attention first to the antiquity of many of the forms of Credit, a point upon which much fresh light has been cast by recent discoveries in, and ability to decipher the cuneiform writing of, the ancient Assyria and Babylonia. It is to the credit of Credit, that the earliest of civilized men seem to have perceived its nature, to have seized upon its powers, and to have realized for themselves some of its advantages. Credit is natural and legitimate. The moderns have invented new forms of it, and have tested its capacities to the utmost, but the ancients know it well in several of its instruments, and

vindicate their own insight into the recesses of Exchanges by tablets and documents now known and read of all men.

In an earthenware jar found some years ago in the neighborhood of Hillah, a few miles from Babylon, were discovered many clay tablets inscribed with records relating to banking, and, what is more, to banking as carried on for generations by a single family or firm, which the cuneiform archæologists have translated as "Egibi & Co." These tablets are now deposited in the British Museum. Those who can read them say, that the founder of this banking-house, Egibi, probably lived in the reign of Sennacherib, about 700 B.C. This family has been traced in banking transactions during a century and a half, and through five generations down to the reign of Darius. They were the Rothschilds in the region of the Euphrates: they acted in a sort as the national bank of Babylon.

The Tigris is always associated with the Euphrates and forever will be. Nineveh on the former river, like Babylon on the latter, has yielded from its tablet-records information as to the use of credit in the more northern capital of Assyria. "Within the palace of Asshur-bani-pal, the Sardanapalus of the Greeks, who reigned at Nineveh from 668 B.C., Layard discovered what is known as the Royal Library. There were two chambers, the floors of which were heaped with books, like the Chaldean tablets already described. The number of books in the collection has been estimated at ten thousand. The writing upon some of the tablets is so minute that it cannot be read without the aid of a magnifying-glass. We learn from the inscriptions that a librarian had charge of the collection. Catalogues of the books have been found, made out on clay tablets. The library was open to the public, for an inscription of Asshur-bani-pal says, "*I wrote upon the tablets; I place them in my palace for the instruction of my people.*" The Assyrian tablets embrace a great variety of subjects; the larger part, however, are lexicons and treatises on grammar, and various other works intended as text-books for scholars. Perhaps the most curious of the tablets yet found are notes issued by the Government, and made redeemable in gold and silver on presentation at the King's treasury. Tablets of this character have been found bearing date as early as 625 B.C. It would seem from this that the Assyrians had very correct notions of the promise-character of paper (tablet) money" (Myers).

In the Metropolitan Museum of Art in New York are Babylonian tablets bearing distinct records of credit transactions that took place in the reign of Nebuchadnezzar. The earliest tablet is of the year 601 B.C. On it are memoranda of loans of silver made by Kurdurru as follows: "1 mina of silver to Suta, 1 mina to Balludh, ½ mina to Buluepus, 5 shekels to Nabu-basa-napsate, and 5 shekels to Nergal-dann;—total, 3 minas, 5 shekels of silver." There are more than 50 similar tablets in this collection; the latest dated, "Babylon, 18th day of 14th year of Darius," that is, B.C. 505. M. Lenormant, who can read them, divides these credit documents into five principal types. 1. Simple obligations; 2. Obligations with a penal clause in case of non-fulfilment; 3. Obligations with the guarantee to a third party; 4. Obligations payable to a third person; and 5. Drafts drawn upon one place, payable in another. These last are letters of Credit. They contain the names of several witnesses. They are evidently negotiable, but from the nature of things could not pass by indorsement, because when the clay was once baked nothing new could be added, and under these circumstances the name of the payee was often omitted. It seems to follow from this peculiarity, that the drawee must have been regularly advised by the drawer. One of the credits in this most interesting collection had 79 days to run.

The main elements of their civilization came to the Greeks, and especially to the Greek cities in Asia Minor demonstrably from the Eastward; the Greek West proved itself quick to catch up the thoughts and the modes of the East; accordingly, Isocrates in his plea against the banker, Pasion, describes a formal bill of Exchange bought by Stratocles in Athens, payable in Pontus, and guaranteed principal and interest by Pasion; the practical Romans were pupils of the Greeks in all such matters, and so it came about in course of time, that Cicero wrote as follows in a letter to Atticus,—"Let me know, if the money my son needs at Athens can be sent him *by way of exchange*, or if it be necessary for it to be taken to him,—*permutarine possit an ipsi ferendum sit*"; and after that the Jews and the Lombards carried the Letter of Credit all over the world.

It goes without saying, when the most civilized and advanced people of the world were the first to adopt and have been since the quickest to expand the use of Credit, that there must be pretty obvious and very solid advantages from such use and expansion; and we must now note and weigh a few of these advantages.

(1) There are young men in every advanced community in the world who have integrity and industry and skill, but little or no *Capital*; and when such men are enabled to borrow money, as by the Scotch system of "cash accounts" or otherwise, to start themselves in business or to enlarge a business already in successful operation, the general interests of Production as well as their own personal interests, are greatly subserved by such credit; because in all probability much capital thus passes out of hands which are *less* into hands which are *more* able to use it *productively*. Those who are best able to make capital *tell* by increase are generally those who are most desirous to obtain it, and frequently those who can offer the best security for its replacement. Nothing, therefore, is to be said against, but everything in favor of, such a loaning of capital as shall bring it under safe conditions from the hands of the idle and the aged, from those indisposed or

incompetent to use it productively, into other hands at once competent and honest. Such credits as these are a benefit and only a benefit to all the parties concerned, and to Society at large. The active operators retain something of profit after replacing the capital with current interest upon it; the lenders receive more than if their capital remained idle, or they employed it themselves; and Society is benefited by a more complete development, and rapid circulation, of Services. Despite all the instances of broken faith, it is still an honor to human nature, that men do so gain by good character the confidence of their fellows, that they are and ought to be trusted with capital on their simple word or note; and it is the glory of free political institutions, that under their influence more than elsewhere, young men do rise by the help of so slight a stepping-stone as this, in crowds, to the high places of opulence.

In the important point of view, that thus all of the available capital of a community is brought out into productive activity, too much can scarcely be said of Savings-Banks, which take the surplus earnings of the poor, and not only keep them safely, but pay a fair interest on each deposit, and loan the aggregate at a higher rate on choice securities, thus stimulating frugality in a wide circle of depositors, and at the same time aiding Production by opportune loans to the best class of borrowers. In the year 1881, there were $443,000,000 invested in savings-banks in the State of New York, and $230,000,000 in the small State of Massachusetts.

In this first category of the advantages of Credit, come also the ordinary bank discounts, made for short periods only, holding the debtor to the strictest rules of payment, only professing and only enabled to help customers over the transient hard places in their business, and *not* to furnish the funds on which the business is mainly conducted. Loans drawn from the banks on interest should never be put into the form of fixed capital, and should only be a *part* of the quick or circulating capital, since only the passing necessities of a business having an independent basis and movement of its own, can safely be met by bank discounts. The cash credits of Scotland are quite different both in what they are and in what they imply from the short and sharp discounts of the banks of our own country.

So far as the capital stock of banks is made up, as it usually is, of a large number of comparatively small subscriptions, there is the great advantage just spoken of, of calling a multitude of otherwise idle sums into activity in production; and so far as no undue privileges, unjust to other corporations and individuals, are accorded to banks by law, there is no branch of industry more legitimate and beneficial than banking. It is no essential part of the functions of a bank, that it manufacture and issue paper money; that feature is always rather a source of weakness than a ground of strength; the money the bank circulates should always be the national money; and if that too, unfortunately, should be credit-money, the element of credit in the *money* should be sharply discriminated in the public mind from that other and quite different element of credit by which the bank *loans* it to its customers.

(2) There is another class of advantages in Credit, which do not depend so much on the transfer of Capital from less to more productive hands, as on the facilities which credit affords in economizing the general operations of Exchange. Here the advantages are derived from the convenience of *settling accounts* arising out of exchanges, rather than from the *character* of the exchanges themselves. Look a moment, for example, at foreign Bills of Exchange. They serve to settle up the accounts arising from the Commerce of two or six Continents, with but little transmission of money from any, and with but very little loss of time. Commercial bills drawn in New York on London have been usually payable at sixty days' sight; the New York merchant despatching a ship is able to realize at once the value of her cargo, minus interest for the time his bill has to run; since bankers' bills have so largely taken the place of "commercial" bills, the time is much shortened thereby, and this is one reason why bankers' bills bear a higher price in the market; the merchant or sender is indeed still liable in part to see that his bill is ultimately paid by the drawee; but the commercial integrity of the leading houses and leading banks in all countries is with justice so firmly believed in and acted on, that on the whole but little anxiety springs from this source. It is one of the noble things in international commerce, that men trust each other across the oceans, and lay millions of value on the faith of a single firm.

Inland bills of exchange equally facilitate settlements within the country itself; and cheques, which are of the same essential nature as inland bills, contribute to the same end even more simply and surely, passing readily in payments wherever the parties are known, and through credit and set-off doing the work of money more conveniently and economically than, and within certain limits just as safely as, money itself could do it. The face of a cheque drawn to the amount of his deposit in favor of another depositor in the same bank is transferred in the banker's books from the credit of the drawer to that of the payee by the stroke of a pen, no money at all passes in the premises, while the banker is released from one debt by creating another of equal amount, the drawer is released from one debt by another to be transferred to the payee, and the payee is paid by the drawer by the former's receipt of another debt more acceptable to him.

(3) Besides the two essential functions of all banks, namely, the receiving of deposits and the discounting of bills, most of them perform a variety of other legitimate operations in Credit, which must be classed among the

advantages of Credit. They buy and sell debts of all sorts. They make collection of debts for their customers. They sell their own drafts on distant places. Since 1863, our national banks have done an immense business in handling the debt of the United States: they were instrumental in diffusing the national bonds among all classes of the people: they collect for their customers the coupons at maturity: they have been and still are the factors of the government in exchanging, for those who desire it, one species of bond for another; and the entire debt of the United States has been several times changed, mainly through the agency of the banks, from bonds at high rates of interest and for short times of maturity to bonds at lower rates and for longer times.

(4) The fourth, and probably the chief, advantage of Credit is the fact, that a new purchasing-power is created by means of it, a new Valuable, something additional to all existing before in the world of Values. One can buy other things with Credit, as well as with material Commodities and personal Services. Credit, therefore, becomes a Salable under the two peculiar limitations already explained, those of future Time and personal Confidence, just as Commodities become a Salable under the peculiar limitations belonging to *them*; and, what is more to the present purpose, just as some Commodities (all of them salable) become Capital under the action of the abstinence of their owners, so some Credits (all of them salable) become Capital under the action of the Abstinence of their owners. Some commodities and some credits are expended, that is, sold, for the immediate gratification of their owners, without ever a thought of a future increase to accrue; but also, some commodities and credits are reserved by their owners for use in further production, that is, for future buying and selling; and the motive in all such cases is the same that creates all Capital everywhere, namely, the increase to accrue as the result of such abstinence; and, consequently, we lay down the postulate with all confidence, and enumerate it as one of the main advantages of Credit, that some Credits are CAPITAL, with all the powers in production of that potent agent already exemplified.

It is only fair to apprise the reader right here, that almost all Economists deny that any new capital is created through Credit. These deny *in toto* that the relation of debtor and creditor involves anything more than the exchange between the two parties of certain *titles to tangible goods*. Let the reader now hear, and then judge for himself. Bonamy Price of Oxford University, a professed Economist and a teacher of acknowledged ability, writes as follows: "*Omitting the capital which a joint stock company puts into a bank, the banker possesses no capital, except his premises and any coin that may be in them, however much commercial and monetary literature may ascribe capital to banks. Lines and names in ledgers, cheques at the Clearing-house, debts due to depositors, debts due upon bills by borrowers, are neither wealth nor capital. They are words and nothing more. Incorporeal property, under which these kinds of written words are summed up, is not wealth; it is merely a collection of title-deeds, but from which the reality is absent. The corpus is not in those deeds, but the right to acquire that property, even before possession is obtained, is itself a property. If a title-deed or a mortgage is declared to be actual wealth by Political Economy, then the sooner it is consigned to the waste-basket, the better."*

This passage shows how the word, "wealth," tangles men up inextricably, who, by discarding it utterly, might have become clear thinkers and useful expositors. It also shows, that Professor Price never analyzed Valuables into their three kinds, never thoroughly mastered in a preliminary way the Idea that underlies Economics, never precisely understood what Money is, and certainly never found out the radical nature of Credit. Nevertheless, the passage just quoted really concedes the whole matter in the present dispute,—"the right to acquire that property, even before possession is obtained, is itself a property,"—that is all that we claim, namely, that rights are property, and that new rights (which are property) are created by Credit, and that some of these new property-rights thus created may become and do become a new Capital. These new rights, however, this new and acknowledged "property," are not "*titles*" to any specific valuables whatever, as Price supposed; "*a title-deed or a mortgage*" is a totally different thing from a Credit, since the one always describes and gives a qualified title to *some specific and tangible thing*, while a credit-right is always a claim against *a person*; the Roman law drew this distinction perfectly, a credit-right was a *jus in personam*, while a title-right was a *jus in re*; the common Latin language as spoken and written marked the difference by separate words, a credit-right or true debt was a *Mutuum*, while a title-right or thing loaned was a *Commodatum*; and the Law of our present national banks explicitly recognizes this universal and fundamental distinction, by requiring the banks to loan money *on personal security only*, that is to say, no tangible things whatever, not even real estate, are allowed to be taken as *original* security for any loan. Banks deal only in true debts,—*mutua*,—and when they keep custody of concrete valuables—*commodata*—for their customers, it is as trustees or bailees and not at all as debtors.

Our late Oxford friend was far too well informed in general to contend, that a cheque, for example, is "the right to acquire possession" of any *specific* property anywhere; the drawer has indeed deposited money with the banker on whom the cheque is drawn, but that money became the banker's money the moment it was deposited and no longer his own; the cheque, accordingly, is a general claim on the banker, and not at all on any special fund in the banker's hands; it follows, therefore, that the excess of the banker's average deposits over his average reserves to secure them, is a new creation of Credit, a new resource of Production, a new Purchasing-power now available to the banker not previously and practically available to anybody, a new Valuable which he proposes to use and does use for the sake of profits accruing, consequently a new Capital.

Now let us listen to the objections to this view by a practical banker, J. H. Walker, of Worcester, Mass., in a little book of his on Banking published in 1882: "*A man always borrows something of intrinsic value. What he borrows is not a piece of paper, whatever may be on it, but a farm, a house, a factory, or a part of them; a store, a mine, or goods. No man can borrow or lend anything else. The borrower gets from the lender what puts him in possession of the things he seeks, and it must be some one of these things. So of all money (except coin). It has no value in itself. It adds nothing to the capital of the world. It purports to be and is only a title to property, a convenient device for transferring the ownership of property.*"

This author is led astray by the worse than useless adjective "intrinsic," having never yet learned that there is only one kind of value in the world of Economics, namely, purchasing-power; he sees men as trees walking through the haze cast over paper-money by John Law in the last century, as if paper-money must be "*based*" on something tangible and specific; he makes a narrow and false assumption that the only objects ever bought or borrowed are corporeal "things," denying that the debts in which alone he deals as a banker are *realities* as much as any "thing" can be; and it all comes in his case, as in the case of hundreds of others, from a totally inadequate analysis of Valuables into their three separate and virtually independent kinds, namely, Commodities and Services and Promises. Mr. Walker, although he writes a book on purpose to do this, can not explain at all under his view the Deposits and Discounts of his own bank, and would be as dumb as an oyster when confronted with the "Cash Credits" of Scotland.

(5) The fifth advantage of the use of Credit, and the last one to be mentioned in this connection, is, that it dispenses with the use and wear of large amounts of expensive Money. It is perfectly certain that Credit answers many of the purposes of Money. Suppose A has bought of B $100 worth of goods, and B has bought of A $125 worth of goods. Three ways are open to close up these transactions. A may pay B and B may pay A *in money*. This would take $225. A may pay B in money, and B may send that back with $25 more. This would take $125. Or A and B may mutually balance their credit-books, and B pay the difference in account. This would take but $25. It is clear then, that, as one or other of these general methods prevails in practice, the quantity of expensive money required to do the business of a country is very different. Just so in international trade. Foreign bills of exchange lessen enormously the quantity of metallic money that would otherwise have to be transported.

It is not strange that some thinkers and writers, seeing these unquestionable benefits of Credit even within the peculiar sphere of Money itself, have come, like Herbert Spencer and many more, to think and teach that Credit might answer *all* the purposes of money. Credit *does* take the place of money in part. Can it take the place of money entirely? Let us see. We have defined Credit as *a right to demand something of somebody*, and Debt as *an obligation to render something to somebody*; the denominations of Money are certainly needful in order *to measure* this right or obligation; and how can the denominations of money be established or maintained at all separate from the use of *some* money itself as a circulating medium? Moreover, great as is the undoubted power of Credit, vast as are these five advantages from its current use, still, each particular piece or form of Credit waits for something beyond itself; it waits for its own *extinction* in future time; which can only come about in one of three ways, (a) by *set-off* against another debt with or without a balance, (b) by *renewal* which creates a new debt and extinguishes the old, (c) by its *payment* in money; and now how can these extinctions come about without the current use of some money, at least to settle the balances at the clearing-house?

Furthermore, there have always been heretofore in all commercial countries longer or shorter periods, called "crises" or "panics," during which there was a popular reluctance to accept in exchange the ordinary instruments of Credit. Money, and much of it, was then found to be indispensable. Indeed the very advantages of Credit itself, which have now been explained at length, are dependent on this, that there be alongside of it to sustain and limit it, *a current and legal measure of Services in metallic form*, in whose denominations Values may be reckoned, in whose coins the balances of Credit may be struck, and whose presence secured everywhere by natural laws alone may enable *fulfilment* to join hand in hand with *promise*. If ever Credit should try to usurp the whole domain of Money, a tolerable standard of Value or measure of Services would be no longer possible, Credit itself would lose its foothold, and the vast balloon of Promise, sailing for awhile through the blue, the joy of projectors and the wonder of credulous spectators, would of a sudden descend to the earth collapsed and ruined.

4. There are too some disadvantages inhering in Credit. This admitted fact makes no valid argument against the use and extension of it; because there are disadvantages connected with all human devices whatever,—with all means contrived to reach earthly ends—and even a child may discover many of these; some objections lie against everything, and against everybody, and the practical question always is, Which preponderates, the good or the evil? In respect to Credit there can be no doubt, that the good outweighs the evil many fold; still, in accordance with the purpose in this book of both writer and readers to look on both sides of each significant

point in Economics, we will now give attention to the chief disadvantages inhering in the nature of Credit.

(1) In the first place, when credit is much given by dealers to ordinary retail buyers, the reverse results take place from those but just now characterized as happening under bank credits, namely, capital passes out from the hands of productive operators into hands less able and less willing to use it in further production. Indeed, in most such cases it ceases to be capital, and is expended in immediate gratification. It is much easier for the average man of fair character within the present customs of Society to "get trusted" than to pay "as he goes." Such a man is even called "easy-going." He almost always over-estimates his resources for the future, and under-estimates his obligations at the present. It is always a disadvantage in the long outlook for both parties when such men easily and largely "get trusted." Let us take a sample case: when an industrious artisan or efficient merchant has given credit for six months or a year to dilatory customers, it is so much withdrawn for so long a time from his active capital; and in order to make up his consequent loss of profit to the average and expected rate, there must be an addition to the prices of his wares sold to other parties; and, besides, some bad debts belong to such a system, and there must be additional prices somewhere to compensate for this; and thus the customers who pay promptly bear a part of the burden of the delinquents, who at least do not wholly escape, inasmuch as they ultimately (if they pay at all) pay a price enhanced by their own delay. Thus, if the current and expected profit on his capital be 12%, and the artisan or merchant sells and gets returns four times a year on the average, something less than 3% profit may be charged to each article on the average; while if he only gets returns at the end of the year, at best 12% must be put on everything at the average, and in reality considerably more, because of the bad debts that stick like a burr to that way of doing business. Hence the excellent maxim, "Quick sales and small profits."

(2) There is a greater inherent *uncertainty* in values connected with credits than in those connected with commodities, or than with those connected with personal services. We have already seen repeatedly that Value has its sphere of operations in the Past, in the Present, and in the Future. There is some uncertainty connected with what *has been done* in reference to value, since the market may prove to have been miscalculated, and the commodities to have become unsuitable; there is perhaps more uncertainty connected with what *is now being done* in reference to value, because the services bargained and being paid for may prove to be less steady and skilful than was supposed; but in the very nature of the case there is still greater uncertainty connected with what *is to be done* in relation to its value, because in the first two cases some at least of the conditions are already

fixed, while in the last one all of them are at least open to hazard. There is sufficient certainty in all three of the grand divisions of Time to justify, and probably to reward, operations in each in reference to value under the peculiar limitations and conditions of each, but credits are naturally more sensitive in the law of their value than either commodities or services.

(3) Largely in consequence of what has just been expressed under the last head, credit-exchanges are more likely than commodities-exchanges or than services-exchanges to become unduly multiplied and consequently to fail of ultimate realization. The majority of men are sanguine in relation to the future. Unless they are in actual contact with their limitations, they are apt to belittle the rigidity and inevitableness of such limitations. As the outcome of this, promises are apt to overpass the powers of fulfilment. No more bales of cotton of any one year's crop can be actually delivered to buyers, than have been actually grown and marketed; the services of no more men in any capacity can be contracted for and rendered, than there are men able and willing to work; here are impassable limits; but the field of the future is buoyant with possibilities; and hence credits, whose sphere is the future, though legitimate and potent under the proper conditions, lie in a field whose limits are invisible, and within which *Hope* is ever a tempter to overdoing.

Is speculation proper? Certainly; if by the word "speculation" is meant the buying of anything with an expectation based on rational probabilities of being able to sell it again under different conditions at a higher price. Speculation in this sense is both proper and beneficial to the immediate parties to it, and to the general public as well, because the values of things thus bought and sold neither fall so low nor rise so high as they otherwise would do, which is a public gain. Speculators as a rule buy on a falling market, *which tends to lift it,* and sell on a rising market, *which tends to lower it.* It is better for all concerned, that the necessaries and conveniencies of life should bear as steady a market as is possible in the nature of things, summer and winter, year in and year out; and the ports of every nation should be open with the slightest possible hindrance in the way of tax to the corresponding necessaries and conveniencies from abroad, whenever combinations and "corners" attempt to lift their prices beyond the level determined by a natural and free Supply in contact with the current Demand.

Credits occupy the field of Probabilities; that is to say, probabilities seeming to be such to men of sharp insight and cultivated forecast. When such men *on such grounds* buy and sell "futures" in cotton or corn; when they buy and sell stocks either "short" or "long"; when they seem to themselves to perceive a sound reason for lurching over from the "bulls" to the "bears," or *vice versa;* and when they really think that what they are wont to deal in has touched bottom in price, and they buy now in view of a rise, Economics has nothing to say in blame of any or all of these operations, for they are the same in substance and motive as all other buying and selling; but nevertheless, it has this to say, that all these operations in credit-futures lie adjoining to and in dangerous proximity with another field, for operations within which it has nothing *but* blame to utter. Gambling occupies the field of Chance. There is a great difference between chances and probabilities. Political Economy has no trouble in drawing a fast and hard line between them.

But practically the operators in credit-futures experience an immense difficulty in keeping within this line of rational probabilities. The coolest heads are apt to become heated, and to lose sight of distinctions, in the close air of the Stock Exchange and the offices circumjacent. Some operators openly confess they know nothing which way the index of reason points, by buying "straddles," as they are significantly called. A friend and old-time pupil, who has for years been accustomed to these excitements in New York, said recently to the writer,—"*The Stock Exchange is a great gambling hell, and that's all there is of it!*" In buying and selling of all kinds, both sides gain: in gambling of all kinds, what one side gains the other side loses: therefore, under a sound money, healthful public opinion, and good law, gambling never can become formidable. In every lottery scheme, no matter how honestly managed, the sum of the *prices* of the tickets is greater than the sum of the *prizes* offered, otherwise nothing would be left for the profits of the managers; therefore, he would be a very foolish man, who should buy all the tickets of a given lottery with the certainty of drawing all the prizes; and *he* is a still more foolish man, who should take his *chance* of drawing all the prizes by buying two or ten tickets.

(4) Another and a principal Disadvantage of Credit is seen in its usual action on *prices* through increased Demand, and its consequent tendency to bring about Commercial Crises. Any man's whole purchasing-power is made up of three items: first, the property in his possession; secondly, the values that are owed to him; and thirdly, his credit. He can buy services of the three kinds with these three valuables; and the sum of his power to buy is exactly measured by the aggregate of these three valuables under his control. But while the first two, his property and debts due, are limited and ascertainable, the third (his credit) is indefinite and undeterminable beforehand. Being based upon *confidence*, which is itself sensitive and variable, a man's credit at one time may be vastly greater than at another, compared with his other two means of purchase; and if he have the reputation of doing a safe and regular business, and is favored by circumstances, he will find himself able sometimes to buy on credit to an extent out of all expected proportion to his other capital. When, therefore,

credit is offered and received for commodities, it has the same influence upon their prices as when money is offered and received for them. It follows, consequently, that there is likely to be a general rise of prices whenever there is an extension of credit for the purpose of purchasing; indeed, when money only is used to buy with, there can not be a *general* rise of prices, because while more money may be spent on some things, and they rise in price, there would be less money for other things, and *they* would rather fall in price; but when credit is used freely in addition, and increased purchases go on in all departments at once, there is apt to be a rise of prices as to all commodities and a universal spirit of speculation.

At such times, and while prices are still rising, men *seem* to be making great gains; everybody wishes to extend his operations by means of all his money and all his credit; and forms of indebtedness are multiplied on every hand. By and by it begins to be perceived in certain quarters that the matter has been overdone; speculative purchases cease; banks become particular whose paper they discount; men find it difficult to sell their debts due in order to provide for their debts owed; they fall back on the sale of their commodities, but when holders are anxious to sell, prices always fall; a panic now sets in, more irrational, if possible, than the previous overconfidence; their inflated credits and commodities collapse in the hands of their holders; sales at great sacrifices are inadequate to meet the mass of maturing debts contracted when confidence was high; men fail, and must fail; the banks cannot help them, or think they cannot; and so wide-spread commercial disaster comes in.

Such commercial crises swept over the United States in 1837, 1857, and 1873; and will doubtless recur in the time to come. They always arise from disordered credits, and though not necessarily connected with credit-money, are much more likely to come in connection with that. The more strong and conservative the Banks maintain their ordinary condition, the more powerfully can they operate to prevent or abate a panic. They ought always to be on the shore and never in the stream. From the very nature of banks and of the motives that create and operate them, they are apt to sell for a profit in ordinary times about all of the credit they safely can; unless, then, they foresee a stringency some time ahead, and curtail their loans, and otherwise keep their position strong in reserves and deposits, they will be powerless to help even their most deserving customers when the panic sets in; even then by a special association with other banks in the same city for reciprocal support during a crisis, as was happily brought about in New York some years ago, something may be done for their common constituency and good customers to help them out of trouble by discounts continued to them; especially as it is not money so much that is needed to allay a panic, nor even credit actually given, as it is a general knowledge that abundant credit can and will be given either by some pre-eminent bank, like the Bank of England in London, or by an association of banks for that special purpose, like the agreement just referred to as entered into temporarily by the banks of New York city. As a panic becomes imminent anywhere, some Bank or banks there ought to be in a position to extend their discounts freely, at a high rate of interest indeed, so as to discriminate between customers urgent for and deserving of discounts, and another class whose need of accommodation is not so sore, and a third class who are sure to fail if the Panic stalks forward.

A permission given of the Government to the Bank of England to overpass under these circumstances the Discount-limits laid down by the Bank Act of 1844, has on three several occasions acted like a charm to still the ragings of a commercial storm. On each of these occasions, 1847, 1857, and 1866, the Bank was forbidden by the Privy Council to discount for less than 10%.

As the inclined plane of rising prices is slowly ascended before a Crisis, so the fall of general prices afterwards seems to be rather gradual also till the lowest point of them is reached, from which another ascent is apt to commence. The following table taken from the *New York Public* of the first week of November, 1881, is instructive on both these points. Taking the prices in 1860 of 43 articles of prime necessity, which constituted then and afterwards about ¾ of the commerce of the country, as the normal standard or 100, the table gives the comparative gold prices of the same for four years previous to 1873 and for seven years subsequent, as follows:—

1869	116	1875	107
1870	118	1876	100
1871	120	1878	81
1872	122	1879	98
1873	113	1880	103
1874	115	1881	111

(5) A penultimate Disadvantage of Credit may be noted in the facility which it offers for contracting great national Debts. There are certain aspects, under which a Nation may be properly regarded as a moral person, and as such person may pledge the public faith for the present and the future, becoming a debtor to its own people or to foreigners, and thus a public

debt may be made a sort of mortgage on the national property and income. Now, it cannot be fairly denied, that incidental advantages may spring up in connection with such a national debt: for example, the bonds, which are its evidences, may open up to the people a convenient form of investment for presently inactive capital, and for trust funds of all kinds; there can be little doubt that certain classes of persons holding these national obligations are won thereby to a stronger patriotism and become better friends to stability in government, although this consideration applies mainly to new governments and to those temporarily endangered; both England and the United States now make a portion of their public debt the basis of a national system of Banking, but it is perhaps questionable whether this can be justly put among the incidental benefits of the Debts; and again "a moderate debt adds to the credit of a Nation, and its ability to raise money in an emergency, for bankers and capitalists are more ready to take such securities as they are in the habit of dealing in" (Sidney Homer).

On the other hand, the burdens of a National Debt are very apparent: for example, the annual *interest* charge to the Union at the close of our late civil war was $150,000,000, which gradually declined by the lowering of the interest-rate and by the paying off of principal to $61,368,912 for the fiscal year ending June 30, 1881; between March, 1869, and August, 1873, the United States paid $378,015,065 on the principal of its public debt; the collection of the Internal Revenue alone of the national government cost for the fiscal year 1867, $7,712,089; and in each of the two years, 1870 and 1881, a little over $101,500,000 was paid out to reduce the principal of the Debt. All those vast sums came out of the industry and income of individuals; and taxation to any degree as all this implies is a mighty disturbance to industry, and gives rise to an army of officials who eat out a considerable percentage of all they collect. Moreover, the various expedients of taxation, which are always practically unequal in their operation, are apt to give rise to irritation and political agitation, and even sometimes to threats of repudiation, especially when the occasion has gone by under which the debt was contracted, and another generation is called upon to pay off a debt it had no agency in creating.

Here the vexed question arises, how far has one generation *the right* to throw upon succeeding ones the burdens of a National Debt? The true answer to this question is, *it has a very limited right indeed*. The opposite doctrine implies tacitly when not openly, that the succeeding generations will have no occasion for extraordinary expenses of their own, and, therefore, may rightfully be made to contribute to the extraordinary expenditures of this generation. But it is pure assumption to take for granted, that the next generations will not have, of some kind or other, as much occasion for an extraordinary effort in the way of defence or of improvement as the present generation has had. It is a common but harmful illusion to estimate what has now to be done as of much more importance than what will have to be done. Therefore, to throw the present burden forward on another generation of men, who are likely to have to make their own special exertion, just as great and just as imperatively called for, is a procedure unwarranted by past experience. The view that has long prevailed in practice, that a great War-debt, for example, might be easily and justly cast upon posterity, has again and again given rise to needless and expensive wars; *those* have been called upon to pay the piper, who perceived the utter inutility of the expenditure; and thus bitterness has been added to burden.

Besides, the men to fight the battles, and the capital by which to feed, clothe, and furnish them the munitions of war, *must come from that generation*; and there is always great injustice in the manipulations of a great debt ostensibly incurred to obtain this capital, and the debt itself is usually in large part rather a memorial of the war than of the means by which its expenses were actually defrayed.

The generation of American citizens not yet wholly passed off the stage was called on in the Providence of God to suppress a Civil War of enormous proportions, and to eradicate a social institution that was thoroughly bad; the expense of doing this was many fold enhanced by timorous counsels in the field, by class legislation in Congress, and by wretched financiering in the Cabinet; but the Debt, vast as it was, and needlessly incurred as a large portion of it was, has already in good part been paid off and must be entirely paid off by the generation that incurred it. That this great task may be thus completed, will require (1) an economical administration of the national Government; (2) an avoidance of intervention in the affairs of our Neighbors, and of entangling alliances with Foreigners; (3) a free Commercial System, under which the taxes shall be adjusted only towards the most productive revenue; and (4) a constant and onerous home Taxation.

(6) The final Disadvantage of Credit is this, that it is apt to confuse the minds of men as to its own nature, from its apparent resemblance to something else, which is at bottom wholly unlike it. The people of the United States have suffered greatly from this confusion, and are likely to suffer from it still more in the time to come, both in their property and progress at home and in their good name abroad; and it becomes all good citizens, and especially all those called upon to pronounce on the Law of the Land, to know thoroughly the radical difference between a *Credit* and a *Quittance*, and so to escape the contagious confusion that has entered and stirred up the popular, and even the judicial, mind of this country. All through the present chapter has been insisted on and illustrated the point,

perhaps to the weariness of the reader, that Credit is always essentially the *Promise* of one person to another, and that whatever is thus *Promised* is necessarily and fundamentally different from the Promise itself. To confound those two things as if they were or could be made one and the same thing, is in thought illogical and in practice execrable.

And yet it must be allowed, that there is somewhat in the nature of Credit, that makes this confusion plausible, or else it never would prevail; and also that there is something more still to make it plausible in the nature of Money, which last point can only be cleared up in the next following chapter under that title.

Mr. E. G. Spaulding of Buffalo, in his copious and excellent History of the Legal Tender Act, "all of which he saw and part of which he was," as the chairman of the subcommittee of the Ways and Means at the time the Act was passed, demonstrates the extreme reluctance of everybody concerned to give a forced circulation, that is, a compulsory legal-tender quality, to the first batch of Treasury Notes to the amount of $150,000,000 in February, 1862. We have already noted in another place in this chapter, that two successive batches of similar Notes, each to the same amount as the first, were issued within less than a year. These Notes then and since called Greenbacks, bore at the time four essential features: first, they were both in terms and in reality *national Promises* to pay to the bearer gold dollars of the then and present standard of weight and fineness, because there is no other possible meaning to the words "THE UNITED STATES WILL PAY TO THE BEARER FIVE DOLLARS"; second, in addition to their being a forced loan from the people to the amount of notes authorized, they were given a *forced circulation* as money by means of the clause, "*and shall also be lawful money and a legal tender in payment of all debts public and private within the United States except duties on imports and interest on the national bonds*," which clause still recognizes gold dollars as the only universal and standard money; third, the notes were made *fundable* in sums of fifty dollars, "or some multiple of fifty dollars," in six-per-centum gold bearing bonds of the United States, then called 5-20's, again in this clause recognizing the radical difference between the legal-tender paper promises as money and the gold dollars promised in them, in which gold money the interest and principal of the bonded debt must still be paid; and fourth, these notes were publicly known and acknowledged by the Issuer and the receivers to be presently *irredeemable*, since the Government did not have, and did not pretend to have, any coin with which to redeem them, and everybody knew that they were made a legal-tender *because* they were irredeemable.

These prompt recognitions of the impassable gulf between a Promise and what is Promised, were confirmed by all that happened afterwards. The notes, notwithstanding they were legal tender and all bonds of the United

States could at first be bought with them at par, almost immediately began to droop as compared with gold. The daily quotations showed a pretty steady decline for two years. On Jan. 15, '64, gold in greenbacks was 100:155; April 15, 100:178; June 15, 100:197; June 29, 100:250, that is, 40 cents to the dollar; and July 11, 100:285, or 35 cents to the dollar in gold, their lowest point. From this depth they slowly rose with many fluctuations back and forth from many causes for 14 years. Jan. 1, 1879, they became redeemable in gold, and have so continued till the present time.

When the Civil War was all over, and these startling vicissitudes of the paper money were measurably forgotten; though no prominent man, when they were passed, thought the Legal-Tender Acts constitutional; the paper money began to be popular; the distinction between a promise and its fulfilment began to fade out of the minds of the people; there had always been bank bills circulating as money in the country; these had been called "dollars" equally with the coin; and in December, 1869, a test case, Hepburn *versus* Griswold, was decided by the Supreme Court on the question, whether Congress had the constitutional authority to make anything but gold and silver lawful money in satisfaction of *contracts entered into before the first legal-tender Act was passed.* The question, Can Congress make such notes a legal tender for contracts made *after* the passage of the Act? was not involved in this case; but it was very clear from the Opinion of the court delivered by Chief Justice Chase, that the majority of the justices regarded the Act as being unconstitutional in its application to contracts made *after* as well as *before* the Act was passed. Upon the special question before the Court, the justices were divided in opinion; five, including the Chief Justice, agreed that the Act was invalid so far as it made the notes a legal tender on *contracts executed prior to its enactment*; and the three other judges were of the opinion that it was valid. Of course, the Decision of the Court was rendered by a majority of two, that the Act was unconstitutional. Chase, Nelson, Grier, Clifford, and Field constituted the majority; Miller, Swayne, and Davis, the minority.

Salmon P. Chase was one of the greatest men of the great period of the Civil War. He was Secretary of the Treasury at the time the greenbacks were issued, and they were issued at his instance and advice, but he was opposed to the clause that made the notes a legal tender. He never expressed the opinion that the Legal-Tender Acts were constitutional, nor did he expect that the notes, of which these authorized the issue, would ever become a permanent national money. This is evident from the fact that the notes were made *fundable* at his instance, not so much with the view of keeping up the value of the notes by giving them a present market in bonds, as with the view that they would help the sale of the bonds and would be absorbed by them as soon as the price of the bonds was above par in greenbacks. Afterwards Mr. Chase thought that this *fundability* of the notes into bonds would so far take up the notes as to stand in the way of the negotiation of further necessary loans to the Government, and at his instance this provision of the law was repealed. Consequently, there was nothing inconsistent between his position as Secretary and his later position as Chief Justice. He was undoubtedly right in both of these positions. The making the greenbacks legal tender did not probably add one particle to their purchasing-power, but rather the reverse, because that feature implied a doubt on the part of Congress itself as to the validity and currency of such national promises-to-pay. That he was also right in his judicial opinion and decision, however subsequently overruled in his own Court, may be safely left to the inevitable future appeal to common sense and to the common principles of constitutional interpretation.

This judgment in Hepburn *versus* Griswold was favorably received by the country at large, as being just in the line of the great decisions of Chief Justice Marshall, and as being exactly in accordance with Amendment X of the Constitution, namely, "THE POWERS NOT DELEGATED TO THE UNITED STATES BY THE CONSTITUTION, NOR PROHIBITED BY IT TO THE STATES, ARE RESERVED TO THE STATES RESPECTIVELY, OR TO THE PEOPLE." The State of Massachusetts particularly, which has always maintained and still maintains a strong doctrine of State Rights as over against, though in harmony with, the Rights of the United States under the Constitution, applauded this judgment as sound in law and politics, and as righteous altogether. But the then administration of General Grant, inexperienced alike in law and politics, and linked in entangling alliances with the great corporations of the country, received the Decision with marked dissatisfaction; and it was especially offensive to the huge railroad companies, whose bonds had been executed prior to Feb. 25, 1862, inasmuch as it made the principal and interest of these bonds payable in coin, which they had hoped to pay off in the depreciated greenbacks, made legal tender for all debts.

The Administration lost no time in trying to bring about by fair means or foul, a reversal of this unwelcome decision. E. R. Hoar of Massachusetts, at that time attorney-general in Grant's Cabinet, was the principal agent in accomplishing this end by means so discreditable that he lost in consequence his popularity in Massachusetts and all chance of further political preferment. The means chosen and put into effect was the appointment by the President of two new judges, Strong and Bradley, the first to take the place of Grier, resigned, and the second appointed under a law increasing the number of judges to nine, whose opinions on the point at issue were known beforehand, and who were selected to serve on that very account. "*It was no secret, indeed it was a matter of public notoriety, that these justices were appointed in order that the decision of 1869 might be reversed. Their opinions in regard to the constitutionality of the Legal-Tender Acts had been clearly and publicly expressed. It was therefore pretty well known what the decision would be when the question was again presented."* (Hugh McCulloch.)

The second Legal-Tender case, accordingly, that of Knox *versus* Lee, decided in December, 1870, reversed the judgment of a year before, *no new points therefor being raised either by the new judges or by counsel in the new trial*, the Chief Justice and his three former associates still adhering to their original opinions. It was then five judges to four, the special question being, Is it constitutional to make promises-to-pay a legal tender on contracts executed before the promises were issued? The judicial answer was in this case, Yes; provided Congress regarded such action as a necessary means of preserving the Government in time of War, or any other period of extraordinary emergency. That is to say, *bona fide* creditors were constitutionally bound to receive depreciated notes as legal tender in satisfaction of contracts entered into when no notes were in existence; to receive on contracts specifically calling for "*dollars*" the depreciated notes of the Government merely promising to pay "*dollars*," but on which the "*dollars*" could not be obtained! What is that, but the monstrous incongruity that *a promise* is the same thing legally as its *fulfilment?* What is that but judicial blindness as to the *nature* of Credit? What is it but the old confusion between *names* and *things?* What is it, finally, but the dazed and hazy vision, pardonable perhaps in the popular mind but half-opened to radical distinctions, but unpardonable in learned men professing to lay down the law in a civilized country?

It is scarcely needful to add, that the Supreme Court of the United States suffered in the judgment of good citizens by that transaction; that the best legal and financial opinion of the country yielded little respect to a decision *thus secured*; and that intelligent people do not believe that constitutional law *can* sanction what contravenes at once common sense and common morality.

Judge Field (and his memory the country will not willingly let die), one of the majority in the first decision, and writing the opinion of the dissenting minority in the second, used this strong but just language, "*It follows, then, logically, from the doctrine advanced by the majority of the Court as to the power of Congress over the subject of legal tender, that Congress may borrow gold coin upon a pledge to repay gold at the maturity of its obligations, and yet in direct disregard of its pledge, in open violation of faith, may compel the lender to take, in place of the gold stipulated, its own promises; and that legislation of this character would not be in violation of the Constitution, but in harmony with its letter and spirit. What is this but declaring that repudiation by the Government of the United States of its solemn obligations would be Constitutional?"*

CHAPTER V.
MONEY.

The subject of Money presents few difficulties, or rather none of any depth, to one who has thoroughly mastered the subject of Value. To all others the difficulties are insuperable. Essay after essay and volume after volume has been written in this country upon Money, by men who would have become good economists and good monetaries, if they had only begun their inquiries at the right place and followed them in the right direction. As we saw in the last chapter that it is impossible for anybody to understand the subject of Credit without first comprehending the matter of Value, so we shall see in this chapter that in the order of Nature Value precedes Money, and that the latter can only be learned in the light of the former. The logical reason for this in general is, that Money itself is always a Valuable, and comes to its function as money only through a comparison of itself with other Valuables.

The thin difficulties that confront the student of Money, who has reached the topic along the proper highway cast up for economical inquiries, arise apparently from two sources; and we will begin our present discussion by first looking at these in their order.

In the first place, Money is the only Valuable that may belong to two out of the three possible categories into which Valuables may be scientifically thrown. All Valuables are either Commodities, or Services, or Credits. These categories never change places. Once a Commodity always a commodity, so long as value can be predicate of it; a personal Service can never take on any other valuable form; and a Credit is ever a credit, and nothing else, until it is annihilated by Fulfilment. Now Money is the only Valuable that ever appears in two of these forms. The same Dollar indeed cannot be both a Commodity and a Credit; but some Dollars are a Commodity cut out from gold and silver, and some other Dollars (so-called) are a Credit issued by Government or parties responsible to government; while Money as a general term properly enough covers both kinds of Dollars, the Commodity-Dollar and the Credit-Dollar. In other words, Money is of two kinds, and only two kinds, either a Piece of valuable metal stamped as to weight and fineness by the image and inscription of Cæsar,—a Commodity; or a Promise to pay to somebody some of these pieces,—a Credit. This unique peculiarity of Money, by which, always a Valuable, it may appear and does appear in two out of three possible predicaments of Valuables, makes a little difficulty at the outset of its discussion, and requires continued care in formulating its scientific propositions.

In the second place, a more considerable difficulty, and yet a slight one still, is found in the fact that the choices and the legislations of men have more to do in shaping the propositions of Money than in most other economical propositions. It is true, that Nature and men coöperate in the determination of every case of Value whatsoever; while there is a difference in the cases, though perhaps not a distinction, in respect to the fixedness and universality of the natural laws involved, in contrariety to the purely human impulses concerned. The Providential elements in Economics, both the social and the physical, are of course relatively fixed and unchangeable, otherwise Science could not grapple with and classify them; and so also are those principles of Human Nature related to exchanges, which may be said to be *universal* in their character,—such as, for example, the preference to receive a larger rather than a less return-service, and to render a smaller rather than a larger effort; and at the same time there are other principles of human nature related to exchanges much more *variable* in their character than these, such, for instance, as the nation's choice of the kind of Money it will use, or the kind of Taxation it will impose. It certainly follows from this, that some Economical laws must be more *general* than others, owing to a less variation in the human impulses concerned in them: it follows, for example, that the law of landed rents, or the law of the approach of the price of raw materials to that of the finished products, is more universal in its terms of generalization than most of the propositions of Money and Taxation can be.

It seems like a paradox, that those parts of Economics in which the human elements of variable choice may predominate over the relatively fixed laws of nature and of mind, should be just the parts hardest for men to catch clearly and hold firmly; because, we naturally think, that difficulty and mystery are rather to be found in those departments in which an Infinite Mind has been at work upon an infinite plan, and that there is no such profundity in the works of men; but after all, even those natural laws like Gravitation, which are clear and universal as laws, if they be such as the devices of men have to do with, such as may be modified and in a certain sense controlled by human actions, become from that very circumstance liable to some difficulty and perhaps to some mystery. Now all the truths of Money, and as we shall see in the final chapter all the truths of Taxation also, belong to this class of less general generalizations; still, it is scarcely less than foolish to say, that Money is such an elusive and ideal agent that nobody can understand it. That is the language of indolence and lack of penetration. Money is wholly a matter of man's device, though it comes into constant contact with something greater and more fixed than itself; it was invented, just as any other instrument is invented, to accomplish a certain economical purpose; and it would be strange indeed if men by taking pains could not perfectly comprehend what men themselves have wholly devised. We hope, accordingly, in the following paragraphs to clear up completely to all intelligent readers the whole doctrine of Money. The key to unlock all the superficial difficulties (and there are no others) is this: Money is always a Valuable before it becomes money, and continues a valuable independently of the fact that it *is* money; and, it is always one or other of two kinds, either itself a Commodity or a Promise to pay a commodity. In this chapter, we will not begin with definitions and justify them afterwards, but will come up to them step by step, and, as it were, justify them beforehand.

1. Economical Exchanges may begin, be profitable to both parties, and go forward to a certain extent, without the use of any money at all. As a matter of fact and probably for a long time, while the Civilizations were gathering their inchoate forces for a further progress, men exchanged one Service directly for another without the intervention of any medium. This form of trade is called Barter. King Hiram of Tyre furnished to King Solomon of Judea a certain quantity of cedars from Mt. Lebanon for the building of the new Temple at Jerusalem, and Solomon in return furnished to the Tyrians a certain quantity of wheat and oil, Judea being a fertile agricultural country with no forests, and Tyre a wooded country with no farms. This may well serve us as an instance of Barter, although Money had been in current use in those regions a thousand years before, as is seen in the purchase by Abraham of the cave and field of Machpelah, for which he weighed out "*four hundred shekels of silver, current money with the merchants.*"

It is obvious, however, that while Barter is a good deal better than no exchanges at all, there are inherent and immense difficulties in that form of trade.

(a) Under Barter trade is extremely limited in its *personnel*. Only those parties can engage in it, each of whom is in position to render to the other just such a Service as the other is in direct and immediate need of, and each of whom also wants another Service in kind and quantity exactly what the second man has to render. It is not enough under these conditions, that a man should have some Service to sell, but he must also find some other man, who not only wants that specific service but who also has some service to render in return just such as the first man wants. If A has wheat which he wishes to exchange for a coat, he must first find a party desiring wheat and also having a coat to sell, and moreover who wants just as much wheat as will pay for a coat, no more and no less; if he wants more, he may have nothing to render for the excess which A is willing to accept; if less, A may have nothing besides wheat with which to help pay for the coat. Even in the simpler states of Society the inconveniences of thus hunting up a specific market for each specific service are very great, and in more advanced states of civilization would become intolerable, if it were possible (as it is not) for Society to become advanced under such conditions.

(b) Barter presents insuperable obstacles to trade in point of *place*. While men still exchanged in kind, as it is called, and knew no other mode, the purchasing-power of any Service was necessarily confined to that locality, and would not be parted with except in view of a return service actually there present in the same place. There could be no commercial contact without a local contact. The ultimate parties to every exchange must come together face to face. There could be no middle-men or distributors. The market was circumscribed to the hamlet.

(c) Buying and selling under the scheme of Barter is also wretchedly limited in point of *time*. The fruit-dealer, for example, must dispose of his product quickly, or it perishes on his hands. So of many other commodities. If they are to be sold at all, they must be sold quick. The ultimate buyer must be on hand in time. As the result of these three concomitants of Barter, ten thousand things that are now bought and sold to profit never came to a market or thought of a market, exchanges were so limited in time and place and variety, human associations were so hampered, and the development of all peculiar talents so impeded, that one of the initial steps in the progress of all Civilization has been to hit upon some expedient to lessen these intrinsic difficulties, and so to facilitate Exchanges.

2. The Invention of Money was nothing in the world but the tentative selection by certain people in a certain locality of some Commodity then and there *valuable*, that is, capable of buying *some* things then and there, and gradually giving to that commodity by general consent the capacity of buying *all* things then and there salable. The commodity thus slowly becoming money, whatever it was, had and must have had a *limited* purchasing-power to start with, because no instance to the contrary has ever been shown, and still more because that peculiar comparison between *two* things that lies at the bottom in each single case of Value is exactly the same kind of comparison that holds between money and the *many* things which money purchases; given a *valuable* in common use as a starting-point, and the transition is easy and natural to a *generalized* valuable, that is, to a recognized money; the relation of mutual purchase between the commodity and *some* other things was a common fact to begin with, the making it money was merely the common consent that thereafter it should have a general purchasing-power within the circuit; so that as a simple result, whenever anybody had anything to exchange, he might first exchange it for this selected product, which was valuable before but is now generally

valuable, and then with this money-product in hand he could buy whatever he might want at any time or place within the circuit.

It is impossible from the very nature of Value, impossible from that comparison of two distinct Services, that precedes every Exchange, as well under Money as under Barter, that anything except a valuable anterior to and independent of its becoming money, could ever have become money at all. Money makes no alteration in any law of Value, but only substitutes for convenience' sake in every transaction in which it plays a part, a general for a specific purchasing-power; a book, for example, has a specific purchasing-power, since there is somebody who wants it, and is willing to give a sum of money for it; and the owner of the book by the sale of it parts with a product which has only the power to purchase something from a few persons, and receives a product in return which has the power to purchase something from all persons; it is not true to say that the money is worth more than the book, because they are just worth each other, as is demonstrated by the sale; but it *is* true to say that the seller of the book has substituted in the place of a limited purchasing-power, of which he was proprietor, a general purchasing-power, of which he has now become proprietor; that is, that the command of the money, which has no larger value than the book had, does carry along with it a superior command over purchasable articles generally. In one word, Value in the form of money is in a more available shape for general buying and selling than value in any other form. This is the exact and ultimate expression for all the truth there is in the common vague remark, namely, that Money is something different from all other Valuables; it *is* different from them in just one respect, namely, while they have the power of buying some things from some persons, it has the power derived from the *consensus* of Society to buy all sorts of things from all sorts of persons.

This simple change or substitution, which seems in itself so little and easy and natural, has changed in its ever-enlarging results the face of the world! It makes the valuable now selected to be money seem to the minds of men to be a very different thing from what it was before, although the change in itself is slight indeed. It removes most of the inconveniences of Barter as by a stroke of the hand. So soon as a commodity selected to become money by one people comes to be acceptable as such to all other peoples, as is the case with gold, the advantages of its use are vastly multiplied to all. Experience has shown many times over, and reflection will explain to any one, how that there is no other machine that has economized labor like money; no other instrument that plays so deep and broad a part in Production; no invention whatever, unless it be the invention of letters, which has contributed more to the civilization of mankind. Money makes vast distances relatively indifferent; for it is sufficient to constitute a market for any valuable that it is practically wanted anywhere on the round globe, the middle-man paying the seller for it in money transports it thither, and receives back his investment with a profit from the ultimate buyer. So, also, money generalizes any purchasing-power in point of time. The dealer, exchanging his perishable products for money, may keep its power of purchase locked in this form as long as he lists, putting an interval at his own pleasure between selling and buying, and with this generalized power in his pocket he may buy when he will and what he will and where he will. Money, too, makes any purchasing-power portable, divisible, and loanable. A man may carry the value of his farm in his purse, and may divide it up for a thousand different purchases, and especially is able to loan it in this form in order to receive it back again with interest at a future day.

3. It is important to notice in the next place, that, whatever made the commodity selected as money originally desirable and valuable, it has now become desirable and valuable for other and wider reasons. The tobacco of Virginia, for example, in the early days of that Colony, became valuable at first on account of the demand for it as a narcotic both there and in England; but as soon as it was made a legal money in the Colony by the general consent already described, its value depended in part upon another set of causes. Of course Demand and Supply still controlled its value just as before, only certain parties who had not desired it before as a mere *commodity* thereafter desired it as a current *money*. Its convenience and necessity as money widened the circle of those parties willing to receive it and glad to render a return for it. It is true, that many now received it only because they could pay it out again to buy something else with; but that made no difference so far as Value is concerned; it was valuable before under a certain limited demand, and continued valuable under an additional and broader demand; we cannot certainly say, that it became *more* valuable under this new and wider demand, because we do not know how the then combined demand affected the Supply. We may probably say, that the value became *steadier* if not *larger*, under the double demand than under the previous single one; and the vital point to mark and remember is, that the *value of money*, previously valuable as a commodity only, is still maintained under the law of Demand and Supply, just as all other values are, the only peculiarity being this, namely, as a generalized valuable and consequently a potent social agent money is in demand by everybody who has anything else to sell.

It follows from this in necessary sequence, that Money as such, whatever may have been the ground of its original value as a commodity, *is always received as money in order to be parted with*. It is not bought for its own sake to be used and enjoyed, as most other things are, but is only bought to be sold again. Men will sell everything to buy it, with the sole intent to sell it again to buy something else; and the odd thing about it is, that everybody buys it to sell again, not at all as the speculator buys grain to sell it again at a higher price by the bushel or centner, but, the money remaining constant in their minds, they sell for it something they care less about in order to buy with it something they care more about. Money, therefore, becomes a *medium* in men's exchanges. The word "medium" in this proposition is to be taken in its etymological and strict sense, as something that comes between two extremes and serves also to relate them to each other. This is not the ultimate characteristic of Money, as we shall see, nor can a final definition be founded here, but it is a good step towards ultimates to see that money is exchanged for other things as a means and not as an end, that it is a great help in exchanging all other valuables but is never exchanged for itself in an ultimate transaction.

Small boys, indeed, sometimes swop cents; but men, the miser excepted, who is under a deplorable fallacy of the senses, use and estimate money mainly as the *medium* that facilitates the real exchanges of Society. What is actually and ultimately exchanged is the wheat, the cloth, the lumber, the furniture, the commercial service of every kind, and Money is but the instrument making those exchanges easy, which might perhaps go on in part without it, though with difficulty and loss. In short, money is somewhat like a railroad ticket. Transportation to a given place is what is really bought when one pays for a railroad ticket. The proof of the purchase is the bit of paper exhibited. That comes in as a *medium* between the traveller and the railroad company; and while it facilitates the real exchange, it also partly disguises it. This comparison holds good in the main feature, but in two respects the resemblance fails: Money is not a specific ticket for a single purpose, as the pasteboard is, but is a general ticket (so far as it goes), for all purposes of purchase; and secondly, Money really stands as a value in its own right (so far as any single thing can so stand) at the same time it is serving as a *medium*, while the railroad ticket does not. Still, we are all desirous to get money, not for the sake of the money itself, but for the sake of those things which the money will buy. We part with money freely and constantly for those things which we care more about. What we exactly care for is what our money will buy, is the conscious command over all services and commodities which the possession of money insures to us. If we could give our own commodity or service or claim, whatever it may be, and receive directly in return the claim or commodity or service which we want, whatever that might be, there would be no need of money at all; but this is always inconvenient, and generally impossible; and, therefore, we introduce a middle term, and money is found to be a good mean to help exchange the two extremes.

4. We are now getting on towards a just conception and a true definition of Money, though two or three more points must still be noted as preparatory to that consummation. As a result of the fact already reached, that money serves as a *medium* in men's exchanges, it follows of course that the power of money as such a medium is multiplied by what has been called *rapidity of circulation*, that is, a brisker use of the volume already in circulation will reach the same end as the increase of its volume. As in mechanics, so in money, the whole power is the product of mass and velocity. Money also is like any other tool, the more constant its use the more profitable its agency. The quick movement of a small mass, accordingly, is better than the torpid movement of a large mass, both in what it saves of expense, and in what it presupposes of the general conditions of exchange. The value of the money-volume of any country is a small fraction of the aggregate value of those products which the money helps directly to exchange; and a very small fraction indeed of the aggregate value of all the products which it helps indirectly to exchange through Credit by means of its *denominations*. We shall see better a little farther on, that Money works not only as a medium direct, itself exchanged against other Services, but also as furnishing those denominations of Value, like the *dollar*, which are always used in bargaining; and also used in all cases of Credit, in which settlement is not made by money but by offsetting one piece of indebtedness against another, and these denominations can arise only from the use of money as a direct medium. Therefore, we may say that the hub and the spokes and the rim of the wheel of exchange consist of personal services and commercial credits and all material commodities except money, while, to borrow the famous comparison of Hume, "Money is but the grease which makes the wheel turn easier." It would be a vast mistake to suppose, as some of the ancients did, that the grease is really the wheel.

While Money thus facilitates the revolution of the wheel of Exchange, it follows too from its nature as a medium, that the dimensions of the wheel as a whole are vastly greater than they would have been but for the Money. Money indeed helped to exchange the products that already existed and were coming into existence at its first invention, but by far the largest part of products since have come into existence largely through the agency of Money. We get quite too low a view of the functions of this potent agent, if we think of it merely as an aid in circulating products, that would have existed whether or no; some products would certainly have existed whether or no, and money would surely be of great use and convenience in helping bring these to the ultimate consumers; but this is a partial and wholly inadequate view of the function of Money as a medium of exchange. The fact that such a medium is in universal circulation, and that the present holders of it are ready to exchange it against any sort of Services adapted to gratify their desires, exercises a kind of creative power, and brings a thousand products to the market which would otherwise never have come into existence. Since money will buy anything, men are on the alert to bring forward something which will buy money; and since Money is divisible into small pieces, an incredible number and variety of small services are brought forward to be exchanged against these pieces, for example, into railroad cars and fares of all sorts, which services we have no reason to suppose would ever be brought forward at all were it not for the strong attraction of the money.

5. From this last point of view we may gain another closely connected with it, namely, that Money must be a very important part of the *Capital* of the world. We have already thoroughly learned that Capital is any product outside of man himself from whose use springs a pecuniary increase. Now any one may see that the monetary medium of any country is the most active and the most essential and the most profitable of all those instruments reserved in aid of further production. The axe, the plough, the spindle, the loom, the wheel, the engine, are all instruments, are all Capital, and they each aid respectively some part or parts of the processes of Production; but Money is a form of Capital which stimulates and facilitates all the processes of Production without exception. Just as we have seen that Money is a form of Value generalized, so is it also a form of generalized Capital, that is to say, it is an instrument capable of aiding all processes of Production in every department, while every other capitalized instrument is capable of aiding but few processes in one department. Without Money, for instance, there could be no thorough Division of Labor, because there would be no adequate means of estimating or rewarding each one's share in a complicated process. By means of Money all services small or great contributing towards a common product are neatly measured, and may be paid for by some one, who thereby becomes proprietor of the whole product; or, if the contributors choose, they may wait till the product itself is sold, and then the money received is divisible without loss to each contributor, according to the service rendered. Thus the influence of Money as Capital pervades the whole field of Exchange from centre to circumference, facilitating every transfer and stimulating new transfers.

Now then, if Money be, as it is, a peculiar kind of Capital, since it is a Medium in all Exchanges, the question becomes pertinent, How much of it is wanted? Clearly, only *so much* as will serve the *purposes* which such a medium is fitted to subserve; there should be enough fairly to mediate between the Services actually ready to be exchanged then and there, and also enough fairly to call out other Services proper and profitable in the then circumstances of Society, and whose only obstacle to a profitable exchange then and there *is a lack of a facilitating medium*. All increase of the volume of money beyond this point, which the very nature of Money itself marks out as the boundary, leads to a diminution of Value of every part of it, to a consequent disturbance of all existing monetary contracts, to a universal rise of prices which are illusory and gainless, to unsteadiness and derangement in all legitimate business, and to a spirit of restless enterprise and speculation which seeks to draw off the excess of money in untried and reckless experiments. The only real subjects of Exchange are mutual efforts, mutual services, as these are expressed in Commodities and Services and Credits, and money is the instrument merely that comes in between the real exchanges to facilitate them; and, therefore, it seems to be perfectly conclusive on this point to remark that the quantity of money needed in any country or the whole world is limited by the number of the services ready to be exchanged, to make easy the exchange of which is the good purpose and sole end of Money.

The physical and mental powers of man, which alone can give birth to commercial services, when considered as they must be in this connection as belonging to a given number of men at a given time and place, are strictly limited of course; and although the presence of money then and there is both a stimulus and an aid to all these men to bring forward services of all sorts to the market, there are obvious restrictions both in their powers and in their circumstances; and the quantity of money needed among them is just that quantity which will fairly act as a medium in exchanging the services which they are able and willing to render to each other. All increase in the quantity of money beyond that point would have, and could have, the only effect of increasing the nominal Prices of Services, without making the services themselves any greater in number or better in quality.

It is with Money exactly as it is with any other form of Capital, allowance being made for the fact that Money is a kind of generalized capital. To illustrate, How many ships does a commercial nation need to employ? As many as will fairly take off its exports and bring in its imports. Ships are wanted for one definite purpose; and when enough are secured to answer that purpose, all additions will lessen the Value, that is, the purchasing-power, of ships generally. So of all instruments whatever. Enough is as good as a feast. Enough is better than more. In regard to every form of Capital, and consequently in regard to Money as such, the point of sufficiency is determined by the quantity of work to be done. And as no law of Congress is required to determine how many ships are best to do the transportation for the people of the United States, so no legislation is needed to fix the amount of Money that is best for the same people, or for any people. As the people find out for themselves how many steam-engines they want to do their work of the year, so they find out without any aid from their legislators how much money they want to make their exchanges of the year. The less Law and the more Liberty on all such points the better for all concerned.

Let the reader notice in passing, as a corollary from what has just been shown, that when forms of Credit like bank cheques come into growing use to make payments with and settle balances, they displace to a large extent commodity-moneys, like gold and silver, which would otherwise have to be employed. Speculations, and even scientific discussions, over the needful amounts of gold and silver for money in the United States, have usually overlooked this essential consideration of displacement; and one result of this has doubtless been too large a coinage of the precious metals, to the hazard of their stable value, and especially to the hazard of the permanent maintenance of the gold standard. Men forget in their zeal for Money that it is nothing but a Tool, and that the multiplication of tools beyond the amount of work to be done by means of them always makes the tools a drug; and they are apt to forget also that the cheaper and more convenient substitutes for metallic moneys, namely, forms of Credit, are all the time and more and more taking the place of the older moneys, which, nevertheless, must still be kept at the foundation, though a lessened quantity of them be needful for circulation.

6. We must now carefully sink our analysis one grade deeper, in order to reach the bottom characteristic of Money, and so to formulate an ultimate definition of it.

The only quality common to all valuable things is the fact that they are all *salable*; and if these various and multitudinous valuables are ever to be made in any way commensurable with each other, it must be by means of one of their number assumed as a *standard of comparison* with the rest. Comparisons can only turn on points of *likeness*. The single respect in which all valuables whatsoever resemble each other is their common possession of purchasing-power, be it more or less. Therefore, as a yardstick, itself possessed of length, *and because it is possessed of length*, if assumed as a standard of comparison with other objects that have length, may be used to measure all such objects whatsoever, and may accurately express in units or fractions of itself the simple length of anything and everything; so, any valuable may be selected as a *standard* with which to compare all other valuables, and by means of the terms of which to express numerically the reciprocal relations between all valuables whatsoever. This is just what is done whenever any valuable is selected as Money; and this is the exact and single purpose of such selection.

What is the precise change, then, in the valuable chosen as Money when it becomes money? This: it was a valuable before, else it could not by any possibility serve the present purpose, but now it has become a *standard* valuable, with which other valuable things may be compared in the single point of their *value*. Valuables are now commensurable. That is all. But that is a great deal. As we have already learned to the nail, Valuables are all Services; and now some one Service has been selected from the rest, capable in its very nature of *measuring* all the rest, and so capable of becoming immensely *useful* to mankind.

What, accordingly, is the bottom characteristic of Money? And where shall we find the terms for an immutable definition of it? *The core of Money is this quality of being a Measure of Services, taken on in addition to the usual and universal qualities constituting anything a Valuable.* This additional quality arises under the choices and action of men, just as the ordinary qualities constituting anything a valuable arise under the choices and action of men. But it is an *additional* quality, distinctly conferred, and vastly important. The valuable chosen as Money was a Service to start with, was constantly rendered as such then and there, and was consequently fitted by qualities already possessed to assume a further and a *unique* quality, namely, the capacity to measure and express relatively to itself all other valuable Services whatever.

As each and every Valuable is the outcome of a *comparison* instituted by two persons as between two things, as is thoroughly unfolded in the first Chapter, it is not at all strange, rather it is natural and inevitable, that there should arise in connection with Valuables as a whole class some such further *comparative* measure, as Money is now shown to be; because, without some such common measure of Services in general, itself a Service of the same kind, it would be inconvenient, not to say impossible, to carry on any considerable traffic anywhere. For instance: a baker has only loaves of bread, and wishes to buy a hat, a horse, a house. How many loaves shall he give for each? Unless there be some common Service, in the terms of which these differing Valuables can be expressed, and by means of which they can be brought into commercial relations with each other, it would be an awkward piece of business to effect even the *three* exchanges; and every time the baker wished to buy another article, there must be a rude and slow calculation from independent data, in order to decide upon the terms of the exchange. Let now some Common Service be introduced, in the terms of which each of these values can express itself independently, and the difficulty disappears in an instant. "My loaves are worth ten cents each," says the baker. "My hat is worth ten dollars," says the hatter. Their saying so does not indeed *make* it so; that matter is a preliminary; but each has come to that approximate conclusion by a relatively easy comparison of two Services, his own and another common one; and if the loaves will duly bring ten cents and the hat ten dollars, the terms of their own exchange are one hundred for one, and there is no need of parleying. So of the rest; so of everything that is ever bought and sold. Money becomes by common consent a Measure of them; because it measures them, it makes the interchange of them a very facile matter; because it measures them, it easily becomes a medium between them; and, accordingly, because the money rendered is itself a Service, it is a natural and universal measure of all other Services.

MONEY IS A CURRENT AND LEGAL MEASURE OF SERVICES. With this final definition of "Money" the writer is more than willing to take all the risks. It was new when propounded many years ago in one of the editions of his earlier book. All subsequent testings of it in form and substance have but confirmed the original confidence in it. The word "legal" in this definition is not always to be pressed to its utmost signification, but denotes anything sanctioned by law or usage *equivalent to law*. The other words are to be taken in their full and technical meaning. It is believed that, while this definition is short and simple, it just covers the whole ground and no more. It is not enough that a certain valuable be "legal" as Money; it must also be "current" in order to be a true money. In the United States between 1862 and 1879, to take an example, gold coins, though legal tender all the time for all debts public and private, were not "current" in the full sense of that term, and hence were *not* the Money of the country. Till the last-mentioned date, the gold dollar of 25 ⅘ grains standard fine was required by law to pay customs-taxes with and the interest on the public debt, and was used to a small extent in a few branches of private business, and was not otherwise in the hands of the people. These dollars, accordingly, were not strictly money, but bore a premium over the "current" money of the country. To be Money, then, a Valuable must be recognized as money by law or custom as strong as law, and also circulate among all classes of the people as a medium in their exchanges.

But we are bound to observe that Money becomes a *medium* in men's exchanges, because it first became a *measure* in their Services. Some economists think that these two functions are separate, and are of equal rank; but it is easy to see that one only is original, and that the other is derived from that. Even Aristotle perceived that Money is a Measure, inasmuch as he defined property "*anything that can be measured by money*." We may be pretty sure, in opposition to Professor Jevons, in his Money and the Mechanism of Exchange at page 13, who thinks there are *four* characteristics of Money, that Money as such has but *one* primary characteristic difference from other forms of Value, namely, this *measure*-quality, this *standard*-quality, this publicly recognized function as a *common measure* to which all other valuables are constantly referred. This additional attribute put upon a money-valuable by law or custom is not what *makes* it valuable, since an ounce of uncoined gold standard fine is worth within a very small fraction as much as an ounce of gold coins, but it makes the money a far more convenient instrument to purchase with, inasmuch as money, having now the attribute of making all other valuables easily commensurable with itself, becomes at once something which everybody is ready to receive, because everybody knows in general what its power will be to purchase all other things. In other words, Money becomes a *medium* in exchanges just because it has already become a *measure* of Services in general; and there are not consequently two prime functions of Money, still less four, but only one. This view seems to simplify the whole subject of Money very much; and we may be sure that it will be found to be scientifically correct, and that we shall find many means of testing its accuracy as we go on.

To maintain, as we do, that "Money is a measure of Services," is much better than to say, in connection with many economists, that "Money is a Measure of Value." That phrase is objectionable because Value is always relative to two Services exchanged for each other; and to say that money is a measure of that *relation* is neither so simple nor so ultimate as to say that it is a measure of each of the Services entering *into* that relation. The Services may be conceived of and spoken of separate from the Value into which they merge, although they come into existence solely for the sake of that resultant Value, and it is more exact and final to propound that Money, itself a Service, is a measure of all other Services considered as constituent elements of the Values into which they fall. We are not without strong hopes, accordingly, that competent economists will concede, that here is a radical improvement in the nomenclature of our Science.

In the place of our expression and definition, and the foregoing explanation consequent upon its use, President Walker in his Money, pages 280 *et seq.*, prefers the mathematical and excellent phrase, "*the common denominator in exchange*"; Professor Bonamy Price, in his Practical Political Economy, page 363, shows his fondness for the formula (and it is a good one), "*the tool of exchange*"; and Henry Dunning Macleod, in his Elements of Banking, page 17, insists with much less reason, that "*Money is the representative of Debt.*" He says: "The quantity of money in any country represents the amount of Debt which there would be if there was no money; and consequently when there is no debt there can be no money." The unfortunate use by some countries of a paper money, which is indeed a form of debt, gives some plausibility to the notion that Money is a representative of Debt; and perhaps the fact that Money is often used to pay debts previously contracted, and that debts are almost always contracted in the terms of Money, may give some additional plausibility to this view; but as Macleod himself goes on to say that "no substance possesses so many advantages as a metal for money," and that "all civilized nations therefore have agreed to adopt a metal as money, and of metals, gold, silver, and copper have been chiefly used," we do not see how he can logically hold that a gold dollar, or a gold sovereign, whose value is as substantive and independent as that of any Valuable in the world can be, becomes through coinage and circulation "a representative of Debt." Instead of saying as he does, "where there is no debt there can be no money," it may be confidently asserted on the other hand, where all transactions are settled at once in solid money there can be no debt.

7. Having thus looked into the nature of Money, and seen what is its one essential characteristic, and its one obvious and universal function as the result of that, it will help us now in our further discussion, to examine some of the material commodities that have served as Money at different times and places.

Cattle appear to have been the earliest money of which there remains any record. Homer, near the middle of the sixth book of the Iliad, indicates in the following lines that oxen were an incipient money in the Heroic age:—

"Then did the son of Saturn take awayThe judging mind of Glaucus, when he gaveHis arms of gold away for arms of brassWorn by Tydides Diomed,—the worthOf fivescore oxen for the worth of nine."

We cannot certainly infer, when it is said in Genesis that "Abraham departed out of Egypt very rich in *cattle* and silver and gold," that any of these were anything more than articles of valuable merchandise; but on the other hand it is certain from the Latin name of Money, *Pecunia*, which is derived from the root *pecus*, which means "*cattle*," that Cattle were the Money of the early Romans; and Pliny writes expressly that King Servius Tullius stamped the first bronze money of Rome with the *image of cattle*, undoubtedly indicating by that some equivalence in current value between the two. At any rate cattle have been used as Money among pastoral peoples very widely in place and in time, and are still so used in various parts of Africa.

In the region of the Euphrates and Tigris the precious metals became money in very remote antiquity; for the art of coining, and all other arts, came thence westward to the Greek cities of Asia Minor, and to Greece itself, and we learn that Pheidon, King of Argos, coined silver money on a scale derived from the East in 869 B.C.; and a better proof still is the fact that burnt clay tablets are found in the Royal Library at Nineveh, discovered by Layard, which are really credit-money, notes issued by the Government, and made redeemable in gold and silver money on presentation at the king's treasury. Tablets of this character are extant bearing date as early as 625 B.C. But the gold and silver money must have been circulating a long time in their own right as valuables, before such a credit-money, such a promise-money, as those tablets are, could have originated in connection with them. Abraham, who himself migrated from "Ur of the Chaldees" about 2000 years B.C., not long after reaching the Mediterranean, "weighed unto Ephron the silver which he had named in the audience of the sons of Heth, four hundred shekels of silver, current money with the merchant." This is expressly said to be "money" and "current money." Perhaps it was coined money. At any rate, it was cut and piece money. It was indeed weighed out, and not counted out. This is still the more accurate and speedy manner, when the facilities for the weighing are present. The Bank of England at this day weighs, and not counts, the coins received and paid out. The Romans first coined silver money in 269 B.C., and gold money in 207 B.C., and gold coins were stamped in Greece about the time of Alexander the Great, say 333 B.C.

Other metals than those called precious were also early used as money. Long before Pheidon's silver coinage in Greece, *copper skewers* were used as money in that country, of which six made up a *drachm*, which was afterwards both a coin and a unit of weight, the coin being worth about 17 cents of our money, and the weight being about 66 grains avoirdupois. The word drachm is derived from δράγμα, *a handful*; and the sixth part of it, called an *obol*, from the Greek word meaning a *spit*, became also both a coin and a weight, all which makes it evident that these were used in connection with roasting meat, and that one skewer or obol was originally a unit both of value and of weight. In Adam Smith's day, in certain districts in Scotland, *nails* were still used as small money, which is a forcible reminder of these old Greek skewers. Iron became money in Sparta; money of lead was known to the ancients, and is still current in the Burman empire; the earliest Roman coins were of copper, which were cast rather than stamped, for no die would have sufficed for pieces so large and heavy, and the *denarius* was the unit divided into ten *asses*, the *denarius* being nearly the equivalent of the Greek *drachma* whether of copper or silver, because the Romans reckoned from the first the ratio of copper to silver as 250:1; bronze is a mixture of copper and tin, and brass of copper and zinc, and copper coins with both these admixtures—used for the purpose of hardening the copper, it being a general law of metals that a mixture of two is harder than either—have been very common in ancient and modern times; Sicilian, Roman, and old British coins of tin alone are known to have been struck; and Herodotus makes the statement that the Lydians of Asia Minor were the first to make a coinage of *electrum*, which, as some claim, was a mixture of gold and silver, and of which ancient specimens are still existing.

Cowry *shells* are still used in the East Indies, and also in Africa in the place of small coins, and have sometimes been imported into England from India to be exported in trade to the coast of Africa, being reckoned in Bengal at about 3200 to a silver rupee, which is about 46 of our cents. The New England Indians also used beads or shells of periwinkles (white) and of clams (black), of which 360 made up a belt of *wampum*, as they called it, the black being counted worth twice as much as the white; and the English colonists accepted the wampum in their exchanges with the Indians, regarding a string of white as equal to five shillings, and a string of black to ten shillings, and afterwards made it legal tender among themselves for small sums, and even counterfeited it. Cakes of *tea* have passed as money in India, and elsewhere; and it is said, that at the great annual fair at Novgorod, in Russia, the price of tea has first to be determined before the prices of other things can be settled upon, since that is a kind of standard of Values in that great mart. *Salt* has been current money in Abyssinia; *codfish* in Ireland and Newfoundland; and *beaver-skins* in New Netherlands, New England, and the western parts of America.

We do not here try at all to give a full list of the things that are known to have been used in the early states of society as money; and there would be no ground for surprise in any list, however large and varied, when we remember how great is the need of some such form of value generalized in order that exchanges may grow to any considerable size and vigor. Two points only need now to be noted, (1) that the tendency everywhere has been sooner or later to come to the metals as the best form of money, and among the metals to reach gold and silver as the only ultimately satisfactory materials for Money; and (2) that no instance has ever been found in the whole stretch of inquiry over all the earth, of anything becoming a Money that had not been previously a Valuable. We might be perfectly sure of this beforehand, without any search at all among the moneys of primitive times and states of civilization, because, from the *very nature of the case* nothing could ever serve the purpose of Money except what was already a valuable to make the comparison with,—nothing could ever possibly serve as a measure of services except a service. It has several times been claimed, that actual exceptions to this law have been historically discovered, but when the alleged exceptions have been closely scrutinized they have been found to be apparent only. To take two or three of the most plausible examples: the Carthaginians had a kind of leather money, which originally enclosed bits of the precious metals, and circulated in virtue of them, though they afterwards came to circulate as bits of leather only, as counters and pledges, in a way that will be explained later. According to the Venetian traveller, Polo, China had in the thirteenth century a money made of the bark of the mulberry tree, cut into round pieces and stamped with the name of the sovereign, which money it was death to counterfeit or to refuse to take in any part of the empire. If we had the whole history of this money, it would surely ally itself either with the other commodity-moneys now being treated, or with the modern credit-moneys made legal tender to be treated hereafter. It is just as certain as anything can be, that these circles of stamped bark did not start out as money in their own right. The French writer, Montesquieu, asserted that there was in use in the last century among the people of the coast of Africa, what he called "an ideal money," "a sign of value without money," the unit of which was called a *macoute*, which was subdivided in ideal tenths, called *pieces*. This statement was startling, as implying a denomination without the thing denominated, as implying a standard of value which had no basis in a valuable thing. It was afterwards discovered, however, that this money of account had its origin, just as we should suppose it must have had, in an actual *macoute*, a piece of stuff, a fabric, which they had used first as a commodity-money, and afterwards its *name* as a money of account. A valuable thing may become money, and then its name may become a *denomination* of value, and still later a bit of leather or a bit of paper may be called by the same name, and in a certain sense take the place of the same thing. All this will be as clear as day pretty soon.

8. Contrary to what has often been affirmed by Economists, the real measure of Services is the service itself, the *thing*-dollar and not the *denomination*-dollar. The denominations are used in bargainings and calculations as representatives of the money itself, and thus indeed in a secondary sense serve as *measures*; but the subtle connection between the thing and its name, between money and its denominations, and the differences between the two, need to be clearly unfolded, because most of the current fallacies about money take their rise just at this point. An illustration will best serve us here. The original measure of Services in France and England and Scotland was the pound weight of silver. No coin of that weight was ever struck; but the pound of silver was cut into 240 coins called pence. Twelve of these pence were called a *solidus* or shilling. Thus, as applied to silver, the symbols lb. and £ denoted equivalent weights, the former of uncoined metal, the latter of metal coined. But in course of time, more "pence" than 240, and at last in Elizabeth's reign 744 "pence were coined out of a lb. of silver." Yet all the while 240 of these pence were called a £. £ and lb., both a contraction of the Latin *libra*, were no longer equivalent. The lb. of weight continued stable; the £ of money had dwindled to less than one-third. Yet the *name* pound continued to attach to 240 pence, although the pence embodied a less and less quantity of silver. Each actual penny had less silver in it, and though it was still called a penny as before, the *denomination*, though spelled and sounded as before, represented less silver, and therefore less *value*, than before. The denominations, then, always follow the fortunes of the coins, whose names they are, to the frequent loss and shame of the unthinking, who suppose the same *name* must represent the same *thing*. Unfortunately it does not.

Take another illustration. In 1834 the gold eagle of the United States was reduced in weight from 270 to 258 grains troy, and the alloy increased from one part in 12 to one part in 10. These changes took out more than 6 parts of gold from every 100 parts in all the gold coins of the country. Yet all these coins bore the same names as before. The things denominated changed, but the denominations changed not. Other things remaining equal, the coins lost six *per centum* of their purchasing-power, or in other words, general prices rose in that proportion; the *measure* became so much smaller; and the names, *eagle*, *dollar*, outwardly unchanged, varied simultaneously and equally with the change in the coins.

Also, coins are liable to change in their function as a measure of general Services from unavoidable changes in the general purchasing-power of the precious metals themselves. If for any reason an ounce of gold will buy less of general Services than formerly, of course the coins cut from that gold will buy less than formerly; and this change in the *measure* is followed instantly and inevitably by a corresponding change in the meaning, though not in the spelling, of the *denomination*. Not so with all other tables of denominations. These have a *basis* independent of the things which they help to measure. The French *metre*, for example, is not variable by the lengths or breadths or heights of the things it measures, but is an invariable unit of length the world over; so is one of Troughton's inches; but this feature does not hold at all of the denominations of Money; because *sovereigns, dollars, marks, francs*, are denominations of *Value*, which is itself a variable relation. Such denominations, consequently, are *not* an independent standard to which values themselves can be referred, as lengths are referred to metres and inches, but vary with the varying purchasing-power of the coins themselves. The "*dollar*," as a denomination, means more or less, just according as the "DOLLAR," as a coin, buys, that is, measures, more or less.

Still, essential as is the point now made to any just understanding of the subject of Money, it is vastly important for all the interests of Exchange that the accepted measure of Services be as little liable to fluctuations as possible, especially in all cases in which lapse of time is involved before the exchange is fully consummated. An inflexible standard there cannot be from the very nature of the measuring, but also from the very nature of all measuring, the money-standard should be and should be kept as nearly inflexible as it possibly can be. For the same reason in kind, only multiplied a thousand-fold in force, that the bushel-measure should be of the same capacity in sowing-time and in harvest-time, to sell and buy by, always a bushel, no more and no less; and the yard-stick an inflexible measure of length, always 36 of Troughton's inches, no more and no less; so, as far as it is possible in the nature of Values, ought the current measure of Services, and hence its denominations, to represent, year in and year out, a uniform degree of purchasing-power.

9. This brings us logically to the historical fact, that, no matter what measure of services any people may have adopted in their primitive times, there has always been a steady force at work tending to displace these in favor of gold and silver. This has become the universal result the world over among all advanced peoples. Governor Bradford in his History of Plymouth Colony gives a quaint account of the origin of money among the Pilgrims, and in connection with that of the fee-simple in lands: "*The Pilgrims began now highly to prize corn as more precious than silver, and those that had some to spare began to trade one with another for small things, by the quart bottle and peck; for money they had none, and if any had, corn was preferred before it. That they might, therefore, increase their tillage to better advantage, they made suit to the governor to have some portion of land given them for continuance and not by yearly lot, for by that means that which the more industrious had brought into good culture (by such pains) one year came to leave it the next and often another might enjoy it; so as the dressing of their lands were the more sleighted over and to less profit; which, being well considered, their request was granted.*"

The neighboring Colony of Massachusetts, settled about ten years later, used Bullets for small change, reckoning them at a farthing apiece, and made them legal tender for debts of less than one shilling; for larger exchanges Wampum and Beaver-skins were long used; but the steady force just spoken of induced Massachusetts in 1652 to supplant these with a silver coinage of her own, called the Pine-tree shillings and sixpences and threepences and twopences. This mint existed (sometimes idle) for over 30 years, but all the pieces coined bore the dates of 1652 or 1662. In 1691, the two Colonies were forced into one government through a new charter granted by William and Mary; and after lengthened trials of inferior moneys, not needful to be described now, Massachusetts determined in 1749 to have no other than silver money circulate in the Colony, and became thereafter till the Revolution the so-called "Silver Colony," and business rapidly and steadily revived and enlarged in consequence of the change, and in contrast with the rest of New England.

Gold and silver, thus ever urging their way in to take the place of tentative and transient standards, and ever coming back again to stay if displaced for a time by cheaper and changeable moneys, have never been anywhere of equal value, weight for weight. An ounce of gold has always been more valuable than an ounce of silver. Probably in the Euphrates country where coinage began, and certainly in Asia Minor deriving thence its weights and measures, gold was strictly the standard with silver as subsidiary to that; in Greece, when Philip's victories established a double standard there, gold was reckoned relatively to silver as $1:12\frac{1}{2}$; in the Roman world, where silver had been the standard after 217 B.C., Augustus Cæsar legalized gold as a co-standard in the ratio of 1:12; in 1717 a double standard was established in Great Britain, gold being rated in the coinage as 1:15⅕ of silver, but in 1816 by a law still in force, gold was made the sole standard for the United Kingdom, the legal use of silver being limited to 40s. in any one payment; in France the legal relation of gold to silver was fixed in 1803 as 1:15½, and so continued till 1876; in the United States the ratio first established, in accordance with the recommendation of Alexander Hamilton as Secretary of the Treasury, was 1:15, but in 1834 this was changed to the relation of 1:15.98, and so it remains to this day; in 1871, the new German Empire adopted the sole gold standard, and limited silver to the amount of 20 *marks* in any one forced payment, still allowing the old silver *thaler* to circulate at the rate of three marks to a thaler; and since 1875, the Scandinavian Union permits gold alone to be coined for private persons, and limits the debt-paying power of silver to 20 *crowns*. A crown is 26.78, and a mark 23.82, of our standard cents.

Moreover, the relative value of gold in silver never continues the same for any great length of time, even after the law has sought to ascertain and fix it. Indeed, any law fixing the ratio between the two has very little, if any, effect towards maintaining the ratio. Demand and Supply determine the value of the precious metals each in each at any one time as absolutely as they decree the value of Hindoo rice in silver. France managed to maintain her legal ratio at 1:15½ for 73 years, because all the conditions were on the whole favorable; but when the Germans threw a portion of their silver on the world's market in hopes to reach the single gold standard, and the mines of Nevada poured forth on the same market their millions of silver, the ratio could no longer stand, the right of private individuals to have silver coined for them was taken away in behalf of the government, and only the five-franc silver pieces continued to be legal-tender to all amounts, the other silver coins becoming then (1876) only legal to pay debts to the amount of fifty francs. A franc is 19.29 of our standard cents.

And this brings us to notice what are called *subsidiary coins*. France, England, Germany, and the United States have debased their smaller silver coins in weight, so that the *nominal* value of these coins is from 7 to 15% above their *bullion* value. For example, two halves, four quarters, ten dimes, of our silver since 1875 weigh 385.8 grains, which is also the exact weight of the French five-franc piece, while our standard silver dollar weighs 412½ grains, both ⁹⁄₁₀ fine, so that our "subsidiary" silver is debased in weight 6.48%. There are three advantages in thus treating the smaller silver: (1) there is so much clear profit to the Government minting them, thus lessening taxation; (2) a security to the peoples that they shall not lose their convenient small change by export to neighboring countries; and (3) this scheme allows a very considerable rise in the market value of silver without tending to throw the subsidiaries out of circulation. As these are never legal-tender except to very small amounts in domestic trade, there are no serious objections to their use in limited quantities. The English can pay debts in their silver to the amount of £2, and we in ours to the extent of $5. Coins of copper and of other inferior metals are also *subsidiary* in principle and motive. Our 5-cent and 3-cent nickel pieces are 75 parts copper and 25 parts nickel, and the 1-cent piece is 95 parts copper and 5 parts tin-zinc; and debts of 4 cents can be paid in 1-cent pieces, of 60 cents in 3-cent pieces, and of 100 cents in 5-cent pieces.

10. The steady experience of civilized men for two milleniums and a half seems to demonstrate, that gold and silver constitute the best Money; and we must now investigate the reasons, one by one, *why* they are the best money. The reasons appear to be three. Of these the first is by much the most important.

(1) The first and main reason why gold and silver make the best money is to be found *in their comparatively steady general Value*. Since Money is a Measure of all other valuables, its success as a measure must depend on its own *steadiness* of value, and gold and silver meet this test better than anything else. Money is a valuable, and not in any sense a *representative* of value; except as to the subsidiaries, a coin does not owe its value at all to the *stamp* impressed upon it or to the *law* authorizing it, since the metal in it is worth as much out of the coinage as in it; coin-values arise under the same conditions as all other values, and are variable by any change in any one of the four elements which alone can vary the value of anything; and it would seem that nothing more is needed in order to remove the last vestiges of the dark cloud which has so long overhung this subject of Money, than to familiarize ourselves first of all, as we have already done, with the true doctrine of Value in general, and then to hold fast the truth exemplified on every hand, that the value of Money is just like every other value. Let us examine then, first, why the value of gold and silver is so steady.

(a) On account of the comparatively steady Demand for these metals. Gold and silver are wanted for two general purposes: first, to be used as money, and second, to be used in the arts; and the usual estimate is, that about ⅖ of the aggregate quantity in the world is in the form of money, and the other ⅗ in the form of plate and utensils and ornaments. Now, so far as the element of Desire controls Value, the purpose for which any article is desired is a matter of indifference. The aggregate desire for it for all purposes, accompanied with the offer of something with which to buy it, constitutes the Demand; and the more universal the desire, no matter for what use, the steadier the Demand and so far forth the steadier the Value.

It is a point still too little noticed, that the combined demand for the precious metals for all uses is what helps determine their general value, and not the demand for them as coin alone; just as the value of barley is regulated partly by the demand for it for food, and partly by the demand for it for malting purposes. Hence an ounce of bullion of the standard fineness destined for the smelting-pot of the artisan is worth within a very trifle as much as an ounce of coined money.

For example, by the law of the Bank of England an ounce of standard gold ($^{11}/_{12}$ fine) is coined into £3 17s. 10½d., and the Bank is obliged to buy all bullion and foreign coins of the standard fineness offered to it at £3 17s. 9d. per ounce,—a difference of only three half-pennies. Now, gold and silver are so indispensable in the form of money, so beautiful in the form of ornaments, so well adapted to serve the purposes of luxury and love of distinction, and so really useful in the arts, that the Demand for them is constant and well-nigh universal; and should there be in the progress of civilization a lessened demand for them for purposes of personal ornamentation and luxury, and a less quantity be required for coins on account of the multiplied use of cheques and other credit-forms, as seems likely in both cases, a greater quantity will doubtless be required for all the other uses old and new, and so, as the Demand in the past has been steady, and probably steadily increasing, there is every reason to expect the same course of things for the time to come. Moreover, it contributes to the steadiness in value of the gold and silver coin, that there is at hand at all times, in the form of plate, a reservoir from which a chance chasm in the coin may be replenished, or an extra demand for it answered.

(b) On account of their tolerably uniform Cost of Production. Not Desires only but Efforts as well determine Value. Supply is the correlative of Demand; and when to a steady demand there answers a steady supply realized under conditions of pretty uniform difficulty, there will be as a matter of course a pretty steady Value. Nature herself, that is to say, God himself, has indicated in a manner not to be mistaken the intention, that these precious metals should be the Money of the nations. They are scattered all over the earth, and so scattered that the cost of their production has been on the whole pretty steady ever since civilization and commerce began in earnest. God is a God of order throughout all His works. Corresponding to the nature and necessities of men is the whole structure of the outward world. Science builds only on these predetermined lines of Order. Induction is only possible where original Resemblances run through great departments of phenomena. To be enabled to buy and sell to any considerable extent in order to meet their subjective wants, men must have an objective measure of mutual Services, and this measure must be a valuable steady in its purchasing-power: very well; such a possible measure was all provided for beforehand, when the foundations of the earth were laid.

The precious metals have always been obtained in one or other of two ways: by surface diggings and washings, and by rock-mining. Both were employed in the very beginnings of Civilization. There is a description in the book of Job (chapter xxviii) of the way in which the ancient mines were wrought, and of the worth of the ores:

"Truly there is a vein for silver,And a place for gold, which men refine.Iron is obtained from earth,And stone is melted into copper. Man putteth an end to darkness;He searcheth to the lowest depthsFor the stone of darkness and the shadow of death,From the place where they dwell they open a shaft.Forgotten by the feetThey hang down, they swing away from men.The earth, out of which cometh bread,Is torn up underneath, as it were by fire.Her stones are the place of sapphires,And she hath clods of gold for man.The path thereto no bird knoweth,And the vulture's eye hath not seen it;The fierce wild beast hath not trodden it;The lion hath not passed over it.Man layeth his hand upon the rock;He upturneth mountains from their roots;He cleaveth out streams in the rocks,And his eye seeth every precious thing;He bindeth up the streams, that they trickle not,And bringeth hidden things to light."

These methods and difficulties in rock-mining, thus poetically and beautifully delineated, have been substantially the same from that early day to the present time; and, consequently, there have been but two or three striking changes in the general value of gold and silver in the commercial world during the last 500 years, at least changes owing to easier and larger Supply. The discovery of the mines of Potosi in 1545, and the large influx of silver into Europe from those and other American sources, together with the irrational stimulus thereby given to the working of European mines under the false impression not even yet wholly dissipated that Value can be clutched bodily in mining, so increased the stock of silver, that its value as measured in grain or other commodities declined in Europe in 70 years after 1570 to about 25% of its previous purchasing-power. Adam Smith expresses the opinion in his Wealth of Nations, that silver did not perceptibly fall before 1570, nor continue to fall further after 1640. The discovery of gold deposits on the Pacific coast of the United States in 1848, and a similar discovery in Australia in 1851, enlarged the annual supply of gold for the world from $40,000,000 in 1848 (*Chevalier*), to an average of $136,000,000 for the five years ending in 1859 (*Jevons*); and the latter writer estimated the fall of gold in general commodities from 1845 to 1862 at about 15%. But with exceptions like these, and similar ones are perhaps not likely to recur, the precious metals have always maintained and seem likely to maintain in the future a considerable uniformity of Value, as estimated by their power to purchase other valuables, so far forth as Cost of Production goes to determine their value. Even the great changes just noted in the cost of the metals issued only gradually in a rise of Prices, which many were able to foresee and thus to provide for, but by which many more were caught and brought into distress and even pauperism. The two classes that suffer the most under a fall in the Value of Money are the wages-receivers and the holders of long annuities and other similar obligations.

(c) On account of their Quantity. The amount of gold and silver in circulation in the commercial world, to say nothing of the quantity so easily brought into circulation from the reservoir of plate, is so vast, that it receives the annual contributions from the mines much as the ocean receives the waters of the rivers, without sensible increase of its volume, and parts with the annual loss by detrition and shipwreck, as the sea yields its waters to evaporation, without sensible diminution of volume. The yearly supply and the yearly waste are small in comparison with the accumulations of ages; and, therefore, the relation of the whole mass to the uses of the world, and the purchasing-power of any given portion, remain comparatively steady. It is probable, that production at the mines might cease altogether for a considerable interval without very sensibly enhancing throughout the commercial world the value of gold, as it is certain, from experience, that a production very largely augmented only very gradually and after a considerable interval of time diminishes its value. The mass of the precious metals has been aptly compared with the heavy balance-wheel in mechanics, which preserves an equable and working condition of the machinery under any sudden increase of the power, and even when the power is for a moment withdrawn.

Just at this point a caution is needful. Because it is affirmed that the great amount of the precious metals is a ground of their firm value, it must not be supposed that we are going beyond our general doctrine, and introducing another element, namely, Quantity, besides the four elements, which, as we have so often alleged, can alone vary the value of any Service. Quantity, in itself, is not an element capable of varying the value of anything, but taken in connection with durability, it is an element of what might, perhaps, be called with propriety the *Inertia* of Value, and tends to keep the purchasing-power of gold and silver where it is. *Value and Steadiness of Value are two distinct ideas.* The present value of an ounce of gold is decided by four things alone, two Desires and two Efforts; but other elements besides these may help determine that that ounce of gold shall have ten years from now a purchasing-power approximately the same as now. It will depend of course in the last analysis upon the relation of the then Demand to the then Supply; yet the vast quantity of the precious metals in existence, combined with their durability, prevents those fluctuations in the Supply which are so destructive to a steady value. It is not with them as with the fruits and the cereals, whose value varies perpetually with the seasons, and which are so perishable that they must be sold quick or never. Gold and silver are almost indestructible, and the existing mass is not liable to be lessened except by wear and accident, and in so far as the annual production from the mines exceeds the yearly waste there is a natural provision made for the natural increase of Demand to supply the wants of the world for money and for the arts without much disturbing the relation of the Demand and the Supply; and so Quantity in connection with durability helps preserve to them a tolerably steady value from generation to generation.

(d) On account of their Fluency. Gold and silver are in demand the world over. Having great value in comparatively small bulk, they are easily transported from Continent to Continent; and whenever from any cause they become relatively in excess in any country, and so lose there a portion of their previous purchasing-power, there is an immediate motive in profits to export them to other countries, in which their power in exchange is greater, and thus the equilibrium tends to restore itself. The proposition is, The value of gold and silver is kept pretty steady throughout the commercial world by the facility with which they are carried from points where they are relatively in excess to points where they are relatively in deficiency. In any country or place where the precious metals are temporarily in excess, the prices of general commodities as measured in them will rise of necessity, because the unit of measure is smaller than it was; and for the same general reason, the country temporarily lacking in these will experience in consequence a fall of general prices. There is, therefore, a private gain in carrying these metals to those countries in which their power of purchase is the greatest owing to the lack of them, because more commodities can be obtained in exchange for them than at home; and private motives here coincide, as indeed they generally do, with public welfare, since what the traders do in carrying gold and silver abroad with an eye to their own interest only, helps maintain at home and abroad the steady value of these commodities.

This law of the distribution of the precious metals by Commerce, and the equilibrium of their general value resulting therefrom, is as natural and beautiful as the law which preserves the level of the ocean, or that which balances the bodies of the planetary system. This has come at length to be recognized by the nations, and the laws which used to forbid by heavy penalties the exportation of gold and silver are all swept away, and these metals are now free to go and do actually go wherever they can obtain the most in exchange. It is absurd to suppose that their owners would carry them out of a country unless they were worth more abroad than at home; and, therefore, the prejudice which still exists in this country (the relics of itself) is a senseless prejudice. The gold is not given away, it is *sold*, and sold for more than it will buy at home; otherwise nothing in the world could start on its foreign travels. There is the same kind of gain in this as in all other exchanges of commodities, with this great incidental advantage in addition, that its general value is by this means kept pretty uniform throughout the commercial world.

Unluckily for the darker and middle Ages, so far as they took their cue and thought from the Romans, the latter, in the teeth of the sound view of Aristotle, looked upon Money as something quite different from other forms of salable things, looked upon it in short as an *end* in itself, as something to be gained and not readily to be parted with. If this were the right view of Money, as it is not, then the policy to spring from it might well be,—Get all the money possible into the country, and let as little as possible out! Just this came to be the policy of the Romans. In one of his Orations, Cicero says, "*The Senate solemnly decreed both many times previously, and again when I was consul, that gold and silver ought not to be exported.*" The other and the true opinion, that money is bought and sold like any other valuable, and that its sole peculiar function is as a *means* to further sales, was indeed held and argued at Rome, as we learn incidentally from a passage in the Institutes of Justinian; but the false though plausible opinion, that money is *ultimate*, and not *mediate*, is said in the same passage "to *have prevailed*"; and accordingly this superficial view of money, and that it "*ought not to be exported,*" constitute what may be called the Bullion Theory, and it is the first general theory of Sales ever promulgated. The Romans brought it forth, and other nations took it from them. It could never stand in the light of Reason, and still less amid the exigencies of practical Commerce.

It is an illustration of the continuity of human thinking as well in wrong as in right directions, that the second main theory of Sales, which has long been styled the Mercantile Theory, is a prolongation and expansion of the first. *That* gave an undue weight to gold and silver over other goods in trade, and forbade their export: *this* did the same thing too, but also tried to swell the exports of other goods beyond the worth of current imports, *so as to get back a balance in gold and silver:* both alike interfered with the international fluency of the precious metals, to the constant detriment of all parties to the restrictions. The common principles of both Theories may be thus expressed: *Gold and silver are the things to get; they are worth more than what they will buy; therefore let us get all of these in that we can, and let as little of them out as we can; and let us work all our trade so, that others shall have to give us a balance back in gold and silver.* These false postulates and inferences wrought centuries of woe in the world of commerce, because all the leading nations became devotees simultaneously to this scheme of each shrewdly plundering the rest. The germs of this Mercantile Theory appear first in France, when Phillippe le Bel, in ordinances of 1303 and 1304, put his hand in as king to mend the movement of trade, to forbid the export of gold and silver, to fix the price of wheat and to forbid its export, and to lessen imports by prohibitions of them. "*Considering that our enemies might profit by our provisions, and that it is important to leave them their merchandise, we have ordered that the former should not be exported nor the latter imported.*" The famous Colbert, who laid down many financial maxims that are good, thought nevertheless, that he could so manage the foreign trade of France that she should get the better of her neighbors, and embodied his plan in the tariff of 1664. We will let him state his plan in his own words: "*To reduce export duties on provisions and manufactures of the Kingdom; to diminish import duties on everything which is of use in manufactures; and to repel the products of foreign manufactures by raising the duties.*" The principle of the Mercantile Theory was never better or briefer expressed than by Ustariz, a Spaniard, in 1740: "*It is necessary rigorously to employ all the means that can lead us to sell to foreigners more of our productions than they will sell us of theirs, as that is the whole secret and the sole advantage of trade.*" Too many nations knew the "whole secret" at the same time, and accordingly the "sole advantage" to any became exceedingly small. England was as deep in the sloughs and wars and losses of this false system as any of the rest.

It may be laid down as an axiom, that no country will ever export for the sake of buying other things those things which are more needful for its own welfare at home. So long as human nature continues what it is, what it always was, what it always will be, no persons in any nation will ever export gold and silver except to buy therewith other valuables then and there more important to them and consequently to their country. There need not be the slightest fear that any nation which cultivates its own commercial advantages under freedom will ever lack for a day a sufficient *quantum* of the precious metals; because under freedom these metals will always go, and go in just the right proportions, to and from those countries which produce and offer in exchange those desirable Services which other countries want. The greater the enterprise and skill, the keener the development of all peculiar and presently available resources, the more honorable and free the commercial system, so much the surer is any nation whether it be a gold-bearing country or not, of securing all the gold and silver which it needs. This is so, because *there* will be a good market to buy in, an abundance of good and cheap goods will be there, and they who have gold will resort thither to buy. But such a free and enterprising nation will also want to buy other things besides gold and silver, and other things than those itself can make or grow to advantage, and when enough of the precious metals is secured for money and the arts, the residue will be exported, perhaps to the very countries from which it originally came, in payment for some products which *those* countries have an advantage in producing.

The United States, for example, is a gold- and silver-bearing country, and exported in the years 1850-60, both inclusive, $502,789,759 in coin and bullion, according to the official Report on the Finances, 1863; and during the same period imported from other countries $81,270,571 in coin and bullion. Where was the famous and fallacious "balance of trade" in that case? The United Kingdom, on the other hand, is not a gold- and silver-producing country at all, but it is the central market of the world for the precious metals all the same, its imports and exports of them are immense in all directions, because it is an enterprising country within the lines of Nature in agriculture and manufactures and commerce, and is not afraid to allow its people to buy and sell freely with all the world. Where lies in the technical sense the "balance of trade" between Great Britain and the rest of the world? Who can tell? All that is known, and all that is worth knowing, is, that all that trade is immensely profitable to all the parties to it wherever situated.

Now, there is always a double advantage in these free movements of coin and bullion in exportation and importation. In the first place, more and better commodities are secured to the countries exporting, whether they be gold-bearing or not, than the gold could have bought in those countries, otherwise it would not have been carried abroad, that being the sole motive that stirs it from its present haunts; and in the second place, the benefit to the countries importing is the market for their own commodities created by the gold brought in, for we must never forget that a market for products is products in market, is a benefit also in naturally and easily filling up a chance deficiency in the quantum of coin there, and incidentally too a benefit to the world as tending to keep *in equilibrio* the purchasing-power of the metals everywhere. This last is especially seen when new and pregnant sources of supply are opened in any country. For example, in the United States about the middle of the century the stock of gold was more than doubled in ten years' time; unless by much the larger part of this had been carried abroad in commerce, it would have inevitably depreciated the whole mass and disturbed the prices of everything; but by causing the new gold to impinge on the whole world's stock, the shock of the new production on the measure of Services, though perceptible, was reduced and deadened. The world's mass of the precious metals is comparatively torpid beneath the action of an accretion which would break down by its weight the metals of a single nation. Therefore, in conclusion on this topic, the Fluency of gold and silver, by which they pass easily in commerce to those places where their present value in exchange is greatest, or to such countries as India and China which have shown for centuries a wonderful power to absorb the metals of the West, and return as easily when the conditions are reversed, or when a larger use of paper-credits releases some portion of the coin, tends powerfully to make their general value uniform throughout the world, and consequently to make them the best medium of Exchange and the best measure of Services.

(e) On account of this Circumstance, that every general rise or fall in the value of gold and silver tends quickly to check itself. This principle, indeed, is applicable more or less to the value of all commodities, but owing to their quantity and durability and fluency pre-eminently applicable to the value of the precious metals. The check is double in either direction. First, let us suppose that the purchasing-power of an ounce of gold or silver be rising: then, production will be stimulated at all the mines, and the more stimulated as the rise is more; and this new and enlarged Supply will tend to check a farther rise, and unless the permanent Demand has been in the meantime intensified, to bring back the value to the old point; moreover, when there is a rise in the value of the coin, a less quantity is required to do the same amount of business; and the demand for gold which causes the rise tends to be checked by the rise itself, because a lessened quantity is needed for money-use in consequence of the rise. If the exchanges mediated by money have become permanently greater than before, then of course the Demand will continue greater than before, and the rise in value may be maintained.

And just so, *mutatis mutandis*, of a fall in the purchasing-power of the coin. The production of the metals is thereby slackened at the mines, and the lessened Supply tends naturally to enhance the value; and if the same amount of business is to be done as before, there is a stronger demand for money while the fall continues, and this new Demand helps also to bring back the old value. All this is in the interest of a steady value.

(f) On account, lastly, of this Circumstance, that a stronger Demand for Money is met in either one of two ways, by increasing the stock of coin, or by an increased rapidity of circulation of that on hand. It is exceedingly fortunate that a brisker demand for money, especially if it be but temporary, does not necessarily enlarge the Supply or alter the value, but only hurries round the existing money. Oscillations in the Demand are responded to by a slower or a more rapid circulation. This tends admirably to keep the value of the existing-stock of money steady within certain limits. Ignorance of this principle, or indifference to it, has caused mighty mischiefs in the United States. In General Grant's administration, for instance, the cry that a larger *volume* of money was needed "*to move the crops*" was disastrous in its results. The truth is, that the volume of Money in the

United States was then, and has been ever since, by much too great, considering its character, as we shall see by and by. The multiplying and fructifying nature of Rapidity of Circulation has never been understood by our national financiers. When, however, enterprises are multiplying and Exchanges are being permanently increased in number and variety, then there must be a larger volume of money, and this larger amount is secured in the ways already indicated, with perhaps slight disturbances of value, but the temporary ebbs and flows of business should have no effect at all on the mass of money, but only on its movement, and its value consequently would scarcely be disturbed.

These Six grounds appear to be satisfactory and sufficient to account for the superior steadiness of the value of gold and silver, so far as their value is determined by considerations relating to these metals themselves. We now proceed to the two reasons additional to this why gold and silver constitute the best Money.

(2) The second general reason why gold and silver make the best money is found in the fact *that Governments have little to say or do about the Value and Quantity and Mode of Circulation of such Money.* In respect to Credit-Moneys, like our own Greenbacks and national Bank-Bills, the Government has everything to say. When we remember how governments are constituted, that they are only a transient Committee of the citizens for special purposes; of what sort of persons they commonly consist; the variety of subjects they are obliged to consider during short periods of office; the absence for the most part of expert knowledge among them; the enormous blunders they have made in the past in all financial measures; and that those who know the most about their action in the past and present in such matters have the least confidence in their ability to act wisely; the better we shall see the strength of the grounds of this second reason. In all essential respects money of gold and silver regulates itself. These metals came to be money and continue to be money in the main sense independent of the enactments of any Government. The people chose them: they choose them still. As we have seen, coins do not owe their value to the stamp of the Government, since the metal in them is worth within a trifle as much before coinage as after. Coinage publicly attests the quantity and quality of the metal in the coin, and that is all. Of the value of their coins governments say nothing. They can say nothing. That depends on men's judgments, and not on edicts at all. No law of the United States can add directly an appreciable fraction to the value of a gold dollar. The law makes it consist of $25\frac{4}{5}$ grains troy of gold $\frac{9}{10}$ fine, the mint so stamps and attests it, and thereafter it takes its own chance as to value.

Some Governments charge a little something for coining for their People, and some do not. What is charged is called *seignorage*. England coins gold for all comers at a seignorage of .032%, which is practically a free coinage. France charges for gold .216%; and by the law of 1874, the United States charge nothing for coining gold. It is left to the People to say *how much* money they will have coined; and, having received it back from the mint, they may do just what they please with it; they may hoard it, they may melt it, they may sell it at home in purchase, and they may export it in foreign trade, at will. Now, it is a great gain, an immense relief, to have a Money with which the Government has nothing to do except to mint it; a money that asks no favors, needs no puffing, never deceives anybody, knows how to take care of itself, is always respectable and everywhere respected.

(3) The last general reason why gold and silver make the best Money is to be found in their physical peculiarities, in accordance with which they are (a) *uniform in quality*, (b) *conveniently portable*, (c) *divisible without loss*, (d) *easily impressible*, and (e) *always beautiful*.

Pure gold and pure silver, no matter where they are mined, are exactly of the same *quality* all over the earth. Not so with iron and coal and copper. Gold is gold, and silver is silver. The gold mined to-day in California differs in no essential respect from the gold used by Solomon in the construction of the Temple, and the silver out of the Nevada mines is the same thing as the silver paid by Abraham for the cave of Machpelah. Nature with her wise finger has thus stamped them for the universal money; and a universal coinage, that is, coins of the same degree of fineness, and brought into easy numerical relations with each other in respect to weight, and current everywhere by virtue of universal confidence in them, though bearing the symbols preferred by the nation that mints them, is one of the dreams and hopes of economists, that will be realized in some

"Fair future dayWhich Fate shall brightly gild."

Gold and silver are sufficiently *portable* for all the purposes of modern Money. Their weight is little relatively to their value. A thousand dollars in gold are not indeed carried so easily as a Bill of Exchange or a Bank-note; and expedients are easily adopted, and have been in use since the days of the Romans (really since the later days of the Assyrians), by which the transfer in place of large masses of coin is for the most part obviated; and these expedients have all been explained at length in the foregoing chapter on Commercial Credits. But for the ordinary exchanges for which they are designed, gold and silver coins are portable enough. The writer has carried across the ocean, incased in a glove-finger and borne in a vest-pocket, a troy pound of English sovereigns, worth about $230, scarcely conscious of their weight though easily reassured of their presence by a touch of the hand. The experience of those countries, like France and Germany, in which the Money has been and is still mostly metallic, has not pronounced it onerous on account of its weight; and, at any rate, it is better to accept all the other immense advantages of gold and silver money, together with some inconvenience as to weight, if one chooses to insist on that, than to adopt substitutes every way inferior as money, except that they are lighter in our purses. They are unfortunately "lighter" in other respects also.

Moreover, gold and silver differ from jewels and most other precious things, in that they are *divisible* without any loss of value into pieces of any required size. The aggregate of pieces is worth as much as the mass and the mass as much as the pieces. This is a great advantage in Money, because for the convenience of business a considerable variety of coins is required, and the proper proportion of each kind to the rest is a matter of trial, and if any kind be minted in excess of the demand nothing more is required than to remint in other denominations, and the whole value is thus saved to the country in the most convenient form.

Then, gold and silver are easily *impressible* by any stamp which the Government chooses to put upon them. Indeed in their natural state they are too soft to retain long the impress of the die. Accordingly for coinage purposes they are always alloyed with another metal, chiefly copper, since by a chemical law whenever two such metals are mixed together the compound is harder than either of the two ingredients. Most of the Nations now use in their gold and silver coins $\frac{1}{10}$ alloy, but England still adheres to her ancient rule of $\frac{1}{12}$ only. So compounded coins receive readily and retain for a long time with sharp distinctness the legend and other devices chosen for them to bear. In monarchical countries the head of the reigning sovereign is usually stamped upon the current coins; in all countries national emblems of some sort; quite recently some of the coins of the United States have been made to bear the appropriate legend "In God we trust"; so that patriotic and even religious associations are connected with the national Money. Although the alloys harden the coins, yet after long usage they will lose a part of their weight by abrasion, and Governments usually indicate a short weight, after coming to which the coins are no longer a legal tender for debts. Thus an English sovereign weighs 5 pennyweights 3 $^{17}\frac{1}{623}$ grains, containing 113 $\frac{1}{623}$ grains of fine gold, and when it falls below 5 pennyweights 2¾ grains, it loses its legal-tender character.

Lastly, gold and silver when coined into Money are objects of great *beauty*. This is no slight recommendation of these metals for the money of the world. They are clean. They are beautiful. People like to see them, and to handle them, and to have them. Their perfectly circular form, the device covering the whole piece, the milled and fluted edges, the patriotic emblem, whatever it be, the religious or other legend, and their bright color, are all elements in their beauty. The educating power over the young of a good coinage well kept up, æsthetically, historically, and commercially, is a matter of consequence to any country. A whole people handling constantly such money cannot fail to receive a wholesome development thereby. The new German coinage, for example, in contrast with the old moneys of the German States, furnishes a good illustration of all this. The new German coins from highest to lowest are very beautiful, and have already tended and will tend more and more, other things being equal, to a true German nationality.

11. Silver is much inferior to gold as a metal for Money, for this main reason, that it has proved itself much less steady in its general *value*; and its value is less steady, because it is subject to greater changes in its Supply and greater variations in its Demand. As an example touching Supply, we cite the fact, that the annual silver product of the world *doubled* in the third quarter of this Century, rising from an average of $40,000,000 yearly, 1851-61, to $80,000,000 in 1875; and that Nevada alone yielded in 1876 as much as the whole world yielded twenty years before. Then, too, Demand, that is, effective public opinion, does not hold to silver as it does to gold for a standard of Values. The action of England in 1816, of the United States in 1853, of Germany in 1871, of Scandinavia in 1874, and of the Latin Union in 1876, *in legally making gold the sole standard of Services and silver subsidiary to that*, of course affected more or less the Demand for silver as Money, and thus varied its value. We have at hand the data to demonstrate the effect of these two causes combined: the average price of silver in gold from 1833 to 1874, in the London market, which is the bullion market of the world, was for the 40 years just about 60 pence per ounce, never falling below 58½ and never rising to 63. At 60 pence per ounce (444 grains of pure silver, standard English silver being .925 fine) the ratio of gold to silver is 1:15.716. But between May, 1875, and July, 1876, when both the above causes had come into full action, silver dropped in the London market to 47 pence per ounce, a fall of 21%, and a ratio of gold to silver of 1:20. The price gradually rose again to about 53 pence per ounce, and remained in that general neighborhood till 1882, between which date and 1890 the *sagging* process went on to the general result of 25% discount as compared with the old average of 60 pence in gold per ounce of silver.

These facts settle the question adversely to the fitness of silver to become an independent Measure of Values. When, however, it is designed that gold and silver shall circulate together in some numerical relation to each other as Money, it becomes needful that Government shall fix as well as it can, not the general value of either but the relative value each in each for the time being. But this specific value, too, goes on to regulate itself independently of government edicts. No matter how well the work is done at first by ascertaining the actual ratio in which they are exchanging in a free market, it will certainly require revision from time to time. This is what is called *Bimetallism*. The reader will now perceive the fundamental and ineradicable difficulty with the bimetallic system, which has led by bitter experience nearly all the European nations to abandon it. It especially becomes us to understand how the United States have fared in a century's attempt to keep *in equilibrio* as a conjoint and legal Measure of Services both gold and silver in a fixed numerical relation.

Alexander Hamilton as the first Secretary of the National Treasury, entering upon excellent preparatory work done both by Robert Morris and Thomas Jefferson, guided the action of Congress in establishing the Mint in 1792, and really determined the weight and fineness of the first federal coins and their relative value each in each, the silver coins being struck in 1794 and the gold ones in 1795. The silver dollar was copied from the Spanish milled dollar of commerce, which contained 371.25 grains of pure silver, and that has been the exact content of our national silver dollar from that day to this. The halves and quarters and dimes were exactly proportioned in weight and fineness to their units. Hamilton supposed that gold was then worth in Europe 15 times as much as silver, and advised consequently that the gold dollar should contain 24.75 grains pure, and that both dollars should be alloyed at the English rate of $\frac{1}{12}$, thus making the silver dollar weigh 405 grains and the gold dollar 27 grains; but Congress, while enacting the gold dollar just as the Secretary recommended, preferred to *alloy* the silver dollar by 44.75 grains instead of 33.75, thus making its weight 416 grains. Alloy is of no account in value.

From the ratio of 1:15 fixed by the act of Congress in accord with Hamilton's opinion as to the relative value of gold in silver to be maintained in the coins, unforeseen and important consequences followed, since that was not the true ratio of their value at the time in the markets of the world; an ounce of gold was worth more at that time than 15 ounces of silver, and, accordingly, was worth more out of the coinage than in it, and was therefore exported in preference to silver in payment of foreign balances, especially after France had changed the relative legal value to 1:15$\frac{1}{2}$, which happened in 1803; and of course the gold refused to circulate here under those circumstances, being *undervalued* in the coinage, thus giving a neat illustration of the economical law to be unfolded under the next numerical heading, namely, that the cheaper money will always push the dearer out of the circulation. Not till 1834 was the attention of Congress so strongly drawn to this fact and consequence, as to secure an enactment to remedy it; and this coinage law of 1834 rated gold to silver as 1:15.98. The weight of the gold dollar was at the same time reduced from 27 to 25.8 grains, and the alloy increased from $\frac{1}{12}$ to $\frac{1}{10}$. These changes of 1834 increased the relative legal valuation of gold in silver 6.53%. But this in turn was going too far in the opposite direction; gold was not worth 1:15.98 in the bullion markets of Europe; France was holding steady her ratio of 1:15.50; and, consequently, the commercial current of the metals was now reversed, silver passing in preference to Europe to liquidate the balances of trade, and gold beginning to come to the United States, where it would buy more than 3% more silver than in Europe.

Three years after the above changes, that is, in 1837, the standard of $\frac{9}{10}$ fine instead of $\frac{11}{12}$ was applied by law to silver also, and this altered fineness made a change in the weight of the silver coins necessary, if the ratio of 1:15.98 was to be maintained between the gold and silver. Accordingly, the weight of the silver dollar, and of two halves, four quarters, and so on, was reduced from 416 grains to 412½, that is to say, less alloy was put into the silver coins, but the fine silver to the dollar was kept just as it was, namely, 371.25 grains. Since 1834 there has been no change in the gold dollar and its multiples, and since 1837 there has been no change in the silver *dollar-piece*, and the legal ratio of value between gold and silver in our coins is still 1:15.98, since the silver dollar of 1878 and onwards to 1890 corresponds in weight and fineness with the dollar of 1837.

Still, notwithstanding the pains taken and the changes made from time to time to keep the two metals in legal *equilibrio*, there never has been any considerable period in the century now drawing to a close, during which gold dollars and silver dollars have circulated freely and indifferently in the United States. Sometimes it has been the one kind, and sometimes the other kind, but never both kinds at the same time. The present writing is in the spring-time of 1890: both kinds of dollars are legal tender for all debts public and private in the old-time ratio; the national Government professes to be indifferent whether it pay out gold or silver in redemption of its paper-moneys, but after all, with the exception of the Pacific States and a few special branches of business in the cities of the East and of the Middle, gold coins are not now in common circulation, the bank drawers crowded with silver dollars feel little of the weight and see little of the shine of the gold coins, and if any of these chance to be paid out to ordinary bank-customers they are pretty certain to return in speedy deposit. The theoretical bimetallism of the United States has been a practical though alternate monometallism with various incidental and concurrent disadvantages and losses.

By 1853 these disadvantages of a long-attempted double Measure of Services made legal tender for all debts had become plain enough to everybody, for experience had demonstrated that the Value of gold and silver each in each was not constant but constantly variable; and Congress then wisely determined to make Gold alone the legal tender, except in sums below $5. In connection with this great change in the coinage, a lesser one was introduced at the same time, namely, to reduce the weight of the silver half-dollar and its subdivisions, so that their nominal value in the coinage should be considerably above their metallic value, and their exportations be thus prevented. Accordingly, the half-dollar was reduced in weight from 206¼ to 192 grains, and the smaller coins proportionally. This was in imitation of the English legislation of 1816, and brought into this country a *subsidiary* silver coinage, which still continues, and of which a nominal dollar's worth weighed 6.91% less than the Silver Dollar, which was not mentioned one way or the other in the law of 1853, but which was then worth about three cents more than the gold dollar, and was of course wholly out of circulation.

Through the influence of the late Samuel B. Ruggles, these subsidiary silver coins were brought in 1875 into harmony with the silver-system of France and the Latin Union. Their five-franc silver piece which is also 9/10 fine, weighs just 25 *grams* or 385.8 *grains*; a dollar's worth of our subsidiary silver, as we have just seen, weighed 384 grains; and it was, therefore, needful to add only a slight fraction of weight to our smaller silver coins in order to knit a real connection between them and much of the European silver. Two halves, four quarters, ten dimes of our silver since 1875, are debased in weight (not in fineness) 6.47% as compared with the standard silver dollar. A more important coinage connection with Europe was knit through our first five-cent nickel pieces, each of which weighs just five *grams*, and five of which laid along in order measure exactly a *decimetre* in length. These were the first official applications of the Metric System on the part of the United States. The nickel pieces, both the five-cent and the three-cent, are 75 parts copper and 25 parts nickel; and the one-cent piece is 95 parts copper and 5 parts tin-zinc. Debts of 4 cents can be legally paid in one-cent pieces, of 60 cents in three-cent pieces, of 100 cents in five-cent pieces, of 500 cents in *subsidiary* silver, and of any amount in gold coins or in silver *dollars*.

12. *A money inferior in general value will, so long as it circulates locally, drive a superior money out of the circulation.* This proposition is a fundamental and universal one in monetary Science. The only exception to it is found in *token-coins*, and in subsidiary silver so far as that has the *token*-quality, that is, so far as its *nominal* is above its *bullion* Value. The main motive in coining tokens is to make sure for its own local uses of a nation's small change. Token-money is worthless for export, is only designed for the smaller exchanges, is legal tender only for very small sums, and is acceptable only on local and conventional grounds. The exception aside, the above proposition is a pervading and controlling Law of Finance and has been illustrated over

and over again in every Age and Nation. It is as solid as the substance of truth can make it, although it looks at first sight like a paradox. We naturally think that what is excellent all round tends rather to displace what is inferior in spots, but with Money the exact reverse is the law; and the perfect coin of full weight, instead of driving out the light and the debased pieces, is always itself driven out of the circulation by them.

The reason for this becomes obvious the moment we ponder the nature of Money. Money is always a Valuable, taking on in addition under Law or Custom the function of serving as an instrument of Exchange. As money, nobody wants it except to buy with, and so long as the Government and the community treat light coin and full coin as of equal value, receiving them indifferently in payment of debts and of taxes, it is clear that nobody will give in payment of debts and of taxes that which is really worth more so long as that which is really worth less will go just as far. The inferior pieces will abide in a market where they will fetch just as much as the superior pieces, while the superior pieces will take on a form or migrate to a place in which some advantage can be gained from their superiority. Thrown into the crucible, or exported in commerce, this superiority immediately manifests itself; and therefore into the crucible or into the channels of foreign trade it might be confidently predicted beforehand that such money would be thrown, and all experience testifies with one voice that exactly those are the destinations of such money.

Aristophanes, the Greek comic poet, in the 5th century before Christ, seems to have been the first writer who noticed that good coins of full weight are apt to be crowded out of the circulation by the lighter and poorer pieces, and he, mistaking the cause of this, satirized his countrymen unmercifully for preferring bad coins to good, and demagogues, like Cleon, to honorable citizens for rulers. The following are the verses:—

"Oftentimes have we reflected on a similar abuse,In the choice of men for office, and of coins for common use;For your old and standard pieces, valued and approved and tried,Here among the Grecian nations, and in all the world beside,Recognised in every realm for trusty stamp and pure assay,Are rejected and abandoned for the trash of yesterday;For a vile, adulterate issue, drossy, counterfeit, and base,Which the traffic of the city passes current in their place!And the men that stood for office, noted for acknowledged worth,And for manly deeds of honor, and for honorable birth;Trained in exercise and art, in sacred dances and in song,All are ousted and supplanted by a base, ignoble throng;Paltry stamp and vulgar metal raise them to command and place,Brazen counterfeit pretenders, scoundrels of a scoundrel race,Whom the State in former ages scarce would have allowed to standAt the sacrifice of outcasts, as the scapegoats of the land."

Sir Thomas Gresham, financier of Queen Elizabeth and founder of the Royal Exchange and of Gresham College in London, was the first thinker to understand fully and explain scientifically what Aristophanes and others had noticed as a fact, and what in its explanation may hence properly be called "*Gresham's Law.*" We will append a few historical illustrations of the fact and the law as instructive in many ways.

(a) The City of Amsterdam founded its famous Bank in 1609, because no other way seemed to open of preventing the clipped and worn foreign coins then and for a long time circulating in that great Mart of Trade from driving out completely the good money of full weight, which the Mint of the City had been constantly pouring in. The Bank was devised as a municipal Institution with this intent; it was a Bank of Deposit only; it took in all the old coins at their *bullion* value only; and then had them reminted at full weight; it gave the depositors credit on its books in the terms of the *new* money for all of the *old* they chose to bring in; it then adjusted accounts between merchants and all other of its customers by mere transfers on its books; the City required all debts falling due in Amsterdam to be paid in the new "bank-money," which took away all uncertainty from Bills of Exchange drawn on Amsterdam, which were previously liable to be paid in the clipped and worn coin, and were therefore sometimes at as much as 10% discount in other cities; this simple requirement brought these foreign bills to par, and kept them there; the full-weighted money now stamped by the city Mint abode in the circulation, being now the sole Measure of Services there; and thus it became the interest and convenience of every business man in Amsterdam to have these simple dealings with the Bank, which in turn enjoyed unlimited credit in the commercial world for almost two hundred years.

(b) The great English Recoinage of 1696 was completed under the imperatives of Gresham's Law. Graphically does Macaulay describe the causes and the effects of this in his 21st Chapter. The old silver coins had been stamped under the hammer; few of them were perfectly circular; the edges were neither milled nor fluted; the legend was not so near the edge as that the letters were impaired by a little clipping; it was easy to pare off a pennyworth or two, and then pass the coins along; it was profitable to do it, and in vain that Elizabeth enacted that the clipper must suffer the penalties of high treason; nearly all the coin of the realm became mutilated, and about 1660 a new process of coinage was brought in. A mill worked by horses fabricated the new coins on better principles. They were exactly round, and the edges were inscribed with a legend, and they were all of just and equal weight. They were thrown out to pass current with the hammered money, and it seems to have been expected that they would soon come to displace it. But they did not. Both were received at first without distinction by the individual traders and by the public tax-gatherers. But the milled money soon came to be scarce, and the old money grew constantly worse. The lighter the old coins became, the scarcer became the new ones; for who would pay two ounces of silver when one ounce was legal tender? The new money was melted, was exported, was hoarded, but circulate it would not. At length the lightest pieces began to be refused by some people, and other people demanded that their silver should be paid to them by weight and not by tale, and there was wrangling over every counter, and a dispute at every settlement, and the coin was really so diverse in its value that there was no longer any measure of value in the kingdom; business was in utmost confusion, society was by the ears, poor people were unmercifully fleeced, and shrewd ones grew enormously rich; and the Jacobites secretly exulted in the hope of being able to avail themselves of the prevailing discontent to overthrow the scarcely established revolutionary government of William and Mary; when, by the joint counsels of two such philosophers as Locke and Newton, and two such statesmen as Somers and Montague, the government took the bold resolution of recoining all the silver of the kingdom. An early day was fixed by Parliament after which no clipped money could pass except in payments to Government, and a later day after which it could not pass at all.

(c) Gresham's Law has had beautiful illustrations in the monetary history of the United States. We have already seen the reason why the first silver dollars of 1794 could not compete in currency with the gold coins of 1795,—the silver was under-valued in the legal ratio 1:15,—it would have been much nearer the European market at 1:15.5. There was another reason operative in the same direction from the beginning, which did not, however, come to the notice of the Government till ten years later. Only 321 silver dollar-pieces were coined in the year 1805; and May 1, 1806, there stands an order from President Jefferson to the Director of the Mint,—"*that all the silver to be coined at the Mint shall be of small denominations, so that the value of the largest pieces shall not exceed half a dollar.*" The presidential reason given for this order is,—"*that considerable purchases have been made of dollars coined at the Mint for the purpose of exporting them, and that it is probable that further purchases and exportations will be made.*" The coinage of silver dollars thus suspended was not resumed for 30 years. What was the matter with these dollars? Nothing, only they were too valuable. Hamilton had adopted for his new dollar the exact weight in fine silver of the normal Spanish-Mexican dollar, then and for a long time the unit of the thriving West India commerce; clipped and worn coins of this popular stamp had slipped into circulation in large numbers throughout the United States, and driven out the new and good pieces in accordance with a principle much better understood now than then; the President's order itself was not very intelligent, inasmuch as two halves, four quarters, or ten dimes, were then equal in weight and purity with the dollar-pieces, and as a matter of fact were almost (if not quite) equally driven out by the smaller Spanish-Mexican coins. The "four-pences" and "nine-pences" ("York shilling") of that coinage were almost exclusively the small change of New York and New England during the first half of this century. The "dimes" and "half-dimes" of our own mintage, though long legalized, were but slowly naturalized. The coin-changes of 1853, already described, gave a fair chance for the first time to our smaller silver coins.

The last native illustration of Gresham's Law will force us to anticipate here the discussion under the next numerical heading, so far as to assume that there is such a thing as paper money, and that the Law now in hand works in connection with that as well as with diverse forms of metallic money. In 1862, Treasury notes, commonly called Greenbacks, made a legal tender for debts though not bearing interest, were issued by the national Government to the amount of $450,000,000. Of course, under these circumstances they depreciated in value as compared with the gold dollars, which gold dollars *they were unfulfilled promises to pay.* Just so soon as the greenback dollars fell fairly below the gold dollars in value, the latter left the channels of trade in a very few days' time. Down sank the greenbacks gradually below the *subsidiary* silver coins in value, and the latter obediently and utterly abandoned the commercial field. At last the greenbacks went down even below the level of the copper cents, which at that time cost the government about half a cent each, and this invariable law of money swept the circulation bare of coppers, and the people had to resort for their smallest change to postage-stamps and shin-plasters and other abominations. Happily, the country survived to see these processes exactly reversed, and the old law confirmed on its other side. When, after a considerable interval, the paper dollar appreciated to the proper height, it was interesting to watch the copper cents put in a prompt re-appearance; after a still larger appreciation of the paper, back came in abundance the subsidiary silver; and as the day of the redemption of the paper drew near, silver dollars and gold dollars greeted smilingly their old acquaintances of the street.

13. So far we have treated only of Coin-Money in its two forms, *substantive* and *subsidiary.* The latter may now be dismissed as of little consequence in itself, and as already elucidated fully: the latter is the only Money that stands in its own right as a *commodity*, and the only Money that can give birth to the *Denominations* of Value, such as sovereigns, dollars, marks, and francs. *What is a Dollar?* A dollar is 25⅘ grains of a metal compound coined, of which nine parts are pure gold and one part a hardening alloy. It is a definite

quantity of a thing definitely and legally described. It is a visible and tangible and well-known *commodity*. Government is competent, if it pleases, to alter the quantity of gold that shall constitute a dollar, although the People will quickly and roughly readjust the prices of Services to a changed measure of them; it is competent even to make a dollar out of silver, as our Government has tried to do (for the most part vainly) for a century, though it is *not* competent to cause both dollars to circulate as such at the same time; but civilized and advanced Governments are not practically competent to make a Dollar out of anything else than gold and silver.

Money is a current and legal Measure of Services; for the end and in the way in which Money alone originates and becomes current its material must be a valuable commodity; and after centuries of experiments and exclusions no civilized People now tolerate any other commodity in this relation than gold or silver. Such a selected commodity becoming in the manner already explained an actual medium passing from hand to hand in Exchanges, impresses its *name* on the minds of men as an ideal *measure* of services, which measure they can use, and do constantly use, without handling at the time the commodity itself. But these ideal-dollars, these denomination-dollars, need to be kept in check by a constant recurrence to actual, palpable thing-dollars. The denomination only comes into existence in connection with the use of the thing, cannot possibly exist independently of it, and needs constantly to be reduced to it (as it were by actual contact) in order to be useful as a measure. Just as men talk about inches, and calculate by inches, in thousands of cases in which no actual inch is used as a measure, and in every case of doubt, dispute, or difficulty have recourse to the actual inch, and thus the ideal inch is kept steady in the minds of men by frequent reference to the outward standard; so the mental measure of services, which men insensibly acquire from the use of the objective measure, needs to be kept true by actual and frequent contact with that measure.

But besides this Thing-Dollar and its Denomination, which always go together like a man and his shadow, there is one other kind of Money, namely, the Promise-Dollar. We must now attend to this. What is a Dollar-Bill? How does it read? It is always a Promise of some Issuer to pay to bearer One Dollar, that is to say, this legal and definite quantity of a precious metal. There is no mystery here. There can be none. A Dollar is a tangible and weighable commodity. A Dollar-Bill is a Promise to render this commodity to bearer on demand. The difference is the same in kind as that between a bushel of corn and a man's promise to his poor neighbor to give him a bushel if he will come for it. It depends on the *man*, on his ability and character, how much the corn-promise is worth; and so it depends on the *issuer*, on his ability and character, how much the coin-promise is worth.

The Issuer may be of such standing as to be able to secure for his promises that they become "a current and legal measure of Services"; and if so, they become Money under the definition.

There is, then, such a thing as Paper-Money, though many high authorities are reluctant to concede, that any mere promises can be money at all. For ourselves we cannot refuse the courtesy of the term "money" to paper-promises-to-pay-coin, which our Country makes a legal tender for all debts, public and private. The making them legal tender, however, does not alter their nature one particle. They are still promises,—and nothing more. Their *Value* depends in all cases upon the character and resources of the Issuer; their *Currency* may be quickened (at some rate of value) by their being made a legal tender. Nothing can by any possibility become a Money unless it first be a Valuable. The essential characteristic of Money is its possession of a *generalized* purchasing-power. The Value of a promise depends on one set of causes, with which we are now very familiar,—the same causes on which the value of everything depends; the Generalization of any purchasing-power into money depends upon another set of causes, of which the action of a Government in legislation may be one.

Paper-Money, as now defined, may be issued by Banks with or without an indirect government sanction, or through the direct action of Government. The Bank of England has been issuing since 1694 paper-money under a series of Charters granted by the Government, which becomes thereby in a manner responsible to the bearers for the redemption, that is, the fulfilment, of the direct promises of "The Governor and Company of the Bank of England"; since 1863 the so-called National Banks of the United States have issued promises-to-pay, designed to circulate as money, under the direct authority and quasi-endorsement of the national Government; and since 1862 that Government has been putting out directly its own promises commonly called "greenbacks." These last have rested and now rest for their value solely on the good faith of the People as between themselves. By a separate and additional act of legislation, which it is mischievous as well as unscientific to confound with the original promise-legislation, this particular paper-money was and is legal tender for debts, which collateral circumstance whether wise or unwise neither changes the nature nor lessens the obligation of the original promise to pay coin. No so-called Decision of the Supreme Court can abolish or abridge a natural and scientific distinction. Money is at bottom of two kinds only: the first kind is an intermediate and equivalent merchandise, COIN; and the second kind is Promises to pay this to a bearer on demand, PAPER MONEY.

The only way to make any promise respectable is to fulfil it in due time. The only way to make Paper Money a decency is to hold sacred in action the promise that distends it. The United States undertook in 1862 and onwards to make its own plain promises respectable by a different method, namely, by legally asserting in substance that the *promise* is its own *fulfilment*, and needs no other; and in this persistent undertaking encountered a miserable failure throughout; because the People also persisted in *estimating* the promise solely in the light of the *prospect* of its literal fulfilment. The greenbacks at one time lost two-thirds of their normal value under the working of such estimation. This question of the relation of two kinds of Money to each other is a question of Economics, and not of Constitutional Law; or rather, it is a question of common sense and common honesty, and the judgment upon it of nine men learned in the Law is no whit better than the judgment of nine other intelligent men.

As Money is analyzable into two varieties only, Coin and Paper, so Paper Money falls into two classes, Convertible and Inconvertible. A convertible paper money consists of promises that are always *kept* by the issuer according to their terms, that is to say, that are paid in specie at the will of the holder. An inconvertible paper money is only another name for unfulfilled promises. Is it any wonder that unfulfilled promises to pay invariably become less valuable than *that* which they promise to pay? They are valuable to start with, else they could not become money, and they are valuable because men suppose the promise will be kept: they are commonly valueless to end with, because men lose faith in the fulfilment of a promise long delayed. This is the simple secret of the depreciation of inconvertible money so soon as the amount of it passes a certain limit, and so soon as a certain time has elapsed after its issue and the issuer shows no signs of keeping his word. As money is only a measure of Services, and as possible Services are limited at any one time and place, and consequently as the amount of money needed for healthful business is limited also, a steadily convertible paper money, provided the limit of quantity be not overpassed, will constitute a tolerable money. But this limit of quantity is apt to be overpassed, whether the paper money be convertible or inconvertible, and especially in the latter case, because the temptation to issue promises to pay in excess of the means of promptly redeeming them always besets the issuer on account of the *gain* to him in such issue at least for a time. This temptation has been yielded to first or last by every nation, and probably by every corporation, that has ever issued paper money. The Bank of England has been on the whole the best managed Bank of Issue in the world, and its Bills (Promises) have gained the most confidence and the widest circulation. This is because they have been kept by the Issuers *convertible* from the beginning, with the exception of two comparatively brief intervals of time. As already related under the last general proposition, the silver coins of the realm were much worn and clipped when the Bank was established in 1694, the Bank, however, had received them on deposit of customers at their full nominal value; but after the Recoinage began in

1696, it was obliged under the law to redeem its Bills in new coin of full weight, that is, for perhaps 9 ounces of silver received, it was now bound to pay 12. Consequently its enemies, the Jacobites, made a "run" upon the Bank by collecting up its Bills to a large amount and presenting them for payment. The Bank was obliged to suspend payment, at first partially, and then generally. In February, 1697, the Bills were 24% below par. The Promises could not be kept, and therefore they drooped in value according to man's estimation of the probability of their becoming again *convertible*, which happened in the course of that year under a new charter and privileges from Government to the Bank.

Just 100 years after the first suspension of specie payments, in 1797, when the War of the French Revolution made such demands upon the English for money, the Bank broke its solemn promises the second time, and did not formally resume payments until 1821. Government and the business men of London did their best to hold up the credit of the notes during the suspension, *but they were not made a legal tender for debts.* Government received them at par for taxes, and provided that business payments in notes would be held as payments in cash if offered and accepted as such. Debtors, having tendered bank notes, which the creditor refused, had certain privileges before the law which other debtors had not. The notes therefore had a *quasi* legalization, but not a forced circulation. The bank was also authorized at this time to issue £5, £2, and £1 notes. Cautiously issued at first, bank paper continued at par for several years after the suspension, which proves that when government possesses the monopoly of issuing paper money, and carefully limits its quantity, and both receives and pays it out at par, it may keep an inconvertible paper at par, or even by sufficiently limiting its quantity carry it above par. But this truth does not make an inconvertible paper a good money, because it does not make it a self-regulating money, and because government is not wise and firm enough to fix and maintain a proper limit. Though Parliament intended in successive acts to confirm to the Bank of England the monopoly of banking by enacting that no partnership of more than six persons should take up money on its own bills, yet the common law assured to private persons and smaller partnerships the right to do this; and private bankers multiplied after the suspension, since they were allowed to pay their notes in Bank of England notes. Thus the quantity of paper money gradually increased till in August, 1813, the Bank of England notes were at 30% discount in gold.

The United States, both as Colonies and as a Country, have had varied and instructive experience with inconvertible paper Money. We will glance at two or three specimens only. The first issue of Treasury Notes, commonly called Greenbacks, given by Congress the quality of legal tender for all debts, public and private, except duties on imports and interest and principal of the national bonds, was made in April, 1862, and was justified in Congress and out solely as a war measure. An aggregate of $450,000,000 was put out in all, of which $87,000,000 were afterwards taken in, and the balance was still circulating in 1890. In one month after the first issue of $150,000,000, these greenbacks began to droop in value as compared with gold; in four months, when the second batch of $150,000,000 was authorized, their depreciation was already marked and firm; and in nine months, when President Lincoln reluctantly gave his approval to the third issue of the same amount in order to pay off the soldiers and sailors, he uttered a solemn protest against the policy of thus inflating the current money, which, he said, "*has already become so redundant as to increase prices beyond real values, thereby augmenting the cost of living to the injury of labor, and the cost of supplies to the injury of the whole country.*" In March, 1863, $50,000,000 of paper promises for fractions of a dollar were authorized, redeemable in sums of not less than three dollars in greenbacks, and receivable for all dues to the United States less than five dollars, except for duties on imports. Subsidiary silver coins have since taken the place of these fractionals. In July, 1863, the greenback dollar had lost one-quarter of its nominal value; in July, 1864, it had lost almost two-thirds of its nominal value, as its lowest point was reached in that month, namely, 35 cents as compared with the gold dollar; in July, 1865, it had risen to 70 cents; in July, 1866, it stood at 66 cents, just two-thirds of a dollar proper; and from that time it slowly rose, with many fluctuations, till New Year's, 1879, when it became legally and actually redeemable in gold and silver. Its variations for the sixteen years, however, cannot be counted by the number of years, nor even by the number of days; for they were numerous on each business day, and, as Comptroller Knox says, "*can only be numbered by tens of thousands.*" What a Measure of Services that was!

Between 1863 and 1879 the Bills of the new national Banks were redeemable in the greenbacks only, that is to say, one species of national promises-to-pay were paid on demand by another species of similar promises, both alike inconvertible into coin; and, as a natural consequence, the bank-bills bobbed up and down in value in servile obedience to the inconvertible legal tenders.

Massachusetts Colony was the first constituent of the present United States both to mint silver, and to issue irredeemable promises to pay it. Under the false impression that only Money made inferior to Sterling would stay in the Colony, Massachusetts began to mint in 1652 silver shillings and sixpences and threepences purposely debased in weight (including seigniorage) 22% below sterling. The silver for these coins came in mostly from the trade with the West Indies, to which were now shipped peltry, fish, various forms of lumber, beef, pork, pease, cattle, and horses, for which they took mainly sugar, molasses, rum, and silver. "*They would have brought more silver and less rum and other merchandise, had the first been in greater request at home.*" (Bronson.) John Hull, the mint-master took out 15 pence out of every £ for his own pay, and grew rich by the process. That was over 6%. In 1662, a twopenny piece was added to the series, and the mint existed (sometimes idle) for over 30 years, but all the pieces coined bore the dates of 1652 or 1662. This paucity of dates is commonly and perhaps properly accounted for on the ground that coining in the colony was contrary to the prerogative of the Crown; but it is to be added that John Hull was not a man to get new dies so long as the old ones would answer his purpose. The law forbade the exportation of these pieces under the penalty of thereby forfeiting one's whole visible estate; because, though this money was much worse than sterling, there was a worse money than this circulating in the colony, and Gresham's law began to crowd it from the first, and to some extent it was both smuggled out and clipped down. But it furnished a sort of standard, nevertheless, and tended to keep the later money within distant sight of the silver, and became the reason why in New England there were six shillings to the dollar. The Spanish pillar dollar, which was the standard in the West Indies, was worth 4*s.* 6*d.* sterling; and in 1672 a law was passed in Massachusetts allowing these dollars to circulate at 6*s.* provincial, which was a discount on the home pieces of 25%. Ever after there were six shillings in a dollar in New England. Hull's money is called the "pine-tree" coinage, and was the only coin money minted in the country till after Independence.

Also in 1690 Massachusetts set the first example, which was imitated 20 years later by the other New England Colonies and by New York and New Jersey, of issuing "Bills of Credit" to meet the expenses of the two disastrous Expeditions against the French in Canada. Those Bills were not made legal tender in private payments, and pains were taken to keep up their credit, but they were depreciated from the first, and came to be very much depreciated. Massachusetts and Connecticut made their bills receivable for taxes at a premium of 5%, laid special taxes for their redemption, and from time to time called in portions of the issues. In 1718 Connecticut enacted that a debtor tendering these bills should not be liable to legal execution on his estate or person for the payment of that debt, an expedient, as we have seen, resorted to by England in the great Bank restriction of 1797-1821. These early New England bills bore no interest, were not loaned out by the colony, and were a convenient though dangerous means of anticipating the income of future taxes; but after 1712 a paper money scheme originating in South Carolina came into favor in the colonies, which was, to open loan-offices for the issue of colony bills on the mortgage of land, the interest on which helped to pay the colony expenses, the principal of which at first, and on being paid back and reloaned, furnished a capital to borrowers, while the bills themselves furnished a money for the people. Pennsylvania had the best luck with this scheme of all the colonies which tried it: as early as 1729 Benjamin Franklin became thoroughly possessed of John Law's notion, that paper money may be "based" on land or other valuables, saying in a pamphlet of that year that "*bills issued upon land are in effect coined land*": Pennsylvania bills nevertheless were at 46% discount in 1748. Some of the later colony bills bore interest, some were of a "new-tenor," so-called, designed to take up the old ones,— Virginia in 1755 made hers a legal tender for debts,—some were issued in bounties for Indian scalps and for various manufactures and fisheries, but all ran one road of depreciation and gave birth to one set of results. Connecticut managed her issues the best of the colonies, and yet Bronson says of the state of things in that colony in 1749, "*Trade was embarrassed and the utmost confusion prevailed: no safe estimate could be made as to the future, and credit was almost at an end: no man could safely enter into a contract which was to be discharged in money at a subsequent date: prudence and sagacity in the management of business were without their customary reward.*"

John Law, a shrewd Scotchman, born in Edinburgh in 1671, son of a goldsmith, with an innate talent for finance and well educated, was the first to give scientific form and color to the false theory that paper money *represents* commodities of some sort, and may be issued to an amount equal to the value of these. "*Any goods that have the qualities necessary in money may be made money equal to their value. Five ounces of gold is equal in value to £20, and may be made money to that value; an acre of land is equal to £20, and may be made money equal to that value, for it has all the qualities necessary in money.*" The fallacy in these words of Law is patent enough to any one who will stop to think a moment about the *nature of Money*. Because land, for example, has value, it does not follow that it has "*all the qualities necessary in money*"; and, as a matter of fact, it lacks the precise quality necessary in money, because, though it has purchasing-power, it cannot from its very form and nature become *a generalized and current* purchasing-power. Money is indeed a valuable thing, but that does not prove that all valuable things can be money. With this radical vice of Law's view was wrapped up another, namely, that there may be in any country as much paper money as the sum of the values of all its valuable things. Now, we have learned perfectly, what escaped the acute intellect of John Law, that Money is only a valuable *measure* of all other salable Services; and therefore, that the amount of it that can be made useful at any one time and place is strictly limited, and bears very little relation to the sum of the values present at that time and place.

Scotland fought shy of Law's idea when he published it there in 1705, and so did Paris the first time he visited that city, in which and in other cities he gambled successfully and talked finance to princes and statesmen fascinatingly; but when he returned to Paris in 1715 with his ill-gotten fortune, he gained the ear of the Regent Duke of Orleans, who permitted him to found a bank there, in which were incorporated some sound principles of monetary science as well as the prime fallacy of his system. The bank bought a portion of the State Debt, just as the Bank of England had done, and laid in also a fair stock of coin, and thereupon issued a paper money. For a couple of years, or so, the bank surpassed all hopes, for Law had touched a spring till then but little known in France, the potent spring of Credit. But his whole thought, meditated on for years, could not be expressed through a private bank. The State should be a banker; it should collect all its revenues into a central bank, and attract the money of individuals to it as deposits; besides, the State has public property of vast value, on the strength of which paper money can be emitted and made legal tender; and thus the State, instead of borrowing, should lend to all on easy terms and the profits thus accruing would lessen or abolish taxes. Nor was this all. The State should also be a merchant; the whole nation should form a commercial company, a body of traders, whose common treasury should be the State bank. Commerce by individuals creates great wealth; why should not the organized commerce of a State make everybody rich? The discounts of the bank, and the profits of the trade, would surely provide for the public service without taxation. These vast ideas were actually carried out. Law's bank became the Royal Bank, issuing a paper money guaranteed by the State and resting back upon the value of all national property. The money was receivable in taxes, nominally redeemable in coin, and made a legal tender. It actually bore at one time 5 and 10% premium over gold and silver. People were anxious to exchange their coin for notes. Meanwhile a commercial company was formed in connection with the bank, to which the State ceded at first the monopoly of the commerce of Louisiana and of the Canada beaver trade for twenty-five years, and the soil of Louisiana forever; under the auspices of which NEW ORLEANS was founded, and named from the Regent, the patron of the grand system; and in succession, the monopoly of tobaccos, the rights of the Senegal Company, of the East India Company, of the China Company, and of the Barbary Company; until, having almost all the commerce of France outside of Europe in its hands, it entitled itself the COMPANY OF THE INDIES. Its shares rose from a par value of 500 francs to 10,000 francs, more than forty times their value in specie at their first emission. To support such speculations, which completely turned the heads of all classes of the people, the amount of paper money reached at last the sum of 3,071,000,000 francs, 833,000,000 more than had been legally authorized to be emitted. The collapse of this most gigantic bubble of history was terrific. Before the close of 1720, the shares of the Company could be bought for a louis d'or, or twenty shillings sterling, and the paper money of course became worthless.

The ghost of John Law reappears gibbering and chattering in some human shape once in a generation or two in all civilized countries. In March, 1890, Senator Stanford of California, himself reputed to be worth $30,000,000, propounded the question in the Senate of the United States, whether it were not advisable for the Government to issue legal-tender notes on the basis of the real estate of the country. His interrogative argumentation implied, (1) that there was a scarcity of Money causing great hardship to individuals and depression to business, (2) that if national bank bills are properly issued on government bonds it is equally proper to base legal tenders on real property, (3) that there is no natural and strict limitation to the amount of Money in a country at any one time, and (4) that as far as he knows there may well enough be as much money in amount as the estimated value of the real estate. All this is John Lawism pure and simple. All this utterly ignores the nature of Money as a valuable measure of all other Services. It also ignores the truth, that an advancing country needs less rather than more Money in amount as it advances, because cheques and other forms of non-money Credits are constantly increasing both absolutely and relatively. It is because this Senator's monetary notions seemed to correspond with those of a majority of the Senate, that it is perhaps proper to give them here a moment's attention.

These supposed legal-tender notes would be secured by a government lien on land and buildings, and by the direct credit of the Government as well; just as the national bank bills are secured by the bonds of the nation held in reserve for that purpose, and also by the direct image and superscription of Cæsar upon every bill. People holding mortgaged real estate could accept a non-interest bearing government lien instead of a 6% or 8% private mortgage, that is, could pay off their mortgages with the legal tenders given them by the Government, the latter taking the lien or new mortgage; and people owning real estate clear could, if they chose, execute a perpetual mortgage to the Government, that is, give up the fee simple to their lands, and receive legal-tender notes to the full amount in return. This would at least relieve the "scarcity" of Money! The volume of national Money at that moment was in round numbers $1,400,000,000; the assessed valuation of the real property of the country was at the same moment at least $15,000,000,000; so that, on this scheme, perhaps $10,000,000,000 of additional legal-tender Money could be issued! Here is paternalism and socialism and John Lawism all combined. Here is a Government of strictly limited and carefully enumerated powers, under a written Constitution as precise as language can make it, containing the solemn declaration that all "powers not delegated to the United States are reserved to the States respectively or to the People," owning or soon to own not only the railroads and the telegraphs but also the major part of the lands of a free country, and going into the mortgage business on the heroic scale!

If this honorable Senator and his like-minded colleagues were tolerably familiar with the financial history of their country, and perhaps they were, they would have known that this precise scheme had had a practical trial in Rhode Island, just before the adoption of the national Constitution. The Legislature authorized the issue of $500,000 in scrip-money based upon the value of the real estate of the farmers of the Colony. The law required a mortgage for twice the amount of scrip-money based upon it, and it was therefore supposed the money would be as good as gold or better. But somehow or other the merchants of the towns could not see the matter in that light. The depreciation of the scrip-money began at once, and the prices of wares ran up in a way that should have set business in active motion, according to all the views of the "scarcity" school. It was therefore enacted by the Legislature, that anybody who refused to accept the scrip at its face value should be fined $500 and lose the right of suffrage! They made it a legal tender! But business refused to boom. The merchants shut up their stores, the farmers could not market their crops, and idleness and rioting set in all over the State. Then the farmers organized a boycott against the towns, and food became scarce. Meanwhile the mortgage legal tenders would not pass at the best for over 16 cents to the dollar! There was more of "enforcing" legislation, and appeal to the courts, but nothing could boost the mortgage-money. The chief result of the experiment was, that Rhode Island gained in this way the title of "Rogues' Island."

No matter how good the cause, how patriotic the People, an inconvertible paper money is sure to run down at the heel. In June, 1775, one week after Bunker Hill, the Continental Congress voted to emit $2,000,000 in "Bills of Credit" issued on the faith of the "Continent." Eleven separate Colonies, New Hampshire and Georgia issuing none, began about the same time their revolutionary issues of the same sort, amounting in all during 1775-83 to $209,524,776. The vice of such irredeemable scrip is, there is no economical limitation of the Supply. The middle of 1777, when Burgoyne was prosperously advancing from Canada towards New York, saw a general fall of the notes both Continental and Colonial, and of course and in consequence a universal rise of the prices of other products. At the close of that year, the average depreciation from silver was not far from 3 to 1; at the close of 1778, it was not far from 6 to 1; at the end of 1779, it was about 28 to 1; the Continental press then rested, after $200,000,000 nominally had been put out, but actually about $40,000,000 more than that, a usual if not universal accompaniment of such issues. When the stuff dropped out altogether in the spring of 1781, the country found no more lack of silver for Money than Massachusetts had found in 1749, when and after she redeemed her outstanding bills of credit at 11 for 1 in sterling silver, £138,649 of which, the share falling to her from the capture of Louisburg, was shipped to the Colony in coin, and she became for the next

25 years the "Silver Colony." Assuming that only $200,000,000 Continental had been issued, Thomas Jefferson carefully estimated that the Nation realized from them $36,367,720 in specie value, or 18% of the nominal value.

14. Whether the Money of any Nation be coin or paper or both, when once it is in the hands of the People, Government has properly nothing to say *about the rate of interest at which one person loans this money to another.* Usury Laws so-called, prohibiting the lender from taking more than a prescribed rate % for the use of money loaned, under penalties sometimes of the entire interest and sometimes of the entire debt have disfigured the statute-books of all Nations and of all the States of this Union. Such laws cannot justify themselves for a moment in the light of sound principles of Political Economy. Their origin may be explained by a reference to two false views, now happily exploded.

(a) The laws of Moses forbade to the Israelites the taking from one another any *interest* on money loaned, but at the same time it allowed them to take such interest freely of strangers; the permission in the one case going to show that there is nothing in the taking of interest that is unjust or sinful, and the prohibition in the other being readily explainable from the general purpose of the municipal regulations of Moses, which was to found an agricultural and not a trading commonwealth, in which every family was to possess land that could not be permanently alienated or sold, in which it was a great object to maintain the personal independence and equality of these families, in which the law for the recovery of debts was very summary and effective, lessening the risk of losing the principal, and which was to be and was sedulously separated in its usages from the surrounding nations. It has been well understood for a long time that the municipal code of Moses was local and peculiar, not necessarily applicable at all to the circumstances of other States, and in no sense binding on the conscience of legislators; and yet there doubtless sprang from the prohibition referred to a prejudice against interest, and this prejudice was perhaps deepened in the Middle Ages and onwards by the conduct of the Jews themselves, who, in addition to their sin of persistently growing rich in spite of the endless disabilities laid on them by the people of Europe, always demanded, in accordance with the permission of their great lawgiver, a good rate *per centum* of interest from those strangers to whom they became money-lenders. The Jews were everywhere hated, and consequently the usury which they practised was hated also. The fundamental absurdity of forbidding in trading communities the taking of interest on sums loaned to a borrower which he was at liberty to use for his own profit, deterred the nations from going to the length of prohibition, unless it might be in the case of the hated Jews. There is a clause of Magna Charta, interesting as showing how early the children of Abraham became the money-lenders of Europe, to the effect that, during the minority of any baron, while his lands are in wardship, no debt which he owes to the Jews shall bear any interest.

(b) Governments formerly deemed themselves competent to determine and fix the *general* purchasing-power of their own money. Even the Constitution of the United States uses this language: "to coin money, *regulate the value thereof, and of foreign coins.*" There was formerly, and there is still to some extent, a curious and harmful confusion in the public mind in respect to this term, "the value of money." In the only proper sense of the term the *value of money* means its power of purchasing services in general, and the value of money is *high* when a given sum of it will purchase much of general services, and *low* in the contrary case; and a high or low value of money in this true sense depends on a very distinct set of causes from those which determine the high or low rate of interest on money loaned; nevertheless, so long as governments supposed that they could regulate the former, it is very natural that they should also suppose that they could regulate the latter; and although all intelligent governments have given over the idea of being able to regulate the general value of the money they furnish to the people, many of them still adhere to the notion, equally false with the other, that they *are* able to regulate the loanable value, or the rate of interest, at least to prevent any more than their prescribed maximum rate from being taken. A few simple considerations will sufficiently condemn all usury laws.

(1) It is at once needless and invidious to deny by law to money-lenders, who offer just as honorable and useful services to society as any other class of men, the privilege of selling *their* service for what it will bring in the market, while other men in every department of business are allowed to exchange their services on the best terms they can make without interference or control. Let us see precisely the nature of the transaction when one man loans money to another. It is a clear case of value. The lender does a service to the borrower, and for this service justly demands a compensation. The service is this: The lender might himself use the money to gratify his own desires. It is his money; he may use it, as he pleases, for his own gratification. Or he may himself employ it productively, and, at the end of the period, receive back his principal with the customary rate of profit. If he surrenders this advantage to the borrower, if he passes over to him the right to use this money, say, for a year, he practises what we call in Political Economy *abstinence.* For this abstinence he has a right to claim a reward, precisely as the man has a right to claim a reward who foregoes working for himself in order to work for another. This reward of abstinence is *interest.* The money-lender foregoes an advantage. He performs a service for the borrower; and, therefore, the right to interest stands on just as unassailable ground as the right to wages. Moreover, the

loanable value of money varies under Supply and Demand just like other values; there are always those who want to borrow, and always those who want to lend; both parties must be assumed to know their own minds, and to be equally competent to make their own bargains; it is a case of mutual exchange for a mutual benefit, like all other trade; and the current rate of interest is determined at any one time by the actual free exchanges between borrowers and lenders. Now for any government to try to compel a lender by law to take only 6% when his money is worth 8, is a direct violation of the rights of property. It is a forcible and pernicious interference with the freedom of contracts. It is based on the false premise that the loanable value of money is uniform, and that government is competent to determine what it is. No value is uniform. And no government is competent to determine even the maximum price of money loaned, any more than the maximum price of commodities.

(2) Usury laws are almost uniformly *disregarded*, both by the governments which make them and by the people for whom they are made. Indeed, such laws cannot be enforced in a commercial community. Common sense is outraged by a law which requires a man to part with his property at less than the actual value; and when common sense is against a law, it stands a slim chance of observance. If the legal rate be six, and the actual worth be eight, who lends at six? Not the banks. They require deposits of their customers, the use of whose money shall make up to them the difference between the legal and the actual rate. The modes of evasion are various, but they are adequate and universal. Besides, governments themselves have shown a noteworthy inconsistency in this matter, which incidentally proves the unsoundness of their whole action. While announcing pains and penalties to those who take more than a given rate, they are careful never to bind themselves down to any given rate. Governments are always more or less borrowers, and if usury laws are necessary in order to help borrowers in a pinch, there ought to be a clause in the organic law of every country, forbidding the government to pay and its lenders to take any more than a certain rate per cent. There is no such clause in any organic law. Governments wisely follow the natural market, and borrow low when they can, and pay high when they must. In the last months of Mr. Buchanan's administration, the United States paid 12% on a public loan, and could get but little at that. Sauce for the goose is sauce for the gander, and if usury laws are good for the citizens, some solid reason ought to be rendered why they are not good for the government. The truth is, they are not good for either, since natural laws are perfectly competent to regulate the rate of interest, and do regulate it substantially in spite of a factitious, impertinent, and mischief-making interference.

(3) If Usury laws were *not* disregarded, they would be even worse in their effects than they are now. We must suppose that their aim is to aid borrowers, and make it easier for them to contract loans. But are borrowers, as a class, any more deserving of the fostering care of government than are lenders? Even if it could make its interference effective, as it cannot, is there any reason why government, leaving these borrowers to make all other bargains, sales, and transfers according to their best skill and judgment, should rush to their rescue only when they propose to borrow money? If they are competent to do their other business for themselves, government pays their capacity a poor compliment in undertaking to help them in the single matter of making loans; and the borrowers in turn have reason to pray to be delivered from their friends, since they, of all others, would be the men especially injured if all the lenders obeyed the usury laws. Suppose that a borrower is in great need of a loan, and that for some reason his credit is now a little weak. Many men would be willing to loan him at 9%, which affords a margin for the extra risk, but at 6, which we will suppose the maximum allowed by the law, he cannot borrow a dollar, because his credit is not quite equal to the best. If, therefore, the lenders obey the law, he, and such as he, must fail. And because it is unlawful to take over 6% he will be obliged to pay those who are willing to violate the law 10 or 12, to compensate them for the risk and odium of such violation, while, under freedom, he could borrow at 8. Moreover, if the loanable value of money at the time be actually 9, while the law only allows 6, many men will attempt to use their own capital productively, who would otherwise loan it, in order to realize the high rate; and this action of theirs still further restricts the loan-market and makes it more difficult to borrow. If, then, the purpose of government be to aid borrowers, no means could be more unskilfully chosen for that end than to pass usury laws, since such laws, so far as they are obeyed, have necessarily the opposite tendency; and even when violated redound to the disadvantage of borrowers, so long as the laws themselves are popularly regarded as of any legal or moral force.

In 1716, the Bank of England, as a great loaning institution, was exempted from the operation of all usury laws: why the bank only, and not other people as well, the Act of Parliament does not state. In 1867, the State of Massachusetts repealed all its usury laws, though 6% is to be understood in the absence of special agreement, and the result has been entirely satisfactory to all classes of the people. Rhode Island had done this previously, and Connecticut did it subsequently, and both have experienced equal satisfaction in the result. Other States will soon follow in their lead; and this relic of ignorance and prejudice will pass away. Adam Smith left the Wealth of Nations disfigured by the concession that governments might properly enough pass usury laws; but it is gratifying to be able to add that he was convinced of his error in that by Bentham's book on Usury, and fully acknowledged his conviction in the spirit of a genuine lover of truth. We conclude, then, that usury laws are needless, since interest, like all other prices, will perfectly adjust itself. They are disregarded, since lenders will loan or withhold their money according to their own keen sense of interest. They are pernicious, since they infringe the rights of property, and tend to prevent weak borrowers from having a fair chance in the market.

The present writing is at midsummer, 1890; and, in order to complete the entire discussion so far as this country is concerned, it is needful to add, that, between 1878 (when specie payments were resumed) and 1890, the circulating medium of all kinds is proven by official statistics of the highest authority to have increased from $805,793,807 to $1,405,018,000, or more than 57 *per centum*. This circulating medium consists of six formal kinds; namely, gold, silver, greenbanks, bank-bills, gold-certificates, and silver-certificates. Each of these differs in important respects from each of the rest, but all come alike under our fundamental classification of Moneys, as either an intermediate merchandise or promises to render it. This increase is way beyond any increase in the population of the country, and way beyond any apparent or proven increase in the national business; while at the same time the banking facilities of the country, which always spare the use of Money by substituting cheques therefor in the wholesale business and in a large share of the retail business also, have been increasing in equal measure. The number of national banks, especially in the West and South, has been multiplying. The use of cheques has been enlarging in every commercial community in the land. Yet up to the present time all of this vast volume of Money has been kept at par with gold, and consequently at the highest state of efficiency for commercial purposes.

What about the immediate future? Science is not prophecy except in a quite subordinate sense. Congress is loudly threatening at this very moment to more than double the enforced monthly coinage of silver dollars at the public expense for the sole benefit of a comparatively few miners of silver. If this threat be executed upon a long-suffering people of tax-payers, who will have no one to blame but themselves if they tolerate the outrage, Science is willing to venture the prediction, that the monetary standard here will drop from gold to silver within a twelvemonth or two; that general prices will rise much beyond the appreciation of money implied in that drop, though they will be illusory and gainless; that prudent debtors will hold high carnival for a time at the expense of their creditors; that the country will become as empty of gold as a contribution-box is of other money between Sundays; that foreign trade (soon to be explained), already in a sickening decline, under restrictions and prohibitions, will hasten to a practical demise; and that the United States, at once the laughing-stock and the victim to the superior intelligence of other nations, will come through alternate fever and chills to a position of common sense and ultimate recovery.

CHAPTER VI.
FOREIGN TRADE.

Wonderful is the continuity in the growth of any great Science, and equally so the persistency of any radical error that once gets fairly imbedded within it. As we saw fully in the last chapter Money is nothing in the world but a convenient, intermediate, equivalent, and easily measurable merchandise; but almost as soon as men began to analyze Sales and to generalize from their data, a notion nestled way down in their work, that Sales against Money were somehow or other different from Sales against other merchandise; and thence sprang up, particularly among the Romans, what we have called the Bullion Theory. The broad and the true view was held indeed from the beginning, and was maintained even among the Romans, as we learn from an interesting passage in the Roman Law,—"*Sabinus and Cassius think Value can dwell in another thing than money too, whence is that which was commonly said, Buying and Selling is carried on in the exchange of goods, and that view of purchase and sale is very old; but the opinion of Procullus has deservedly prevailed, who says, Exchange is a particular kind of transaction different from Selling.*"

Science has indeed sloughed off this old and vital error, and most of its sequels; but Public Opinion in many countries is full of it still; and Legislation, in our own country at least, is all the time trying or threatening to transmute merchandise (say silver) into money, as if that could raise its value or change its nature.

It was but a single step from the Bullion Theory to the Mercantile System. If money be somehow different from and better than merchandise, then each nation should strive to handle its foreign trade so as to get back from other nations more money than it renders to them in exchange: in other words, each nation must try to sell to the rest more goods than it takes goods back in pay, so as to have a "*balance*" come in of gold and silver. How natural the transition from Bullionism to Mercantileism! And it was a step of genuine progress too. Goods are good, and there is profit in their exchange; but gold is somehow better than goods, and we must manage somehow to get a "balance" in that! If this position had only been sound, and one nation only been in possession of the precious secret, how nicely it might have worked for that nation! But all the leading Nations of Europe made the transition from Bullionism to Mercantileism at one and the same time, and they vexed and impoverished each other for three half-centuries, and went to war with each other besides, under the double illusion, (1) that gold could be practically gotten in that way, and (2) that if gotten it were one whit better than the goods for which it would have been at once spent.

Economics as a Science is now free from every taint of Mercantileism also, but it lingers on more or less in half-informed minds, and in the less-experienced nations; and the system itself merged itself three half-centuries ago into another, which is not another, namely, into Protectionism. If nation A must sell more goods to nation B than it takes back in goods, so as to get the coveted "balance" in gold from B, would it not help that cause along to put obstacles in the way of restrictions or prohibitions against the introduction of goods from B to A? Less goods, more gold, argues A. A forgets that the same mental processes are going forward in B's mind towards the same conclusion in relation to A. Now, cogitates A, what kind of goods from B had we better restrict or prohibit? A, by the way, consists of some millions of individuals, some of whom are always on the watch to get their axes ground at the government grindstone. What kind of goods shall we prohibit from B? Why, of course, those kinds which we are now making or growing. We can supply these for ourselves. It does not escape the notice of these makers and growers, that the restriction or prohibition of similar goods from B will raise the price at home of their own goods. Scarce is ever costly. On go the restrictions, ostensibly at first in behalf of an imaginary "balance" in gold, which fragile reason soon passes out of mind in the presence of a very real reason for such restrictions, namely, artificial high prices for certain domestic goods, paid indeed by the entire home community to the comparatively few makers or growers of the goods now "protected," as the current phrase is. Mercantileism has passed over into protectionism. The feeble friends of a "balance" have now become the strong friends of a "monopoly." Personal greed to grow rich at the expense of one's own countrymen thus becomes the single or combined force that puts on and keeps on and piles up the so-called "protective" restrictions and prohibitions.

Scientifically Protectionism is as dead as Mercantileism and Bullionism. There is not an Economist in Christendom, of any international or even national reputation, who now undertakes fairly and squarely by means of analysis and induction, to propound or defend a scheme so contrary to common sense and common honesty as this is, and which, universally applied, would annihilate the commerce of the world. But many of the nations are still tinctured more or less by the old subtlety, and powerful classes within them and specially within the United States, classes grown rich and powerful by what is nothing else than public plunder, are strenuous and successful advocates, not in open discussion and fair debate but by clandestine and corrupting methods and combinations, to maintain in the light of the nineteenth century an outworn and decrepit "something" worthy only of the dark ages. The old and foolish cry for a "balance of trade" is merged now in the United States into the insane and hateful clamor for the destruction of public trade in the behalf of private gain.

This is the sole reason why we must now undertake a careful chapter on Foreign Trade. There is no reason in the nature of things, or in the nature of trade, why Foreign Commerce should be treated of separately from Domestic Commerce. The two are precisely alike in all their principles and in all their results. In one as in the other, in every case and everywhere, there are (1) two persons, each of whom has a Service in his hands to sell against a Service in the hands of the other; (2) two reciprocal estimates, by which each owner concludes that he prefers the Service of the other to his own; (3) two mutual renderings, by which each Service comes into the possession, present or prospective, of the new owner; and (4) two personal satisfactions as the result of all, constituting the ultimate motive and the sole reward of Buying and Selling.

There are two possible differences in certain cases between Domestic and Foreign trade, both superficial and but barely worth the mention here. Foreign countries engaged in trade *may* be more remote from each other than places exchanging products within the same country. The distances, however, between Bangor selling ice to New Orleans for sugar, and Boston selling boots and shoes to San Francisco for fruits and wine, are much greater than those between Liverpool and St. Petersburg, or those between Stockholm and Palermo; so that, it may be said in general, that the trade between all the European countries confronts less distances, and presumably less costs of transportation, than the trade within the United States. And another thing is to be said in this connection: Foreign trade as a general rule is conducted by water-routes, and domestic trade under the same rule is carried on by land-routes; and, therefore, the costs of transportation by the latter are much more expensive.

The other possible difference is more considerable, and considerably more in favor of Foreign as compared with Domestic trade. We have learned perfectly already, and the point is fundamental, that all trade proceeds on the sole basis of a relative Diversity of Advantage as between the two parties exchanging. This relative superiority of each exchanger over the other at different points depends in domestic trade partly upon divergent natural gifts to individuals, partly upon their concentration of mind or muscle or both on a single class of efforts each, and partly upon the use and familiarity in the use of the gratuitous helps of Nature aiding that class of efforts. But in foreign trade there are commonly some additional grounds of Diversity, since the various countries of the earth have received from the hands of God a diversity of original gifts, in climate, soil, natural productions, position, and opportunity. And besides these original international differences, there has been developed of course in the history of the inhabitants of these countries a diversity of tastes, aptitudes, habits, strength, intelligence, and skill to avail themselves of the forces of Nature around them. International trade, accordingly, is somewhat more broadly and firmly based than the home trade can be, inasmuch as these international differences are apt to be more inherent and less flexible than domestic differences between individuals; it is on these diversities, original, traditional and acquired, that international commerce hangs; it could never have come into existence without them; and it would cease instantly and completely were they to fade out. Men engage in foreign trade,—not for the pleasure of it,—but for the sake of the mutual gain derivable to both parties; they desist from it so soon as that mutual gain disappears; and there is no gain in any series of exchanges, unless each party has a superior power in producing that which is rendered, compared with his power in producing that which is received.

With these few preliminaries, we pass now, in the first place, to unfold in order the COMMON AND UNIVERSAL PRINCIPLES OF FOREIGN TRADE. For the sake of illustrating these, we will now take a simple supposed case, a trade between England and France in cottons and silks, and follow it through clearly to the end.

1. When will it be mutually profitable for England, that is, for certain English merchants, to send cottons to France to buy silks with, and for France, that is, for certain French traders, to send silks to England to buy cottons with? Money and all other commodities except these two, silks and cottons, are wholly out of the question now and should be wholly out of our minds the while, though for simplicity's sake we shall use the *denominations* of money for comparing the respective efforts, translating pounds and francs into dollars. The answer is easy: the trade will be mutually profitable, when efforts bestowed in France upon silks will procure through exchange with England more of cottons than the same amount of efforts bestowed in France upon cottons will produce of cottons directly; *and* then, when efforts bestowed upon cottons in England will procure more of silks through exchange with France than the same amount of efforts bestowed in England upon silks will produce of silks directly. It is not a question of the absolute cost of either commodity to the parties producing it, or of a comparison of those absolute costs at all, but a question of the relative cost of that produced in either country compared with what would be the cost of the other commodity were it to be produced in that country. So long as there is a difference of relative efficiency in the production of the two commodities in the two countries, so long, setting aside the costs of carriage, may there be a profitable exchange of the two. A demand in each country for the product of the other is of course presupposed in the illustration.

Suppose now, that Efforts in England on certain cottons be gauged at $100, and that Efforts in France on certain silks be gauged at $80, and that these finished commodities then exchange even-handed against each other: is that a losing trade for England and a gainful trade for France? That is more than we can tell yet. That depends upon the further decisive question, whether the Efforts gauged at $100 if expended in England in the manufacture of silks will procure as many and as good silks as the same obtain in exchange with France; and whether the Efforts gauged at $80 if expended in France on cottons directly will secure as many of them as if expended on silks directly and then traded off for cottons. In effect the Frenchmen ask, Can we get more and better cottons by working on silks and then trading them off for English cottons than we can get by equivalent Efforts in working on cottons at home? Likewise the Englishmen ask, Can we get more and better silks by working on cottons at home and then trading with France for silks than we can get by trying to make silks directly? France by climate and soil and habitudes is better adapted to silks than cottons: England by virtue of the same is better adapted to cottons than silks.

2. How does the Diversity of relative Advantage practically work in foreign trade? Let us suppose that while the cottons cost $100 in England, it would cost $120 to manufacture there as good silks as can be made in France for $80; and that while the silks cost but $80 in France, it would cost $96 to make cottons there as good as the English can make for $100. On this supposition France can make both the silks and the cottons at a cheaper absolute cost than England can. What of it? Does that destroy the motive and the gain of an exchange between the countries in these two articles? Let us see. By an exchange with England, France gets for $80 in silks, cottons which would otherwise cost her $96, which is a handsome gain of 20%; while England gets for cottons costing her $100 silks which would otherwise have cost her $120, which is another handsome gain of 20%. Although France can make each commodity for less absolute money than England can make either of them, there is a Diversity of relative Advantage; and, therefore, there might be in this case, as there is actually in many such cases, a very profitable trade. The efficiency of France in making silks relatively to the efficiency of England in making silks is in the ratio of 80 to 120, namely, a difference of 50%; while the aptitudes of France in making cottons relatively to that of England in making the same is only in the ratio of 96 to 100, namely, a difference of $4\frac{1}{6}$%. So long as England offers in cottons a good market for French silks, how utter the folly and large the loss of France in going to work to make cottons!

In the majority of cases, doubtless, foreign trade takes place in articles, in the production of one of which each of the respective countries has an absolute advantage over the other; but an every way advantageous trade may be carried on in commodities, in the production of *both* of which one nation shall have an absolute superiority over the other, provided only that this superiority be *relatively diverse* in the two commodities, as has just been shown. This is an effectual answer to the ignorant clamor of some, we take it, who make objection to importing articles which might be made at home for the same sum of money as foreigners expend in making them; admitted, that they might be so made, does it follow that the country importing them would get them as cheaply by making them itself? *By no means does that follow.* Let no nation, then, be in haste to drop a trade, because it thinks it can make the goods received in exchange as cheaply as the other nation makes them, so long as it has an advantage absolute or relative over the other in making the goods rendered in exchange; and when that advantage ceases, it may be sure, that the trade will drop of itself; because it always takes *motives* to make the mare go.

3. What are the extreme limits of the Value of cottons and silks in the case supposed, and when will a third nation be able to undersell either in the ports of the other? This is the answer: the extreme value of French silks in English cottons will be 80 and 96; they cannot fall below 80 because they cost the French that to manufacture them; they cannot rise above 96, because at that rate the French can make cottons, and there would be no motive, that is, no *gain*, in their exchanging for cottons. Nations, that is to say, individuals, will never get themselves served at a greater effort than that at which they can serve themselves. If a given effort does not realize more through exchange than it would do directly, then that exchange ceases of necessity, as fire goes out for lack of fuel. The extreme limits of the value of English cottons in French silks will be 100 (lowest) and 120 (highest) for reasons precisely similar in the case of the English. Therefore, the highest profits possible to both nations under the conditions of the trade are 20% each. France would be glad to take the cottons at a return of 80 in silks, at which rate her gain would be 20%, and she cannot under any circumstances offer quite 96, at which rate her gain would disappear.

No third nation, accordingly, in a trade of silks for cottons can expel the French from the English ports, until it is prepared to offer nearly 96 (or more) in silks in return for English cottons; that is to say, until its efficiency in making silks relatively to that of England in making them presents a greater difference than the difference of efficiency between France and England in making silks, which is a difference of 50%. England would be glad to take the silks from France at a return of 100 in cottons, at which rate her gain also is 20%, and she cannot possibly offer quite 120 in cottons, because at that rate her gain would wholly vanish. England could be undersold in the French ports, when somebody is ready to offer nearly 120 (or more) in cottons against the French silks, whose *quantum* in the exchange may vary from 80 towards 96. Here is the whole doctrine of one nation underselling another in the ports of a third nation. Silks stand here for sample of all French commodities of whatever name and cottons for all English goods whatsoever; and England and France stand in the illustration for any and all nationalities. Any nation obtains any share or a greater share in the commerce of the world solely in virtue of a greater relative efficiency in producing *something* valuable, as compared with some other nation's power in producing something *else* that is valuable.

4. How does the varying play of International Demand affect the value of articles in foreign trade? The answer is clear and easy: if the demand for French silks in England just answers to the demand for English cottons in France, so that the silks offered by France just pay for the cottons offered by England, then, cost of carriage aside, the gains of the trade will be equally divided between the two sets of merchants, and each will realize 20% profits, because neither will have any motive to lower the value of its commodity below its highest value. The Frenchmen from their point of view will offer 80 in silks and take 96 in cottons: the Englishmen from their standpoint will offer 100 in cottons and get 120 in silks. Demand and Supply are equalized at a point of value most favorable to both parties, and one really determined by the relative cost of production.

This case of equalization, though possible, is likely rarely to occur in practice. On any terms of exchange first offered, there is likely to be a stronger demand in one country for the product of the other than in this country for the product of that. This will of course lead to a change of Value, and a new division of Profits. The product for which the demand is less will find its market sluggish, and in order to tempt further and brisker exchanges will be compelled to offer more favorable conditions. He who enters a market in quest of what is *more* in demand with a service which is *less* in demand, will have to lower his terms, or not trade. The equalization of Supply and Demand will only be reached in this case, by quickening the demand for the commodity now less in demand through an offer of better terms in trade. Thus, if the demand for French silks in the English ports be slack, in comparison with the demand for English cottons in France, at the rate of exchange first established, say, 80 for 96, the French merchant has no resource, if he wishes to continue the trade, but to agree to give more silks, for the same amount of cottons, say, 85 for 96. If this actual reduction prove sufficient to cancel the account in cottons with the account in silks, then the trade will proceed on this new basis for a while, because the equalization of demand and supply has been reached through a new valuation of the two commodities, and there is now consequently a new division of the profits. France gains less than 13% by her trade with England, while England gains 27% in her trade with France.

Under these new terms of exchange, it is quite possible that silks may again become heavy in reference to cottons, and a new decline take place in their relative value. If the French are obliged in consequence to offer 90 for 96, in order to obtain the cottons they want, their own profits will sink to 6%, while the same causes will lift the English profits to 35%. If, in any contingency, the French were driven by the state of the market to concede something near to 96 in silks for 96 in cottons, the trade would cease in that case, just as every transaction ceases when the motive for it ceases. We must remember of course, that the cottons of England are just as likely to become slack in reference to silks, as the silks are relative to the cottons; and when this happens, the English dealers will have to lower their terms, and thus surrender a larger share of the profits to the French. By this ceaseless play of Supply and Demand, within the outermost limits drawn by the relative Cost of Production at the time, is the Value of commodities determined in Foreign Trade; and no degree of complication in the variety of articles, or in circuitous exchanges, affects, for substance, these fundamental principles.

5. What are the causes deciding the exportable articles of any nation, and their order of precedence in Export? Watch a little at this point, and the true answer will loom up steady and certain. If, instead of one article, say cottons, England sends two or ten kinds of goods to France in payment for silks or wines or whatnot, she will of course send in preference that commodity in which her own commercial efforts are relatively most efficient, so long as the French demand will receive it, because her own profits will be the greatest on that; then, when obliged to lower terms on that down to the point of relative advantage at which her next available article stands, she will send that next in quantities regulated by the demand for that; and so on down to the end of the list of possible exportables to France. France is guided as to her exportables to England by precisely the same principles and prospects of profit. So of all commercial nations whatsoever. No matter whether the articles be one or many; no matter whether the trade be a direct or indirect trade; the profits in international commerce depend in all cases, first, upon the ratio of the cost of what is rendered to what would otherwise be the cost of what is received, secondly, upon the relative intensity of the two Demands.

It follows logically and necessarily from all this, that what a nation purchases by its exports, it purchases by its own most efficient Production, and consequently at the cheapest possible rate to itself, and at the highest possible profit to its merchants. Under a decent freedom of international choice and action, of sale and delivery, only *those things* are ever exported, for the procuring of which a nation possesses decided advantages relatively to other nations, and relatively to its own advantages in producing directly what is received in return; and hence, the return cargoes, no matter what they have cost their original producers, are purchased by this nation as cheaply as if they had been produced by its own most advantageously expended Effort. This is a wholly impregnable position; and the advocates of restricting and prohibiting Foreign Trade are challenged to try their hand a little or a good deal (as best suits them) at its bristling defences.

It follows also from the discussion under this head, what shallow thinkers are they, who deem it needful that each nation should be able "*to compete*" with other nations in every branch of production. Why are they not consistent enough to apply their favorite catchword, "*compete*," to domestic exchanges also, and require that the clergyman shall have artificial and governmental facilities for "*competing*" with the lawyer, the tailor with the blacksmith, the farmer with the manufacturer, the publisher with the author? Will folks never learn that *all* Exchanges, domestic as well as foreign, hang on relative superiority at different points, and that any Nation trying to make its success in production equal at all points would be just as stupid as an artisan trying to learn and practice all the trades at once? Suppose the said nation to succeed, what then? It would supply its wants at a certain low average efficiency of effort; whereas, by a thorough development of all its own peculiar resources, it could command by exchange the products of the whole world at a cost not exceeding that of its own most productive and efficient Exertion. The precious metals, whether produced at home or obtained from other nations by another series of exchanges, whether coined or in the form of bullion, stand here in the same relations as other commodities, and are frequently the most profitable articles that a nation can export. In one word, whatever justifies individuals in selecting diverse paths of production according to their capacities and opportunity, the same (and even more) justifies the Nations in fully drawing out their own best capabilities under the conditions in which God has placed them; and then, exchanging what costs them little for what would otherwise cost them much, in enjoying all that the world offers at the least possible expenditure of irksome effort. Such wise and wide action promotes the common good of all the nations, and makes the best of all accessible to all, and arms each with the power of all; while the narrow and senseless policy of drawing into one's own shell after putting up barricades against one's neighbors, by lessening everywhere the Diversities of relative Advantage, so far forth incapacitates all for profitable and progressive Exchanges.

6. How do new improvements in machinery and other enhanced facilities of Production in one country affect its foreign trade? A cheering response will be drawn out, if we now apply this question to the conditions of our old trade in silks and cottons. Suppose France by new methods of silk

culture to become able to make the silk which before cost $80 for $50, cottons in France and silk and cottons in England remaining in natural cost as before, does France alone gain the entire advantage of the increased cheapness of silk? Wait a minute, and we will see. The production of silk in France is greatly quickened by the cheaper methods, more is produced, more is carried to England to buy cottons with, but at the old rate of 80 for 96, the English will not take any more silks, and the French who can now abundantly afford it, since their nominal 80 is really 50, will offer more silks for 96 in cottons, in order to tempt a brisker and broader sale. They offer, say, 96 in silks for 96 in cottons, and if that reduction of Value of silks in cottons be enough for the equalization of the respective Demands, the trade will proceed on that basis, at least for a time; and as there is now a larger difference of relative advantage than before, there will be, as always in such cases, larger profits to be divided between the two parties. The 96 now in silks to the English is really only 60 in cost to the French, so that the French gain in the trade is largely increased; because they now get for what costs them 60 what would otherwise cost them 96, a clear gain of 60%. Before the new methods of silk culture were introduced they could gain but 20% at the utmost.

But the English have also reaped largely from the ingenuity and diligence of their neighbors. Before, they gained only 20% in the exchange at best; but now they get for what cost them $100 that which would otherwise cost them $144, a handsome profit of 44%. Indeed, it might easily happen, through the incessant changes in International Demand, that even a larger share of the benefit of the French improvements should accrue to the English than to the French themselves; the share of the French all the while being large, and much larger, than if, greedily endeavoring to keep all the benefit, they should refuse to trade at all. Thus we reach again from another outlook, a grand and universal doctrine of Exchange, *that each party is benefited by the progress and prosperity of the other.* Indeed, the only possible way in which all nations can share in the thrift and enterprise and improvements of each other, is through mutual international exchanges; and when each nation sees to it that it have a few commodities at least for which there is a strong demand among foreigners, and in the production of which themselves have a strong superiority, it may rest assured that it buys all it buys from abroad, gold included, at the cheapest rate to itself, and shares a part of the prosperity of every nation with which it trades.

7. Which party in foreign trade pays the Costs of Carriage, or do each pay them in equal proportion? It is plain, that the aggregate cost of transportation to the foreign markets is just so much added to the Cost of Production, and is a deduction of so much from what would otherwise be the whole gain of the Commerce; but it is plainly not true, that each party

necessarily pays the whole of his own freights; and, therefore, that the party carrying bulky articles is at a disadvantage compared with the other. He may or may not be at a disadvantage on that account. That will depend on the effect of the new expense for freight, however divided, on the Demand in each country for the product of the other. We will suppose, that in the outset England pays the whole cost of carrying cottons to France, and France the whole cost of sending silks to England; but as cottons are many times more bulky than silks proportionably to value, a larger bill of freights would fall of course to England; and cottons would therefore fall in value relatively to silks; but cottons and silks have both risen absolutely, that is, with reference to any given effort, or with reference to a money standard.

Suppose now that France, instead of 80 for 96, has to render 82 for 96; and England, instead of 100 for 120, now has to give 105 for 120. The French gain in the trade is reduced from 20 to nearly 17%, and the English gain from 20 to nearly 14%; but it is by no means certain, that the commerce would go on precisely on these terms; the enhanced value of silks might well deaden the demand for them in England, more than the relatively less enhanced value of cottons in France would affect the demand for them. Silks have risen in England 5%, but cottons have risen in France only 2½%; it is therefore very likely that thereafter the demand for cottons will be stronger than the demand for silks, and if so, the French will have to offer better terms, or, what is the same thing, to be obliged to pay a part of the English freights; so that there is nothing in the true state of the case to justify the conclusion jumped at by some people, that they who carry heavy goods are at a disadvantage compared with those who carry light goods. That will depend wholly upon the Equation of International Demand as between the two kinds of goods. Nothing in the nature of things hinders, that each party shall in effect pay the freights of the other, or one even really pay the freights of both.

8. Lastly, what is the effect upon international commerce of the constant play of the Par of Foreign Exchange. This is a point of great importance, that has been but little discussed in this connection, because it has not been popularly understood or scarcely even popularly explained. In the light of the full unfolding of "Credits" in our Fourth Chapter, and in the light of these simple principles now under discussion, there will be no great difficulty to any intelligent reader in fully understanding this matter of Foreign Exchange,—a matter never before so vital to the commercial interests of the United States as now. For the sake of general illustration we will take the "Exchange" as between the United States and Great Britain, since the same fundamental principles apply as between all commercial countries.

When merchants export goods, say from New York to London, or *vice versa*, they do not wait for their pay till the goods be actually marketed abroad, but draw at once Bills of Exchange to the amount of the home value of the goods on the parties to whom the goods are sent, and then put these bills on present sale with brokers or middlemen at home. There thus becomes a market or prices current in New York for commercial bills drawn on London, and similarly a market in London for bills drawn on New York. The New York exporter, accordingly, is not certain of getting in money the full face of his bill *minus* interest for the time it has to run, because a great many such exporters may have thrown their similar bills upon the market the same day, which always tends so far forth to depress the price of the bills in accordance with an universal law of Economics. Scarce is ever costly: plenty is ever cheap.

Who buys these bills when exposed for sale in New York? Who wants them? Clearly, only those who have commercial debts to pay in London. A bill of exchange drawn in New York on London is nothing but a debt due from somebody in London to anybody whom the drawer in New York chooses to make the payee. The debtor lives in London, and it is every way cheap and convenient for all parties, that he settle his debt with a creditor living in London. So it happens, that parties in London who have sold goods in New York and drawn bills on them for present payment, expose those bills for sale in London to the parties who have debts to pay in New York. If now, London or those whom London represents in these transactions, have sold but few goods to New York or to those whose business is settled in New York relatively to the amounts sold by New York to London, then London bills will be relatively scarce as compared with the New York bills drawn on London. In other words, New York has more debts to pay in London than London has in New York, and, consequently, the parties in London who want bills to pay New York debts with, have to buy them in a relatively scarce market. They have to *bid* for them, as it were. The effect of this is always to carry up the price of that, for which the buyers are many and the sellers relatively few. So, under perfectly natural causes, London bills on New York come to a premium; that is to say, the London sellers get more than the face of their bills drawn, and the trade with New York becomes *extra* profitable to them.

Suppose London bills of Exchange on New York are selling for 101, thus giving 1% extra profit to English exporters; for precisely the same reasons that they are so selling, New York bills on London are selling in New York for 99, thus subtracting 1% from what would otherwise be the gains of the New York exporters to England under the common principles of Foreign Trade. It is evident, therefore, that the causes of the course of the international Par of Exchange are an essential part of the principles of foreign Commerce; and whatever tends to derange or upset the natural course of the Par, as a constant or constantly recurring cause, must receive careful attention in a book like the present. We have begun at the very beginning of this matter, and we are now going to follow it up to the very end.

The Diversity of relative advantage in the Production of the two commodities exchanged, is the first and chief ground of mutual Profit in foreign trade; the varying Intensity of relative Desire on the part of each exchanger for the product of the other, is the second and secondary ground on which foreign trade must go on; and the third and final difference as between the two parties, which goes to make or mar the profit of each of them in the trade, is the current Price of the Bill of Exchange drawn by each creditor on his debtor abroad. It is plain that these three things must always be taken into account simultaneously by prudent exporters and importers, in order to estimate the prospect of a profitable trade then and there; and it is plain also, that one or even two of these three differences of relative advantage might fade out for a time, and a profitable trade still proceed, provided the other two or one of these differences were sufficiently pronounced. For example, to take an extreme case, silks from France might still go to England for cottons to the advantage of both countries for a time, though "exchange" were exactly at "par" between them and the "demand" for silks were precisely met by the "demand" for cottons, on the strength of a marked and persistent diversity in relative cost of production of the two textiles.

Here is another of the trinities of Political Economy. Here is complication indeed, but a complication regulated and beautified by inflexible laws of Nature and the scarcely less inflexible laws of human Motives.

So far the argument has proceeded on the supposition of a common standard of Value, say gold, between England and France, London and New York, and by implication all other commercial countries. Commerce rejoices in, and progresses by, a common measure of Values. By an experience of 2000 years the world has proven gold to be the best international Measure. From a simple comparison of the weights of pure metal in the standard coins of the nations is established a fixed monetary "par" as between them. Thus the dollar of the United States contains 23.22 grains of pure gold, and the English pound sterling contains 113.001 grains of the same; consequently, there are $4.8665 to the £ sterling, and this is and has been since 1834 the monetary "par" between the United States and Great Britain. Similarly, the par between France and the United States is $1 to 5 fr. 18 centimes, since the franc is 19.29 cents gold for gold. The monetary par, accordingly, as between any two nations using the gold standard, is a matter easily ascertained and kept in mind; while the constantly variable prices current of Bills of Exchange are reckoned in and from this monetary par. Thus, if a commercial bill drawn in New York on London sells for $4.8665 *minus* current interest for the time it has to run, English "exchange" with us is said to be at "par"; if it sell for more than that, exchange is technically said to be "*against*" us, although the excess in price is just so much additional profit to the American exporter; and if it sell for less than that, exchange is said to be in our "*favor*," although the difference is just so much subtracted from the gains of the American exporter.

The close of the second week in July, 1890, found in New York "Sterling exchange dull but firm, with actual business at $4.84¾ for 60-day bills and $4.89 for demand bills: the posted rates were $4.85½ and $4.89½ respectively." Exchange, accordingly, had turned "against" the United States, that is to say, American exporters could get a little more for their bills on London than the monetary par. Under such circumstances it may be cheaper to send the gold to liquidate a British debt than to buy bills and send *them*. Just this happened last week: $2,000,000 in gold went (mainly under this impulse) from New York to London. There is a limit, therefore, to any further rise in the price of "exchange," when it reaches in an upward direction the then present cost of sending gold to foreign creditors. The limit in the downward direction to the price of exchange is the last margin of profit to the exporter as such. Thus, when the New York exporter can only get, say, $4.83 for his sight bill of exchange on London, his loss in the trade so far forth is 1%; and it may be doubtful, whether his possible gains at the other two points, namely, relative cost of production and relative intensity of demand, will overbalance this certain loss and leave a sufficient margin of profit.

This chance of profit or loss from casual turns in the commercial "exchanges" is a very small matter in foreign trade in comparison with the other two grounds of possible profit or loss. The main thing for every commercial nation to see to is, that it have at least a few (the more the better) commodities in general use throughout the world, *in the cost of the production of which it has a relative advantage over all competitors, and the demand for which by foreigners is relatively intense and constant.* And it will never come amiss for any nation with these two crucial advantages to keep a sharp watch over a class of its own citizens, lest they, shrewdly and greedily, for special reasons of their own, get laws passed the result of which can only be *to increase the costs of production of these few exportables, and at the same time lessen the foreign demand for them.* ETERNAL VIGILANCE IS THE PRICE OF LIBERTY OF COMMERCE.

As a general rule for the last half century commercial "exchanges" have been "against" Great Britain, that is, her exporters have been able to get more than "par" for goods sent abroad in the price of the bills drawn on them, and her commerce has been *profitable* to her so far as this cause is concerned; which during the same interval of time the "exchanges" have been "in favor" of the United States, that is, her exporters have been obliged to sell their bills drawn for less than "par," and her commerce so far forth has been *unprofitable* to her. We may only briefly indicate here the causes of this state of things.

(a) Great Britain has been during this period a vast loaner of Capital to other countries, and particularly to the United States; while the United States has been a vast borrower of Capital, particularly from Great Britain. The interest on these loans from Britain, and the principal also so far as it has been repaid, has been constantly remitted thither in goods for the most part, and bills of exchange drawn on these goods have been sold at all ports, and particularly at New York; the abundance of these bills has tended of course to lower their price at the place of sale, and so far forth to heighten in effect the relatively less abundant British bills drawn on exports thence; and the *creditor* country for this reason is apt to sell its bills above "par," and the *debtor* country its bills below par. It makes no difference at this point how the borrowed funds have been invested by the borrowing country, since the interest and the principal must be repaid at some time chiefly in the manner just indicated.

(b) With the exception of a dozen or two articles customs-taxed for simple revenue, Great Britain in this period has kept her ports absolutely open to imports from all the world, and of course to all imports from the United States, which has tended to swell the volume of imports into that country, and the volume of foreign bills drawn on them, particularly of United States bills; while the United States during the same time has excluded imports by customs-taxes designed for that very purpose, to the number of over 4000, and in many cases to a height of tax involving prohibition of import. The Constitution of the United States expressly forbids customs-taxes upon exports, so that goods may indeed go out freely, so far as tariff-barriers are concerned; but as the only impulse that ever carries goods *out* is to get *back* more desirable goods in pay, and as these return-goods are greatly restricted or virtually prohibited by the United States, the Constitutionally-free exports are not large enough to help much in keeping down below "par" the price of bills of exchange drawn here. It should also be said that Great Britain is restrained in her exports to the United States by the latter's legal unwillingness to receive them, which tends of course to keep the price of bills drawn on the exports she can and does send still more above "par."

(c) The enormous customs-taxes in the United States on ship-building materials and on almost everything else have practically destroyed the ocean merchant-marine of the country. The bulk of the Freights, therefore, on what foreign commerce there is left to us under the Chinese-wall policy of our Government,—the bulk of the freights both ways,—has to be paid to foreigners, mostly to the British, and these payments too are made in exportable goods, which wretched fact (looked at in its causes) increases exports hence relatively to imports hither, and of course diminishes *pro tanto* the current price of mercantile bills drawn here. So far as these *extra* exports to meet freight charges are carried to England, they tend to lift there in the usual way the price of bills drawn on British exports. It is a million pities, no matter from what point of view one looks at it, that the present governing classes of this country totally misapprehend the Nature of foreign trade, and by short-sighted legislation minimize its Benefits to the people.

So far we have been unfolding the causes and courses of foreign exchange on the hypothesis, that both the nations exchanging employ the same standard in measuring Values. While the present paragraphs were in process of composition, the President of the United States signed (July 14, 1890) the so-called "Compromise Silver Bill," which is to go into operation after thirty days, and the effect of which in the judgment of some of the best economists and financiers of the country *may be* to bring down the national measure of Values from the gold dollar to the silver dollar. We are bound at this point, therefore, to explain the action and reaction on the course of the "exchanges," of a monetary standard lower in general value than the standard prevailing in the commercial world. We have all the data needful for clearing up this matter completely, at once in the inflexible laws of Money and in the actual experience of several of the Nations. For example, England has the gold standard, and India the silver standard; there is an immense commerce between the two countries; silver is merchandise and not money in London, and gold is merchandise and not money in India; every cargo, accordingly, to and from either has to have its value "changed" through the price of current bills into the current money of the other country; the price of silver in gold in London (average) between 1852 and 1867 was $61\frac{1}{3}$ pence per ounce; at 60 pence per ounce the ratio of gold to silver is 1:15.716; between 1875 and 1882 silver drooped (with many fluctuations) in the London market, bearing about the average of $52\frac{1}{3}$ pence per ounce, which is a ratio with gold of 1:18; during the first half of 1890 the price of silver in London was as nearly as possible 43 pence per ounce, which is a ratio with gold of 1:21.93; so that, the prices of India bills in London and of London bills in Bombay have yielded up to the careful observer all the secrets of the "exchanges" between high-standard and low-standard countries.

But we have no need to go out of our own country for illustrations of all this. Between May, 1862, and January, 1879, the "Greenback Dollar" was the measure of current Values. It was depreciated every day of that interval as compared with the gold dollar, and it fluctuated in the comparison more or less nearly every business day. The New York importer bought his foreign goods for gold, paid the customs-taxes on them in gold, and then sold them against greenbacks. How much must he charge for his goods in order to make himself whole? The current premium in gold over greenbacks was posted every day, and perhaps every hour, but was that a safe guide to greenback prices for our importer? Wholesales are rarely for immediate realization in money, and even if they were, the money would have to be rechanged into gold in the future for repurchases abroad. In the uncertainty of greenback values, the importer must *insure himself* in his prices to-day against a possible further depreciation next week, or next month. In other words, *he must speculate in the prospective gold premium.* Suppose his industrial cycle to be one month. If he sell his foreign goods in greenbacks to-day as these stand in comparison with gold, and greenbacks fall still lower before the month is out, he will lose money in those transactions; if greenbacks should rise in the interval, he would gain money, because he could get more gold for them in the next turn. To the credit of human nature be it said, that in 9 cases out of 10 a merchant will raise the present prices of his goods in order to make himself as sure as possible in a case where all is uncertain. There can be no reasonable doubt that in the fifteen years of depreciated greenback units, retail prices to ultimate consumers were lifted 10% above the average reckoning of goods in greenbacks from this cause alone.

In regard to exports at that time the facts and principles are still clearer. These exports were sold in Europe for gold. But the bills of exchange drawn on them were sold in New York for greenbacks. Take wheat, for example, of which there was a large export in all those years. The New York broker or banker in buying these bills was obliged to make the conversion from greenbacks to gold. He had to estimate as well as he could what the value of greenbacks would be when the gold-bill became payable in London. In other words, he had to speculate in greenbacks, because he had to take the risk of their declining or advancing value for an interval of time, say, one month. He would not take this risk without virtually making a charge sufficient in his judgment to cover it, and leave him a good profit in any case. This charge came out of the price of the wheat ultimately paid to the growers thereof. The bill of exchange was sold in New York or Chicago in order to get present pay for the farmers who furnished the wheat, and present profit for the commission-merchants or middlemen. But the bill brought less greenbacks than the quoted premium on gold would warrant for that day, on account of the risk, the uncertainty, the speculation. Therefore, less went to the farmers for their wheat per bushel or centner. *The masses of the people lose the immense losses of that depreciated money.*

And during these very years also the Government put customs-taxes to a then unheard-of height on imports from abroad, not primarily for the sake of the revenue to come from the taxes, but chiefly with a view to keep certain foreign goods out of the country altogether, in order that *some* citizens might be able to sell their own product *to the rest* at artificially enhanced prices. Thus the natural market abroad for wheat and pork and petroleum and other provisions was enormously lessened by the prohibition of imports,—a market for products is products in market,—at the same moment when the actual prices for products exported were still further diminished by the action of depreciated money on the par of commercial exchange.

Our neighboring Republic of Mexico has had for a long time the so-called bi-metallic standard of Money, the same as the United States have had. When the great fall of silver in gold took place in the London market as indicated above, gold was rapidly exported from Mexico, and soon disappeared from circulation, in accordance with Gresham's Law. For many years now the simple silver standard has prevailed in Mexico. Its entire working in foreign trade through the "exchanges" has been sufficiently demonstrated; and as there is more than a possibility, more even than a bare probability, that the United States under the law of 1890, and other and earlier extremely complicated laws of Money, may drop from bi-metallism to silver monometallism in the near future, in the way of premonition and warning to our own people we may fitly close our discussion of foreign "Exchanges" by briefly stating what of hazard and disaster under the silver standard is now going forward among our neighbors to the southward.

The effect of estimating Mexican transactions in silver money, while all the nations with which they trade estimate theirs in gold, is seen in an artificial enhancement of prices to the Mexicans on all their imports, and an artificial depression of prices to them on their exports. Look first at imports. There is of course a current discount on Mexican silver as compared with the gold in which the imported goods are bought. This discount is now over 20% throughout the commercial world, the London price of silver in gold giving the key to that song. But this is not all by any means; the discount is variable from day to day and from month to month; in changing his gold prices present into silver prices future, the Mexican importers must insure themselves. This necessitates a speculation in the future of silver. What the risk may be will depend somewhat on the activity of the silver market: if silver be rapidly fluctuating in price, the importer will add more to his silver prices additional to the current premium on gold, than if silver be comparatively stable; but in all cases he will add enough to cover all prospective risks. It is quite likely that five *per centum* is added on the average to wholesale prices by Mexican importers on this ground alone, which addition with all the usual increments must be borne by retail and ultimate prices.

Now look at Mexican exports. The larger part in value of these exports is silver in some form, mostly in the form of silver dollars. But these silver dollars are merchandise in London, and quite variable in price there, as has already been shown; and bills of exchange drawn on this silver in any form, and sold in Mexico to parties remitting gold values to London, are subject to constant depression on account of the uncertainty as to the value of silver in gold when the bills reach London. It follows from this, that the use of the silver standard in Mexico actually depresses the value of silver there. By means of the "exchanges" both ways, silver tends to be still further depreciated in comparison with gold, retail prices of all importables enhanced in silver, and the chief exportable (silver) depressed in value all the while! Truly, the Mexicans are between the upper and nether millstones. Poor Money never pays.

In confirmation of this fact that Mexico has not lifted the relative value of silver by making it the sole Measure of Value, we have the corresponding fact that the herculean efforts of the United States since 1878 to advance the value of silver to a parity with that of gold in the legal ratio of 1:15.98, have issued in the constant relative decline of silver here; and, what is more surprising, in an almost constant increase of the yearly production of silver here. The following table tells the whole instructive story: the figures are official: commercial "fine ounces" are .915 of technically "fine" silver.

Year.	Production (fine ounces).	Average Price.	Year.	Production (fine ounces).	Average Price.
1878	34,960,000	$1.15	1884	37,800,000	$1.11
1879	31,550,000	1.12	1885	39,910,000	1.06
1880	30,320,000	1.14	1886	39,440,000	.99
1881	33,260,000	1.13	1887	41,260,000	.97
1882	36,200,000	1.13	1888	45,780,000	.93
1883	35,730,000	1.11			

These Seven, then, are the essential Principles of Foreign Trade, brought out, it is hoped, as clearly and consecutively as the relative and complicated nature of the transactions will allow; in the light of these Principles it is very clear, that Foreign Trade is just as legitimate as, and may be more profitable than, Domestic Trade; that it rests on the same ultimate and unchangeable grounds in the constitution of Man, and in the Providential arrangements of Nature; that the Profit of it is mutual to both parties, or it would never come into being, or, coming into being, would cease of itself; that to prohibit it, or restrict it, otherwise than in the interest of Morals, Health, or Revenue, must find its justification, if any at all, wholly outside the pale of Political Economy; and that for any Government to say to its citizens (of whom Government itself is only a Committee), who may wish to render commercial services to foreigners in order to receive back similar services in return, that such services shall neither be rendered nor received, is not only to destroy a Gain to both parties, but also to interfere losingly with a natural and inalienable Right belonging to both.

If the reader pleases, we will turn now, in the second place, to the METHODS AND MOTIVES IN VOGUE TO RESTRICT AND PROHIBIT FOREIGN TRADE. The instrument for this purpose is called a *Tariff*. The origin of the word Tariff, its nature and kinds, will throw much light upon what has been a vexed question, but is one easily solvable, and indeed long ago resolved.

1. Origin.—When the Moors from Africa conquered Spain in the year of our Lord 711, they fortified the southernmost point of the peninsula where it juts down into the Straits of Gibraltar, and by means of their castle and town, called in their Barbary language *Tarifa*, compelled all vessels passing through the Straits to stop and to pay to these Moorish lords of the castle a certain part (determined by themselves) of the value of the cargoes. This payment appears to have been blackmail pure and simple; it was certainly extorted by force; and whether there were any pretence of a return-service in the form of promised exemption from further pillage or not, that made no real difference in the nature of the transaction. Eleven centuries later, the United States demonstrated what they thought about similar extortions on American commerce practised in the same waters by the descendants of these same Moors, by despatching Commodore Decatur with a strong fleet to Algiers and Tunis and Tripoli; to which piratical states they had already paid in twenty-five years two millions of dollars in "tribute" or "presents" for exemptions of their Mediterranean commerce from plunder; who captured the pirate ships and compelled the terrified Dey of Algiers (and the rest) to renounce all claim thereafter to American "tribute" or "presents" of any kind. The word *Tarifa*, accordingly, in English and other modern languages, a word which seems to be very dear to some men's hearts, does not appear to have had a very respectable origin, though that is not sufficient of itself to condemn the thing described by the word. That will depend upon its nature and purposes.

2. Its nature.—There never was one particle of doubt on the part of those compelled to pay the Moorish demands at Tarifa, or on the part of the United States compelled to pay "tribute" to the Algerines for a quarter of a century, about the *nature* of the transaction. The sign at Tarifa was *minus*, and not *plus*. To the credit of those pirates let it be said, that they never pretended to take what they took for the *benefit* of those from whom they took it. They took it for their own benefit. The action was abominable, but it was aboveboard. There was no deceit and no pretence about it. Both parties knew perfectly what was going on. What was delivered was just so much *out* from what would otherwise have been the *gains* of the voyage. And the truth is, the thing, tariff, is always true to the origin of the word, tariff, so far as this, that a tariff always *takes*, and never *gives*. The only phrase a tariff speaks, or can speak, is, *Thou shalt pay*! There is lying open on the table of the writer at this moment a stout volume of 417 pages, printed, with nearly as many more interleaved, entitled Tariff Compilation, published by the United States Senate in 1884, containing every item of all the tariffs passed by Congress from 1789 to the present time. One may read this volume from beginning to the end, or he may read it from the end backwards to the beginning, or he may begin in the middle and read both ways, and all he will find between the covers is a series of *Demands* made upon somebody to *pay* something. These demands, of course, are made upon, and realized from, the citizens of the United States, who are the only people under the authority and jurisdiction of the Congress. A tariff, then, may be correctly defined as *a body of takings or taxings levied upon the people of any country by their own government on their exchanges with foreigners*. How anybody can intelligently suppose that a body of *taxes*, which their own countrymen will have *to pay*, can be so cunningly adjusted as to become to them a positively productive agent, a blessing and enrichment to the payers, a spur to the progress of their Society, *they* may be properly called upon to explain who pretend to believe such an absurdity in the nature of things.

3. Its kinds.—There are two kinds of Tariffs under our general definition, very diverse from each other in their respective purposes, principles, incidence, and results.

(1) There is a tariff for Revenue. The sole purpose of a revenue tariff as such is to get money by this mode of indirect taxation out of the pockets of the People for the coffers of the Government, in order to be then expended, governmentally, for the general benefit of those who have paid the money in for that single end. The underlying thought of this kind of tariff, a tariff for revenue only, is, that the Government itself shall get all the money which the people are obliged to pay under these taxes, except the bare cost of collecting them; that only *such* taxes shall be levied at all as will come bodily and readily into the general Treasury for public uses; and

no intelligent and justice-loving people will long tolerate tariff-taxes laid with any other intent than the economical support of their government, or laid in any other way than shall bring into the Treasury all that is taken out of the People. A Revenue Tariff, therefore, may be properly defined as *a schedule of taxes levied on certain imported goods with an eye only to just and general taxation.*

There are three vital principles on which a revenue tariff as such must always be levied. (a) As the sole object is to get money for the national treasury, and as money can only be gotten as the foreign goods taxed are allowed *to come in,* such taxes must be levied at *a low rate* on each article taxed, so as not to interfere essentially with the bringing in of that class of goods with a profit to the importers, and not at all to encourage the smuggling of them in. (b) A varied experience of all the commercial nations has shown, that it is not needful in order to derive a large and growing revenue to lay even low rates on *all* goods imported, but only on certain classes of them, so as to burden at as few points as possible the successful ongoing of international exchanges; since the prosperity ever induced by commercial freedom enables a country to import and to pay for in its own quickened products vast quantities of the articles subjected to the tax, so that large revenues come from low rates levied at few points. Here we lay bare the ground of a great income in the exemption of the bulk of imports from any tax at all. (c) Custom-taxes should be laid wholly or at least mainly on articles procured from abroad, and not also produced at home; for otherwise the incidence of the tax on the portion imported will necessarily raise the price also of that portion made or grown at home; and thus the people will pay *more* money in consequence of the tax than the Government *gets* from the tax in revenue. Three points, then, in a revenue tariff, namely, *low duties on few articles, and these wholly foreign.*

The best modern example of a purely revenue tariff is that of Great Britain since 1860. All duties are on one or other of the following sixteen items, namely, Beer, Cards, Chiccory, Chocolate, Cocoa, Coffee, Fruit, Malt, Pickles, Plate, Spirits, Spruce, Tea, Tobacco, Vinegar, and Wine. Of these, Spruce yielded no revenue in 1880; Cards, Malt, Pickles, and Vinegar, yielded in the aggregate that year only £1.491; leaving the other eleven items to furnish practically all the customs revenue; but of these Coffee and its three substitutes with Beer and Plate, furnished only £337.258, so that, the remaining five articles yielded £18.915.489, or 98% of the whole income in 1880. In other words, Fruit, Spirits, Tea, Tobacco, and Wine, brought in all but 2% of the customs-taxes of Great Britain in 1880. In 1890, the duties on certain Wines and Spirits having been lifted, there was a large surplus of revenue over the Estimates, which has just been devoted to the enlargement of the Navy. Every other European commercial country had a deficit that year as compared with its Estimates of the year preceding. The figures are not now at hand for an exact statement, but there can be little reasonable doubt that the "Five Articles" rendered at least 98½% of the tariff-taxes of England last year. If there be also some domestic production of any article taxed by the British tariff, a corresponding excise-tax on that part produced at home, which part would otherwise be raised in price by the tariff-tax to no advantage of the Revenue, enables that Government to get easily all that the people are made to pay in consequence of the tariff-tax on the imported part.

(2) There is a tariff under Protectionism so-called. The ruling aim in this second kind of tariff is not at all to obtain income for Government in order to promote the general good, but on the contrary by means of heavy taxes on *foreign* articles to raise the prices of corresponding *domestic* ones for the exclusive benefit of a few producers of these home goods at the expense of all home buyers of them. If these special tariff-taxes be so high and complicated as to keep out altogether the foreign articles, and so the Treasury realize nothing at all from the taxes on them, so much the more "protectionist" do they become, and so much the better pleased are the special domestic producers with the entire monopoly of the home market at their own prices. Such taxes are prohibitory and protectionist at the same time. Prohibition is the perfection of Protectionism. A Protectionist Tariff, accordingly, may be justly defined as *a body of taxes laid on specified imported goods with a single eye to raise thereby the prices of certain home commodities.*

The vital points of a protectionist tariff are also three, but these are the exact opposites and antipodes of the three points of a revenue tariff, so that it is self-contradictory and impossible to combine in one tariff-bill the two sets of contrary elements. A revenue tariff with incidental protectionism is a solecism. (a) If a tariff-rate is to be protectionist in character, that is, competent to raise the price of home products, it must be *high*, so as either to exclude altogether the corresponding foreign products, in which case there is no revenue at all, or else to make their price by means of the duty added reach the point at which the home producers plan to sell their own, in which case there will be very little revenue. For instance, when the Bessemer steel companies asked in 1870 for two cents a pound tariff-tax on foreign steel rails, they called it in terms in their "confidential" statement to the Ways and Means "*exceptional protection*," and admitted in so many words that they expected to supply the home market entirely, and so the Government would get *nothing* in revenue and the people be compelled to pay $44.80 *extra* for their home steel rails per ton. It is a little bit of comfort to think, that they only obtained $28 per ton, or 1¼ cents per pound, which was not quite prohibitory, so that the Government got a little revenue on steel rails, and the people paid for some years only about *double* for their rails what they were worth in a free market! To reach its end a protectionist tariff-tax must be *high* of necessity.

(b) No system of protectionist tariff-taxes can be entered upon or continued in any country except by means of many persons who all alike want their special products artificially lifted in price by legislation, and who are obliged *to combine* in order to get and keep what they want, so that protectionist taxes on a few things only were rarely or never found in a tariff; so contrary are such taxes to the common sense and common interests of man, that only strong combinations of many special interests can begin or maintain them, whence there must be *many* taxes if any under this strongly selfish scheme; and by an actual count of them by the writer in 1868 there were found to be 2317 distinct rates of tax assessed on different foreign articles in the Tariff of the United States, which was strikingly in contrast with the Revenue Tariff of Britain in point of the number of things taxed. So needful is log-rolling to the maintenance of protectionism, that the passage of the "knit-goods bill" in the summer of 1882, for example, was contingent on the contemporaneous passage of the famous "River and Harbor bill" of that year.

(c) While Revenue Taxes select by preference things wholly imported, Protectionist Taxes are placed of course on such foreign goods as are also and especially made or grown at home, otherwise their plain and sole purpose would be thwarted, which completes the contrast between the two kinds of tariffs. For illustration, Tea and Coffee are the best things possible to tax in a tariff for revenue, because (1) they are in universal consumption, and (2) they are wholly imported, and taxes upon them do not raise the price of anything else, and so the Government gets all that the people pay under them; for this very reason the taxes upon Tea and Coffee, which had yielded for years some $20,000,000 of revenue yearly, were thrown off in 1872 under protectionist leadership, by the deceptive cry of "*a free breakfast table*," in the subtle interest of commercial bondage; seeking to give the impression on the one hand that everything on the breakfast table was to be free, whereas nothing on it or around was to be free except the two beverages mentioned, and on the other hand that the removal of these two taxes was a great boon to the people, whereas the motive for the removal of these was *to continue* on the people burdens tenfold heavier. Eighteen years have rolled away since then, and Tea and Coffee are still upon the free list; the incompatibility of the two kinds of tariff-taxes is demonstrated in the fact, that there has not been for years a single tax primarily for revenue in the United States tariff, the opposite protectionist idea having logically wrought itself out there; and the same incompatibility is shown in the British tariff, in which there has been no protectionist tax since 1860. Each aim logically carried out completely excludes the other aim.

The best and worst specimen of a protectionist tariff that the world has ever seen, has been in operation in the United States for thirty years, 1861-1890. Its inner history is not yet fully known by the public, but enough is known to expose the motives and to condemn the action of all those, whether constituents or congressmen, who knowing what they were doing, contributed to build up gradually that mass of incongruities and iniquities, under which the entire agricultural class of the country (nearly one-half of the people) has become impoverished, by much the larger part of the farming lands of the Union covered by heavy mortgages, and the ocean-marine of a naturally nautical people almost totally destroyed. Attempts more or less successful have been made at various times and at different points to conceal from the Public the impulses really behind the provisions of this tariff, and even the amount and the mode of the incidence of its taxes; many of the most protectionist taxes have been complex, combining upon the same article *specific* and *advalorem* rates, as for instance, upon blankets "*50 cents per pound and 35% advalorem,*" so that it was difficult or rather impossible for the common reader or buyer to ascertain how much the tariff-tax really was; much of the language of the tariff-bills has been to the last degree involved and uncertain, often leading to perplexing disputes and costly litigations, and sometimes covering up a half-hidden purpose; importers have been bribed, as it were, in cases of doubtful legality, to pay the maximum rates demanded, by the prospect and promise that the extra sums if ultimately found by the courts illegal should be repaid bodily *to them* and not to the people who in the mean time had bought and paid for the goods thus enormously enhanced in price, and millions of the people's money have gone back in that way to importers and to spies and informers; a careless wording in tariff-descriptions has again and again covered goods not designed to be touched, as the lastings and rubber webbings of the shoemakers to the consternation of that great interest, which asked for no protectionist privilege for itself, but wanted its raw materials at their natural price; and the iron industry of Pennsylvania was bitterly angry at Secretary Sherman, who construed a line of the tariff relating to cotton ties used at the South more favorably to the planters than to the iron-workers, although the latter were strongly privileged at every point of the tariff (even at this) in the teeth of the interests of the consumers of iron, and the later honorable ambition of the Secretary to become a candidate for the Presidency of the United States was largely thwarted in consequence by the hostility of these miserable and revengeful monopolists.

There were fifty descriptions of iron and steel taxed by the tariff in 1879, and the average rate of tax on these at that time was 77% *advalorem*, and this was about the average rate for the thirty years under the consideration. On special articles of prime necessity and universal consumption, as steel rails, the tax varied under the rate of $28 per ton put on in 1870 from 85% to

100% *advalorem*; and the purpose of this particular tax was plainly seen in an average price of domestic steel rails in this country $24.44 a ton higher than in England for better rails under a longer guarantee for the eleven years, 1870-80; in other words, 87% of the tax paid on the smaller and better part imported was added to the average price of the larger and worser part produced at home during those eleven years. That the English rails were better and even regarded as cheaper under their guarantee with the $28 a ton added to their price, is proven by the fact that the N. Y. Central railroad company relaid their tracks with the English rails, and were putting them down in Detroit in plain sight of simultaneous track-laying across the river in Canada, where the same kind of English rails were costing $28 a ton less. Every passenger and ton of freight carried by steel-track roads in the United States in this interval contributed his and its share to make up to the roads this *extra* price paid for steel rails. In 1883 the tariff-tax on steel rails was reduced to $17 per ton. That this enormous artificial price of iron and steel products under tariff-taxes redounded wholly to the profit of the capitalists concerned, and not at all to the benefit of the laborers concerned, is shown by the Census of 1880, which gives $393 as the average pay for that year of the persons employed in the iron and steel industries of the country; and the late Senator Beck of Kentucky demonstrated on the floor of the Senate, *nemine contradicente*, that only 8.8% of the value of the products of the Bessemer steel industry in 1881 went to the laborers employed in it, while 66.9% of the same went to the capitalists as profits. Let the thoughtful reader remember at this point, that iron and steel products are only one of an indefinite number coddled and privileged by the tariff at the expense of the masses of consumers.

It is impossible to tell exactly *how much* more the people of the United States were compelled to pay for their commodities under tariff-taxes, whose ground-thought was to compel them to pay more and the more the better, than the Treasury received as the direct product of these taxes during 1861-90, but an approximation can be made within the truth whose results are fitted to startle the minds of all good citizens. For convenience' sake only, and because the official figures are complete for the shorter period, let us take for comparison the twenty years, 1863-82. The annual average tariff-income for those 20 years was in round numbers $158,000,000; but the ground-thought of the tariff-scheme in all those years was not to get an income for Government, but factitious prices for capitalists privileged by law; and during the last half of the time there were no tariff-taxes on Tea and Coffee, which had been before the principal revenue taxes. If, now, we may fairly suppose, that for each *one* foreign article paying a tax into the Treasury there were *four* domestic articles raised each in price as much as the foreign article paid in customs-tax, then it follows, that the People paid in each of those 20 years under customs chiefly protectionist, $632,000,000, or $12,640,000,000 in all, no penny of which went into the Treasury of the United States. That this supposition of 4:1 is wholly reasonable, appears partly from the known proportion (officially reported) between Domestic and Imported as to several leading articles, for example, of steel rails in 1880 the Domestic was 20 times the Imported, and the People paid 19 times more under the tax than the Treasury got; and on woollen blankets in 1881 the Treasury took in less than $2000, while the People paid in the *extra* price of blankets more than 1000 times that sum that year; and on iron and steel goods of all kinds the average tariff-taxes were about 77% in that interval of time and the vast bulk of the iron and steel goods consumed was boasted to be of domestic production.

Let us confirm these striking results by another more than reasonable supposition taken from the opposite quarter. The census of 1870 gave $4,232,000,000 as the value of home manufactures for that year, which we may fairly take as the average of the 20 years under consideration; now, if we throw off one-third of those home products as not affected by the tariff at all, and reckon that the rest were only raised in price 22%, which was only one-half of the average rate of tax on dutiable goods,—the average rate on these was officially pronounced in 1880 at 44%,—then almost precisely the same results will follow as before: two-thirds of $4,232,000,000 is $2,880,000,000, and 22% on that sum is $633,600,000. An acknowledged statistical expert of national reputation, Mr. J. S. Moore, calculated from data quite diverse from our own, that the People paid $1,000,000,000 in the one year, 1882, *extra* to the sum reaching the Treasury that year, under protectionist tariff-taxes. We see, then, clearly the *methods*, by which Protectionism reaches its ends, and we cannot but conclude, that these methods issue in monstrously unjust burdens on the masses of the People.

It remains, under this second general head, to examine the *motives* of those men, who have gotten the protectionist tariff-taxes put upon the different classes of imported goods in this country. Fortunately we have data of unquestionable authority, covering the entire first century of our national existence, which prove these two propositions: first, *that no protectionist tax has ever been* PUT ON *by our Congress from the first day until this day except at the instance and under the pressure of the very men personally and pecuniarily interested to secure thereby an artificial rise of price for their own domestic wares*; and second, *that these very men have been almost, if not quite, as active and determined* TO KEEP OFF *protectionist taxes on other goods used by them in their processes of production, whether raw material, machinery, or accessories*. These two propositions, taken together, demonstrate beyond a cavil the motives of the protectionists as a class. Of course, they have had their dupes and tools. Out of their own mouths and out of their own actions are they to be judged. One hundred years is long enough of time in order to display perfectly the motives of a prominent and persistent class of men, under that Government of the world, whose key-note is Exposure, and under that maxim of the world, Actions speak louder than words.

Thomas H. Benton, a United States Senator from Missouri for 30 years, 1820-50, himself in all that time a prominent leader and debater, and always an indefatigable investigator, published an *Abridgment of the Debates in Congress from 1789 to 1856* in 15 large volumes. Each important tariff Debate for the first 70 years of our national history is distinctly brought out in these volumes, and the impulses and motives behind each leading speaker may be discerned as clear as day. The present writer has been over these debates with great care, and has mastered them in their substance and motives on both sides; and he has been besides a deeply interested reader and excerptor of all Congressional tariff-debates for more than 30 years just past; and now invites his present readers to take a cursory glance over this broad field, and satisfy themselves as to the motives personal and associate of the protectionist debaters from the first to the present time.

Because the new Constitution prescribed that "*all bills for raising revenue shall originate in the House of Representatives,*" the main debates on the first tariff-act of 1789 were in that branch of the national Legislature. Nothing could be simpler or sounder than the basis of the new tariff as proposed by Madison, the acknowledged leader in the debates, namely, the so-called Revenue System of 1783, as adopted by the old Congress, and ratified by all the States in succession, excepting New York. That was, small specific taxes on eight articles, namely, Wines, Spirits, Tea, Coffee, Cocoa, Molasses, Sugar, and Pepper. In the earlier part of the discussion no other end than revenue was mentioned in connection with the taxes. Madison said: "*I own myself the friend of a very free system of commerce: if industry and labor are left to take their own course they will generally be directed to those objects which are most productive, and that in a manner more certain and direct than the wisdom of the most enlightened legislature could point out; nor do I believe that the national interest is more promoted by such legislative directions than the interests of the individuals concerned.*" It is significant of after times that the first word in this debate respecting any other word than revenue through the tariff-taxes came from Pennsylvania; and equally significant, that the next and strongest words for something else than revenue came from Massachusetts; and more significant than either was the junction of the two States in influence and votes when it came to the final adjustment of the actual tariff-rates. Pennsylvania had already gotten well forward in the manufacture of iron and steel products, particularly of nails, and wanted "*encouragement,*" that is, protectionist taxes upon the foreign products corresponding. Said Hartley of Pennsylvania: "*I am therefore sorry that gentlemen seem to fix their mind to so early a period as 1783; for we very well know our circumstances are much changed since that time: we had then but few manufactures among us, and the vast quantities of goods that flowed in upon us from Europe at the conclusion of the war rendered those few almost useless; since then we have been forced by necessity, and various other causes, to increase our domestic manufactures to such a degree as to be able to furnish some in sufficient quantity to answer the consumption of the whole Union, while others are daily growing into importance. Our stock of materials is, in many instances, equal to the greatest demand, and our artisans sufficient to work them up even for exportation. In these cases, I take it to be the policy of every enlightened nation to give their manufactures that degree of encouragement necessary to perfect them, without oppressing other parts of the community."*

Massachusetts was not a whit behind Pennsylvania in asking for discriminations in her own favor at the obvious expense of the rest of the country. New England rum was made out of molasses, and Jamaica rum was its competitor in public favor; distillers in the neighborhood of Boston and Salem wanted therefore a *high tax* on Jamaica rum, and a *low one* on the imported molasses used in the home manufacture. Madison was willing to discourage rum-making and rum-selling both in the interest of temperance, and proposed a tax of eight cents a gallon on molasses and fifteen cents on Jamaica rum, which called out this indignant burst from Goodhue of Massachusetts: *"Molasses is a raw material, essentially requisite for the well-being of a very extensive and valuable manufacture. It ought likewise to be considered a necessary of life. In the Eastern States it enters into the diet of the poorer classes of people, who are, from the decay of trade and other adventitious circumstances, totally unable to bear such a weight as a tax of eight cents would be upon them. I cannot consent to allow more than two cents. Massachusetts imports from 30,000 to 40,000 hogsheads annually, more than all the other States together. Fifteen cents, the sum laid on Jamaica spirits, is about one-third part of its value: now eight cents on molasses is considerably more: the former is an article of luxury, therefore that duty may not be improper; but the latter cannot be said to partake of that quality in the substance, and when manufactured into rum is no more a luxury than Jamaica spirits."*

The Senate in the First Congress sat with closed doors, and was thus more open than the House to the influence of interested petitions which soon began to pour in upon it, asking for amendments to the House bill in the line of protectionism; and through such amendments the Massachusetts and Pennsylvania members, with a few other members similarly inclined, partially carried their points into the first Tariff. The tax on molasses was fixed at 2½ cents a gallon, and on Jamaica rum at ten cents a gallon; nails were taxed one cent per pound imported; and an accepted Senate amendment classed Hemp and Cotton together as two products of the soil worth "encouraging," hemp at ⅗ of a cent per pound and cotton at three cents a pound; yet hemp constantly "encouraged" to this day at the cost of ship building and other industries has never risen to the rank of a staple.

Coal was also taxed protectionistly, at the instance of Virginia, then the coal-producing State. Note the three universal features of Protectionism in the original application of it to the United States; (1) the purely selfish call to tax one's neighbor in order to lift the price of one's own wares (nails), (2) the equally selfish resistance to such a tax as falls on one's raw materials (molasses), and (3) the final log-rolling among those legally privileged at different points (Massachusetts and Pennsylvania and Virginia).

Take a second instance of the same general point from our second Tariff, passed in 1816. Two Massachusetts young men, Lowell and Jackson, brothers-in-law, had started a modern cotton-mill in Waltham, near Boston, in 1813, and constructed in it, with the help of an ingenious mechanic named Moody, a power-loom; as soon as the war with England was over, and Congress in consequence began to talk about a new Tariff, Lowell went to Washington, and by personal influence with Mr. Calhoun, then the leading man in the House, with Mr. Lowndes his colleague from South Carolina, who afterwards reported the new bill, and with other members of Congress, contributed largely to the introduction into this Tariff of protectionist features towards *cottons*. Lowell struck strong at the start. He represented (doubtless with entire honesty) to Calhoun and Lowndes, both from a cotton-planting State, that a domestic market for raw cotton *in addition* to the foreign market would raise the price of that agricultural staple. Both were easily convinced that such would be the case, although both found ample reasons afterwards for altering their opinion in that regard. Lowell, the "cotton city" on the Merrimack, founded in 1821, was named from the successful lobbyist of 1816. Lowndes reported a tax on cottons of 33⅓% *advalorem*, with a proviso *that all cottons should be assumed at the custom-house to have cost at least 25 cents to the square yard*. This was the famous principle of the "*minimum*," a device to increase the protectionism without *seeming* to do so.

The debate on this feature of the bill was a marvel in many ways. The penetrating reader will not be at a loss for the reason of this. John Randolph moved to strike out from the bill the proviso for the cotton *minimum*, and argued at some length "*against the propriety of promoting the manufacturing establishments to the extent and in the manner proposed by the bill, and against laying up 8000 tons of shipping now employed in the East India trade, and levying an immense tax on one portion of the community to put money into the pockets of another.*" Calhoun rejoined: "*Until the debate assumed this new form, he had determined to be silent; participating, as he largely did, in that general anxiety which is felt, after so long and laborious a session, to return to the bosom of our families. It has been objected to that bill, that it will injure our marine, and consequently impair our naval strength. How far it is fairly liable to this charge, he was not prepared to say. He hoped and believed it would not, at least to any alarming extent, have that effect immediately; and he firmly believed that its lasting operation would be highly beneficial to our commerce. The trade to the East Indies would certainly be much affected; but it was stated in debate that the whole of that trade employed but six hundred sailors. The cotton and woollen manufactures are not to be introduced: they are already introduced to a great extent; freeing us entirely from the hazards, and in a great measure, the sacrifices experienced in giving the capital of the country a new direction. The restrictive measures and the war, though not intended for that purpose, have by the necessary operation of things turned a large amount of capital to these new branches of industry. But it will no doubt be said, if they are so far established, and if the situation of the country be so favorable to their growth, where is the necessity of affording them protection? It is to put them beyond the reach of contingency."*

Thus Calhoun goes on, making the greatest mistake of his life which he regretted to his dying day, to give plausible reasons for his insistence and his vote, but he does not even touch upon the *real reason*. If he had detailed his conversations with Lowell, it would have been far more to the point. His motive, like that of every other man in Congress who has urged protectionist schemes, was the special benefit of some of his constituents at the more or less concealed expense of their countrymen. But, as always happens when men really act from unavowed motives, he was suspected of having them; and he guarded himself: "*He was no manufacturer; he was not from that portion of the country supposed to be peculiarly interested. Coming as he did from the South, and having in common with his immediate constituents, no interest but in the cultivation of the soil, in selling its products high, and buying cheap the wants and conveniences of life, no motives could be attributed to him but such as were disinterested.*" But Randolph still charged, that the discussion showed "*a strange and mysterious connection*" between this measure and the National Bank bill which had just passed. This was a loophole of escape for Calhoun: "*he wished merely to reply to the insinuation of a mysterious connection between this bill and that to establish the Bank. He denied any improper or unfair understanding, and could challenge the House to support the charge.*"

A beautiful instance of the *confession*, which all protectionists make in action when it comes to the pinch, that a rise of price is at once the object and the result of protectionist tariff-taxes, is found in the awkward attempt of Congress to relieve indirectly the burnt-out citizens of Chicago in 1871. The great fire occurred in October of that year. In the winter following a bit of legislation took place in Congress in consequence, which is too instructive to be passed by without notice, because in all the parts of it taken together we have in epitome the motives and the processes and the prompt confessions of Protectionism. Contributions were taken up all over the country, and even in Europe, for the relief of the people of Chicago. As Whittier puts it:

"From East, from West, from South and North,The messages of love shot forth,And, underneath the severing wave,The world, full-handed, reached to save."

But cannot Congress do something to help rebuild the ruined city? April 5, 1872, President Grant set his signature to a congressional bill enacted to last one year only, and for the express benefit of Chicago alone, *to exempt all building materials except lumber from the operation of tariff-taxes.* As a public and emphatic confession on the part of Congress, that tariff-taxes raise the prices of protectionist goods, and that the remission of such taxes lowers the prices of such goods and becomes a boon to the buyers, all this is refreshing and satisfactory; but why was *lumber,* by much the most important of the building materials needed, *excepted* from the bounty of the legislators to the unfortunates of Chicago? The bill applied to Chicago only, and was to last but one year at best! The bill as drawn and debated included *all* building materials. Why was lumber excepted? Because, while the bill was still pending, a special car filled with the lumber-lords of Michigan and Wisconsin was rolled to Washington in haste, and the potent influence of these men was sufficient to cause the express exemption of their product from the intended cheapening (for one year) of the building materials for desolated Chicago. The brief official record of this curious transaction will be found in U.S. Statutes for 1872, page 33. It needs no comment but the obvious one, that here is the whole matter of protectionism in a nutshell;— the motive, the open confession, the greedy lobby determined to thrive on their neighbors' misfortunes, the inhumanity, the spirit of monopoly, the infernalism,—a game of grab from beginning to end!

Shameless as the protectionist debates in Congress have been from the start, in letting it be plainly seen, that the sole motive of their efforts is an artificial rise of price in certain goods which their fellow-citizens would be compelled under the law to pay, the debate in the House of Representatives in the spring of 1883 was by far the most shameless and avowed in this respect of any that ever transpired there. In the last days of that debate all pretence of any action for the good of the country at large dropped utterly out of the discourse: the old fallacies and disguises and subterfuges of "home markets" and "higher wages" and "commercial independence" were no longer put forward even in word under the clash of selfish interests, and in the eagerness to secure for their wares a factitious price to be paid by their countrymen; proposed reductions in tariff-taxes were fought off by these men, and in many instances still higher taxes were urged on, under their unabashed avowal that, unless home prices were thus stiffened and uplifted, they could not make and sell their wares at a profit; one honorable member from New Jersey brought his pottery wares upon the floor of the House, and tried to demonstrate to his fellow-members that, unless these very goods were hoisted in price, by taxes on his foreign competitors, he could no longer tread his clay and work his wheels with profit to himself: in other words, he and others like-circumstanced, by lobbying and log-rolling, persuaded Congress to pass so-called laws to compel their countrymen *to hire them to carry on what they publicly alleged were unprofitable branches of business.* By their own confession, the only trouble with their goods was, that they were inferior in quality and superior in price to otherwise similar goods in the open market of the world.

One more, and the latest instance, out of hundreds equally accessible and equally conclusive, will suffice for a demonstration of the point in hand. In the early summer of 1890, a Massachusetts member of the House of Representatives, an avowed protectionist from an alleged protectionist district of that State, waxed so warm in arguing against a protectionist tax upon a certain raw material useful in tanning leather, that he took off his coat and proceeded in his shirt-sleeves! One would suppose, both from his zeal and the tenor of his speech, that he was a veritable free-trader! But no! He had argued a hundred times that protectionist taxes (to be paid by other people) were a good thing for the payers, and enriched the whole country; but lo! it turned out in this case that he himself was a buyer of this particular material, and lo! he did not relish the tax-lifted prices caused by the tariff. They were all wrong. They must be fought off at all hazards, even in the hottest weather! This is a very respectable gentleman, well thought of by his neighbors in Worcester County, but his protectionism is *not* respectable. It is chameleon-colored. It is one thing in one light, and an opposite thing in another light. Indeed, the protectionist congressman has never yet been discovered in this country, who was fond of paying protectionist taxes himself, or willing that his immediate and powerful constituents should pay them! It has been proven many times over, that the very strongest friends of a Free List in this broad land have been certain so-called protectionist Senators and Representatives.

From these few sample-examples, the reader of penetration will perceive, that there is no element of logical coherence or moral decency or even outward respectability in Protectionism. There is no *principle* in it or of it. It does not hang together. It walks in darkness and not in light. It is full of deceit. It is fond of disguises. It is contrary to common sense. It offends justice. Morality frowns at it. It has no basis in any Science, least of all in the Science of Buying and Selling, whose best impulses it feebly tries to deny, and whose largest and most innocent gains it fain would destroy.

Next in order we will examine, in the third place, a few of the chief FALLACIES AND FALSEHOODS, by which Protectionism has striven to give itself a standing in the commercial world. In our day at least, these are, without exception, afterthoughts and subterfuges. We have just seen under the last head the real impulses, plain as a mountain peak, which put on and keep on and pile up these taxes on the masses of the people; but these real motives will not bear inspection and public criticism, and so plausible reasons must be found or at least propounded, which shall do the double duty of covering the real reasons, and of seeming to convince while they only perplex the victims of the scheme. These plausibilities we propose now to analyze and to expose. The test of any alleged truth is its harmony with acknowledged truths: the test of any propounded error is its incongruity with and contradiction of acknowledged truths. On a logical comparison, therefore, of any false proposition with any known truth, the latter will be sure to fling out its flat contradiction and floor the falsehood forever. Protectionism contradicts economic truths at practically innumerable points, but we will now watch the collisions at the principal points only.

Fallacy A: *that a nation may still sell to foreign nations while prohibiting the buying from them.* Protectionism is multiplied prohibitions on the buying of goods from foreigners. Between four and five thousand of such prohibitions deface our national Statute-book at the present moment. All the while, however, the assumption underlies this policy, and the express proposition is often heard in different forms along the lines, that our citizens may still sell their products to foreigners, nevertheless. England has *got to buy* our cotton or starve: the Continent *is compelled* to take our pork products, for they are the cheapest food in the world: how can China or India *help* taking the silver from our mines? Softly. Buying and selling from the very nature of it is never compulsory, but always voluntary. A commercial service is never rendered but in plain view of a return-service to be received. The mental estimation of each buyer is couched in the very terms of what is offered in return by each seller. Buying and selling from its inmost nature is always one act of two persons acting conjointly and inseparably to the advantage of each. How, then, can the individuals of one country *sell* anything to individuals of another country without at the same instant *buying* of these in return? The act of selling is just as much buying as it is selling, and the act of buying is just as much selling as it is buying. As we have abundantly seen already, the introduction of Money as a *medium* in the transaction makes no difference in the *nature* of the exchange of commodities internationally. The postulate, therefore, that the people of one country can continue to sell products to the people of another while refusing to take their products of some kind in return, is an *absurdity* in the nature of things and an *impossibility* in the world of facts. *A market for products is products in market.*

All known facts confirm this irrefragable reasoning, and discredit utterly the fallacy in hand. When France and Germany a few years ago gave back to our protectionists a dose of their own medicine, and prohibited American pork-products, ostensibly because they feared the trichinæ but really to cajole their own farmers under the plea of protectionism, their brethren in the faith have made up all sorts of faces ever since, have wound up the respective diplomatic clocks to strike twelve against the too presumptuous countries which ventured to restrict American products in their ports, have protested and proclaimed. What is the matter? Is not sauce for the goose sauce for the gander also? Have not American protectionists shut out French and German products 100:1 under the same plea now used on the Continent? "*But we cannot sell our products abroad,*" cry the angered Western farmers. Of course they cannot, because restrictions on buying *are* restrictions on selling; and additional restrictions of the same kind put on French and German buying are of course still further restrictions on American selling. And the farmers are, as usual, the victims both ways.

To hear an ordinary American protectionist talk, one would think that Great Britain is the enemy of mankind for admitting into her ports practically without let or hindrance the goods of all the world. *Free Trade England!* Let us look a moment. England has to pay for all these goods received from all quarters. In what does she pay? In her own goods, of course. What is her market? The whole world. Is that market ever slack on the whole? Never. Is she ever flooded with cheap goods? The more she buys the more she sells of necessity. How much does she sell *per capita* of her people? More than twice as much as the United States sells *per capita*. How can she sell so much of her own stuff? Because she buys freely other stuff from all the world. What are the limits to her capacity to sell her own goods to foreigners? Precisely the limits of her willingness to take in pay other goods from foreigners. Cannot these limits be overpassed in either direction? By no possibility: when people can no longer pay for what they buy, the buying ceases; and when they are not permitted to take their pay for what they sell, the selling ceases. Is this free trade profitable to Great Britain? Immensely so in every way. Whither has it carried up her ocean-marine? To the topmost notch. Is capital abundant in England in bulk, and are its loanable rates low? England is the richest country in the world, and all nations resort thither to buy. What is the source of this vast volume of Capital? The only source of Capital is savings from the natural gains of Buying and Selling.

Is Great Britain willing to take in goods from the United States? Certainly, under the universal conditions of taking in foreign goods at all. Is the United States willing to take in British goods in pay for her own goods exported thither? She is not, except over protectionist barriers averaging 47%. Is it a good thing for the United States, that Great Britain takes in her goods freely? We should suppose so! Does the former already sell to the latter and through the latter more goods than to all the world besides? Much more. Could this profitable trade be easily increased? It could be quadrupled in a very short time. How? By simply according to our citizens a decent liberty, which is their inalienable right. Would the United States like it to be commercially treated by Britain exactly as the former treats the latter? It would bankrupt the United States in six months. Would our protectionists like it? It would make them howl. Is it the commercial salvation of the United States that Britain is immovably for free trade with her and the rest of the world? Nothing else saves her from commercial ruin. Can the ghost of a reason be given, commercial or other, why the United States should continue to fling double fists into the face of British goods seeking a market and so making one? Not a shadow of a shade of a good reason was ever given for such folly, or ever can be.

It is more than a pleasure to acknowledge at this point the great service done by James G. Blaine, Secretary of State, during the summer of 1890, to Country and Commerce, by his courageous avowal contrary to his own personal record and to the vehement behest of his party, that the economic principle just enunciated is sound, and should be at once applied by the United States in connection with all the countries of Latin America. In a letter to the Senate on the results of the recent Pan-American Conference, he said: "*The Conference believed that while great profit would come to all the countries, if reciprocity treaties could be adopted, the United States would be by far the greatest gainer.*" The principle of reciprocity is the principle of free trade applied by both parties to the trade. It is the sound principle, that goods buy goods and pay for goods at the same instant to a mutual profit. Manifold reiterations of this principle came from the Secretary that summer, especially in vigorous protestations against the McKinley tariff-bill then pending, alleging with truth that "*there is not a line or a section in the bill which opens a market for another bushel of wheat or another barrel of pork.*" The unequivocal statements of a favorite statesman have roused the somewhat indifference of thousands of citizens, and make certain the speedy prevalence in the United States of the unassailable doctrine, that any People must buy freely if they would sell broadly.

Fallacy B: *that tariff-taxes are needful in order to start infant industries.* There is no analogy whatever between Child-bearing and Child-growing and any form of Buying and Selling at any time, but the deceit in the wretched simile has cost the world billions of dollars of pure loss. To bring up infants from birth to maturity is indeed a good deal of a task for the parents, but it is not in any sense an economical task: the parents neither ask for nor receive a return-service in kind: the transaction is wholly moral in its character, and not economical at all: there is no party of the second part in the premises: there is a free giving, and that is all. Buying and Selling, on the contrary, has no infancy, and no maturity and no old age. This particular Minerva springs at once full-grown and full-armed from the brain of Jove. The conditions of Trading are forever the same; with no reference to the age of the parties, the antiquity of the industry, or any other such irrelevant thing. If any person anywhere (old or young) has got something to sell, and finds (directly or indirectly) any other person anywhere who wants his wares and can pay for them,—all the conditions of mutual profit are present, and everything else is an impertinence.

Much more than this. Tariff-taxes have to be paid by somebody. Their payment is inexorable at the custom-house, and interest and other charges are added before the sum reaches the ultimate payer. But the ultimate sum however made up is exactly so much *out* of the commercial gains of the payer. The sign is every time *minus* and *not* plus. When egregiously high tariff-taxes are multiplied in number, and all the additions are made to them, they become an incalculably large sum, every cent of which *has to be paid* out of the gains of current Industry. Now, what a queer way that is to foster industries! What a queer way to help start them! It takes Capital to start new industries, and to carry on old ones; but tariff-taxes (with all their accretions) take just so much *out* from what would otherwise naturally become Capital. That is to say, all Capital is savings from the gains of Exchanges; and these gains are *reduced* by every tariff-tax that touches them directly or indirectly. Taxes from their very nature can help nobody. They hurt everybody. What a device this is to start new industries with, namely, to pick the pockets of the very men, who are to start the industries, if they ever are to start at all! Lower your reservoir to begin with, in order to give head and force to your faucet flow!

But this is not half of it. On what industries do the protectionist taxes fall at first to weaken and discourage them? Of course on the natural and profitable ones, which only ask to be let alone in order to maintain a healthful life and growth. If, under natural conditions, any industry is in existence, one may be perfectly sure it is profitable, since Profit is the only thing in the world that can start and build up an industry: when the profit ceases, the trade ceases of necessity: the motive to it is *gone*. In behalf of what sort of industries are these taxes ostensibly and plausibly levied? Only, if we are to believe the protectionists, the weak and presently unprofitable ones. *It is the infant industries that need the nursing-bottle!* That is to say, tax down and perhaps destroy the *profitable* industries, the industries that *pay*, that can paddle their own canoe and no thanks to anybody, in order to bring forward certain other industries, which by confession and open proclamation are *unprofitable*, and can only *start* by taxing their neighbors! Of course, there is a cat in this meal, and we shall let her out of the bag in plain sight presently; but we are taking now our friends, the protectionists, at their own word, and exhibiting their marvellous wisdom under the terms of their own choosing. What a blessed way for a nation to grow rich, to smite down with high taxes the active and enterprising and independent and therefore profitable industries with one hand, and grope around with the other to find some poor and inactive and unfrugal and naturally unprofitable industries, in order to fetch forward these by means of the plunder filched from the others!

To go back for historical illustration to Washington's first administration, when the first (extremely mild) protectionist taxes were levied in this country, we have the highest authority for knowing that many of the leading branches of manufactures were prosperous and profitable. They had no artificial help in order to start, but on the contrary had had continual discouragement for a century under the miserable protectionist policy of the mother country. Washington himself was inaugurated in a dark brown suit of woollen cloth of American manufacture: so was John Adams inaugurated first Vice-President of the United States about the same time in a garb of wholly native manufacture. This was in April, 1789. In November of the same year, Washington returned to New York from his first tour in New England *"astonished both at the marvellous growth of commerce and manufactures in New England and the general contentment of its inhabitants with the new government"* (Schouler, p. 117). Alexander Hamilton, the first Secretary of the Treasury, in his famous Report to Congress on Manufactures, in 1791, enumerated seventeen branches as then thriving so as to fairly supply the home market, and settle into regular trades. These were, skins and leather, flax and hemp, iron and steel, brick and pottery, starch, brass and copper, tinware, carriages, painter's colors, refined sugars, oils, soaps, candles, hats, gunpowder, chocolate, snuff and chewing tobacco. It is plain enough from the debates of the time as well as from the nature of the case, that the protectionist taxes in our first two Tariffs, already considered here in detail, although they were comparatively slight in number and amount, fell in the way of discouragement on these incipient yet independent manufactures as well as upon all the farmers of the land. There can be but little rational question, that the woollen industry was sounder at the core in 1789, when Washington was inaugurated in native woollens, than in 1889, when Harrison was inaugurated in the same, the ostentatious gift of a firm of protectionist woollen manufacturers shortly afterwards adjudged to be bankrupt and fraudulently so.

The best point, after all, to make against this hollow fallacy, is the practical one, that no industry whatever, whether "infant" or other, has ever come in this country into an acknowledged self-sustaining position under a whole century's tariff-taxes. Salt, hemp, coal, cottons, woollens, nails, and iron and steel products generally, were the chief articles protectionized at first, and have been protectionized ever since, but no one of them all has ever come into a condition of self-support according to the view of the privileged beneficiaries. Each one of them was an old industry, and a relatively rich industry, when it was taken under the "fostering care" of the tariff-taxes, levied for their further enrichment on the masses of the people; and it was only greedy and secret combinations among these for that purpose, which put them at first and has kept them ever since in the rank of public beneficiaries. The simple truth is, that diversity of employments is rooted in human nature and in the circumstances amid which God has placed men, and so far is it from being true that taxes and restrictions are needful in order to foster manufactures, taxes and prohibitions cannot prevent them from springing into life! They are just as natural to men and to colonies as agriculture is. Indeed, agriculture can scarcely take a step without them. The farmer must have ploughs and carts and other implements; and, depend upon it, there are some natural mechanics in that colony. Clothes are as needful as food, and spinning and weaving in some form will begin at once, and prohibitions will be powerless to stop them.

Deadly to the fallacy in hand is the word of unquestionable History. Any one may read in Palfrey and Bancroft and Hildreth such facts as these, scattered all along through the noble volumes. The manufacture of linen and woollen and cotton cloth was begun in Massachusetts in 1638, in Rowley, by some families from Yorkshire; and became so remunerative in a couple of years that some acts of the General Court designed to stimulate it were repealed. Brick-making and glass-works and the manufacture of salt were all begun in Massachusetts before 1640. In 1643, the younger Winthrop established iron-works in Braintree and Lynn, which after some losses were successfully prosecuted. Within less than twenty years thereafter, tannery and shoemaking had made such strides, that boots and shoes became articles of export. That these were no fancy beginnings in manufactures, we may strikingly learn from an Act of Parliament passed in 1698. Notice the date. This law is a sample of many more:—"*After the first day of December, 1699, no wool, or manufacture made or mixed with wool, being the produce or manufacture of any of the English plantations in America, shall be loaden in any ship or vessel, upon any pretence whatsoever,—nor loaden upon any horse, cart, or other carriage,—to be carried out of the English plantations to any other of the said plantations, or to any other place whatsoever.*" Thus the fabrics of Massachusetts were forbidden to find a market in Connecticut, or to be carried to Albany to traffic with the Five Nations. "That the country which was the home of the beaver might not manufacture its own hats, no man in the colonies could be a hatter or a journeyman at that trade, unless he had served an apprenticeship of seven years. No hatter might employ more than two apprentices. No American hat might be sent from one plantation to another." In 1701 the three charter colonies are reproached by the lords of trade "*with promoting and propagating woollen and other manufactures proper to England.*" In 1721 New England alone had six furnaces and nineteen forges, and there were many others in Pennsylvania and Virginia. Parliament enacted in 1750 that no more mills should be erected in America for slitting or rolling iron, or forges for hammering it, or furnaces for making steel; and in certain cases, agents of the crown were authorized to tear down such establishments as "*nuisances.*" How far all the arts of navigation had been carried in the Colonies before the Revolution, every one may read in Burke's famous speech on Conciliation with America. How far the products of the loom, the forge, and the anvil, were already being exported, in spite of British legislation, to other countries, any one may see in Lord North's last proposals and concessions to ward off Independence.

Protectionism having once fed its petted beneficiaries from the public crib, that is to say, from taxes wrenched from the many to enrich the few, invariably clamors for more and more rations for its pets from the same public source. Not only does no industry become self-supporting by its bite and its sup, but each becomes according to its own facile representations and representatives, more and more helpless in itself, more and more shameless in its demands, more and more *entitled* to public charity, and less and less inclined to surrender one iota of past or present privilege. The daughters of the horse-leech cry continually, Give! Give! The following schedule relates to woollens mainly, but it is a fair sample of many other protectionized classes of goods under the successive tariffs in this country, in point of increased taxes on the people in their behoof. While these lines are being written, the McKinley tariff-bill, so-called, having passed the House, is pending in the Senate. It is significant, that this piece of legislation, whether it be finally enacted or not, proposes to open the second century of the United States Protectionism by largely hoisting the tariff-taxes along the main line. Infant industries indeed!

ARTICLES.	RATE OF DUTIES UNDER THE TARIFF OF					
	1791.	1859.	1861.	1864.	1883.	1890.
	Per cent.	Per cent.				
Dress goods of cotton and worsted, costing 15 cts. the sq. yd.	5	19	30	55 per cent.	68 per cent.	88 per cent.

Same, costing 20 cents sq. yd.	5	19	30 "	50 "	60 "	90 "
Same, all wool or of mixed materials, costing 24 cents sq. yd.	5	24	30 "	47 "	77 "	100 "
Same, costing 30 cents sq. yd.	5	24	30 "	55 "	70 "	90 "
Same, costing 60 cents sq. yd.	5	24	30 "	45 "	55 "	70 "
Same, weighing over 4 oz. sq. yd.	5	24	25% and 12 cts. per lb.	40% and 24 cts. per lb.	40% and 23 cts. per lb.	50% and 44 cts. per lb.
Ready-made clothing	7½	24	25% and 12 cts. per lb.	40% and 24 cts. per lb.	35% and 40 cts. per lb.	60% and 50 cts. per lb.
Tapestry Brussels carpets	7½	24	30 cts. sq. yd.	50 cts. sq. yd.	20 cts. sq. yd. and 30%	28 cts. sq. yd. and 30%
Tapestry velvet carpets	7½	24	50 cts. sq. yd.	80 cts. sq. yd.	25 cts. sq. yd. and 30%	40 cts. sq. yd. and 30%
Brussels carpets	7½	24	40 cts. sq. yd.	70 cts. sq. yd.	30 cts. sq. yd. and 30%	40 cts. sq. yd. and 30%
Druggets and bockings	5	24	20 cts. sq. yd.	25 cts. sq. yd.	15 cts. sq. yd. and 30%	20 cts. sq. yd. and 30%

Silk goods, including velvets and plushes	7½	19	30	per cent.	60	per cent.	50	per cent.	Average probably 90%
Woollen hosiery and underwear:									
Costing 32 cents per lb.	5	24	30	"	90	"	77	"	214	per cent.
Costing 42 cents per lb.	5	24	30	"	79	"	79	"	175	"
Costing 62 cents per lb.	5	24	30	"	62	"	74	"	135	"
Costing 82 cents per lb.	5	24	30	"	54	"	82	"	120	"
Linen goods	5	15	30	"	Average 37½%	35	"	50	"
Cotton hosiery:									
Costing 62½ cents per doz.	7½	24	30	"	35	per cent.	40	"	110	"
Costing 2.10 cents per doz.	7½	24	30	"	35	"	40	"	76	"
Costing 4.10 cents per doz.	7½	24	30	"	35	"	40	"	64	"

It is also significant in this connection to read an extract from the Report of Mr. William Whitman, President of the National Association of Wool Manufacturers, dated March 29, 1890, to the Stockholders of the Arlington Mills, Massachusetts. "*I have been your Treasurer for a consecutive period of twenty years. During this period the average earnings have been 20 $^8/_{10}$ per centum upon the capital. The earnings of the last year were nearly three and a half times those of the year* *previous, and there is every indication that the current year will be the most profitable one in the company's history."*

Fallacy C: *that a home market is better and broader than a foreign market.* Professor Thompson of Pennsylvania has publicly and repeatedly stated, that, by a persistent policy of Protectionism a "home market" would be created for all the bread-stuffs that this great country produces; and John Roach, the shipbuilder, expatiated at length before the Tariff Commission of 1882 on the advantages the farmer derives from the better "home market" already created by Protectionism. To come nearer home in place and further down in time, there was organized in Eastern Massachusetts with headquarters at Boston in some connection with the national election of 1888, a so-called "Home Market Club" of large proportions. It is generally understood in the State, that a large minority, if not a majority, of the members, are displeased with the McKinley Bill of 1890, declaring that the mustard is carried to fanaticism in this bill, that neither the "home market" nor any other can profit by such a series of prohibitions.

However this last may be, it is plain, that a ridiculous and most harmful fallacy underlies all references to a "home market" in any connection with foreign trade. It is simple Gospel charity to believe, that Thompson and Roach and the founders of the Home Market Club and all others, who repeat this wretched stuff, never stopped in their thoughts long enough to inquire what a "market" really is, never analyzed into its simple elements that composite thing called a "market," but each and all in turn have taken up a catch-word carelessly which seems on the surface to have some significance though in reality it has none.

All will agree, if they will stop to think, that a "market" is always made up of *buyers* with return-services in their hands. A bigger home market than before consists only in more domestic buyers than before, all ready with acceptable pay in all their hands. More persons than before, more services-in-return than before. Now, if Protectionism *can enlarge the home market,* it must be (1) either by increasing the number of births or diminishing the number of deaths in a given time in a given country. Precisely how big bundles of big taxes, which the whole population must pay in one form or another and over and over again, may be made to stimulate births or prolong lives, no reasonable man can see, and it is not unreasonable to deny that a protectionist can see it. But conceding that he can see and show this, his task is then but half done, for he must proceed to see and show how these same onerous taxes are able (2) to multiply the return-services in the hands of this increased population!

If he think at all, the protectionist is compelled to remember, that his system is always and everywhere a series of prohibitions on profitable trade.

A profitable trade always gives birth to gains. It always gives birth to Capital. It always gives birth to Plenty. That is the nature of it, and the Divinely ordained blessing on it. But when the greater part of these gains are artificially cut off, when the possible capital is reduced in volume, when the scarcity comes in which is the primary *purpose* of Protectionism to create, it shall go hard if there be even as many return-services as when the process began. Not a better "home market," but a more meagre one, is the inevitable issue of restrictions and prohibitions.

If our protectionist try to get out of this snug place, in which he now finds himself, provided he is able to feel the force of any logic whatever, by claiming that his broader "home market" is to be made by new immigrants with old-world values in their hands to buy with, he certainly cannot escape by this route, because (1) he must in order to do this see and show what there is in big taxes enormously multiplied to invite immigrants here at all; and (2) our typical protectionist is scared to death by the *handiwork* of foreign "pauper labor" wherever exposed for sale, and of course he is not prepared to welcome the pauper laborers themselves, of which class as described by him the immigrants would mostly consist; and besides, the tariff would not admit to our shores the old-world values, which would be the immigrants' sole *return-services* to help make up the new market!

Within a week of the present writing, Senator Morrill of Vermont has broached from his place the idea in debate, that the industries of the United States can be so stimulated by protectionism as to cause the consumption of all the agricultural products of the United States. Well, when? The stimulus has been applied now just thirty years under Mr. Morrill's own eye, and by a tariff called by Mr. Morrill's own name, increasing its rates every little while, even in 1883, when the public pretence was to diminish them; and agricultural products of all kinds, including lard and pork and wool, have never been so "deadly dull" as in this interval of high protectionism. Scores of thousands of bushels of well-ripened Indian corn were burned for fuel in the more western States and Territories the very last winter, because the market for it was too poor to pay for its transportation to Chicago over protectionized rails, and in cars built of tariff-cursed lumber, every nail and bolt and screw in which doubled in price from the same general causes. If Mr. Morrill were not in his dotage, or if in his prime he had ever closely analyzed a single case of trade, foreign or domestic, he would see that the abandoned farms of his own State reckoned to be about one-third of the cultivated land on the eastern slope of the Green Mountains to the Connecticut River,—Mr. Morrill's own native region and residence,—abandoned farms for two years past assiduously sought by State officials to be filled in if possible by immigrants from Sweden virtually giving them the lands and farm-buildings,—fling out their flat contradictions to this senatorial drivel; that the constant decline for a quarter of a century of the farming population in every State in New England gives the lie to this miserable proposition; and that the constantly increasing area of mortgaged farms in every agricultural State in this Union is an overwhelming proof that the "home market" for farm staples has been growing constantly worse for years under this boasted protectionism.

The year 1890 is likely to prove the pivotal point of time in the swing of this whole proposition of Deceit, for two reasons, namely, (1) it is the year of the decennial Census, in which at least a half-hearted attempt is being made to bring out the aggregate area in each State of the mortgaged farming lands, and nothing can prevent the appearance in which of the lessening volumes of population in the purely agricultural communities; and (2) the year has already been marked by the political revolt from the party of protectionism of the masses of the farmers in the Mississippi Valley, and their organization into "Farmers' Alliances," naturally and demonstrably hostile to all Restrictions on the sale of farmers' produce.

Fallacy D: *that protectionism tends to raise the wages of general laborers*. In our third chapter, the whole doctrine of Wages was clearly and carefully laid down, and it is only needful now to remind the reader of two or three of those fundamental principles. The Labor-giver and the Labor-taker only touch each other at the old points of reciprocal Desires and Renderings. There are two persons standing in that relation each to each. A rate of Wages is always a result of a Comparison. If the Labor-takers, whoever they may be, more strongly desire the services of the Labor-givers, whoever they may be, other things remaining as before, there will be a rise in the rates of Wages, because Effects always follow the operation of Causes in Economics, as in all other scientific spheres; and if the Labor-takers, for any reason, desire less than before the services of Laborers, other things being equal, the general rates of Wages will decline of necessity.

Now, what is the necessary effect of Protectionism upon the general Demand for Laborers? How is the whole class of Labor-takers affected by prohibitory tariff-taxes? Note every time, that it is the presently and independently *profitable* industries, the industries that ask for nothing except to be let alone, that are struck and restrained by these tariff-taxes; the fact that any industry is successfully going forward under its own motives is sufficient proof of its own profitableness; these are the industries, in every case, which are curtailed by restrictive tariff-taxes, their former gains are lessened of course and by design, and their *motives* consequently to hire Laborers to carry on these branches of business now taxed and tormented are *lessened*; less Desire for Labor-givers gives laborers less every time round; the so-called argument of Protectionists is, to introduce alleged *unprofitable* industries by means of taxing down *profitable* ones; and pray, what effect must that have upon the general Desire to employ Labor-givers, and consequently what effect upon general rates of Wages?

Take one look further along this same line. Tariff-taxes of this character are designed to keep out, and do keep out, foreign wares, which are the natural and profitable market for domestic wares: how will this forced exclusion affect the Demand for laborers to make or grow the domestic wares whose market is now lost? And what is the influence on the Wages of those whose services are now in lessened Desire along the whole line? Causes produce their Effects everywhere and every time.

Dissatisfaction among, and actual disaster to, Labor-givers as a class, have always followed the imposition of protectionist tariff-taxes in this country, as a matter of plain observation and record; have followed increasingly and more disastrously increased restrictions and prohibitions on profitable trade; "Strikes" on the one hand to resist a lowering or secure a lifting of Wages, "Lockouts" on the other to bring laborers to terms, "Shut-downs" for pretended repairs in order to gain time to tide over the gluts that always accompany artificially restricted markets, semi-hostile relations between Employers and Employed, interruptions to travel and transportation, timidities of Capital fatal to new and enlarged enterprises, have never characterized this country so strikingly as during the quarter-century of Protectionism culminating in 1890.

The following table accurately compiled by Editor Philpott of Iowa, from the National Census, shows in remarkable figures the relatively slow rate of progress of the Nation in thirteen essential items of growth under the Morrill Tariff, as compared with the rapid rates of progress in the leading lines under the Walker Tariff. *The comparison lies in the per centum of increase over the previous decade of the period 1850-60 relatively to each of the two periods 1860-70 and 1870-80: the average of the last two periods is taken for the sake of an easier comparison of the progress of the one decade (Walker) with the average of the two later ones (Morrill).*

Lines of Progress.	1850-1860.	Average each Ten years—1860-1880.
Population	35.5	26.2
Wealth	126.6	61.0
Foreign commerce, aggregate	131.0	45.6
Foreign commerce, per capita	70.3	15.2

Railroads, aggregate	240.0	69.0
Railroads, per capita	150.0	34.0
Capital in manufactures	90.0	66.0
Wages in manufactures, aggregate	60.3	58.2
Wages in manufactures, per hand	17.3	9.4
Products	85.0	69.6
Value of farms	103.0	23.6
Farm tools and machinery	62.0	27.7
Live stock on farms	100.0	17.3

The State of Massachusetts has been diligently and scientifically taking the Statistics of everything relating to Laborers as such for many years; and we take now by way of confirmation of what has just been written a few statements of fact from the official Reports. *One-third of Massachusetts wage-earners were out of work one-third of the time under the benign influence of Protectionism . Wages went down in Massachusetts on the whole average 5 per centum 1872-83, while in the same interval of time they went up 9 per centum in Great Britain . Wages in Massachusetts advanced in 1830-60 (Walker) 52 per centum and in 1860-83 only 28 per centum (Morrill). What is called the needful cost of living increased in Massachusetts between 1860 and 1878 (Morrill) 14½ per centum in spite of immense cheapenings in costs of production and transportation .*

The U. S. Government has been gathering for a long time important Statistics relating to Laborers and their Wages and their Costs of Living, not only in the decennial Censuses but also in Consular Reports and in the Reports of a national Commission established for that purpose. We excerpt a few relevant statements from these almost at random. *Wages in free-trade England are from 50 to 100 per centum higher than they are in any protectionized country on the Continent of Europe. The aggregate Values of this country increased 1850-60 (Walker) 126 per centum, and in 1870-80 (Morrill) only 80 per centum, after reducing the census values of 1870 to a gold basis. Vessels American-owned and American-built controlled three-fourths of our foreign carrying trade in 1856, and less than one-sixth of it in 1886.*

The Census of 1880 gives the total number of persons employed in the great subdivisions of industry in the United States as follows:—

Trade and transportation	1,810,256
Manufactures, mechanical and mining	3,837,112
Professional and personal services	4,074,238
Agriculture	7,670,493

The following table compiled from the censuses of the last four decades will be found to yield food for thought in the light of the present paragraphs. *It relates solely to manufactured goods at the four successive epochs.*

	1850.	1860.	1870.	1880.
Value of products	$1,019,109,616	$1,885,861,676	$4,232,325,442	$5,369,579,191
Value of materials	555,174,320	1,031,605,092	2,488,427,242	3,395,823,547
Wages paid out	236,759,464	378,878,966	775,584,343	947,953,795
Materials to products, per cent	54	54	58	63
Wages to products, per cent	22	21	18	17
Average wages earned	$247	$289	$377	$346
Capital to products, per cent	52	53	50	50
Number of establishments	123,029	140,433	252,148	253,852

Average hands each	7.79	9.34	8.16	10.79

Our manufactures were put down in the Census of 1880 as in value $5,369,579,191. But this sum contains $1,670,000,000 that does not strictly belong to manufactures, such as flouring, lumbering, blacksmithing, sugar-refining, coffee-roasting, slaughtering, and a few others. This sum being taken out, there is left in round numbers but $3,700,000,000. This is not a great amount for 50,000,000 of people, and for a land with such natural advantages for manufacturing as our own.

Fallacy E: *that the costs of Wages to employers and of Materials to manufacturers somehow justify Protectionism.* The harmful confusion is constantly made here between Rates of Wages and Costs of Labor—two very diverse matters. Rates of Wages depend on a very different set of circumstances from Costs of Labor. Failure to draw this distinction, and a desperate desire to clutch even at a straw with which to bolster up absurd Restrictions, have made a hotch-potch and a caricature of attempted argument at this point. Rates of Wages have always been relatively high in this country as compared with the countries of Europe for two general reasons: (1) the country is new, with enormous natural advantages of every sort, with comparatively few laborers competing steadily with each other for work, large numbers of persons passing constantly out of the employed into the employing classes; and (2) there has almost always been from the first, and there is likely to be again in the immediate future even if there be not at the present moment, a Money in this country depreciated below the gold standards of Europe, in which the rates of current wages are always reckoned, and which makes them *seem* to be higher than they actually are in purchasing-power. On the other hand, Costs of Labor have always been, and are now, low in this country as compared with Europe, for two general reasons also: (1) all classes of laborers are more efficient and skilled in this country than in Europe, working with more energy more hours in the week, under less cost of superintendence, being as a rule more temperate and healthful and educated persons, so that employers *get more for what they give* than do employers abroad; and (2) the cost of that to the employers in which the laborers are paid, whether money or other valuables, is always less here than abroad, because the money usually is depreciated money which costs less in commodities, and even if it be not, the current prices of general commodities are higher here than there, so that the cost of wages paid directly or indirectly in commodities is less here to employers.

A second and distinct and wholly convincing proof, that the Cost of Labor to employers has been less here than abroad during the first century of our national existence, has been the unquestioned fact, that the Rate of Profits has been higher. A constant stream of foreign Capital has come hither for investment, drawn solely by the higher rates of Profit. But if the rates of Profit have proven to be higher, the costs of Labor must have been lower, because laborers and capitalists divide the whole returns between them. Nobody else has any claim upon the conjoint proceeds. *Profits are the Leavings of the Costs of Labor.* If, therefore, these Leavings are larger in one country than another, then of necessity the Costs of Labor are lower in the first country.

Now, Protectionists have had the effrontery (largely the result of ignorance) to contend, that they are at a disadvantage as employers of laborers on account of the rates of Wages they are obliged to pay to them! *Exactly the reverse is the truth.* Instead of being at any disadvantage at this point, it is a matter of absolute demonstration, that American employers pay the smallest costs of Labor in the world! Employers as such have no interest in the rates of Wages as such, but only in the costs of Labor to themselves as capitalists. High rates of Wages not only usually accompany low costs of Labor, but also are a proof of them! The patient (not to say stupid) American People have consented for thirty years past to be abominably taxed for the exclusive benefit of a set of brazen mendicants, on the ostensible ground, that the said public beggars were unfortunately placed in comparison with European competitors, when the simple truth has been, that they had a constant advantage in the best, and cheapest (in cost to themselves), and steadiest and most intelligent (on the whole), laborers in the world.

What is the truth about raw materials in this country? Especially raw materials in those branches of industry, which have been most steadily protectionized from the first, like iron and copper, and cottons and woollens? Can any reason be found for legislatively excluding foreign products of these classes on the ground of any disadvantage of our producers on the score of raw materials? Look at iron ore, for example, now protectionized to the extent of 75 cents per ton. No country in the world possesses such deposits in quantity and quality and accessibility of iron ore as the United States of America. Vast beds of the best ore in the world, especially in wide regions along the whole course of the Tennessee River, lie directly upon the surface of the ground; and the so-called "Iron Mountain" in Missouri is said to have ore enough above the general surface of the country round to supply the wants of the entire United States for two centuries! Yet every ton of this ore is artificially lifted in price to the very People to whom God gave it in exceeding abundance. The average cost of mining, washing, screening, and loading upon steam freight-cars for transportation to market, of brown-hematite ore at one of the Mines in

Tennessee during the summer and autumn of 1890, was 33 cents per ton, with a constant downward tendency in cost as machinery was multiplied and methods improved. This included the rent paid to the owners of the land holding the ore-beds, and every other item of cost carefully computed by the owner of the capital and manager at the mines. This statement is made on the authority of the said owner and manager over his own sign manual, with his consent given that it be printed as at present in the interest at once of Science and Righteousness.

It has often been publicly stated by experts, that there is more coal in deposit in the United States than in all the rest of the world put together. Nevertheless, bituminous coal has been protectionized since 1874 to the extent of 75 cents per ton, and slack or culm (another form of coal) 40 and 30 cents per ton. The bounty of God to the people of this country has been so far forth thwarted by the greed of mine-owners acting on the subservience of members of Congress to the few rich combined for that purpose to the impoverishment of the unorganized masses. Especially has every interest of New England both popular and manufacturing been sacrificed to the short-sighted selfishness of the mine-owners, because the British Provinces, just to the northward, are full of bituminous coal waiting for a market against New England goods.

Limestone is a second indispensable requisite for the reduction of iron ores. God has put the ore and the coal and the lime in unfailing quantities in close proximity with each other throughout the entire valley of the Tennessee. So small is the natural cost of making iron in that favored region, that it has been transported this summer to Savannah by rail (freights heightened by tariff-taxes on steel rails and lumber), and then exported 3000 miles to Liverpool with good profits to the makers by their own confession.

Steel rails are protectionized at present to the extent of $17 per ton, formerly $28 per ton. Fortunately, we have at present a competent National Labor-Commissioner, heretofore in the service of Massachusetts in the same capacity, Carroll D. Wright, who has just made a Report to Congress on the comparative cost of producing steel rails here and abroad. The following table is national and official and indisputable. It shows the Element of Cost in one ton of steel rails in Eleven distinct establishments, the first Two being located in the United States, the next Seven in countries on the Continent of Europe, and the last Two in Great Britain. The first column gives the Cost of the Material in the several districts, the second the Cost of Labor, and the third the total cost of the rails.

Distinct Establishments.	Materials.	Labor.	Total Cost.
1	$21.10	$1.54	$24.79
2	25.11	1.38	27.68
3	17.67	1.04	19.57
4	18.06	2.51	22.18
5	18.06	4.64	25.65
6	18.23	2.58	23.12
7	18.10	2.68	23.19
8	18.66	2.97	23.74
9	23.42	2.01	27.02
10	18.05	2.54	21.90
11	16.39	1.36	18.58

The reader who knows how to read between the lines will observe the strong confirmation of this table to the point already made in these pages, namely, that the "pauper labor of Europe" costs much more at a given point than the more highly paid labor of England and the United States. Thus: the average Cost of Labor in a ton of rails in the two latter countries is $1.70; the average in the seven Continental countries is $2.63. The average total cost per ton in the nine foreign countries is $22.77; the average in the two establishments here is $26.23. It must be remembered, that the cost of the material and of all the processes of manufacture here is greatly enhanced by the device of the tariff-taxes: still the difference in cost is even then only $3.46 per ton greater than the foreigners' cost: considering that these foreign rails must be carried 3000 miles over sea, how comes it that a tariff-tax of $28 or $17 per ton is needful in order to foster rail-making in this country? Take off all the tariff-taxes the rail-makers and transporters have *to pay out*, and could they not well forego the additional taxes they now impose on their fellow-citizens? Is there anything anywhere in the natural costs of Materials and Labor here to put American manufacturers at any disadvantage in their natural lines of business as compared with foreigners in *their* natural lines of industry?

Fallacy F: *that artificial tariff-burdens placed at one point may become a compensation for other such burdens placed at another point of the same general line.* This fallacy has been luridly illustrated in this country since 1867, when in the Wool and Woollens Tariff of that year additional protectionism was accorded to Woollens ostensibly to compensate the manufacturers for protectionism then first accorded to raw wools. For a number of years the woollen manufacturers had succeeded in persuading the wool-growers not to demand of Congress tariff-taxes on raw wools, thus publicly confessing that such taxes raise the prices of materials to the manufacturers thereof. But the wool-raisers argued naturally, if protectionism be good for woollens, it must also be good for wools; the truth was, it was equally baneful to both, and to every other beneficiary of it in the long run; but the wool-workers had no answer to the simple logic of the wool-growers,— they gave their case away when they alleged that *they* could not live without government aid,—and so they were obliged to surrender to their already angered brethren of the fleeces in 1867, and higher tariff-taxes were put on the woollens in order to compensate the manufacturers for the anticipated rise in the price of wools. Of course it was supposed that the patient people would bear the now doubled burdens put upon them by *two* privileged sets of their fellow-citizens. If protectionist taxes made the manufacturers rich, why should they not also enrich the rural herdsmen? In short, why may not such taxes make everybody rich?

There were those at the time, and the present writer was one of them, who foresaw and foretold just what has actually happened, namely, that both allies in this scheme of popular plunder were going in to their own death as well as in to the impoverishment of their countrymen. How would any level-headed man, capable of seeing beyond the point of his nose, have prognosticated in the premises? Something like this: it takes many kinds of wools mixed, say six or eight, to make the best woollen cloths, and several kinds to make good cloths at all; the United States could only furnish two or three kinds, and these in quite limited quantities; the tariff-taxes would raise the price of the foreign wools by just so much, to the detriment of the manufacturers, who could no longer buy the foreign wools, needful for good cloths, and must consequently drop down to inferior cloths in their mills, using shoddy and cotton and what not: how will that affect the market for native wools, especially the fine Ohio and Vermont wools? Only as the manufacturers are prosperous in making good cloths that find a quick and wide market at home, can the growers find a good market for their wool; from these heavy taxes on their material and machinery and lumber and dye-stuffs and so on, the manufacture will surely droop, and employ itself on poor goods from cheap materials, and the market for native fleeces will droop in consequence, and the prices of home-wools will go down and down and down of necessity.

Precisely this has happened. The gold prices of wool were never before so low in this country as since the unholy alliance of 1867, and as a rule they have gone down lower and lower and lower. Why? Because the manufacturers *could* not, under the tax-laws of their country which they themselves had egged on, make the cloths demanding the native fine wools. Sheep-raising became unprofitable. Millions of fine-woolled sheep were slaughtered in a few years for their pelts and mutton in Ohio alone. The following official table from the Department of Agriculture exhibits the relative number of sheep in thirteen States of the Union, at the two epochs 22 years apart:—

States.	Feb. 1867.	Feb. 1889.
Maine	895,884	547,725
Vermont	1,335,980	365,770
New York	5,373,005	1,548,426
Pennsylvania	3,456,568	935,646
Kentucky	933,193	805,978
Virginia	700,666	435,846
Missouri	1,005,509	1,109,444
Illinois	2,764,072	773,468
Indiana	3,033,870	1,420,000
Ohio	7,159,177	4,065,556
Michigan	4,028,767	2,134,134
Wisconsin	1,664,388	793,146
Iowa	2,399,425	540,700
	34,750,504	15,475,839

The effect of the tariff-taxes on wools, accordingly, even during a period when the population of the country increased 65 *per centum*, has been *to diminish the number of sheep in the hands of the farmers by more than one-half.* The wool clip in the entire country has indeed increased since 1867, but it has been in Texas and on the free ranges of the extreme boundaries of civilization in the West, where about one pound in three of the gross fleece is clean wool, and the most favorable estimate of the present clip would only suffice to clothe about one-half of the people of the country. Does this look like becoming "*independent*" of the rest of the world in the matter of woollen clothing for our great People? Will our folks never learn that there is nothing "*dependent*" in Buying and Selling, that the more any individual or nation Buys and Sells the more *independent* they become of course, and that the hermit in his poverty-stricken cell is the best image of Protectionism?

The extra barriers heaped up in 1867 against foreign woollens not only did not lessen their importation, but in connection with the discouragements thrown upon the domestic manufacture as just explained increased the importations; so that, in 1877, imports of woollen goods stood at $25,000,000; and in 1882 had increased to $42,000,000, the latter being an increase in one year, from 1881, of 34 *per centum*. The people must be clothed at some rate, and many people will have good cloth at any cost; and the whole result of this imbecile policy of Prohibitions on wool and woollens has been demonstrated right before our eyes, (1) to kill off the sheep, (2) to compel the manufacture of poor goods, (3) to multiply foreign woollens in domestic use, and (4) to double in general the cost of clothing the American People. It is difficult to say whether the grangers as a class, or the manufacturers as a class, or the consumers of woollens, are more put out by this state of things. They are all in the slough together, and have only themselves to thank for their condition. And it is growing worse and worse. As a mere and small example, less than one-half the amount of woollen machinery is now in operation in Berkshire County, Massachusetts, that was running here 15 years ago; and three-fourths of all the woollen manufacturers doing business in the County have failed in the 20 years just now past. In one word, *it is no compensation to one industry for artificial burdens piled upon it, to pile corresponding burdens upon other industries affiliated with it.* ALL LEGITIMATE INDUSTRIES EVERYWHERE ARE INTIMATELY AFFILIATED WITH EACH OTHER.

Fallacy G: *that because some kinds of prosperity sometimes accompany and follow after Protectionism, therefore they are caused by it.* This is at once the commonest and the hollowest of the forms of false argumentation employed in this country to bolster up a monstrously unjust Privilege. The rapid growth of Chicago, for example, in the ten years following the first imposition of the Morrill tariff-taxes, was often referred to, as if the Taxes caused the Growth. Admitting for argument's sake, what would be the height of folly to admit in reality, that these Taxes were *among* the causes of that Growth, how absurd to refer to one antecedent the result of one hundred or one thousand antecedents! So of the growth of national population in the twenty years following the Wool and Woollens Tariff of 1867: population increased about 65 *per centum* in that interval: tariff-taxes on most of the necessaries of life increased in the same interval just about in the same proportion: was there any tie of Cause and Effect as between the rise of taxes and the rising tide of population? Any *tendency* in the one to bring the other? Because one thing *follows* another in point of time, is that any proof that the second is the *result* of the other in point of cause?

In the old classification of Logical Fallacies this particular one was called by the Romans "*post hoc ergo propter hoc*," that is, *after something therefore on account of that thing*. The thoughts and the speech of civilized men have always been full of some form of this incongruity of inference; but it is the stock in trade, the staple and body of protectionist argumentation. But it is utterly devoid of any significance whatever. Unless some natural tie of connection can be shown, as between precedent and consequent, unless it can be probably shown that *nothing but* the precedent could cause the consequent, unless taxes are adapted in their very nature to increase riches, unless repeated subtractions can be shown to be the same thing as multiplied additions, then all this sickening talk of cheapening prices and intensified activities and diffused popular blessings under an odious scheme of subtle taxes that only *take* and can never *give*, is to be treated with a silent and pitying contempt, whether used by the duped or the duping. A good instance of this empty form of reasoning,—much better because more uniform than any one ever sought to be applied in the realm of Trade,— would be this: the Day has uniformly followed after the Night ever since the dawn of Time, and therefore the Night is the cause of the Day!

It has been indeed hard work to destroy the commerce utterly of a great People by legal restraints however multiplied and by mountain-barriers however piled up, and some prosperity has pushed itself into prominence after all these and in spite of all these. Behold! cry the logical protectionists, behold in such prosperity the *effects* of our beautiful legislation! Immeasurable areas of fertile land to be had by all Immigrants for the asking; endless deposits on every hand of coal and of all the useful and precious metals; primeval forests and streams leaping with power from their mountain springs to mill-wheel and intervale; commodious land-locked ocean harbors on every side but one, and vast chains of inland "unsalted seas"; a salubrious climate, and an ingenious, well-trained people; self-organized and liberal governments, guaranteeing all rational liberties to the people—but one; all these antecedents and accompaniments go, as it were, for nothing in the minds and on the tongues of some of our citizens, as causes of accruing prosperity, in comparison with (as a cause) the commercial bondage at the one point possible under our liberal and blessed institutions.

These are seven of the fundamental Falsities of Protectionism. They might easily be made seven times seven, and even seventy times seven. But not one of them is to be forgiven. They are unpardonable sins against Science and Liberty and Progress. Any radical and comprehensive Falsehood, like Protectionism, practically contradicts the Truth at innumerable points. The test of any proposed truth is its harmony with other and acknowledged truths: the test of any suspected error is its contradiction to such truths. Enough has now been said to settle the place of any pretended right of a part of the people commercially to enslave the other part, and ultimately themselves also.

It only remains in this chapter, in the fourth place, to indicate briefly at a few points the course of OPINIONS in relation to commercial Restrictions and Prohibitions in general, such as exist at present in their most exaggerated forms within the United States, on the part of those best entitled by study and intellect and opportunity to form and formulate a candid judgment in such matters.

In respect to the personal motive and circumstances of those combining to frame such legal interferences with the natural liberty of their contemporaries, and the inevitable results of them, we will quote first from Sir Thomas More, a man of men, in his Utopia, written in 1516. "*The rich are ever striving to pare away something further from the daily wages of the poor by private fraud, and even by public laws; so that the wrong already existing, for it is a wrong that those from whom the State derives most benefit should receive least reward, is made yet greater by means of the law of the State. It is nothing but a conspiracy of the rich against the poor. The rich devise every means by which they may in the first place secure to themselves what they have amassed by wrong, and then take to their own use and profit at the lowest possible price the work and labor of the poor. And so soon as the rich decide on adopting these devices in the name of the public, then they become law. The life of the labor-class becomes so wretched in consequence that even a beast's life seems enviable.*"

The utter folly of supposing that a Parliament or a Congress or a Committee of either is fit to determine, or to have any voice in deciding, what shall or what shall not be manufactured or grown, what shall or what shall not be exported and imported, was never more happily exposed than by Adam Smith in his Wealth of Nations, published in 1776. "*The statesman who should attempt to direct private people in what manner they ought to employ their capitals, would not only load himself with a most unnecessary attention, but would assume an authority which could be safely trusted not only to no single person, but to no council or senate whatever, and which would nowhere be so dangerous as in the hands of a man who had folly and presumption enough to fancy himself fit to exercise it.*"

Alexander Hamilton, our first Secretary of the Treasury, and in some respects the most brilliant of all our statesmen, has often been claimed and referred to as a protectionist by those unfamiliar with his writings; but the paragraph of those writings, or the phrase of any authenticated conversation of his, has never been quoted and never can be, because they do not exist, which proves him to have been a "protectionist" in the modern, or any other proper, sense of that word. On the contrary, his deliberate and well-founded opinion in the premises is given at length in number XXXV of the Federalist, this number printed early in 1788: "*Exorbitant duties on imported articles serve to beget a general spirit of smuggling; which is always prejudicial to the fair trader, and eventually to the revenue itself: they tend to render other classes of the community tributary, in an improper degree, to the manufacturing classes, to whom they give a premature monopoly of the markets: they sometimes force industry out of its most natural channels into which it flows with less advantage; and in the last place, they oppress the merchant, who is often obliged to pay them himself without any retribution from the consumer. When the Demand is equal to the quantity of goods at market, the consumer generally pays the duty; but when the markets happen to be overstocked, the great proportion falls upon the merchant, and sometimes not only exhausts his profits, but breaks in upon his capital. I am apt to think, that a division of the duty between the seller and the buyer more often happens than is commonly imagined. There is no part of the administration of the Government that requires extensive information, and a thorough knowledge of the principles of Political Economy, so much as the business of taxation. The man who understands those principles best, will be least likely to resort to oppressive expedients, or to sacrifice any particular class of citizens to the procurement of revenue. It might be demonstrated that the most productive system of finance will always be the least burdensome.*"

Shrewd old Benjamin Franklin, impersonation of common sense and common honesty, ridicules in his sly way the whole wretched business in the columns of the "Pennsylvania Gazette" in 1789. "*I am a manufacturer, and was a petitioner for the act to encourage and protect the manufacturers of Pennsylvania. I was very happy when the act was obtained, and I immediately added to the price of my manufacture as much as it would bear, so as to be a little cheaper than the same article imported and paying the duty. By this addition I hoped to grow richer. But as every other manufacturer, whose wares are under the protection of the act, has done the same, I begin to doubt whether, considering the whole year's expenses of my family, with all these separate additions which I pay to other manufacturers, I am at all the gainer. And I confess, I cannot but wish that, except the protecting duty on my own manufacture, all duties of the kind were taken off and abolished.*"

In the first congressional debate on the Tariff after the new Government went into operation, that is, in 1789, Fisher Ames of Massachusetts, who had just before made the strongest plea against the Molasses Tax, the raw material of New England rum, became also the strongest stickler there for the protectionist view, that artificial manufactures may properly enough fasten and fatten upon Agriculture, like shell-fish upon ship-bottoms, and went to the root of the whole matter of that inevitable antagonism in a few frank and radical words, the best because the most truthful words that can be found upon that side in the century that has followed. "*From the different situation of the manufacturers in Europe and America, encouragement is necessary. In Europe, the artisan is driven to labor for his bread. Stern necessity, with her iron rod, compels his exertion. In America, invitation and encouragement are needed. Without them, the infant manufacture droops, and those who might be employed in it seek with success a competency from our cheap and fertile soil.*"

Gouverneur Morris, one of the youngest and among the most gifted of the Revolutionary statesmen, had a clear insight into Economic realities. "*Whatever saves Labor rewards Labor.*" "*Those who will give the most for money, in other words, those who will sell cheapest, will have the most money.*" "*Taxes can be raised only from revenue: push the matter further, and their nature is changed: it is no longer taxation, it is confiscation.*"

CHAPTER VII.
TAXATION.

Political Economy is the Science of Buying and Selling. It must include of course in its discussions the Motives, the Methods, the Obstacles, the Rewards, relating to Sales, which are themselves first to be defined as furnishing the sole Field of the Science. We have now gone through with painstaking all of these topics in order, but we have not yet fairly struck Taxation, which is indeed in all its forms an obstacle to Sales, and in some of them the annihilation of Sales, but which in its nature is something much more than an obstacle, namely, a Condition of something higher than itself. In the very strictest sense of the terms, Taxation is not a part of the Science of Political Economy, because it is not an essential part of any one of those natural processes by which men buy and sell and get gain. It is rather a Condition through Government of the successful ongoing of all those processes. There cannot be, therefore, a *science* of Taxes, as there is unquestionably a science of Sales. The facts of Taxes are artificial and governmental, the facts of Sales are natural and original.

All forms of Production, as we have now seen, go forward in accordance with positive natural forces and motives, which God has appointed, and which men have a natural impulse to ascertain and generalize and profit by; for it is Nature bids men work and save, buy and sell, invent and transport, navigate and grow rich; but Nature has given no whisper anywhere, at least that we can hear, about any Taxes. That is the work of Society. That seems to be something negative, not positive, so far as Buying and Selling is concerned. Taxation is indeed something necessary to the social order, as men are; it furnishes means of defence against greater evils than itself is; but in itself considered, it is an economic evil, because it takes away from exchangers a part of the gains of their exchanges; strictly speaking, therefore, it cannot be made a part of Economic Science.

But, on the other hand, as we shall see at length in the exposition that follows, all the relations of Taxation from the beginning to the end are so ultimately connected with Exchanges, are so founded on and limited by Exchanges, its true principles are so exclusively economical, and its abuses are so instantly and constantly harmful to all the ongoings of natural and profitable Trade, that Taxation must always be treated as if it were a part of Economics. The latter is a science, the former is an art; but the art is almost exclusively dependent upon the principles of this one science; and a comprehensive treatise on the science, accordingly, must exhibit all its main bearings upon those practical rules of Taxation, which are so vital to the happiness and prosperity of any People. All scientific Economists, therefore, have considered the subject of Taxes to lie within their legitimate beat. They have, however, justified the inclusion upon very different grounds, one from another; and so far as now appears, the present writer was the first technical Economist to disclaim in the name of his Science direct jurisdiction over Taxation.

A careful discussion of a series of distinct though related Questions belonging to Taxes will exhibit the whole practical matter in the light of well-established principles of economical Science.

1. What is the fundamental GROUND of Taxes? *Government* is an essential prerequisite to any general and satisfactory Exchanges, since it contributes by direct effort to the security of person and property; and justly claims, therefore, from each citizen a compensation in return for the Services thus rendered to him. We do not mean to say that government exists solely for the protection of person and property, or that all the operations of government are to be brought down within the sphere of exchange, for government exists as well for the improvement as for the protection of society, and many of its high functions are moral, to be performed under a lofty sense of responsibility to God and to future ages; nor do we mean to say that government has not also a deep ground for its existence, in virtue of which it may on extraordinary occasions demand all the property of all, and even the lives of some, of its citizens; but we do mean to say that, whatever may be conceded as the ultimate ground of government, the matter of taxation, by which government is outwardly and ordinarily supported, and by which it takes to itself a part of the gains of every man's industry, finds a ready and solid justification in the common principles of Exchange. If, as far as the tax-payer is concerned, the exchange does not seem to be voluntary, on a closer analysis it is seen to be really voluntary; for in effect the people organize government for themselves, and voluntarily support it, and there is no government separate from the will of the people.

In a very important sense, accordingly, a tax paid is a reward for a service rendered. The service which government renders to Production by its laws, courts, and officers, by the force which it is at all times ready to exert in behalf of any citizen or the whole society when threatened with evil in person or property, is rendered somewhat on the principle of division of labor, one set of agents devoting themselves to that work; and, notwithstanding some crying abuses of authority which no constitution or public virtue has yet been found adequate wholly to avert, is rendered on the whole economically and satisfactorily. Taxes, therefore, demanded of citizens by a lawful government which tolerably performs its functions, are legitimate and just on principles of Exchange alone.

2. What is the SOURCE out of which Taxes are actually paid? The answer is, out of the gains of Exchanges of some sort. Gifts aside, and thefts which are out of the question, no man ever did, no man ever can, pay his taxes, except out of the gains of some sales which he has already made. Even the man who lives wholly on the interest of his money must make a true exchange in lending it (a credit transaction), and must already have gotten his return-service in interest, before he can pay his taxes; personal and professional servants must receive their wages, the outcome of exchanges, before they can possibly pay their taxes; and men can realize nothing for taxes or other payments from their farms or foundries or stocks in trade except as they sell either them or their products. The more sales, the more gains, and the greater reservoir whence taxes may be drawn. Political Economy, as the vindicator of sales, as the defender of all legitimate gains whatsoever, is the best possible friend of tax-payers and tax-gatherers as such. Whatever thought or force restricts sales, makes it *pro tanto* the harder to pay and collect taxes, so much the harder for a government to keep its head above water and reach the ends of its being.

It follows from all this, by a necessary inference, that the annual Taxes of any country must come out of the annual Earnings of the people of that country, using the word "earnings" in its general and proper sense. The greater the earnings *per capita*, the easier are the taxes paid. Sir Richard Temple read an address not long since in the Section of Economic Science and Statistics of the British Association, some of whose results are not only interesting but also astonishing. For instance, taking the whole population of the United Kingdom (England, Scotland, and Ireland), without division into classes, he demonstrates that the average of yearly earnings per head of the population is £35 4s., or $171.28. This exceeds the average earnings in the United States by 30%, £27 4s.:£35 4s. It exceeds also the average on the Continent of Europe by 95%, £18 1s.:£35 4s. It falls below that of Australia only, £43 4s.:£35 4s., or 19% less. Canada's average earnings *per capita* are $126.80, or 5% less than those in the United States, £27 4s.:£26 18s. According to the same unimpeachable authority in the same paper, the annual income from investments is in Great Britain and the United States as nearly as possible one-seventh of the aggregate Property in each (all kinds), or 14%. In Canada and Australia, 18% and 22% respectively. Undoubtedly the most profitable country in the world at present is Australia, and Great Britain stands next. The only apparent reason why the United States, whose natural resources of every kind are vastly superior to either, takes the third rank is, that profitable exchanges here are forcefully suppressed by law, and that to an enormous extent, neutralizing natural resources and glorious opportunities for easily acquired and widespread gains. This violent suppression of commerce by national legislation makes it just so much the harder for any man to pay his taxes, whether these be due to Nation, State, or Municipality. If the reservoir be diminished the flow from it through every pipe becomes feebler.

3. In what PROPORTION ought the individual citizens to contribute to the fund annually necessary to be raised by Taxation? The usual answer has been, that a man should be taxed according to his *Property*. That is the radically correct answer, though most who have given it have not understood clearly the meaning of the word *property*. We have already seen that the ultimate idea of property is the power and right to render services in exchange, and defined it as *anything that can be bought and sold*. Robinson Crusoe, while solitary upon his island, did not and could not have property, in the true sense of that word. It is not the fact of appropriation that makes anything property; it is not the fact that a man has made it or transformed it, that makes anything property; it is not the fact that a man may rightfully give it away, that makes anything property; but it is the fact that a man has something, no matter what it is, for which something else may be obtained in exchange, that makes that something property, and gives government the right to tax it. In other words, property consists in Values, in a purchasing-power, and not in possession, or in appropriation, or in the esteem in which a man holds anything he has as long as it is his own.

The test of property is a sale; that which will bring something when exposed for exchange is property; that which will bring nothing, either never was, or has now ceased to be, distinctively property. This view may not seem to be as novel as it is, or it may be prejudiced by its very novelty, but at any rate it carries along with it that strongest of the criteria of truth, that it simplifies and illumines a confused section of the field of human thinking; and at the same time justifies a practice which governments have reached, as it were through instinct, the practice, namely, of taxing men who have neither real estate nor chattels, on their incomes from industry and from credits.

To the general question, then, in what proportions shall the citizens contribute in taxes to the support of government, the general answer comes, that they ought to contribute *in proportion to the gains of their exchanges*, of whatever kind they may be. The farm, the foundry, the mill, the railroad, the real estate of every name; personal property of every kind; and personal acquirements and efforts of all descriptions, best appear, for the purposes of taxation, *through the gains realized by means of them*. If, for any reason, any of these become unproductive, taxes should cease to be derived from them; indeed, must cease to be derived from them, because their owners can no longer pay by virtue of them. It may be objected that lands, for example, presently unproductive, may be held untaxed under this principle, held for the sake of a prospective rise of price. Very well; when they are sold at a profit, let the owner be taxed on that profit: it will be time enough then, especially as men do not like to hold unproductive forms of property. It may also be objected, that, under this principle, wages, the result of personal and professional exertion, would be taxed just the same as profits and rents, the result of previously accumulated property. Very well; they ought to be so taxed. Can anybody give a solid reason why they ought not to be so taxed? One may say, that a professional man earning a large income, on which taxes are paid the same as on a similar income of a land proprietor, dying, leaves to his children no further means of earning, while the land-proprietor, dying, does leave such means. Granted; but the land income continues to pay taxes, while that professional income does not! Other members of the profession will do the business which the former one would have done had he lived, and they will pay taxes on the income from it. What a man transmits to his children, whether a great name or a great estate, has nothing to do with the amount of taxes that he ought to pay while he lives.

There is an illusion about lands and real property that needs to be dissipated before men will understand clearly the whole matter of Taxation. Without constant watchfulness and foresight, without constant efforts in improvements and repairs, almost every form of realized property will rapidly deteriorate and become unproductive. Land even in Great Britain, where land is scarce, is only worth about twenty-five years' rent; and without the exercise of intelligence and will property ceases to be. *Property has its birth in services exchanged; services exchanged give rise to gains; taxes can only be paid out of these gains; they ought to be proportioned to the amount of these gains without any reference to the class of exchanges producing them; while the right to tax on the part of the government is connected with a service rendered by government, and both grows out of and is limited by the right to exchange on the part of the citizens.* These considerations, though they may exclude the propriety of a poll-tax, are consistent with most other forms of taxation, and give unity to them.

4. Does it not follow from all the preceding, that a single and universal INCOME-TAX would prove the best form of what is in its own nature a subtraction from the gains of the governed for the maintenance of Government? If the approximate amount of Income could in all cases be ascertained, and if no other form of tax were levied upon the same persons, this would seem to be a perfectly unexceptionable mode of Taxation. The only sources of Income are three: Wages, Profits, Rents. It does not seem that gifts are legitimately taxable; they lie outside the field of exchange; they spring from sympathy, from benevolence, from duty; and while exchange must claim all that fairly belongs to it, it must be careful not to throw discouragements into the adjacent but distinct fields of morals. Hence, it may well be questioned whether legacies, bequeathments, gifts to charitable and educational institutions, and gifts to individuals proceeding from

friendship, gratitude, or other such impulse, are properly subject to taxation. The property is taxable in the hands of the donor, and may be in the hands of the recipient, but the passage from one to the other ought to be unobstructed by a tax. Gifts, then, excepted, and plunder, which is out of the question, the sources of income are few and simple, and there is no great difficulty in every man ascertaining about what his annual income is. Because this income, exactly ascertained, exactly measures the gains of his exchanges for that year, a tax upon that income is the fairest of all possible forms of taxation, and might be made with advantage, in time, to supersede all other forms.

Superficial objections may be easily raised, and are raised constantly in the United States, against any form of an income-tax. Reference is often had to our national experience with such a tax during and just after the late Civil War. The truth is, that tax was thrown on in addition to, and in no proper relations with, a large number of other national taxes of all sorts, good and bad; it was no possible experiment in Taxation, because there was no opportunity of watching its operation separate from that of other and confused forms; industry of all kinds was demoralized by the war, and still more by a depreciated and abominable paper money made legal tender for all debts; and the tax became unpopular in influential quarters for certain reasons not inherent in the nature of the tax, and was discontinued in consequence. In order to be fairly tested, an income-tax should either be exclusive, all other taxes being intermitted for the time being; or at least levied simply in itself in connection with a few other simple taxes, each of which can be watched in its incidence and results separately from the others.

Great Britain derives its national revenues almost wholly from five sources; namely, (1) Excises, say £27,000,000 annually; (2) Customs, say £20,000,000; (3) Incomes, say £12,000,000; (4) Stamps, say £12,000,000; (5) Postals, say £9,000,000. The remaining, say £10,000,000, come from miscellaneous sources. One feature of the English Income-tax is, that it is varied from time to time according to prevailing national needs, the rate having been lifted from 2d. to 16d. per pound of income, according to estimated expenditures. In 1857, it realized in our money $80,255,000. In 1866, the largest year, our own national income-tax realized $60,894,135. By varying the rate to the pound of income according to the prospective wants of the Exchequer, the English have found for about forty years their income-tax to be the most uniform, unfailing, expansive, and responsive to control, of all their fiscal expedients.

The Prussians, too, are applying an income-tax as a means of raising revenue with good success. There, as in England it is somewhat complicated with other kinds of taxes, and cannot exhibit itself altogether in its own nature as if it were *exclusive*, such as all scientific economists would like to see it tried somewhere on a large scale; and the Germans have a different method from the English, of making the tax more or less flexible as circumstances vary. The English change the *rate* of the tax to the unit of income: the Germans *graduate* the tax to different classes of income-receivers. For example, those persons having an income between 420 and 660 *marks* a year pay 84 pennies (*pfennige*) as income-tax; persons in the next higher class pay 164 pennies a year; those in the class, whose maximum income is 6000 marks, pay 44 marks and 80 pennies a year; and all persons whose income does not rise above 420 marks are not subject to this tax. On account of hard times a few years ago, Bismarck brought it about, that all the classes included between 420 and 6000 marks of income should be wholly exempted from one-quarter's taxes. A *mark* is 23.82 of our cents; and a *pfennig* is one-hundredth of a mark.

Besides the complete harmony of an Income-tax with the general principles of Taxation, as already unfolded, it has several specific advantages over other forms of Taxes.

a. It has no tendency *to disturb prices*. Were there no taxation except on Incomes, and were all the incomes rightly ascertained, the prices of everything would be just as if there were no taxes at all. Taxation would then be like the atmosphere, pressing equally on all points and consciously on none. It is through tricks wrought on Prices, that the greatest and most widely spread injustices have been done and suffered in this country during the past thirty years: a depreciated Money, whether of paper or silver, raises some prices and not others, and some prices before others, and thus distributes its mischiefs unequally; protectionist tariff-taxes play of design fantastic tricks with prices, raising some and depressing others, thus working monstrous injustice on a vast scale; and almost all forms of taxation become unequal and unjust through their diverse action on Prices. But a universal Income-tax exclusive of all others, properly levied and fully responded to by the payers, would have no influence at all upon prices, could by no possibility work essential injustice, and would be certain to be very productive without becoming burdensome.

b. A second great advantage of such an Income-tax in such a country as this, would manifestly be, that all men would be obliged to keep exact pecuniary accounts; more orderly methods of Business would generally prevail; most men would know much better than they do now how they stand themselves, and whom of others to safely trust; sudden commercial failures, indeed failures at all, would be less frequent and severe; and everything in the business world would be more aboveboard and better known.

c. A third advantage of such an Income-tax, and the chief, would be its tendencies *to fiscal simplicity*. Complexities in the Exchequer are always and in many ways expensive to the People. In this country, where distinct taxes have to be paid, first to the local municipality, then to the State, and last to the Nation, Income-taxes, were all others abolished, would have this striking advantage, that the local municipality might best ascertain the incomes of all its legal residents once for all, no matter from what sources local or other the incomes be derived; and, having collected its own local *per centum*, the State and then the Nation would each have to collect an additional *per centum* on the same income for themselves. Or, better still, by an amicable arrangement, neither party yielding up its inherent right to tax, one set of officials might ascertain the incomes and also collect the tax for all three governments once for all. It may be long, it doubtless will be, before we shall ever come to such economy and simplicity and fiscal beauty as this is; for the pride of sovereignty is very strong both in State and Nation; each is jealous of the powers of the other, each is fond of the pelf and patronage and officialism connected with the gathering of the taxes, and each would be disinclined to yield anything to the other; but the fact remains, that, as it is of acknowledged moment to have the single Cæsar's image and inscription on every piece of the national Money, so it is of almost equal moment in point of cheapness and clearness and simplicity to have the hand of Cæsar seen but once in taking in the Taxes.

Objection has been often raised to any form of Income-tax from the publicity of private affairs resulting from it. It was just this that proved fatal to our own first experiment along this line of national action. But there seems to be some confusion of ideas in connection with this phrase, "publicity of private affairs," for really, so far as taxation is concerned, there ought to be nothing "private" about the amount of any man's income, or the aggregate of all forms of his property, inasmuch as every man has a *right* to know, that all his neighbors are contributing *pro rata* with himself to support that Government, which is *common* to him and them. There is nothing, at least there should be nothing, "private" in connection with Government; that is the one absolutely "*public*" thing of the world; least of all should there be anything private in the matter of public taxes, since in bearing up the burdens of Government all the citizens are alike copartners, and in this view and for this purpose each has a right to demand a look into the books of all the others.

Another objection has often been raised, namely, that some men will never give in a true return of their Income. Ah! but they can be made to do so, as the forms are perfected, as fraudulent returns are promptly punished by additional assessment and collection, and as the memory and conscience of the payers are quickened by the action of a healthful public opinion brought to bear through the annual publication of the list of their returns. Men are not so isolated from each other as that a man's neighbors do not know pretty well the general amount of his income. There is the additional security of an oath, of the fear of punishment, and of the wish to stand well with one's class. At the worst, it may be said, that evasions and fraud accompany also all other forms of Taxation.

5. What is the difference between DIRECT and INDIRECT Taxes? This is an old and proper division: we must now see what is the economical basis of it. A direct tax is levied on the very persons who are expected themselves to pay it; an indirect tax is demanded from one person in the expectation that he will pay it provisionally, but will indemnify himself in the higher price which he will receive from the ultimate consumer. Thus an income tax is direct, while duties laid on imported goods are indirect. There has been a great amount of discussion on the point whether direct or indirect taxation be the more eligible form; but the reader of penetration will perceive that there is not at bottom any very radical difference between them; each is alike a tax on actual or possible exchanges, with this main difference, that men pay indirect taxes as a part of the price of the goods they buy, without thinking perhaps that it is a tax they are paying, and consequently without any of the repugnance that is sometimes felt towards a tax-gatherer who comes with an unwelcome demand. Thus indirect taxes are conveniently and economically collected. Especially is this true of impost taxes; since one set of custom-house officers may collect easily and at once the government tax which is ultimately paid by consumers all over the country. The taxes also levied by the present United States internal revenue law are indirect taxes, whereby the government gets in a lump what is afterwards distributed over many subordinate exchanges. The countervailing disadvantage of indirect taxation, however, is, that the price of the commodity is usually enhanced to an extent much beyond the amount of the tax, partly because it is a cover under which dealers may put an unreasonable demand, and partly because the tax, having to be advanced over and over again by the intermediate dealers, profits rapidly accumulate as an element of the ultimate price.

Direct taxes are laid either on Income or Expenditure. As the difficulty of a tax on a person's whole expenditure is much greater than one on his whole income, inasmuch as the items are more numerous and more diffused, it is only attempted to levy a few taxes on some special items of expenditure, such as those on horses, carriages, plate, watches, and so on; but as these do not reach all persons with any degree of quality, they are so far forth objectionable. A house-tax, levied on the occupier, and not on the owner, unless he be at the same time the occupier, would be a direct tax on expenditure every way unobjectionable. Taking society at large, the house a man lives in and its furniture are probably the most accurate index attainable of the size of his general expenditures. They are open to observation and current remark; they are that on which persons rely more perhaps than on anything else external for their consideration and station in life; the tax could be assessed with very little trouble on the part of the assessor; and it is well worthy the attention of our State and National Legislatures, whether such a tax, if more taxes should be needed, would not be more equal and more easy of collection than any others now open; or whether it might not with advantage take the place of some of the complicated and objectionable taxes now laid. Direct taxes have this general advantage over indirect, that they bring the people into more immediate contact with the government that lays the taxes, and subject it to a quicker supervision and more effectual curb, whenever its expenditures grow larger than the people think it desirable to incur; perhaps they have this general disadvantage over indirect taxes, especially over imposts, that the number of officials required to assess and collect them is larger, thus swallowing up a part of the proceeds of the taxes, with this liability also of bringing the people into an attitude of hostility to the government and to its contemplated expenditures. But whether the taxes be direct or indirect, or whatever be their form, except it be a poll-tax, which is questionable at best, they are laid upon Exchanges, and are designed to withdraw for the use of the government a part of the Gains of exchanges.

6. Are CREDITS a legitimate subject of Taxation? The answer is very easy. Unless this whole treatise from beginning to end be unsound, Credits stand upon the same economical grounds as Commodities and Services, and so may be taxed for the same reasons as those may be taxed. Whatever is bought and sold is properly enough taxed, if the needs of the government require it, and if such taxation would be productive and not too unequal. As Values always spring from the action of individuals, so the incidence of taxes is upon persons rather than upon things; and the question is what can a man sell, or what has he already sold, on the gains of which sale the government may lay some claim? If I have a note and mortgage on my neighbor's farm, I can sell it at any time to a third party; it pays me interest *ad interim*, and I can collect it at maturity. Government therefore properly taxes me for that credit in my possession. It is a part of my property. The holders of the government bonds occupy an economical position exactly similar. They have a lien on the national property and income. The credits they hold are vendible commodities. They are a paper bearing interest. They can be collected at maturity. They are indeed exempted by law from municipal and State taxation. That was a legitimate inducement held out to everybody alike to invest in the bonds. But there is no reason why the nation, having withdrawn them from town and State taxation, should not itself all the more subject them to their fair share of the national burdens,

unless indeed it be claimed, as perhaps it fairly may be, that the exemption enables the government to borrow at a just so much lower rate of interest. The income at any rate derived from the bonds should be taxed as soon as any other income is. It is no longer any ground of merit, even if it ever has been, for persons to buy the government debt. It is a mercantile transaction, and should be so considered in relation to taxes. So of other mercantile credits. They are taxable. Massachusetts has had a great deal of trouble of late years both in the Legislature and otherwise about the taxation of mortgages on taxed Massachusetts farms and other real estate. The question is intricate and full of difficulty. Some things about it, however, are clear. The note and mortgage is a different *piece* of property, and a different *kind* of property, from the real estate. It is a peculiar sort of credit. The owner of it is a different person from the owner of the real estate. Either bit of property may change hands without changing the *status* of the other. The question of taxing the note and mortgage, like the question of taxing the bonds, seems to hinge on the effect it would have on the rate of interest of the obligation secured by the mortgage. If the holder of the mortgage expects to have to pay a tax upon it, he will try to get a higher rate of interest on his money loaned and thus secured. Whether mortgagees taxed as such *can* throw off the tax upon the mortgagors in a higher rate of interest on the money loaned is a point much disputed and at least doubtful. General principles would lead us to favor the taxation of note and mortgages in the hands of their holders, so long as such cumbersome forms of taxing as prevail in Massachusetts are maintained. A universal income-tax would solve this difficulty also in a moment of time.

7. Has Political Economy anything to say about the RATE of taxes per unit of that which is subject to tax? Yes; it has an important word to say upon that point. From the very nature of Taxes in general, and in order that they may be most productive in the long run, as well as discourage as little as possible the Exchanges which would otherwise go forward, the Rate of taxes ought always to be *low* relatively to the amount of Values exchangeable. A high rate of tax not infrequently stops exchanges in the taxed articles altogether, and of course the tax then realizes nothing to the government. As the only motive to an exchange is the gain of it, the exchange ceases whenever the government cuts so deeply into the gain as to leave little margin to the exchangers. The greater the gain left to the parties, after the tax is abstracted, the more numerous will the exchanges become, and the greater the number of times will the tax fall into the coffers of the government. In almost all articles, consumption increases from a lowered price in even a greater ratio than the diminution of the rate of tax; so that the interests of consumers and of the revenue are not antagonistic but harmonious. On articles of luxury and ostentation, and on those, such as liquors and tobaccos, whose moral effects are clearly

questionable, very high taxes may properly enough be laid, because their incidence will hardly tend to diminish consumption, and it would scarcely be regretted if it did; but with this exception, duties and taxes should be levied at a low rate *per centum* as well for the interest of revenue as of consumers. It is to be added, however, that the taxes even on these articles may be too high to meet either a revenue or a moral purpose. The internal tax of two dollars a gallon upon distilled spirits was of this character. Experience has demonstrated that a less tax will produce more revenue, and the drinking of whiskey, bad as that is, is less culpable than the endless frauds on the government provoked by the high tax.

8. What is the difference between SPECIFIC and ADVALOREM Taxes, and why should the student take careful note of these both singly and combined? These terms are used more particularly in relation to Tariff-taxes, but there is nothing in the distinction itself so to limit its application. A Specific tax is a tax of so many cents or dollars on the pound, yard, gallon, or other *quantity* measurable: an Advalorem tax is a tax of so much *per centum* on the invoiced or appraised *money value* of the goods subject to the tax. Specific taxes, accordingly, are far simpler and steadier in their operation than the others; it is easy to ascertain the weight or number or other quantity of valuables, and then to apply a fixed ratio to them in the way of tax; the payer knows or may know beforehand precisely how much the tax will amount to, and consequently just how it is to affect the profitableness of his current trade; and on these and other grounds specific taxes are preferable to advalorem ones. To be sure, this form of tax involves that high-priced grades of an article pay no higher taxes than low-priced grades of the same, but this consideration is largely overbalanced by those of convenience and productiveness.

Advalorem taxes, on the other hand, are never calculable beforehand; because Values from their nature are variable, and as a matter of fact do constantly vary. Imported goods, for instance, bring with them the invoice of the seller giving the values at the place of exportation. But the importer is by no means sure that the tax will be levied upon that valuation. The home valuation will of course be higher, otherwise the goods would not be imported. Whenever it becomes the policy of a country, as of the United States at present, to keep foreign goods *out* to the utmost extent possible under the law, which law is itself devised on purpose to keep them out, there will always be suspicions and charges of undervaluations at the place of export; there will always be a motive on the part of the foreign seller or agent thus to undervalue the goods in the interest of the importer, so as to lessen his tax, and so increase the seller's market; such abnormal tariff-taxes are the enemy of mankind in general, and, therefore, there will be no end of deceits and evasions at both terminals of the ocean-route, and "custom-house oaths" will become a by-word of course; the importing, or rather the non-importing, country will keep in pay an army of spies and informers on both sides of the water in order to prevent what is called "frauds," and another army of "appraisers" at its custom-houses in order to discredit the invoices, and to jump at a valuation of the goods, on which the tax shall be levied; and honorable merchants and importers, without any fault of their own, are liable to get entangled in the miserable meshes of such goings-on, as happened in a memorable case in New York a few years ago, and be mulcted in fines (perhaps to immense amounts) one-half of which shall go to the informer.

There are too many practical difficulties connected with either of these two forms of tax to make it proper to combine the two upon the same article of merchandise. To combine them thus is one of the tricks and traps of Protectionism. That makes it next to impossible for any importer to tell beforehand what the two taxes will aggregate, and quite impossible for any ultimate consumer to tell how much of his price paid is due to the demands of his Government. Opening the official tax-book at random, we quote as follows from a single page: "Webbings, pound 50 cents, and 50 per cent"; "Buttons, pound 50 cents, and 50 per cent"; "Suspenders, pound 50 cents, and 50 per cent"; "Mohair cloth, pound 30 cents, and 50 per cent"; "Dress trimmings, pound 50 cents, and 50 per cent." Besides these, on that same page, there are 14 other articles under similar compound taxes, mostly at 50 cents a pound and 50 per cent additional, this as under the Tariff as it was 1874-83; but all these 18 articles were put in 1883 at "*pound 30 cents, and 50 per cent.*"

9. What are the economical reasons for an EXCISE or INTERNAL-TAX in connection with Tariff-taxes for revenue? A tariff-tax, whether for revenue or other purpose, raises the price by so much of the article subjected to it and actually imported; now, if similar articles of the same quality be made or grown at home, and be not subjected to a corresponding tax, these will inevitably rise to the price of the foreign, with the tariff-tax added, for there is no possible competition or conceivable impulse that can keep it lower than that; so that, in that case, the government gets in revenue, only the taxes paid on the part imported, while the people are compelled to pay in addition virtually the same taxes on all that part produced at home. Why should not the government have the proceeds of the last as well as of the first? The last is the direct result of the first. If now, a corresponding excise-tax be put on the domestic product also, the government will get in revenue all that the people are obliged to pay in consequence of government-tax. This is just: the other is wantonly unjust.

Take an illustration, please. The national Census of 1890 gives the Pig-iron production of the Census year as 9,579,779 tons of 2000 lbs. each. This is an increase over the production of the Census year, 1880, of 255 *per centum*,—3,781,021:9,579,779. Fortunately the present Census adds the net imports for the two years respectively, with these results: the *per capita* consumption of Pig-iron in 1880 was 196 lbs., of which 126 was home production, and 70 of foreign import; while in 1890 the consumption was 320 lbs. *per capita*, of which 299 was domestic, and 21 foreign. That is to say, in 1880, 65% of the pig-iron consumed in this country was of home production, and 35% was of foreign production. At that time the tariff-tax on imported pig was $7 per ton. Government secured this tax on a little more than one-third of what was consumed, while a small circle of citizens banded together for that purpose secured for themselves this tax on the remaining two-thirds of all pig-iron consumed that year, *and the whole people paid the tax on the entire three-thirds.* As we shall see fully a little further on, our national Government has no constitutional or other right to tax the people one penny except to supply its own needs as such; if, therefore, the $7 impost per ton were put on as a legitimate tax, there should have been an *excise* or internal-tax to the same amount put on the pig-iron produced at home. That would have cost the people no more, and the Government would have gotten twice as much more as it did get from the tax. If there be an axiom in Taxation, one point indisputable by any rational human being, it is this: *The Treasury should receive all that the people are made to give up under a public tax.*

In 1890, this particular matter came to be much more flagrant. Only 21 parts out of 320 parts were in that year foreign pig-iron; that is, a little less than 7%, while 93% was domestic pig-iron; the tariff-tax at that date was .3 of a cent per pound, or $6.72 per ton of 2240 lbs.; the tax was sufficient practically to exclude foreign pig, although the Scotch pig as more fluent is very much desired here in some branches of the iron manufacture, particularly in making steel rails; Government received the proceeds of its own tax on only one-fourteenth of that, which really paid the tax on its whole fourteen-fourteenths; where did the tax on the thirteen-thirteenths go to? If this were a matter of genuine taxation, ought there not to have been an *excise* on the domestic corresponding to the *impost* on the foreign?

Precisely that is what we do in the case of other articles not *protectionized*. For example, in the fiscal year 1889, the excise or internal-tax on "distilled spirits and wines" realized to the Treasury $74,312,200, and the tariff-tax on the same realized $7,123,062, total, $81,435,268; on "malt or fermented liquors" the same year, the excise was $23,723,835, the impost only $663,337, total, $24,387,172; and on "tobacco" the excise was $31,866,860, the impost $11,194,486, total, $43,061,346. These figures are official.

An ostentatious display of private figures and price-lists is often made, with a design to show that the prices of home-made products protectionized are not lifted so high to consumers or buyers as those of foreign-made products with the tariff-taxes added. The main sophistry in these figures is this: the pure assumption, that the *quality* of the home-made products alleged to be cheaper than the tax-added price of the foreign, is *the same* as that of the foreign. Unluckily, things are often called by the same names, and even described by the same technical terms, which are very different sorts of things in reality. A subordinate sophistry in these figures, often allowed to pass, but not requiring any sharp insight to detect, is, that the selected price-lists are not the results of an average extending throughout years, but are *picked* at points when (owing to other causes than the taxes) the current prices of protectionized home products are lower than the average of the years. One easy way to expose the putters-forth of these figures, as not themselves really believing in them, is, gravely to propose to lower or remove the tariff-taxes, which (it is alleged) do not have the effect to lift much, if any, domestic prices. This simple experiment has several times been tried, with ludicrous effect upon the figure-mongers; they cannot spare one iota of present taxes on foreign products: if the smallest fraction be removed, they can no longer make and vend their wares; indeed, heavier tariff-taxes are needed at this very moment, in order to lift the domestic prices higher; and, presto! another set of figures are forthcoming at once to prove the disabilities, either in respect to Labor or Capital, under which the poor protectionized producers are staggering in order to keep the home market!

Another complete refutation of the false position of the protectionists, namely, that the domestics are not lifted in price on the average to the price of the foreigns of the same quality with the tariff-taxes added, is their utter failure and inability to project any reason in the nature of things or the motives of men, why the *home-prices should* NOT *be thus lifted!* What impulse, pray, on the earth or under the earth, can serve to depress them on the whole average *below* that point? Does any one say, that "domestic competition" will depress and keep depressed the prices of home goods of the same grade below the prices of the foreign taxes paid? Did this astute objector ever hear of "domestic combination" to keep prices up to the highest possible point? To shut down mills and factories, to avoid depressing prices? To sell surplus stocks abroad for what can be gotten for them, in order to make prices at home up to the usual scarcity point? In July, 1890, the Boston Commercial Bulletin, the special organ of Protectionism in New England, and special spokesman for the wool-and-woollens industry, spoke thus of that industry, after 30 years of public hiring the growers and manufacturers to carry it on with a *bonus*, just at a time when the worsted tariff-taxes had been advanced, alleged custom-house frauds stopped, and still higher tariff-taxes on their way from the so-called McKinley Bill in Congress: "*The woollen goods industry was probably never in much worse condition in this country. The slowness of its development may be judged from the fact, that, despite an average yearly increase of over a million in population, the increase in the number of wool cards in this country is less than a hundred a year, while the proportion of woollen machinery shut down between June 1 and September 1 bids fair to be the largest ever known. The market is dull, deadly dull. The large amount of silent machinery is making its presence felt. The sluggish sales of wool are due to most of the big mills being closed. Depression in business is the cause of so many woollen mills closing, and the news comes this week of four woollen mills, three in the Bay State and one in Pennsylvania, that will close for periods ranging from two weeks to several months."*

Not only is it true, that the purpose and usual effect of tariff-taxes is to hoist the price of domestics protectionized up to the limit of the corresponding foreigns with the taxes added, but it sometimes happens that the home products are carried for considerable periods at a level a good deal above that. A conspicuous instance of this, commented on at the time by all the Boston papers, was brought to notice a couple of years ago in connection with the steel beams purchased by the city for the new and noble Boston Court-House. The beams were bought in Belgium at $28 a ton, paid at the Boston Custom-house *"one and one-fourth cents a pound,"* that is, just $28 a ton, making their cost to the city $56 a ton. But domestic steel beams of the same general description were selling here at $73 a ton. Their price had been raised here twice in one summer, about fifty cents a ton each time. One of the conglomerated curses of cutting off by law the natural competition in such products is, that the unnatural competition still permitted by law is sluggish in coming into operation, and the monopoly becomes even more such than was intended by the law.

The tariff-tax on steel rails is $17 a ton, formerly $28 a ton, proposed in the McKinley bill to be reduced to $11.20 a ton. That even this last is wholly needless, or any tax at all on steel rails, is proven by the fact, that in March, 1890, Pittsburg rail-makers sold 5000 tons of rails at Vera Cruz at lower prices than the corresponding European rails were offered for in Mexico. Another fact that proves the same thing is this: James M. Swank, the mouth-piece of the Pennsylvania iron and steel interests, describes the year 1885 as one of unprecedented prosperity in the steel-rail industry, and gives a formidable list of new establishments opened in that year. But steel rails were much lower in that exceptional year than in any year before or since. A tariff-tax of $5 a ton would have been in that year absolutely prohibitory, for steel rails were worth less than $28 a ton the greater part of that year. Yet that very year was the year of greatest prosperity, Mr. Swank being the competent witness! But the fact in general, which ought to overwhelm the iron and steel protectionists with confusion, if they were capable of any such emotion, is, that iron and steel in every form of both, owing to the unprecedented bounty of God to this good land, costs less both in labor and capital here than in any other country in the world. The official figures of the current Census demonstrate this, authentic statements of practical operators at the iron mines and furnaces and foundries throughout the Tennessee Valley confirm it, and there is not one particle of evidence to the contrary of any name or nature.

Let the reader notice carefully the following quotation from a private letter to the writer, dated July 30, 1890, written by a graduate of this college, in whom all who know him have the fullest confidence:

"*We began to open the mines here just three years ago this Fall, and began shipping the following Spring. Our price for the ore was then about $1.50 a ton, depending on the analysis. We mined in the old-fashioned way—with picks and shovels—and I am safe in saying it cost us all we got for it. I know I was continually making drafts on my father to keep me out of debt. I did not figure on the cost at that time—I was afraid of the figures. My only thought was how to reduce the cost. We had a Steam Shovel in Pennsylvania, and I got my father to send it to me for trial in this ore. We found we could use it to advantage by using also plenty of powder, and I was soon able to buy the second shovel. Of course that reduced the cost of production still lower, and as there was a market for all I could do, I got the third, and am now putting in the fourth, and the fifth is bought and to be delivered inside of 60 days. This doubling up of the shovels made me get locomotives to carry the ore in the mines instead of mules. I have now two locomotives. You will understand how it would make a saving at that point. It would require 15 mules to do that work, and it could not be done so promptly.*

During the month of May we shipped about 14,500 tons with the use of three shovels, and at a cost per ton for labor and fuel and powder of 33 cents. We have reduced the cost on a week's run, in good weather and with no lack of empty cars, to 29 cents, but it never came lower on the month's average than 33. I expect this Fall, with five shovels instead of three, and two locomotives instead of one, to lower the cost of production.

Our average price at the mines is $1.20; we sell some higher. I have just now taken a contract for 40,000 tons to be delivered between now and the 1st of February, 1891, at $1.12½. This is the lowest contract price we have ever made, and likely that has ever been made in this locality; but I did it to get into a different market. That ore is to go to Nashville—a distance of 120 miles. The reason for cutting the price to get the increased quantity I will not need to explain to you. You taught it to me. The freight to Nashville is 75 cents. To our other furnaces in Alabama, at Sheffield and Florence, the freight is only 35 cents. What other contracts I have at present are at $1.25.

With three shovels we make from 600 to 800 tons a day. With one shovel we made from 150 to 250 a day. The variation from day to day depends on the quality of the material we handle.

The ore is all washed and picked and screened before it is loaded on the cars. A very important part of the work is the work done in the washer. It requires very expensive machinery, and the wear and tear is enormous.

We pay unskilled laborers ten cents an hour, skilled men as high as twenty-five. We work eleven hours a day. Our general foreman gets $100 a month."

Sugar and Molasses brought in through the tariff in the fiscal year 1889, $55,995,137. The quantity of domestic sugar and molasses relatively to the quantity imported is so small, that an excise upon it in accordance with the general principle of these paragraphs is not worth while, but would be far more just and rational than to offer bounties to the domestic producers out of the taxes paid by the consumers of foreign sugar. A "bounty" in this sense is at once an abuse of a good word, and an abomination in point of fact. For any Government, which is nothing but a Committee of all the citizens to attend to certain joint concerns of all, to abstract money through taxes from the pockets of a part of these citizens in order to reward another part for carrying on an unprofitable branch of business, is something equally repugnant to Economy and Equality.

10. What, then, is the BOTTOM-PRINCIPLE in the Mode of Taxation? It is this: *Relatively low taxes so adjusted on comparatively few things as not to disturb natural prices.* The principle is simple: the problem is difficult; but wonderfully less so the moment all attempts are given up to foster any branch of industry whatever. Our legislators are not called upon to foster any industries. It is out of their beat. They cannot permanently do it, if they try; and they do immense harm while they try. Their "bounty," instead of being a gift, as the word imports, is a haphazard bestowment of other people's money extorted from them by public taxes. The problem becomes simpler every year of public experience under the practical design of so laying the public burdens as to realize to the Treasury the most money with the least possible interference with what would otherwise be the on-going of Exchanges in all directions. So relatively simple and easy has the English taxing system become, under this one leading design, that Gladstone performed without difficulty the functions of Chancellor of the Exchequer in conjunction with the far more arduous and complicated duties of Prime Minister.

Low taxes on few things. The opposite of this principle at either of its two points becomes at once pernicious. High taxes in general prevent exchanges altogether, by cutting in too deeply in the gain of them, which is the sole motive to them; high imposts prevent importations, and of course destroy the profitable exportations consequent to, and conditioned on, such importations; high taxes even on few things are apt to raise prices of other articles than those on which they are directly levied, and so become objectionable always, and unbearable whenever it is their purpose to raise such prices: taxes on many things, and even on few things every time they change hands, throw an indefinite burden on Exchange, whose weight cannot well be calculated beforehand, either by the consumer or by the government, through uncertainty as to the number of transfers. Once for all, and then an end. Exchanges are indeed the only legitimate subject of taxation, but not every specific and subordinate exchange. An attempt to tax all sales whatever was followed in Spain, and will be followed everywhere, by a sluggish indisposition to trade at all. Let the amount of the tax be definite, and let everybody be sure that when it is once paid government will produce no further claim, and industry will go along under heavy taxes better than under those nominally lighter to which uncertainty as to time or amount attaches. All the more advanced governments have been simplifying of late years their systems of taxation, and collecting their revenue at fewer points, and under more tangible conditions, in order to interfere as little as possible with a free industry and free exchange.

The subsidiary principle is important, namely, that all taxes should be collected by the government in as economical a manner as possible, inasmuch as all direct and indirect costs of collection are so much added to the burdens of the People. This covers two practical points: (1) the number and efficiency of the tax-gatherers, and the whole outward machinery of collection, such as the custom-houses, offices of internal revenue, and so on. These, as they concern the whole people equally, should be separated as far as possible from party politics, and the inevitable corruptions thereupon attendant. All the fiscal officers of the United States, from the Secretary of the Treasury down to the lowest tide-waiter, are liable to be changed every four years, and as a matter of fact are usually to a very large extent so changed, to the great detriment of the service and ultimate expense of the people, to say nothing of the moral losses and crevasses involved. (2) The tax-money should be kept out of the pockets of the people as short a time as possible, disbursement following quick upon collection. It is poor policy to gather taxes at the beginning of the year which will not be disbursed till the end of the year. Let the people use their funds till they are wanted at the treasury; and if the taxes do not then come in as fast as wanted, it is better to issue what are called in England exchequer-bills, and in the United States certificates of indebtedness, to be redeemed at the end of the year from the proceeds of the taxes, than to let the people's money lie idle in the treasury. The Secretary of the Treasury should have nothing to do or say about the circulating medium of the country, or the loanable price of the units of it, under any circumstances whatever. He is neither competent enough in Knowledge nor enough established in Integrity to be trusted with any such functions.

11. Should there be any EXEMPTIONS from Taxation? If the necessities of the State require it, government has the right to demand from all persons who are capable of making exchanges, and who do make them, something in the form of taxes. But it is every way better, when possible, that people of very moderate means should be exempted altogether from direct taxes; and the payment of indirect taxes is a matter more in their own option, since they are at liberty to buy much or little of those commodities subjected to an indirect tax. In the State of Massachusetts, incomes not exceeding $2000 are exempted by the law. If a house-tax should be levied, all houses below a certain grade of style and comfort should be exempted, and the tax pass up by easy gradations from those just taxed to the palatial residences of the rich. In the present age of the world, the well-to-do citizens of every country are able to bear without too great difficulty the burdens of the government, and nothing tests better the degree of civilization which a nation has reached than the care and solicitude it displays for the welfare of its poorer citizens.

12. Who pays the INDIRECT TAXES? At a court ball, Napoleon the First once observed a lady noticeable as richly dressed and as wearing splendid diamonds, and on asking her name, found that she was the wife of a tobacco manufacturer of Paris; it occurred at once to the quick mind of the French ruler, that the State might just as well have those profits as an individual; and the sale of tobacco in all its forms became accordingly a State monopoly, which now yields about 400,000,000 francs a year. That is indirect taxation. So is the British and United States tariff and excise on tobacco. Producers and dealers and bankers and companies add the tax demanded from them, and sometimes more than the tax under color of it, to the price of their wares. But it is not true that they can always realize the whole of this enhanced price. Generally they can, sometimes they cannot. If the article be one of necessity, or a luxury that has become equivalent to a necessity, and there be no other source of supply than the taxed one, then, as a rule, the tax falls wholly on the consumer, and is a matter of indifference to the producer or dealer. But the usual effect of an enhanced price is to lessen demand, and if the article is dispensable, or its consumption can be lessened, or it can be obtained elsewhere, the market will be sluggish under the tax, and producers or dealers will be likely to tempt it by lowering prices, in other words, by sharing the tax with consumers, and paying that share out of profits. This is the principle. Producers and dealers would rather the tax were off. Consumers generally, but do not always, pay the whole of it.

13. What is to be said about the DIFFUSION of Taxes? David A. Wells, an admirable and indefatigable authority on all practical questions in Economics, though perhaps less skilled in scientific classification and

generalizations, several years ago made somewhat prominent in public discussion the tendency of Taxes *to diffuse themselves*. Much more has been written about this than is actually known about it. By Diffusion is meant that it does not make so much difference upon what or upon whom a tax is originally levied, because the tendency of things is to *diffuse it*, that is, to compel others to assist in paying the tax. The result of much personal reading and reflection on this point is the conclusion that taxes do not "diffuse themselves" nearly so much as has been sometimes supposed; and that, at any rate, it is a good deal better to take the taxes from those who ought to pay them, than to lay them at random, and then to trust some unknown forces to make them afterwards just. It is certain that *some* unjust taxes cannot be diffused; for example, the protective tariff-taxes paid by the farmers upon articles of necessary consumption. These taxes have no tendency to raise the price of the farmers' produce, for *that* is determined by the foreign market, to which large parts of the produce are exported. For such taxes the farmers cannot reimburse themselves. Taxes that affect no prices are the best of all; taxes that affect prices the least are the next best; and taxes that are *designed* to affect prices are the very worst.

14. What are the bearings of the UNITED STATES CONSTITUTION on the whole matter of Taxation in this country? We have now seen pretty fully, what the science of Economics has to say about the sources and modes and results of tax-laying: but we are bound to tell also, what the kindred but much less developed science of Politics, and particularly what the Constitution of the Fathers, has to say upon the same vitally important topics.

(1) The first power granted by the People to Congress, which is simply their agent, in that Instrument from which each of the three great Departments of Government derives all its authority, is in these words, exactly copied from the original and official parchment in every particular: "*The Congress shall have Power to lay and collect Taxes, Duties, Imposts and Excises, to pay the Debts and provide for the common Defence and general Welfare of the United States; but all Duties, Imposts and Excises shall be uniform throughout the United States.*" This grant of power, which stands first in order, is followed by seventeen other express powers granted to Congress in the same eighth Section of the first Article.

There never has been any difference of opinion, and there cannot be under such completely explicit language as this, among competent Statesmen and Commentators, as to the exact meaning of this clause, namely, Congress is given power to lay taxes in order to get money, with which to pay the debts and provide for the common defence and general welfare of the United States. That was the opinion and purpose of every member of the Federal Convention, that framed the Constitution in the summer of 1787; of

Alexander Hamilton, who was first called on as Secretary of the Treasury officially to interpret it; of Daniel Webster, often called the "great expounder" of the Constitution; of John Marshall, the great Chief Justice of the Supreme Court; of Judge Story, the first copious and most distinguished commentator upon the Text; of George Bancroft and George T. Curtis, the learned and elaborate historians of the Text; and in short, of everybody else, who has earned any right in any way to have an opinion on any such matter of political interpretation.

Why, then, has there been from the first until now, a feeble flutter of butterfly wings around the clause, as if, somehow or other, it gave Congress by hook or by crook some power or other to do something *else* than to lay taxes in order to get money for the maintenance of the national Government? As if there lay concealed in the language somewhere a power to lay taxes for a purpose precisely opposite to that expressed in the text, namely, *nominal taxes designed to prohibit any money being gotten under them*? And why did Hamilton himself, whose wings were those of an eagle, sweep low and hover uncertainly about these words, and so give color to the political historians of our time to say: "*Once more laying hold of the "general welfare" clause of the Constitution, Hamilton here argued, under color of giving bounties to manufactures, as though Congress might take under its own management every thing which that body should pronounce to be for the general welfare, provided only it was susceptible of the application of money. Though he limited this central discretion to the application of money, and stated some restrictions rather vaguely, the insidious tenor of his report was to show that the Federal power of raising money was plenary and indefinitely great.*"

The true answer to these questions is a point of Grammar. The simple English infinitive, unlike the simple infinitive of any other language with which the writer is acquainted, *often expresses purpose*, as well as the action of the verb without limitation of person or number; so that, it is perfectly good English to say, "To lay taxes to pay," when the only possible sense of it is, "To lay taxes *in order to pay*." Greek, Latin, and German would use here with the infinitive the particle expressing the purpose: the English language does not. It is not true to say, that ambiguity enters this clause, through the common and elegant use of the simple infinitive in English to express the purpose; but it *is* true to say, that superficial confusion has entered here, and a mess of bad logic. What makes it absolutely certain, beyond the possibility of a controversy, that Congress can levy taxes only in order to get money by means of them, is, (a) that is the only English of the clause; (b) the "debts" of the United States can only be paid in money; and (c) if this be *not* the meaning of the clause, its meaning must then be plenary, and there would be no need or place for the remaining seventeen powers, "and all other powers vested by this Constitution in the Government of the

United States or in any Department or Officer thereof"; in other words, any other interpretation of the taxing clause than the plain one would destroy the Constitution root and branch; for, if Congress have the general power "to pay the debts and provide for the common defence and general welfare of the United States," all other possible powers are included in this, and President and Court disappear, and all other clauses of the Text are a nullity.

If the above course of reasoning be sound, and he would be a bold logician who should openly dispute it, then taxes laid for any other end than revenue are clearly unconstitutional. The Supreme Court has never passed upon this bald point, for it has never been mooted in this form; but one would think, there can be little doubt how the judges would decide in any "case" directly involving the constitutional power of Congress to levy prohibitory tariff-taxes, whose avowed or clearly inferrible design it is, *not* to get money with which to pay the debts and so on, but to cut off the possibility of getting any money thereby. The general trend of the decisions of the Supreme Court has wisely been, to leave in their interpretations of the Text the widest margin of discretion to the Legislative branch as to the best means of *raising* revenue; but when it comes to face the question of allowing as constitutional the best means of *preventing* revenue,—well, may we be there to see and hear!

(2) There are prohibitions on Congress in the Constitution, as well as powers conferred, and among these this: "*No tax or duty shall be laid on Articles exported from any State.*" This is a part of the third great Compromise of the Constitution, and was a concession to the southern and planting States to make more palatable to them the power "to regulate commerce," that was expected to be used (and was used) in behalf of the northern and navigating States. But the concession was more nominal than real, as the southerners found out in time to their vexation. To prohibit taxes on exports, and to leave in full vigor the power to tax imports, though consonant with the then prevailing delusion of Mercantilism, is no boon to commerce in general; because, any restriction on buying products is equally and instantly a restriction on selling products. Exemption from taxes on exports is a good thing in itself, but the only reason for selling exports is to take in profitable pay the imports naturally offered against them; and if these be restricted or prohibited, the restriction or prohibition applies instantaneously and inevitably to the would-be exports. A reasonable liberty of exporting is nothing, unless accompanied by a reasonable liberty of importing, because the imports pay for the exports and the exports buy the imports.

The southern States rejoiced for a time in this exemption-clause of the Constitution, for their rice and cotton and indigo found no obstacles in going out; but the only motive in sending them out was to buy something with them to bring back; and after the snare of Protectionism entangled the People in 1816, 1824, and specially in 1828, when the "Tariff of Abominations" was passed, the southern people saw only too distinctly, that taxes on imports which they wished to bring in were the same in effect as taxes on their own exports would have been. Mr. Calhoun and the others were effectually undeceived by the customary on-goings of commerce; and as the northern statesmen unwisely and unpatriotically determined to crowd this iron home in 1828, the party of the other part developed under great provocation the doctrines of Nullification and Secession, which have since caused a plenty of tears and bloodshed. One wrong ever begets other wrongs. The wretched Greed of one section of the country was own father to the wrongful Secession of the other section.

The Farmers of this country have often been congratulated on their privilege under the constitution of exporting their agricultural products without a tax. The congratulation is hollow. Of what use is it to go out free and come back manacled? The ultimate is always the return-service. The farmers are cheated. Their agricultural exports are falling off year by year solely in consequence of outrageous tariff-taxes on imports. In 1881, farmers' produce was exported to the amount of $730,394,943, and that was not one-half what it would have been under a simple and adequate Tariff for Revenues; but in 1889, these exports only reached $532,141,490, a falling off of nearly $200,000,000. This decline was chiefly in meats and breadstuffs. No wonder the farmers have been complaining of terribly hard times of late years: no wonder they are organizing "Alliances" and other machinery for reaching a remedy: they must see clearly first where the disease lies: the truth is, they are tariff-taxed to death: their foes are they of their own household: Vermont, a purely agricultural State, is the only one in the Union, that has actually *retrograded* in property and population in the last census-decade: those excellent people have hugged the Tariff-delusion to their ruin; their senior Senator, whose name is unpleasantly connected with the national tax-laws of a generation, has never yet in the course of a long and reputable life gained a glimmer of the commercial truth,—if men *will* not buy they *can* not sell.

(3) The only other clause of the Constitution, which, as students of Taxation, we are bound to examine, is the following: "*No Capitation, or other direct, Tax shall be laid, unless in Proportion to the Census or Enumeration herein before directed to be taken.*" A capitation tax is a poll-tax, which may be easily "proportioned" to the Census. It is not clear, what is the meaning of the words "or other direct tax"; the Supreme Court early struggled with that question, to this apparent result, that *lands*, as the only form of property that can be "proportioned" in their appraised value to population with any

considerable degree of accuracy, are the only "other" subject of "direct" Taxation. However this may be, it is of considerable consequence to note, that the term, "direct tax," as used in the Constitution, does not correspond in its meaning to the significance of the same term as employed in Economics. With us, a "direct tax" means one demanded from and paid by the person on whom it is ostensibly levied, and cannot be thrown off or forward on anybody else; while an "indirect tax" is one which can be so thrown off or forward.

Attention is called to the distinction here, in order to show that an Income-tax, while in the Economical sense it is a "direct tax," is not such in the sense of the Constitution. Objections were urged against the late Income-tax in this country, that it was a "direct tax," and so, because it could not be proportioned to the population, was unconstitutional. The point is not well taken. It remains, and will remain, after the most searching scrutiny, that an universal Income-tax, all other taxes being abolished, is the form most consonant with the principles of Political Economy, and not at all repugnant to the Constitution of the United States.

15. Finally, are there any hints and guides to thought and legislation in the matter of Taxation through an extremely brief summary of the HISTORY of Taxes? So far as the Greeks are concerned, they showed a practical good sense in their laws of Property in general, and in their laws relating to Taxes in particular. The natural march of industry and commerce was not hindered by taxation: there was no forbidding the export of raw materials or specie; no favoring of manufactures at the expense of agriculture; no hint of the future Mercantilism in any efforts to preserve an artificial balance of trade; and no taxes on imports except for purposes of Revenue. These at Athens itself were usually 2% of the value of the goods, at the ports of her subject-allies 5%, and exceptional cases of higher rates than these were regarded as extortionate.

The Romans also were sensible and moderate in their modes of Taxation. They laid taxes for the sake of getting money for the public treasury, and had no other end in view. They knew nothing of what has since become famous under the name of "Protectionism." Their taxes were both direct and indirect, but especially the latter. The chief direct tax was the land-tax, that is, a claim to the tenth part of the sheaves and of other field produce, such as grapes and olives; and also pasture-money (*scriptura*) demanded of those who made use of the public pastures and woods. In Macedonia and the other larger Provinces, in lieu of the land-tax a fixed sum of money (*tributum*) was paid to Rome each year by each community in its own way. The grain-tenths and pasture-moneys were always farmed out to private contractors or companies on condition of their paying fixed quantities of grain or fixed sums of money. The chief indirect tax was customs-duties.

There never was at any time a general tariff for the whole empire, but there were customs-districts, such as Italy, Sicily, proconsular Asia, the province of Narbo in Gaul, and others, each with a sort of tariff of its own, and some with special immunities. Goods imported by sea into Italy, for example, not for the personal use of the importer, were subject to a tax, which seems to have been mainly a tax on luxuries, since pepper, cinnamon, myrrh, ginger, perfumes, ivory and diamonds, are among the dutiable goods mentioned in one of these tariffs. Sicily had a tariff-tax quite distinct from this, since one-twentieth of the value of the goods (5%) was levied on the frontier on *all* imports and exports; and a similar tax of one-fortieth was laid by the Sempronian law on the province of Asia. These imposts, too, were leased to contractors, which gave, of course, some chance of fraud and wrong. There were other temporary taxes, like those, for instance, which Augustus laid of 5% on legacies and inheritances, and of 1% on articles publicly exposed for sale.

Green's History of England (I., 322 *et seq.*) gives an outline of the taxes there from the beginning of the monarchy. As land was almost the only source of salable things in the early time, so it was almost the only thing on which taxes were levied. Danegeld and scutage and feudal aids fastened only on the land. "But a new principle of taxation was disclosed in the tithe levied for a Crusade at the close of Henry Second's reign. Land was no longer the only source of wealth. The growth of national prosperity, of trade and commerce, was creating a mass of personal property which offered irresistible temptations to the Angevin financiers. No usage fettered the Crown in dealing with personal property, and its growth in value promised a growing revenue. Grants of from a seventh to a thirtieth of movables, household property, and stock were demanded. The right of the king to grant licenses to bring goods into or to trade within the realm, a right springing from the need of his protection, felt by the strangers who came there for purposes of traffic, laid the foundation for our taxes on imports. Those on exports were only a part of the general system of taxing personal property. How tempting this source of revenue was proving, we see from a provision of the Great Charter, which forbids the levy of more than the ancient customs on merchants entering or leaving the realm. Commerce was in fact growing with the growing wealth of the people." This passage shows, that, as a matter of fact, *taxes* have always hinged, and must hinge, on *trade*.

A few facts in the most recent movements of national Taxation in the United States may fitly conclude this Chapter and this Volume. Since 1867, Wool and Woollens have been the ass, upon whose breaking back the most conspicuous burdens have been piled; and the "McKinley Bill" so-called, still pending at the present writing in the Senate, heaps up still higher the groaning loads. The following table shows how futile is the attempt to keep out wools and woollens from such a country as ours, even by the most exaggerated barriers:—

IMPORTS OF WOOLS AND WOOLLENS.
(Calendar Years.)

Years.	Wools.	Woollens.
1886	$17,403,099	$43,995,641
1887	15,645,020	45,065,986
1888	14,542,244	49,984,298
1889	18,696,277	54,080,159
1890	(fiscal year)	56,582,000

Roger Q. Mills of Texas stated from his place in the House of Representatives in 1888, that the United States grows but about 265,000,000 lbs. of wool yearly, while it takes about 600,000,000 lbs. to clothe our own people. Why should more than half the wool needed to clothe the people be taxed in such a way as to double (in general) the cost of the people's clothing? And why should Benjamin Harrison, now President of the United States, have said in that same year, in view of these elsewhere unheard-of taxes, and in view of the average climate of his country, that somehow it seemed to him *that cheap clothing implied a cheap man*? In view of the enormous natural demand for woollens, in order to keep comfortable day and night 64,000,000 of inhabitants, is it not strange, and must there not be artificial causes for it in the kind and mode of national Taxation, that the United States has but 16 sheep to the square mile, while Germany has 92, France 111, and Great Britain 339?

Senator John Sherman stated in his place in August, 1888, and again in substance Sept. 2, 1890, that a line of custom-houses on our joint-frontier with Canada was "*the height of nonsense, and almost a crime against civilization.*" Well might he say this in view of what his colleague, Allison of Iowa, has recently said, namely, that the Dominion bought in 1880 of the United States 8% of its brass goods, 86% of its copper manufactures, 94% of its cordage, 88% of its gingham, 65% of its glasswares, 99% of its rubber goods, 94% of its printing ink, 92% of wooden wares, 91% of tinware, 90% of wall-paper, 72% of paper wares, 98% of ploughs, 97% of engines, 99% of sewing-machines, and 90% of miscellaneous machinery.

The imports and exports of the United States for the last two fiscal years are as follows: —

	1889.	1890.
Imports, free	$256,487,078	$265,588,499
Imports, dutiable	488,644,574	523,633,729
Total	745,131,652	789,222,228
Exports	742,401,375	857,824,834
Gold and Silver, Imports	28,963,073	33,976,326
Gold and Silver, Exports	96,641,533	52,148,420
Total Imports	774,094,725	823,198,554
Total Exports	839,042,908	909,973,254

There two or three noticeable points from this table. First, the large relative increase of free imports over those of former years. Free articles in 1867 were less than 5% of the whole; in 1882, 30%; and in 1890, 33.9%. The Free List, so-called, has indeed been enlarged in the interval, but free goods tend naturally to swell over the taxed goods, so that in 1890 the free were almost exactly one-half of the taxed. Second, of the large total of merchandise exports, it is to be sorrowfully noted, that more than 82% of the whole is made up of the products of agriculture and forests and mines (not gold and silver); while manufactures compose only 17.8%. What ails our manufactures, that we cannot sell them abroad? We have been for 30 years under a vaunted scheme warranted to develop manufactures,— expressly designed and recommended to make them cheap and good,— under an elaborate and artificial scheme that makes everything bend, even the backs of the toiling millions, to foster and propel manufactures! But we do not succeed in selling much of them abroad, except some fractions of them to Canada. The ratio of them to the total of exports of merchandise seems to be growing less: in 1889, 18.9%; in 1890, 17.8%.

The simple truth is, that we are able to sell abroad even this beggarly proportion of manufactures to the total exports of merchandise, only in consequence of a shrewd device working within the Grand Device, namely, the so-called "Free List." Some of the little wheels within the big wheel revolve rapidly. Manufacturers do not like to pay protectionist tariff-taxes *themselves* any better than other people like to pay them. They have by their own open confession in overt act precisely the same opinion of their deadening influence, that other people have. If, however, they can escape such taxes on the things they have to buy, especially their raw material, and *keep* them on their own finished goods offered for sale in a monopoly market, they would be happy. Hence, the Free List. Hear Senator Dawes before the Paper-makers' Convention at Saratoga in 1887: "*There is one other feature of tariff revision much discussed at the present time which must not escape our attention, and that is free raw material. No industrial policy will promote the highest prosperity of both labor and capital in this country, which fails to lay down the raw material at the door of the manufactory at the lowest possible cost. In any new revision of the tariff this rule of preference for our own raw material must be adhered to by those who do not propose to give up the American for the indifferent policy in legislating between ourselves and foreigners.* IT WILL BE FOUND, HOWEVER, TO ADD VERY FEW RAW MATERIALS TO THE FREE LIST, FOR THE REVISIONS OF 1874 AND 1883 HAVE ALREADY MADE FREE ALL SUCH NON-COMPETING RAW MATERIALS AS AT THE TIME OF THE PASSAGE OF THOSE ACTS WERE ENTERING TO ANY CONSIDERABLE EXTENT INTO THE CONSUMPTION OR PRODUCTION OF THE COUNTRY."

Till now, we have been dealing in facts, and figures, and in careful generalizations after the inductive manner: let us, at the very last, indulge in a freak of fancy. Suppose for a moment, that all taxes of every name could be abolished instantaneously, and the Governments, like the Israelites, live on manna for forty years. What harm would ensue? What industry would decline? Who would be impoverished? What stimulus to work and save and grow rich would be weakened thereby? Would not wages, and profits, and rents, all be lifted thereby, with no damage to anybody? A child can see that Taxes from their very nature are a burden, are a subtraction from income, are a *minus* and not a *plus.* Who, then, except from sinister motives, can imagine and represent, that Taxes are a good in themselves, a positive blessing, a spur to the progress of Society?

Taxes of some sort there must be for the maintenance of Governments, which are established for the good of all. Why, then, should not the Taxes be just as few, just as simple, just as comprehensible, just as universal and equitable, as is consonant with the single end of their existence at all?

FOOTNOTES:

Green's Short History of the English People, p. 591.

See on this general topic, Mommsen's Provinces of the Roman Empire, *passim.*

Baines' History of the Cotton Manufacture, as condensed and quoted in Walpole's History of England, Vol. I.

Charles Knight's History of England, III. 292 *et seq.*

O'Reilly's Poem, at Plymouth, 1889.

Green's Short History of the English People, p. 144.

John Jay Knox's United States Notes.

Practical Political Economy, 1877, p. 452.

See an excellent Essay on Mexican Finance by M. L. Scudder, Jr.

Public Statement of Professor Taussig of Harvard College.

See James Schouler's United States, p. 77 of Vol. I.

There were two other authors of some of the papers of the Federalist, Madison and Jay; but Hamilton's authorship of number XXXV was never questioned by anybody; he himself claimed it expressly with his other numbers a few days before he was shot.